Walter Model ranks among the foremost commanders of the German *Wehrmacht* during World War Two. This is recognized by both German and foreign military historians. But Model was also one of the most brutal German Generals. Whenever he assumed a new command, he showered his staff officers with insults which hurt their dignity and led many of them to request their transfer. The higher Model rose in rank, the more offensive his behaviour became.

In the first seven chapters, the author describes the successive stages of Walter Model's career, beginning with his youth and ending with his suicide on April 21, 1945, when he finally woke up to his errors, dissolved his Army Group in the Ruhr Pocket and told his soldiers that they were free to go home.

Walter Model had served with distinction as a junior officer during the First World War. In the *Reichswehr* and after 1935 in the *Wehrmacht*, his service altered between troop commands and increasingly important duties in the *Generalstab*. In March 1938, he reached General's rank with his promotion to *Generalmajor*.

During World War Two, Walter Model rose to the highest ranks. In the campaigns in Poland and France he was Chief of Staff of a Corps and later of an Army. His first troop command was a *Panzer* division during the initial phase of the war against Russia. In the winter of 1941 he rose to corps command, a few weeks later he became commander in chief of 9th Army. As of 1944 he assumed command of Army Groups. In the East, he commanded two of the three Army Groups simultaneously and was also responsible for coordination with the third Army Group, making him, in practice, Supreme Commander East. He was then named Supreme Commander West and commanded Army Group B until the end. Chapter eight is a detailed account of Model's active involvement in the worst war crimes. Chapter nine deals with Model's increasingly absurd orders of the day, some of which can cast doubt on his sanity. Chapter ten deals with courts martial convened by him and shows how he was part of the increasing perversion of military justice.

Researched from a huge array of primary and secondary sources, *A Flawed Genius* is destined to become the primary biography about Model, a most controversial and complex German military figure.

A FLAWED GENIUS

Field Marshal Walter Model

A Critical Biography

A FLAWED GENIUS

Field Marshal Walter Model

A Critical Biography

Marcel Stein

Helion & Company Ltd

Helion & Company Limited
26 Willow Road
Solihull
West Midlands
B91 1UE
England
Tel. 0121 705 3393
Fax 0121 711 4075
Email: info@helion.co.uk
Website: www.helion.co.uk

Published by Helion & Company 2010

Designed and typeset by Farr out Publications, Wokingham, Berkshire
Cover designed by Farr out Publications, Wokingham, Berkshire
Printed by The Cromwell Press Group, Trowbridge, Wiltshire

ISBN 978 1 906033 30 9

British Library Cataloguing-in-Publication Data.
A catalogue record for this book is available from the British Library.

For details of other military history titles published by Helion & Company Limited contact the above address, or visit our website: http://www.helion.co.uk.

We always welcome receiving book proposals from prospective authors.

Contents

Foreword

My German book on Model, *Feldmarschall Walter Model: Legende und Wirklichkeit*, was written in 1999/2000 and published in 2001 by Biblio Verlag, Bissendorf. The book was well received by most of the professional press in German-speaking countries. But soon after it appeared, I began to distance myself from a number of the opinions expressed in it. At the time the book was written, Model was one of the few high commanders who was credited with not having been involved in the Shoah and the worst crimes in the East. But the extensive research by leading German historians during the recent years has shown that he took an active part in the genocide and in all other crimes in which the *Wehrmacht* was engaged in the East. Over the last few years, my friends among the younger generation of German historians have urged me to write a revised book on Model. So I welcome the opportunity of bringing a new biography of the *Feldmarschall* into line with contemporary research on the *Wehrmacht*.

Acknowledgements

L ike every author, I owe a debt of gratitude to all those who helped me with this volume and with the original German edition.

Some of Colonel Günther Reichhelm's personal recollections of the *Feldmarschall* are of value. Reichhelm had served almost uninterruptedly on Model's staffs, after Model became *OB* of 9th Army. He was probably one of the few, perhaps the only high-ranking officer, who managed to live with Model's frequent outbursts. Whenever Model obtained a new command, he immediately requested that "his" Reichhelm be posted to his staff. At the age of 31, Reichhelm became the youngest full Colonel of the *Wehrmacht Generalstab*. In 1945, just two weeks before the end of the war, he became chief of staff of General Walther Wenck's newly-formed 12th Army.

But testimonials by witnesses like Reichhelm must be examined with care. They are seldom entirely objective, personal friendship and animosities tend to influence their content. In his foreword to my German book about Model, Reichhelm writes that "Model was not only a most courageous *Feldmarschall*, (this is true), that more than other high commanders he shared the life of his soldiers in the front line (likewise true) and that he was the most unconditional opponent against Hitler's obstinate military leadership" (an obvious exaggeration). Reichhelm died in March 2007, 93 years old. He could never free himself from the fiction of the "unblemished Wehrmacht". In one of his last talks with me he described the *Wehrmacht* as the "last hoard of decency".[1]

How the members of the "last hoard of decency" viewed themselves is shown by recordings of their conversations in the British POW camp at Trent Park, which were monitored by the British. A few examples, all taken at random from Professor Sönke Neitzel's book *Abgehört. Deutsche Generale in britischer Kriegsgefangenschaft 1941-1945*.

Generalmajor Paul von Felbert: "We had no honour, we were only driven by dirty ambition. No element of conscience remained."

Generalmajor Gerhard Fischer: "We have acted like savages, not like a civilized race."

Generalmajor Ludwig Heilmann (decorated with the Swords to the Oakleaves of his Knight's Cross): "We will remain with the designation 'Huns' for ever."

General Hans Cramer: "During the First World War we could still say that we were decent. But in this war, decency was only on the other side. We were the aggressors, the loudmouths and we behaved like animals."

---

1 In his recollections *Verantwortung und Gewissensnot. Erinnerungen,* Würzburg 2003 (henceforth: Reichhelm), p.161, Reichhelm writes about the situation in autumn 1944: "The German soldier fought. He had no knowledge of the crimes of the dictator." But even worse: "My commander of many years, *Feldmarschall* Model was apolitical, very religious and wholly absorbed by his military duties. He would never have condoned the murder of the tyrant, neither would other high commanders whom I had known like von Manstein, von Bock, Ritter von Leeb." (p.92). In other terms, it was not possible, not even permissible to kill Hitler but the same "religious and moral" Generals had no qualms in participating in the wilful murder of millions of innocent people.

General Dietrich von Choltitz: "The most difficult order I had to carry out – but which I carried out totally – was the liquidation of the Jews." General von Choltitz , at that time a Colonel, commanded a regiment in von Manstein's 11th Army in the Crimea. The shootings he referred to were the mass murder of some 15,000 Jews and Gypsies at Simferopol in December 1941.

General Ludwig Crüwell: "What do the Americans want from us? What business do they have in Italy? Has Germany ever harmed them? As usual, they are making lots of money. They don't like the British and they are aware that the Jewish bacillus dominated their politicians. The Jews stand behind the massive air raid on Hamburg. The Jews are the ones who intend to annihilate all of us. They know that the remainder of the world will finally agree with our ideology and that they will not escape their ultimate destruction." In the eyes of the British monitors, General Crüwell was the head of the Nazi clique at Trent Park. He succeeded in disguising his nature to such an extent that he was under consideration for the post of the first Inspector General of the *Bundeswehr.*

Generalleutnant Maximilian Syri: " We were much too soft. In France we had no problem. The French are degenerates to such a point that when they were told to report to a POW camp the stupid monkeys did just that. But the Russians are clever. During the long marches to the POW camp, many Russians could run away. We should have hacked off one leg from every POW, or, at least, broken a leg or his arms. After that, we would have had no trouble in putting them into POW camps." .[2]

Reichhelm was a very decent man. He had a successful career in business after the war. In 1970, he became chairman of the Düsseldorf industrialists association. Our increasing differences of opinion never affected our personal friendship.

I am also grateful to Winrich Behr, my German schoolmate of the 1930s, for his first-hand recollections of Model. Winrich Behr was a Major in the *Generalstab* at the end of the war, and is another valuable source. Behr was awarded the Knight's Cross of the Iron Cross as a young Lieutenant under Rommel in North Africa. Behr served on the staff of four *Feldmarschalls*, Rommel, Paulus, Kluge and Model. He was with Model's Army Group during the last days in the Ruhr *Kessel*, and added to my knowledge and understanding of the *Feldmarschall*'s attitudes and behaviour. With regard to Model's personality, Behr is a more reliable eyewitness than Reichhelm, there being on his part no personal attachment to the *Feldmarschall*.

I am indebted to Model's son, Bundeswehr Brigadegeneral (ret.) Hansgeorg Model. He is the only son of a *Wehrmacht Feldmarschall* to reach General's rank in the Bundeswehr. He gave me access to the many hundred unpublished documents in the Model estate which he had assembled over more than half a century. He continued to provide me with additional documents while I was completing the manuscript of my first book. Hansgeorg Model started to assemble this estate when attacks against his father gained ground in post war German literature. Since the *Feldmarschall* wrote very little, except for regular letters to his wife and his children and also ordered his papers to be destroyed before he committed suicide, a major part of the estate consists of recorded statements and letters. Of importance are statements by officers of all ranks who had served under the *Feldmarschall*. An estate, which is mainly based on testimonials, can give reason for

---

2 S. Neitzel, *Abgehört. Deutsche Generäle in britischer Kriegsgefangenschaft*, Berlin 2006, pp.107, 247, 258, 286, 309, 310.

doubt, since some writers may adhere to the adage "de mortuis aut bene aut nihil" and refrain from mentioning unpleasantness. Undoubtedly, some documents in the estate are written in an *ex post facto* positive manner. However, the estate contains likewise many documents by subordinates who had to suffer Model's temperament and his frequent outbursts and Model's son has made no effort to hide them from readers. His behaviour stands in sharp and positive contrast to Rüdiger von Manstein, the son of the *Feldmarschall* Erich von Lewinski, named von Manstein, who continues to refuse access of the Manstein estate to most historians, conceivably out of fear that they may reveal documents even more compromising than what is now common knowledge of Manstein's crimes and his involvement in the Shoah.[3]

In 1991, Hansgeorg Model and Dermot Bradley published an album, *Generalfeldmarschall Walter Model, Dokumentation eines Soldatenlebens*, to mark the 100th anniversary of the *Feldmarschall's* birth.[4] The album contains many documents in facsimile, covering all aspects of Model's life and career and many letters which Model wrote to his wife and his son during the war. Like the estate, the selection made by Hansgeorg Model is entirely objective. He made no attempt to hide the increasingly absurd orders of the day which the *Feldmarschall* issued during the last years of the war.

I received additional source material from Professor Martin van Creveld, in Jerusalem, and Dr Manfred Kehrig, former head of the Federal Military Archives in Freiburg. Dr Georg Meyer provided me with judgments about Model by General Heusinger, before his biography of Heusinger appeared. To all of them I send warm thanks.

To the personnel in the Federal Military Archive, above all Ms Carina Notzke, I am most grateful for assistance and speedy preparation of documentary material for this work and my earlier books.

More than usual thanks are due to Dr Johannes Hürter, *Privatdozent* (assistant professor) at the University of Mainz and one of the senior editors of the *Vierteljahrshefte für Zeitgeschichte*, the quarterly review of the *Institut für Zeitgeschichte* (Institution for Contemporary History), Munich. In his review of my German book, Dr Hürter subjected parts of it to severe criticism in the *Frankfurter Allgemeine Zeitung*.[5] As the years passed, I found myself increasingly in agreement with many points raised by him. A personal meeting in Munich, in April 2007, brought our views even closer together. Dr Hürter's recent work about the *Wehrmacht* high commanders in the East, which was published in 2006, is likely to become the classic on this subject. Parts of it are frequently quoted in this book.[6]

I am also most grateful to a number of younger German historians, some of whom I have come to know personally. Through their writing, they have been instrumental in destroying the revisionist views of the *Wehrmacht* and have shown its participation in the vilest crimes of World War II. I have learned much from the works of Andrej Angrick, Michael Wildt, Jochen Böhler, Götz Aly, Christian Gerlach, Dieter Pohl, Martin Cüppers,

---

3   In the footnotes, designated as "Estate", followed by description of the document.
4   H. Model/D. Bradley, *Generalfeldmarschall Walter Model (1891-1945), Dokumentation eines Soldatenlebens*, Osnabrück 1991. (Model/Bradley).
5   *Frankfurter Allgemeine Zeitung*, 19 January 2002 *"Endkämpfer"*.
6   J. Hürter, *Hitlers Heerführer. Die deutschen Oberbefehlshaber im Krieg gegen die Sowjetunion 1941/42*, Munich 2006, (henceforth Hürter).

Peter Klein, Klaus-Michael Mallmann and Oliver von Wrochem, to mention but a few. Their writings, and in some instances our talks, have helped me to review a number of opinions which I expressed in my first books dealing with the *Wehrmacht* leadership.

A number of quotations from literature and archive documents from my book *Field Marshal von Manstein - The Janus Head. A Portrait* (Helion & Company Ltd. 2007) have been reproduced entirely in this book. This was necessary since both Generals followed a parallel career and were engaged, at times, in the same operations.

My thanks and appreciation go to the Helion team in Solihull, Duncan Rogers, Wilf Rogers and all their staff for their support of my writings, their personal kindness, and their professionalism in seeing this new book of mine through to publication.

My son Gabriel has undertaken a final review of my English text. His command of the English language and his profound knowledge of history have given the text its final appearance. I am most grateful for his assistance.

My thanks go to my wife Alla, for her patience, and her assistance with all technical problems, in particular with the recurring computer mishaps.

The responsibility for the contents of this book and of my judgments rests solely with me.

Introduction

"A *Feldmarschall* is not taken prisoner. It is simply unthinkable."
Walter Model to his son Hansgeorg, after *Feldmarschall* Paulus was captured in Stalingrad.

Walter Model remained true to that principle. On 21 April 1945, in a forest in the Ruhr Valley, he shot himself after he had dissolved his Army Group. The other *Feldmarschalls*, those remaining in active service, and those who had been retired, put up no resistance when taken prisoner. Among them were Ferdinand Schörner and Albert Kesselring who had exhorted their soldiers to fight 'to the last moment'. Some of them were tried for war crimes. Wilhelm Keitel was hanged at Nuremberg. The others received prison sentences of between three years and life. However, most were set free after only a few years. A number wrote memoirs, always in a spirit of self-justification.[1]

Model appeared to be the prototype of the German officer, portrayed worldwide by his "Prussian haircut" and ubiquitous monocle. However, his attitude was different to that of other *Feldmarschalls*. He never carried the interim baton associated with his rank. Other *Feldmarschall*s apparently relinquished their baton only when they went to sleep. Model considered the baton to be ugly and cumbersome.[2] During the final years of World War II, Model often wore only a simple field cap and uniform, without a General's stripes. As a result, his troops frequently did not recognize him when he was in the front lines, and did not address him by his rank.

Walter Model ranks among the outstanding Generals of the *Wehrmacht* in World War II. This is not disputed and is recognized by military historians worldwide. Among the highest *Wehrmacht* commanders, only Erich von Manstein exceeded him in military

---

1   Von Kleist, Paulus, Raeder and Schörner were taken prisoner by the Russians. During the last days of the war, Schörner had deserted his troops, wearing civilian clothes, and was captured by the Americans, who handed him over to the Russians. He was sentenced to 25 years. A personal letter from him to Stalin led to a reduction of the sentence to 12 years. After his return to Western Germany, Schörner was sentenced to 4½ years for wanton execution of a subordinate. He served two years. The remainder of his sentence was remitted for ill-health. Kleist died in captivity. Paulus stayed in Eastern Germany for the remainder of his life. Von Blomberg, von Brauchitsch, Busch, Dönitz, Keitel, Kesselring, von Küchler, von Leeb, List, von Manstein, Milch, von Rundstedt, Sperrle and von Weichs were taken prisoner by the Americans and the British. Von Reichenau died of a stroke in 1942. Von Richthofen died of a brain tumour in July 1945. Von Witzleben was hanged after July 20, 1944. Von Greim, von Kluge, Model and Rommel committed suicide. Dönitz, Keitel, von Leeb, List, Kesselring, von Küchler, von Manstein and Raeder were sentenced for war crimes. Sperrle was acquitted. Dönitz, Kesselring, von Manstein and Raeder published memoirs. Raeder's recollections are known to have been written by ghost writers.

2   Hansgeorg Model, "Der Führer dem Generalfeldmarschall Model – die Geschichte eines Marschallstabes", in *Decorations and Militaria Journal*," Notebook 14 September 1976, p. 174.

talent. However, few other high commanders, if any, can be considered to have been Model's equal. In the summer of 1944, while practically serving as "Commander in Chief East", Model simultaneously led two Army groups. Although in 1944, in his last command in the East, he had more than one million soldiers under his orders, he knew many officers of his units personally. When visiting battalions, he would make a point of speaking directly to officers of all ranks.

But with the exception of *Feldmarschall* Ferdinand Schörner, no other high-ranking *Wehrmacht* commander has suffered a worse 'post-war press' than Model, both in Germany and abroad. For this, Model has mainly himself to blame. Even as a young officer, Model was known to be difficult, but during the war he cultivated his offensive behaviour until it knew no bounds. When he relieved a fellow General and assumed command, Model's behaviour was usually contemptible. His first meetings with his new staff members frequently began with an outburst that humiliated them, and that motivated an increasing number to apply for immediate transfer. Walter Görlitz, one of Model's biographers, suggested that Model wanted to be like 'an icy wind' when he took over command, but this explanation is not satisfactory. Model simply displayed atrocious manners, which is surprising, since he had a good upbringing and was polite in private life. Many of his comrades never forgave his behaviour and criticized him in post-war literature. Nevertheless, some officers who had become victims of his temper spoke favourably of him.

Model himself was never known to bear a grudge. He was able to accept sharp criticism, including abrasive words, from his lower-ranking subordinates. If he offended an officer, and that officer took him to task, Model would frequently say that he really had not meant what he had said. Reichhelm wrote of his first meeting with Model in January 1942. The meeting had ended in a clash. "Soon after I arrived, I was asked to report to Model regarding the condition of XXIII Army Corps, and General Friessner's assessment of the situation. Because of the weakness of the individual units of the XXIII Army Corps, and the constant strong attacks by Soviet tanks, my news did not sound very hopeful. Model was enraged. He insisted that I should have come up with at least three alternatives that would lead to a positive conclusion. He insulted me in a way I had never before experienced. I was overcome with anger, threw my files and cards on the ground, saluted and left. He never held this against me, and we never spoke of it again."[3]

In the years that followed, Reichhelm remained a subordinate who was especially valued by Model. Model could seemingly not change his habits even in the last days of the war. As the final destruction of the *Ruhrkessel* was imminent, Reichhelm received an order, signed personally by Hitler, appointing him as Chief of Staff of General Walther Wenck's newly-formed 12th Army. Reichhelm told Model that he would prefer not to leave him and that he wanted to remain in the *Kessel* with him until the bitter end. Model found nothing better to say than to ask him if he was 'afraid to fly out?' Reichhelm replied: "No, I am not afraid, I will fly out immediately on a small *Klemm* plane.". Model: "This is much too dangerous, wait for two hours, I will arrange a *Junker 52* plane for you." As Reichhelm was taking formal leave of Model, he received another reprimand because he had not appeared in 'prescribed uniform'.[4] Model then invited Reichhelm to have dinner alone with him and gave him a handwritten memento: *"Der beste 'Kik' wird 'Kak'!"* (The

---

3   Letter, Reichhelm to author, 3 January 2000. Also mentioned in Reichhelm, p.126.
4   Reichhelm had appeared without his pistol. The pistol was part of the "prescribed uniform".

best comrade inside the *Kessel* becomes the best comrade outside the *Kessel*). When Model accompanied him to the plane, Reichhelm believed he saw tears in Model's eyes.[5]

Model was one of the Generals who often contradicted Hitler in tactical matters, sometimes insistently. Unlike many other Generals, he was often successful because he used the language of the front line soldier, which had a special appeal for Hitler. One has to agree with Hansgeorg Model when he writes: "Throughout his life my father had always candidly expressed his opinions, and he never hesitated to do so when facing Hitler."[6] At times Model acted independently, knowing that he took steps disapproved by Hitler. Later, he justified himself with the convenient argument "that he had acted in the firm belief that what he did was in conformity with Hitler's wishes". In operational matters contradictions were rare. Hitler was at least the equal of most of his Generals in operational knowledge, not to speak of strategy, where the *Wehrmacht* high command was totally deficient. Apart from some elementary notions, at best at battalion level, strategy was not taught at the German war academy. The most outstanding German commander, *Feldmarschall* Erich von Manstein, was a typical example of strategic incompetence. His credo was his 'draw theory', meaning that he could avoid final defeat by forcing a draw, both in the East and in the West, always adding "provided that he would be given Supreme Command." It was a theory to which he remained attached until he was dismissed in 1944 and which he repeated constantly in his memoirs.

Some experts' opinions follow:

Martin van Creveld:

It is hardly a coincidence that all German commanders, with the possible exception of Rundstedt and Kesselring, acted on the operational level only, or at the highest, commanded only Armies and Army Groups. This was also the case with Generals such as Manstein, Guderian, Rommel and Manteuffel, to name but a few. It is as if the US Army had only consisted of Pattons. The German staff doctrine was simply inadequate in training officers for top command positions.[7]

Martin van Creveld again:

Hitler was not an educated expert but, at the highest level, he had a better understanding of all problems of warfare than his Generals. This was his leadership monopoly and his Generals were happy to leave this authority with him. One such example was his decision during the summer of 1941 to suspend the offensive against Moscow and to place the *Schwerpunkt* in the South. *Generaloberst* Halder, head of the *OKH Generalstab*, was furious but felt that he was not the man who could convince Hitler to change his mind. He turned to Guderian for help. Guderian obliged and flew to Rastenburg where he made a plea, lasting some hours, for a continued attack on Moscow. Hitler listened patiently to him and when Guderian finished, he cut

---

5   Reichhelm, p.171.
6   Model/Bradley, p. ix.
7   van Creveld, p.335.

him off with one sentence: 'My Generals understand nothing about war economics.' That was true and both knew it.[8]

Finally, Sebastian Haffner in his perennial, *Anmerkungen zu Hitler* (Comments to Hitler – his book was published in 1971 and has since seen some 90 editions):

> That Hitler was not the 'greatest commander of all times' hardly requires comment. (The slogan 'Gröfaz', *grösster Feldherr aller Zeiten*, was coined by Keitel after the victory over France). In fact, one has to come to his defence against his Generals. According to their memoirs, they could all have won the Second World War, had Hitler not prevented them from doing so. But this is likewise not the truth. Hitler had a wide understanding of military matters. He had learned more from his front-line experience in the First World War than in any other field of knowledge. After the war, he had continued to study military history and military science. Compared with his adversaries, Churchill, Roosevelt and Stalin, all of whom were amateur strategists who often ordered their Generals around, Hitler does not come off badly. True, the concept of an independent *Panzer* force was Guderian's, and the brilliant strategic plan for the victory over France, a much better plan than the Schlieffen plan, was Manstein's creation. But without Hitler, neither Manstein nor Guderian would have prevailed against senior, traditional narrow-minded Army Generals. It was Hitler who understood their ideas and turned them into realities. If Hitler's unimaginative and obstinate strategy during the later years of the war against Russia, was increasingly dominated by his experience from the trench warfare of World War I, one may also ask if Hitler's stubbornness was not instrumental in preventing a total collapse of the *Wehrmacht* during the winter of 1941/42. Hitler was not the military genius that he saw himself, but neither was he the hopeless ignoramus and bungler whom his Generals made the scapegoat for their own failures.[9]

However, the merits of contradicting Hitler should not be exaggerated. In their memoirs, some Generals gave the impression that their life was at stake when they dared contradict Hitler to his face. In reality, contradicting Hitler was no more dangerous for a German commander than for a British or American General who contradicted Churchill or Roosevelt. His ravings against 'old school Generals' and the *Generalstab* notwithstanding, Hitler remained dependent upon them until the very end. The worst that could happen to a General who openly contradicted Hitler, was dismissal, temporary or final. Model did not escape that consequence. By the end of 1943 he was deprived of command for three months. Contradicting Stalin was a different matter. If that occurred, the Red Army General did not know if he would leave the room a free man.

Two other labels that have been affixed to Model can also be disposed of. In his book, "Hitler's Generals",[10] the British historian Richard Brett-Smith has attempted to

---

8   M. van Creveld, *Die deutsche Wehrmacht: eine militärische Beurteilung* in *Die Wehrmacht. Mythos und Realität,* anthology published by the MGFA, Munich 1999, p.330 ff.

9   S. Haffner, *Anmerkungen zu Hitler*, Frankfurt 2000, 22nd edition, p. 80 ff. (Henceforth Haffner).

10 R. Brett-Smith, *Hitler's Generals*, London 1971, (henceforth Brett-Smith).

divide the *Wehrmacht* commanders into separate groups. He called them the Old Guard, *Luftwaffe* Generals, *Waffen-SS* Generals, Cavalry Generals, Nazi Generals, Anti-Nazi Generals, Chiefs of Staff Officers, *Panzer* leaders and "Two Great Commanders".[11] Such classifications are not serious. Only Brett-Smith has been able to include some Generals in the nonexistent group of Anti-Nazi Generals. In many instances *Luftwaffe* Generals commanded ground troops. *Panzer* leaders headed Armies and Army groups which contained few *Panzer*. Cavalry Generals existed in name only. Brett-Smith includes Model among the "Nazi Generals", although he rates his performance as "near great". He adds, "as a field commander Model had few superiors".[12] The label "Nazi General" was adopted by a number of British and American authors. They ascribed some of Model's quick war-time promotions to his proximity to the NSDAP, and to early meetings with Hitler, Goebbels and other dignitaries. In fact, such meetings did not take place. This point will be reverted to, in later chapters dealing with the progress of his career.

In the last chapter of his book on the *Wehrmacht*, the French historian Pierre Masson claimed:

> Toward the end of the war, this class of officer, daring, carefree, exempt from political worries, found their way into the highest ranks of the *Wehrmacht*. They were commanders such as Schörner, Rendulic, Weichs, Manteuffel, and Model.[13]

Both opinions, Model the Nazi General, and Model the new type of officer, can be put aside. Model was certainly a Nazi General but he was not *the* Nazi General. All high-ranking German Generals were "Nazi Generals", as were the ones who participated in the attempted *Putsch* of 20 July 1944. Their gradual but only partial detachment from the NSDAP only took place in the later years of the war.

Among the German Generals who testified at the Nuremberg trials, both *Feldmarschall* von Blomberg and *Generaloberst* Blaskowitz stated that there was no military opposition to Hitler, prior to 1938-1939. There had been no need for it, since Hitler produced the results they had hoped for. *Generaloberst* Reinhardt said that there was hardly a single officer who did not welcome Hitler's extraordinary successes. *Feldmarschall* von Rundstedt emphasized

---

11 Ibid, p. v-vi. The "Two Great Commanders" of Brett-Smith are Manstein, which is certainly correct and Kesselring, which is open to more than doubt.

12 Brett-Smith , p. 201.

13 P. Masson, *Die deutsche Armee – Geschichte der Wehrmacht 1935-1945,* Kirchheim 1996 p. 506 (henceforth Masson). *Feldmarschall* Maximilian von Weichs was born in 1881. In 1940 he was already a *Generaloberst* and in 1943 he was promoted to *Feldmarschall. Generaloberst* Dr. Lothar Rendulic, an Austrian, was hardly "exempt from political worries". In 1936 he had been cashiered from the Austrian Army on grounds of clandestine illegal National-Socialist activities. In 1938, he was reinstated and taken into the *Wehrmacht*. He was one of the few German commanders decorated with the golden party badge. Group qualifications of the kind suggested by Masson are generally off the mark. Model and von Weichs were already Army *OB* in 1941/42. Rendulic received his first Army command on 15. April 1943. We are still more than two years away from "towards the end of the war". Manteuffel obtained his first Army command in 1944. However, he was the scion of a military dynasty which had served Prussia and later Germany over generations.

that restoration of German international equality, and traditional Prussian virtues, were applauded by officers. Erich von Manstein testified at his trial: "The democracy of the Weimar Republic could not impress me. I was at first impressed by the accomplishment of the party. Like most Germans I had hoped that the party would succeed in removing the gap between the working man and the middle class."[14]

At that time, leading members of the plot of 20 July 1944 held similar opinions. *Generaloberst* Beck had already expressed satisfaction with the party's success in the 1930 elections. He wrote to a Ms Gossler after Hitler's appointment: "I have waited for this for many years and I am happy that my hopes were not in vain. Today is the first ray of light since 1918." In 1930, Beck had testified in court in favour of three young Lieutenants who were tried for National-Socialist agitation in the *Reichswehr*. His testimony led Hitler to view Beck with strong approval. During the Blomberg-Fritsch crisis, Beck was Goebbels' candidate to become Fritsch's successor as commander in chief of the Army. Goebbels had a strong dislike of Brauchitsch.

In 1932, Henning von Tresckow had encouraged his fellow officers to educate their soldiers in a National-Socialist spirit. Tresckow would later become the inspirational military leader of the plot of 20 July 1944. Another 1944 conspirator, the future Colonel Albrecht Mertz von Quirnheim, became liaison officer between the Army and the *SA*.

On 4 September 1933, Lieutenant Helmuth Stieff wrote to his wife:

Hitler's ideas about nation and society are remarkable, to the point that one can speak of a real turn…the racial problem is in harmony with Christianity …"[15] After the death of Hindenburg, he wrote to his wife: "… I am entirely convinced of the sincerity of the *Führer* …[16]

As a General, Stieff would become a conspirator in 1944. He was hanged after 20 July. Whether Claus von Stauffenberg led his squadron in 'a triumphant march' on 30 January 1933, has not been substantiated. Some of his biographers have expressed doubt,[17] but his positive attitude toward the regime change and his agreement to the first racial laws have never been disputed. Eleven years later, he planted the bomb on 20 July 1944.

Some Generals were more "Nazi" than others. Manfred Messerschmidt calls the adherence of the German Generals to National-Socialism a partial identification, (*Teilidentität*). A variable degree of identification with National-Socialism could be found among all the officers who later held high commands in the East. The smallest group consisted of National-Socialists by early conviction. That group included Eduard Dietl, Eugen Ritter von Schobert and Ernst Busch. They had shown NS convictions before 1933. Dietl had been a member of the DAP, the *Deutsche Arbeiterpartei*, the forerunner of the

---

14 Manstein Trial (English version) Yad Vashem Library, Jerusalem. A number of pages in the English version are unnumbered. Also in P. Leverkuehn, *Verteidigung Mansteins*, Hamburg 1950, p.3.

15 H. Mühleisen (ed): *Helmuth Stieff Briefe, Berlin 1999*, p.76. (Henceforth Stieff).

16 Ibid, p.89.

17 Peter Hoffmann writes that the parade was led by *Oberleutnant* Hasso von Manteuffel and that Stauffenberg who happened to pass by, joined it. P Hoffmann, *Claus Schenk Graf von Stauffenberg. Eine Biographie*, Munich 2008, p.134.

NSDAP. In 1923 he had a secret talk with Hitler and promised him active support in his *Putsch*.[18] The Generals who favoured a modernization of the Army, in particular the creation of independent *Panzer* units such as Guderian, Reinhardt and Hoth, became enthusiastic followers of the party because Hitler came out in favour of their wishes.

Another group comprised the Generals who, in 1933, were already over the age of 50, among them Fedor von Bock, Gerd von Rundstedt, Wilhelm Ritter von Leeb, Ewald von Kleist, Georg von Küchler, Adolf Strauss and Maximilian von Weichs. Those Generals were in agreement with a number of points of the NS programme and approved of Hitler's appointment as Chancellor. Others, with Erich von Manstein as prime example, were careerists. In private talks with friends they would make jokes about Hitler, deprecate his leadership while extolling their own, but eagerly applaud him when visiting him at his headquarters. (In private conversations, Manstein referred to Hitler as a *Pinkelstratege*. He taught his dachshund to raise his right paw upon hearing *Heil Hitler*. On 20 April 1939, Hitler's 50th birthday, Manstein addressed his Division in a panegyrical praise of the *Führer*.)

Probably the best description of Model's attitude is given by his son: "My father has been a loyal follower, a *treuer Gefolgsmann*, of Adolf Hitler."[19] Model was aged 41 when Hitler became chancellor. At that time he already sympathized with National-Socialism. Gradually his sympathy became progressively unconditional and turned into an exaggerated adherence. His awakening to reality, and to his responsibilities, occurred only the day before his suicide.

The stages by which all German Generals, who held high commands in World War II, were drawn closer to National-Socialism have been analyzed by Hürter:

1. The education of officers in Imperial Germany required an uncritical belief in authority and a one-sided interpretation of credos such as "duty and obedience". Moral values were not yet destroyed, but they had been gradually weakened during the First World War and the revolutionary years that followed.
2. The traditional prejudices against Socialists, Slavs and Jews, gained increasing ground during the same period. Eastern European people were viewed as culturally inferior. Socialists were viewed as responsible both for the disappearance of the Empire and for the weakness of the Weimar Republic. This led to the slogan "Jewish Bolshevism", lurking as a danger from the East.
3. The military doctrine became radicalized with the emergence of total war.
4. The three elements above paved the way to the acceptance of a totalitarian state which could unify the nation and, at the same time, held out prospects for personal careers.
5. Widening of political aims. At first they aimed at the overcoming of the Versailles heritage. Then followed dreams of "greater Germany". In turn those led to the craving for European supremacy, finally giving place to radical plans of conquests in the East. Whatever doubts existed, they were gradually overshadowed by the

---

18 J. Knab, *Generaloberst Eduard Dietl*, in G. Ueberschär (ed.) *Hitlers militärische Elite. Vom Kriegsbeginn bis zum Weltkriegsende*, Darmstadt 1998, p.29.
19 Model/Bradley, p. viii.

fascination of growing power that gradually let 'right' and 'morality' fade into the shadows.[20]

The racial discriminations introduced after 1933 encountered no objections. Anti-Semitism and the exclusion of Jews in the officer corps, whether active or in the reserve, were part of the German officer's *credo*. When Colonel Erich von Manstein lodged a protest against the retro-active introduction of racial laws in the *Reichswehr*, he was not motivated by sympathy for Jews, or "Non-Aryans". His main concern was that the Army should be master of the fate of its members, without intervention from "other bodies". What the narrow-minded Generals overlooked, was that their support of the regime would turn them, step by step, into active accomplices of its crimes, and lead many of them to active participation therein. On 26 July 1945, when Auschwitz and the gas chambers had already become general public knowledge, the US 7th Army recorded a conversation about National-Socialism between *Generaloberst* Guderian and *Feldmarschall* Ritter von Leeb. Guderian had never hidden his sympathies for the swastika, while Ritter von Leeb had succeeded in deluding the IMT that he had been an opponent. Guderian said: "The fundamental principles were fine," and Ritter von Leeb replied: "That is true".[21]

Hürter raises a hypothetical question:

Nobody knows if Beck, von Fritsch, von Witzleben or Blaskowitz would have behaved differently as *OB* in the East than von Rundstedt, von Kluge, Hoth or von Küchler.[22]

Masson's opinion, about the "new types of officers", likewise does not stand up to examination. Walter Model was an "old school officer", like almost all the commanders of Army Groups and Armies during the first two years of the war. The only two exceptions to the typical career followed by "old school officers" were von Schobert and Busch. They had never been members of the *Generalstab*. Not surprisingly, we find their names among the totally convinced Nazis. The most comprehensive analysis of the careers of the highest *Wehrmacht* commanders in the East 1941/42, including Model's, is found in Hürter's recent book, which will be the main source for this introduction.[23]

---

20 J. Hürter, *Hitlers Heerführer. Die deutschen Oberbefehlshaber im Krieg gegen die Sowjetunion 1941/42*, Munich 2006. p.599 (henceforth Hürter).

21 Hürter, p.200 ff.

22 Hürter/Küchler, p. 243.

23 Hürter gives one of the many examples of Hitler's preference for 'conservative old school Generals' in appointments to highest commands. When Ritter von Leeb gave up command of Army Group North on 16 January 1942, Hitler had to choose between two of his Army commanders, Busch and von Küchler. Busch was a convinced Nazi, von Küchler was considered to be a conservative General. He was one of the Generals who had launched the sharpest protests against excesses in Poland. As a result of his attacks upon Himmler and the SS, he was the only Army commander in Poland who was not promoted to Generaloberst after fighting in Poland came to an end. Von Küchler's wife was known for strong anti-Nazi views which she also expressed in public. The Küchler home in East Prussia was known in party circles as the 'Küchler clique'. Yet, when the choice arose between von Küchler and Busch, von Küchler was given preference, because Busch had never been a *Generalstab* officer. After the war, von Küchler was given one of the longest sentences, 20 years, by the IMT (case 12) for crimes committed

As one of Germany's elitist bodies, the Army had established stringent rules of admission to its officer corps. During the first half of the 19th Century, most officers belonged to the Prussian aristocracy, with many being *ostelbische* land-owners (from east of the Elbe, in other words East Prussian). Later, the officer corps was gradually opened to the non-aristocratic middle-class. Wilhelm II, who was more aware of changing times and values than his critics credit him, stated in 1890 that officers should be recruited from aristocracy by birth, and aristocracy by spirit. He defined the latter as men inspired by love for their King and their fatherland, having a warm heart for soldierly values, and possessing a Christian mentality or outlook. The request for a "Christian mentality" was one of the cornerstones of the exclusion of Jews from both the active and the reserve officer corps.

The opening of the Army to members of the middle-class was limited by exclusions. In order to be accepted as an officer, the candidate had to come from *erwünschte Kreise* (desirable social spheres). Among those were officer families, higher level civil servants, clerics, land-owners and large estate tenants, physicians, pharmacists, architects and other professions requiring an academic education. Less desirable, but still acceptable, were independent businessmen, journalists, performing artists, and in Prussia, Roman Catholics, notwithstanding Wilhelm II's call for a "Christian mentality". (*Generaloberst* Reinhardt, whose father was a private banker, barely made it to the desirable social spheres.) Sons of non-commissioned officers and subaltern civil servants were undesirable.[24] Even less desirable were candidates from the lower professional strata, simple employees, craftsmen and factory workers. Members of national minorities and Jews were totally excluded.[25]

To qualify for an officer career, a candidate had either to go through one of the cadet schools, (these institutions were abolished after World War I) or take the *Abitur,* preferably at a *Humanistisches Gymnasium*, a secondary school with special emphasis on Latin and Greek. Other *Gymnasiums*, such as the *Realgymnasium*, still taught Latin, but dropped Greek in favour of English or French. A latecomer among the *Gymnasiums*

---

in Russia. (J. Hürter, 'Konservative Mentalität, militärischer Pragmatismus, ideologisierte Kriegführung. Das Beispiel des Generals Georg von Küchler' in G. Hirschfeld/T. Jersak (ed.) *Karieren im Nationalsozialismus. Funktionseliten zwischen Mitwirkung und Distanz*, Frankfurt 2004, pp.239-253.

24 Only Feldmarschall Friedrich Paulus did not come from 'desirable social circles'. His father was a minor official at a re-education home for juvenile delinquents. The Imperial Navy turned him down because of this family background, the Army showed itself more liberal and accepted him.

25 As World War II progressed and losses of officers began to mount by the day, those criteria were increasingly done away with. One of the most interesting examples is the career of *General der Panzertruppe* Walter Fries. Fries began World War I as a reserve sergeant and rose to reserve second Lieutenant in 1915. No further promotions took place. After the war, Fries joined the ordinary police and became a gymnastics teacher. He rose to Major in the police in 1934 and was taken into the Army as a Major in 1936. His close to meteoric ascension began in 1943, when as *Generalmajor* he was given command of a division. In January 1944 he rose to *Generalleutnant* and in December to *General der Panzertruppe* and commander of a *Panzerkorps*. He was decorated with the Knight's Cross of the Iron Cross with oak leaves and swords.

was the *Oberrealschule*, which taught neither Latin nor Greek, but put the emphasis on mathematics, science and modern languages. It carried less prestige.

After completing their years as Officer Cadets, the future officers had to apply for admission to a Regiment. Thus the final word for their future career rested with their acceptance by the Regimental commander. Marriage of an officer required the consent of the Regimental commander, the officer had to show that neither himself nor his bride were in debt and that his future wife was *standesgemäss* (an unblemished social background). When Hitler attempted to weaken this requirement in a National-Socialist spirit, he was confronted with Blomberg's mésalliance.

All the *OB* in the East, during the years 1941/42, had begun their military careers before World War I and all had served in World War I. Walter Model's father had been promoted to *Oberlehrer* (senior high school teacher). He was given the prestigious title of *Königlich preussischer Musikdirektor*, before Walter Model joined the Army. Model was thus a fully fledged member of the "desirable spheres". (Model's recent American biographer, Steven Newton, is apparently not acquainted with German social hierarchies at that time, when he dismissively refers to Model as "just a son of a music teacher").[26]

Model took his *Abitur* at the *Humanistische Domgymnasium* in Naumburg. He entered the von Alvensleben Infantry Regiment 52 in Cottbus, as a *Fahnenjunker* (Officer Cadet), and was promoted to *Leutnant* in the same year. Still as *Leutnant*, he became *Adjutant* to one of the battalions of his Regiment. In practice, the *Adjutant* of a battalion or a regiment was the equivalent of the chief of staff of that unit. During the First World War, Model served both in combat units and in the *Generalstab* after completing the short "Sedan course". Admission to the 4,000 *Reichswehr* officers, authorized by the Versailles Treaty, was almost exclusively reserved for *Generalstab* officers. Model's acceptance into the new officer corps was hardly ever in doubt. One of the most noteworthy exceptions was Erwin Rommel who had never been a *Generalstab* officer.

Thereafter, Model's career followed the same pattern as the other *OB* in the East, with the exception of Erich von Manstein, who served mainly in the *Generalstab*. Troop service alternated with the *Truppenamt* and later with the *Generalstab*, when it was officially re-established in 1935. Model's highest troop command before World War II was regimental commander. He was promoted to *Generalmajor* in 1938. In 1939, he was foreseen as chief of staff of one of the armies, in the event of a war with Czechoslovakia.

The oldest *OB* in the East in 1941 was von Rundstedt who was born in 1875. He was thus fifteen years older than Model, less than a generation. Most of the other *OB* were of the same age group, with a few years between them. Manstein was four years older than Model, as were Rendulic and Reinhardt. Paulus and Rommel were of the same age.

---

26 Steven Newton, *Hitler's Commander, Field Marshal Walther* [sic.] *Model – Hitler's favourite General*, Cambridge 2006, p.332 (henceforth Newton). Newton further writes that "for a family of such modest means, an officer' career might have been out of reach" and that the Model family had to prevail upon the influence of his uncle Martin Model, a reserve lieutenant(!?), to gain Walter's admittance to the *Kriegsschule* in Neissen (?). p.6. It would be interesting to know from which source Newton obtained his statement, which has no basis in reality.

Related literature and information sources

Germany

Details of military operations involving Model's units are extensively documented in the files of the Federal Military Archives in Freiburg.[27] Amongst those accounts are the war diaries, the orders of the day, and a variety of reports by Model's staff.

In the last fifteen years, many serious younger German historians, men and women in their thirties and forties, have concentrated on the analysis of the *Wehrmacht's* responsibility for starting the Second World War, and on its participation in the most heinous crimes of the Third *Reich*. Such interest was sparked off by the two *Wehrmacht* exhibitions on 'Crimes of the *Wehrmacht*', which were displayed in most major cities in Germany and Austria and seen by hundreds of thousands of visitors. The first exhibition was closed down because a number of the photos shown were incorrectly named and a number of chapters contained significant errors. The second exhibition, of a much higher quality, corrected those unnecessary oversights and other errors.

Much of the research in Germany, over the last fifteen to twenty years, has produced astonishing results. Johannes Hürter's book on the *OB* in the East, during the first two years of "*Barbarossa*", the Russo-German conflict, has already been mentioned.

Less than half of the six million Jews who perished in the Shoah were victims of the gas chambers in the extermination camps in Poland . The majority were murdered by the *Einsatzgruppen,* the police battalions and *Wehrmacht* units.

In his important work, *Kalkulierte Morde*, Professor Christian Gerlach has been able to show that more than half of the civilians, inclusive of Jews in Belorussia, were murdered by *Wehrmacht* officers and soldiers. SS, Police, and local Russian aides accounted for 45% of the victims, the *Einsatzgruppen* of the *SD* accounted for "only" 20%.[28]

Jochen Böhler has shown how the *Wehrmacht* in Poland acted as the forerunner of the future war of annihilation in Russia.[29] Klaus-Michael Mallmann and Martin Cüppers have established that a special *Einsatzgruppe* under *SS-Obersturmbannführer* Walther Rauff, the developer of the gas vans, had been attached to Rommel's *Afrika Armee*. Rauff met several times with Rommel's chief of staff, General Westphal. Rauff's *Einsatzgruppe* was scheduled to engage in the murder of the Jews in Palestine, had Rommel not been halted at El Alamein.[30] Only the lack of shipping space prevented Rauff from deporting the Jews of Tunisia during the months of the German occupation there. The plans were

---

27 Bundesarchiv – Militärarchiv, Freiburg Branch, Collection N/6, (The "N" indicates documents from the estate, *Nachlass*, of an officer. N/6 is a relatively small Model estate.) However, Hansgeorg Model intends to transfer the documents of his estate to the BA-MA at a later date.

28 C. Gerlach, *Kalkulierte Morde. Die deutsche Wirtschafts-und Vernichtungspolitik in Weissrussland 1941-1944,* Hamburg 1999, p.1151 (henceforth Gerlach).

29 J. Böhler, *Auftakt zum Vernichtungskrieg. Die Wehrmacht in Polen 1939*, Frankfurt 2006.

30 K. M. Mallmann/Martin Cüppers, *Halbmond und Hakenkreuz. Das Dritte Reich, die Araber und Palästina*, Darmstadt 2006, and K.Mallmann/Andrej Angrick, 'Immer davongekommen Wie sich Walter Rauff erfolgreich seinen Richtern entzog in Die Gestapo nach 1945', Damstadt 2009.

already drawn up. One will have to agree with the writer Ralph Giordano, who urged the removal of Rommel's name from *Bundeswehr* barracks.[31]

Most early British and US works about World War II were strongly influenced by the writings of Sir Basil Liddell Hart, and his book *The Other Side of the Hill*.[32] It is a collection of talks which the author had, immediately after the war, with a number of German Generals. Before the war, Liddell Hart supported the appeasement policies of the "Cliveden Set". During the war, he repeatedly advocated a compromise peace. Close to unqualified praise of the German Generals became one of Liddell Hart's means to justify his previous positions. Liddell Hart spoke no German and thus had to rely either on the knowledge of English on the part of the Germans interviewed by him, or on the services of an interpreter. Liddell Hart was particularly outspoken in his support of Manstein and he was one of the British contributors to Manstein's defence fund at the *Feldmarschall's* trial.[33] Since no love was lost between Manstein and Model, Manstein's negative views about Model have found their way into Liddell Hart's book. Some examples will be mentioned later.

A majority of the Conservative establishment in Britain, and also the Republican majority in Congress during most of the Truman years, were opposed to the trials of German Generals for war crimes. Many were active in their efforts to obtain their early release. Some British and US works come close to being heroic epics of German commanders, particularly if the author has made their personal acquaintance.[34] The Cold War also played its part. Germany had turned into an ally and the Soviet Union was the potential enemy. Modern German historians must be complimented for concentrating upon analyses of actions by the *Wehrmacht*, and for refraining from the revisionist predilection to set them off against reprehensible actions committed by other armies.

Books on Model

Walter Model has been the subject of four biographies. The first attempts were made by Konrad Leppa, an Austrian author. Prior to the *Anschluss* of Austria to the *Reich*, Leppa wrote articles in Austrian military journals edited by Colonel Dr Lothar Rendulic, who

---

31 R. Giordano, *Die Traditionslüge. Vom Kriegerkult in der Bundeswehr*, Cologne 2000, p.314. Rauff met with Lieutenant Colonel Westphal, at that time chief of Staff of the *Afriakorps*. Plans for action in Palestine had to be abandoned after El Alamein. After the war, Rauff found refuge in Latin America.

32 B. Liddell Hart, *The Other Side of the Hill*, London 1951 (henceforth Liddell Hart).

33 Did Liddell Hart and Manstein ever meet? Liddell Hart refers to conversations with Manstein, while Manstein states in the foreword to his memoirs *Verlorene Siege* that he had never met him. E. von Manstein, *Verlorene Siege*, Bonn 1955 (henceforth *Verlorene Siege*). On the second page of the foreword (unnumbered), Manstein writes: "*Ich selbst habe Liddell Hart leider nicht kennengelernt*" ("Unfortunately I have never met Liddell Hart personally"). One has to believe Manstein's statement, since he would certainly have mentioned talks with Liddell Hart, had they occurred.

34 One such example is *The Last Battle* by Cornelius Ryan, in which he turns *Generaloberst* Gotthard Heinrici, a rather unattractive person, into a knight in shining armour. (C. Ryan, *The Last Battle*, London 1966).

during the war rose through the ranks to become *Generaloberst.*[35] Leppa engaged in serious research and in some instances his book is a reliable source. He intended a three volume biography, but published only the first volume, *Von Genthin bis vor Moskaus Tore,* which ends with Model's command of XXXXI *Panzer* Corps. Leppa soon became embroiled in conflicts with his publisher. He then thought of publishing the remainder of his work himself, but finally gave up. For Model, it was fortunate that Leppa was unable to go beyond his first volume, since the author's enthusiasm for the Third *Reich* would have contributed to attaching the "Nazi General" label firmly to Model's name. Nevertheless, Leppa's volume is an indispensable source for Model's early years and will be frequently quoted.

The first complete biography of Model was written by Walter Görlitz. It was first published in 1975.[36] The paperback edition of the same book was published in 1992.[37] His book is mostly hero worship. All of Görlitz's works, and his books about Model are no exception, are typical examples of an author who has remained primarily a journalist, and who has endeavoured to turn journalistic style into historical reliability. Görlitz never names the source of his statements – at the end of every chapter he has a list of people whom he purports to have interviewed. My talks with a number of them revealed that either Görlitz did not appear at all for an interview or, in some instances, he sent his secretary. Important sources, like Reichhelm and Behr, told me that Görlitz appeared for a few minutes at their homes and promised to return for a more detailed interview, which never materialized. A number of people interviewed by Görlitz have taken exception to the statements attributed to them, either in letters to Görlitz or in conversations with me. Görlitz will have to be quoted frequently, in order to correct a number of manifest errors.

My German book on Model appeared in 2001.[38]

A serious attempt has been made by the American Professor Steven H. Newton, with his biography of Model, published in 2006.[39] His book is the most detailed account published hitherto of Model's military actions, from the beginning of his career until his last day. In fact, one could call it a "Model war diary". For any reader who wants to follow Model's military operations from the first day of World War One until the very end and his suicide, Newton's book is an indispensable source Unfortunately, the book is marred by many errors, some of which should have been deleted by an editor, and also noticed by the author. A number of names of personalities are misspelt. His hero Walter Model becomes Walther Model, (in further quotations from Newton in this book, Model's first name is spelled correctly "Walter"). Adolf Hitler is written Adolph Hitler, Adolf Strauss becomes Adolph Strauss, General Friessner becomes Freissner, Friedrich Paulus is turned into Friedrich von Paulus, Colonel Claus von Stauffenberg becomes Klaus von Stauffenburg, Otto Wöhler becomes Wohler. Model's first regimental commander, Colonel Fromme, is spelled Fromm, which can lead a reader to believe that he was the

---

35   Konrad Leppa, *Generalfeldmarschall Walter Model, von Genthin bis vor Moskaus Tore,* Nuremberg, 1962, henceforth: Leppa.

36   W. Görlitz, *Model – Strategie der Defensive,* Berlin, 1975, henceforth Görlitz.

37   W. Görlitz, *Model – Der Feldmarschall und sein Endkampf an der Ruhr,* Berlin, 1992.

38   M. Stein, *Generalfeldmarschall Walter Model. Legende und Wirklichkeit*, Bissendorf 2001.

39   S. Newton, *Hitler's Commander: Field Marshal Walther [sic] Model – Hitler's Favourite General.* Da Capo Press, 2005.

future commander of the *Ersatzheer, Generaloberst* Friedrich Fromm. City names fare no better, the city Tourcoing becomes Turcoing. Matters become even worse when Newton quotes German texts. *Kriegstagebuch* (war diary) is spelt *Kreitagebuch, Zweckoptimismus* becomes *Zweckoptimisimus*. A General Zorn is described by Newton as one of Model's subordinates who rose to Army *OB*. There were two Generals Zorn, Eduard Zorn and Hans Zorn. Neither rose to Army Commander. Hans Zorn was a Corps Commander and was killed in action in 1943 on the Eastern Front. Eduard Zorn was Division Commander and was killed in action at Colmar in 1945. It would be petty to continue this list, which could take up several pages, especially since such errors can be corrected in future editions.

The designation of Model as Hitler's favourite General is misleading. Perhaps Newton had been inspired by a mention in Görlitz. "In April 1945 Hitler stated that "Model was my best *Feldmarschall*"[40]. He may also have read the chapter about Model "*Walter Model – Hitlers bester Feldmarschall*", written by Joachim Ludewig, in an anthology about the *Wehrmacht* commanders by Ronald Smelser and Enrico Syring.[41] Hitler had no favourite Generals just as he had no friends.[42] For a time, Erwin Rommel was almost the "favourite General", but his aura waned when the *Afrika-Armee* was forced to surrender. Hitler had no hesitation in forcing him to commit suicide when he, wrongly, believed that Rommel had taken part in the 20 July 1944 attempt. Hitler happened to have a weak spot for Ernst Busch, in spite of the General's constant failures. At the end, Hitler may have had a preference for *Feldmarschall* Ferdinand Schörner. Model's personality was too rough and distant to generate genuine friendship.

Other errors and misrepresentations by Newton are more serious and one may wonder from which sources they were obtained. The relations between Model and General Erhard Raus (p. 157 ff), which according to Newton had an influence upon Model's performance, are exaggerated. Raus was one of the three former Austrian Generals who rose to *Generaloberst*, the other two were Alexander Löhr and Lothar Rendulic. Raus was one the many divisional commanders in Model's XXXXI corps and later in Model's 9th Army. Later, as *OB* of 3rd *Panzer* Army, he was for some weeks one of Model's direct subordinates in Army Group *Nordukraine*. He did get along well with Model, but neither had any influence upon the career of the other.[43] He was one of the good *Panzer* commanders but he was never part of the highest command elite and was not considered for the command of an Army Group. (I shall refer to Raus in detail in the chapter describing the battles for Rzhev.) The idea of a "conspiracy" between von Kluge and Model, to present opposite opinions to Hitler in order to obtain Hitler's agreement

---

40 Görlitz, p.230.

41 R. Smelser/E. Syring (ed.), *Die Militärelite des Dritten Reiches. 27 biographische Skizzen*. Berlin 1998. The article by Joachim Ludewig is on pages 368-387.

42 Ernst Röhm was the only man among Hitler's first satraps with whom Hitler had remained with the familiar "*Du*". During the night of the long knives in 1934, Hitler had him shot. Röhm had become politically unbearable. Sebastian Haffner advances the opinion that, given Hitler's strong aversion to intimacy, the "Du" may have been an additional motive for getting rid of Röhm.(Haffner, p.10).

43 The Raus Estate at the Austrian State Archives (Ref. ÖStA, NL/B, C 186) is particularly voluminous and covers all the phases of Raus's life, including the war years. In no file is there any mention of an influence of Model upon Raus's career or vice versa.

to the one desired by both is not serious, given the strong mutual dislike between the two commanders. Also no commander would have dared to play games of that kind with Hitler.[44] Newton is laudatory about Harpe: "Harpe fully justified Model's confidence" (p.259) but he seems not to be aware that Model (also Kluge) had given Harpe the worst possible performance ratings. Harpe was ultimately demoted from Army Group *OB* to Army *OB*.[45] In his account of Reichhelm's departure from the *Ruhrkessel* to take up his duties of chief of staff of Walther Wenck's 12th Army, Newton is guilty of a *damnatio memoriae*, when he writes that "in a fit of spontaneous anger Model accused Reichhelm of deserting the Army Group at a critical moment, and of trying to save himself at everyone else's expense. After curtly 'dismissing Reichhelm'…" (p.353). The circumstances of Reichhelm's departure from the *Kessel* have already been described.

Some of Newton's sources are also of doubtful quality. While describing Franz Kurowski as 'a historian' would elicit a smile from genuine historians, quoting Paul Carell now as a serious source is simply unforgivable. The fact that other US and British authors, among them Brett-Smith, also refer to Carell and that important US dailies had given his books favourable reviews more than half a century ago, does not make Newton's mention of him more palatable. No historian of standing would now quote a man who was indicted for murder in connection with the slaughter of the Hungarian Jews and whose works have long been exposed as pure Nazi lies. Details about Paul Carell's life and writings are given in an annex to this chapter. A glance at Newton's endnotes seems to indicate that he has not consulted the German military archives 'on the spot'. It appears that he contented himself with the material in the US National Archives, mostly with extracts from war diaries, which sometimes are a doubtful source. A number of documents, which are obviously available in the archives, are quoted from books by other authors. One such example is a particularly repulsive order attributed to Model at the beginning of the battle for the *Hürtgen Wald*. This order contains words like "greedy Jew, lusting for gain", "murderous bloodthirsty Bolsheviks". Model has indeed issued a number of horrendous orders, but those words were not his style and he was never vulgar. A production of the original, with archive reference, would have been a must.

Soviet Union

The six-volume *History of the Great Patriotic War* mentions by name all Generals of the *Wehrmacht* who faced the Red Army.[46] However, it is virtually void of any favourable assessments of German Generals. The following comment about Model is one of the few exceptions. "Recently, some West German military historians tried to represent *Feldmarschall* Model, Commander in Chief of the 9th Army, as the 'Lion of Defence,' and to show his retreat from Rzhev as a planned and successful operation."[47] Model's fears for

---

44 Newton, p. 252 ff.

45 Extracts of performance ratings by Model and Kluge, 5 March 1942: Model: "Not enough farsighted in operative understanding. Therefore he can only be permitted to command an Army under strict supervision." Kluge added: "In my view totally unfit for command of an Army" (NOKW 141).

46 Red Army Archives, *Istoria Velikoj Otetschestvennoj Voiny Sovietskojo Sojuza 1941-1945*, Moscow 1963, henceforth: IVOVSS.

47 IVOVSS, Volume 3, p.143.

the failure of Operation Citadel were emphasized and, from the Soviet point of view, of course, were right on the mark because they confirmed the Red Army's effectiveness in counter-measure operations. Then, the typical obligatory last sentence in Soviet military accounts appeared, "The 'Lion of Defence' did not succeed in resisting the Red Army offensive."[48]

The same chapter contains a list of *Wehrmacht* Generals classified as war criminals for having taken an active part in scorched-earth operations, *Feldmarschalls* von Kluge, von Küchler, Ritter von Leeb, von Manstein, Model, and Generals Foertsch, Heinrici, Lindemann, Ruoff, Schmidt, Siewert, and Wagener.[49]

With few exceptions, memoirs written by Red Army Generals were still being written and re-written, under partial or complete censorship, with the assistance of anonymous helpers. Zhukov stressed Model's leadership of Army Group Centre in laudatory terms, but without mentioning Model's name.[50] Rokossovsky mentioned Model in his memoirs by name, and is positive.[51]

Terminology

German Generals' ranks, all ranks of the *Waffen* SS and German military terminology will be given in the vernacular. Only a few ranks and other elements of military terminology lend themselves to exact translation. There is little sense in translating the German *Generaloberst* into Colonel-General, since no such rank exists in the British or US Armies. A German *Generalleutnant* is one rank below a British or US Lieutenant General, since the German Army had no Brigadiers. (In the *Bundeswehr* US/British ranks have been adopted). Further confusions may arise with the Red Army, which contains a number of ranks and terminologies adapted from the German. The Red Army has a Colonel-General (*General polkovnik),* whose rank is lower than a German *Generaloberst.* He is outranked by both Army Generals and Marshals of the Soviet Union. A Russian Marshal of Artillery, Tanks and other weapons is likewise outranked both by Army Generals and Marshals of the Soviet Union.

---

48 IVOVSS, Volume 3, p.277.

49 IVOVSS, Volume 3, p.441.

50 G. Zhukov, *Vospominania i Rasmyschlenia,* Moscow 1969, p.587, henceforth: Zhukov.

51 Soviet Generals, who had been imprisoned in the *Gulag,* were not supposed to mention this in their memoirs, but they found a subtle way around this censorship, which left no doubt with their readers as to their fate. Two examples: Marshal Rokossovsky begins his memoirs with the following paragraph: 'In the spring of 1940, after a holiday with my family in Sochi, I received an invitation from Marshal Semyon Timoshenko. The People's Commissar of Defence received me warmly…Marshal Timoshenko suggested that I resume command of the 5th Cavalry Corps, which I had commanded in 1936-37…' K. Rokossovsky, *Soldatski dolg. Voennie Memuary,* Moscow 1970, p. 5 (henceforth Rokossovsky). Marshal Meretskov was Zhukov's predecessor as Chief of Staff of the Red Army. Shortly after the outbreak of the war, he was arrested and severely beaten. After a few weeks, he was set free and reinstated. In his memoirs, he writes: "In September 1941 I received a new post. I recall how I was summoned to the Supreme Commander in Chief. When I entered his study, Stalin was standing at the map. He turned round, took a few steps towards me and inquired about my health. I replied that I was fit." K. Meretskov, *Na sluszba narodu,* Moscow 1971, p.141.

In German military terminology the rank of *Feldmarschall* comes close to a myth. In the British Army, Field Marshal is simply an additional rank. One could write that at Stalingrad Manstein did not behave like a *Feldmarschall*. However, one could not make a similar statement about a British Field Marshal.

The *Generalstab*

The German *Generalstab* was a unique institution with no equivalent in any other Army. To translate it as 'General Staff' makes no sense. Until the end of the First World War, the *Generalstab* was the highest military authority in the Imperial Army and its Chief outranked the Commander in Chief of the Army. He was the only officer who could turn directly to the Emperor (*Immediatvortrag*). After 1918 this was no longer the case. However, a *Wehrmacht* officer, who had succeeded in joining the *Generalstab* after years of training, enjoyed a particular status.

The *Generalstab* between 1920 and 1939

The term *Generalstab* will be used throughout this section, although the official designation between 1920 and 1935 was *Truppenamt*. However this was only a 'linguistic artefact', chosen to circumvent the clause of the Versailles treaty abolishing the *Generalstab*.

Conditions of admission to the *Generalstab* became more severe in 1920 than they were before the First World War. A first examination, the *Wehrkreisprüfung*, was made compulsory for all active officers. (Before the First World War, it was facultative and reserved for officers who intended to be admitted to the *Generalstab*). When taking the *Wehrkreisprüfung*, officers were between 25 and 30 years of age, and had already served for five years. The rules and questionnaires were established for the whole Army by the T-4 department of the *Generalstab*. The syllabus consisted of military matters, and some general subjects such as history, the constitution and foreign languages. The examination was written, and the candidates were isolated. Immediately after completion, the papers were sent to T-4. No prior review or corrections were permitted. The papers were examined separately and independently by three T-4 officers whose conclusions remained secret. If a candidate failed, the examination could be repeated once, if the candidate failed again, he was excluded from further attempts to join the *Generalstab*.[52]

Officers, who had successfully passed the *Wehrkreisprüfung*, were admitted to a first course (D 1) that lasted one year. It was followed by several weeks of troop service. After completion of the troop service, the candidates joined a second one-year course (D 2). The D 2 course was followed by a two weeks' exercise, which decided upon admission to the third course. Again, the selection was very severe. Only 20% of the candidates were admitted to the third course, the remainder being sent back to troop service. The third course was called the "R-course" and lasted three years. It came under the direct supervision by the Army commander in chief. At the end of the R-course, another two weeks' exercise took place. It came under the direction of a number of very senior commanders and, at

---

52 Even at this stage, conditions of admission to the *Generalstab* were very severe. In his book, *Der deutsche Generalstabsoffizier. Seine Ausbildung und Ausbildung in Reichswehr, Wehrmacht und Bundesheer,* Frankfurt 1968, Hansgeorg Model gives the following example: "1922: At *Wehrkreis* VI 164 officers took the *Wehrkreisprüfung*. 144 were sent home, at the end of the successive examinations only one officer was accepted into the *Generalstab*."

times, the Army Commander in Chief. The results of the R-course and the exercise finally determined the suitability of the officer for entry into the *Generalstab*. Then followed two years of probation. If they were successful, the officers became officially members of the *Generalstab*, added "i.G." after their rank and wore carmine striped trousers and silver collar patches.

Generalstab officers, who were foreseen for the highest ranks, attended the one-year "Reinhardt course" at the Berlin University.[53] At the end of the course, no further examinations took place, but the officers received a performance rating. The Reinhardt course was followed by a two months visit to a foreign country.

Functions of the most important Generalstab officers
- Ia was the first *Generalstab* officer and head of all other *Generalstab* officers in his unit. Since German divisions had no staff, the Ia was *de facto* the chief of staff of the division. He has thus higher authority than the G3 in the US Army divisions.
- Ib was the second officer and responsible for supply.
- Ic was responsible for general intelligence.
- Ic/AO was the subordinate of the Ic and responsible for enemy intelligence.
- Id was the direct assistant to the Ia.
- IIa was responsible for the assignments of officers to his units.
- IIb was responsible for the positions of his units' NCOs.

Designation of German military archive documents
The first comprehensive collection was put together by the Americans during the immediate post-war years. They are now deposited at Nuremberg and are designated by NOKW, followed by numbers, e.g. NOKW 2458.

The archives of the German military at Freiburg (BA-MA) are given in a key which enables an archivist to immediately locate them.

Example taken from Model's 9th Army:
- BA-MA, RH 20-9/542
- BA-MA = *Bundesarchiv-Militärarchiv*
- RH = *Reichsheer* – Ground forces of the Reich
- 20= Second World War
- 9= 9th Army
- 542=File 542 from 9th Army documents.

For most readers this key is unimportant, since the contents of the relevant documents are in the text and the reference of the BA-MA is given in the footnote.

The word "tank" does not exist in *Wehrmacht* terminology. A German "tank" is a *Panzer* and the term *Panzer* covers all types of armoured vehicles.

Gradually, German military terminology developed a separate language of its own. Books that use only translated words tend to be meaningless. For example, the literary translation of *Kessel* would be cauldron. In German military terminology, *Kessel* is a group of ground forces encircled by the enemy. A *Kesselschlacht* is an encounter that results in a *Kessel*.

---

53 The course was named after General Walter Reinhardt, the first *Reichswehr* Commander in Chief.

A *Schwerpunkt* is a massive concentration of forces in a given area.

A *Mischling* (literally half-caste) is a person with some Jewish ancestry. *Mischlinge* were classified in *Grade* (literally stages), depending upon the number of Jewish ancestors. The Nuremberg racial laws provided exemptions for *Mischlinge*, depending upon their *Grad*. In the *Wehrmacht, Mischlinge* were treated differently, depending upon their *Grad*.

I have chosen the following method. At the first mention of a German term, a short explanation in English is added in brackets.

Transliteration

Transliteration of Russian words into languages which use the Latin alphabet is a problem which has not yet found a general solution. Authors in one and the same country go their own ways. In this book the following transliterations will be used:

- Localities: *Atlas of the Chief Administration of Geodosy and Cartography under the Council of Ministers of the USSR*, Moscow 1967.
- Personalities: McGraw-Hill. *Encyclopaedia of Russia and the Soviet Union*, New York 1961
- Albert Seaton, *The Russo-German War 1941-45*, London 1971

As a further assistance to the reader, comparative tables of ranks in the *Wehrmacht*, the *Waffen-SS* and the US and British Armies are given.

Military Ranks

Army

Wehrmacht	**U.S. and British Armies and Air Force**
Leutnant	Second Lieutenant
Oberleutnant	Lieutenant
Hauptmann	Captain
Major	Major
Oberstleutnant	Lieutenant Colonel
Oberst	Colonel
Generalmajor	Brigadier General (one star)
Generalleutnant	Major General (two stars)
General der Infanterie [Infantry], der Artillerie [Artillery], der Gebirgstruppe [Mountain Troops] etc. (The German General appended the name of the military Service arm in which he originally served.) For simplicity's sake, they will be named *Vollgenerale* in this book.	Lieutenant General (three stars)
Generaloberst	General (four stars)
Generalfeldmarschall	There was no *Feldmarschall* rank in the U.S. Army. The equivalent command rank was General of the Armies (five stars). The British Army had Field Marshals.

The *Waffen-SS*

The origin of the *Waffen SS* was the *Verfügungstruppe*, a military unit within the SS that was created to be at Hitler's disposal for any action of his choosing. The name *Waffen-SS* appeared first in an incidental form in an order of 11 November 1939 by the SS leadership which stated that members of the SS could become officers in the *Waffen-SS*. Gradually, the *Waffen SS* developed into an additional German Army of 36 divisions grouped in corps and armies. During the war, the *Waffen SS* units were tactically subordinated to the *Wehrmacht* units in which they were integrated, but promotions and dismissals of officers remained under the authority of the *Waffen SS* personnel department. The supreme head of all the SS was the *Reichsführer-SS*, Heinrich Himmler.

The *Waffen SS* and also the *SD* units, when serving in Army areas, wore the field grey uniforms of the *Wehrmacht*. On their field caps, a death's head was worn below the national emblem. On the *Wehrmacht* uniform, the national emblem would be on the right breast side, and in the *Waffen SS* it was on the left sleeve. The *Waffen SS* uniforms had the SS rank insignia on their collar patch. The shoulder straps were the same as for corresponding *Wehrmacht* ranks.

Waffen SS:	*Wehrmacht:*
SS-Sturmführer	*Leutnant*
SS-Obersturmführer	*Oberleutnant*
SS-Hauptsturmführer	*Hauptmann*
SS-Sturmbannführer	*Major*
SS-Obersturmbannführer	*Oberstleutnant*
SS-Standartenführer	*Oberst*
SS-Oberführer	No *Wehrmacht* equivalent
SS-Brigadeführer und Generalmajor der Waffen-SS	*Generalmajor*
SS-Gruppenführer und Generalleutnant der Waffen-SS	*Generalleutnant*
SS Obergruppenführer und General der Waffen-SS	*General*
SS Oberstgruppenführer und Generaloberst der Waffen-SS	*Generaloberst*

There was no *Waffen SS* rank equivalent to *Feldmarschall*. All *Waffen SS* officers would be addressed by their SS rank, without preceding it by "*Herr*."

Wehrmacht Naval Flag Ranks:

German Navy:	**German Army:**
Konteradmiral	*Generalmajor*
Vizeadmiral	*Generalleutnant*
Admiral	*General*
Generaladmiral	*Generaloberst*
Grossadmiral	*Generalfeldmarschall*

An important source for an analysis of the *Wehrmacht*'s fighting power is Martin van Creveld's classic *Fighting Power* which has been published in Germany under the title *Kampfkraft*.[54] With the exception of Martin van Creveld, all the experts consulted by the Pentagon were American officers and military historians. Since Martin van Creveld's book extols the fighting power of the *Wehrmacht*, it has become close to a bible for German revisionist authors. The background of the study is ignored and van Creveld's book is presented by them as a kind of whitewash of the *Wehrmacht*. Sentences like: "and the foremost Israeli military historian Martin van Creveld confirms ..." are repeated *ad nauseam*. The fact that Martin van Creveld is a Jew presents such authors with an additional convenient argument. They would be well advised to read the prefaces of the two German versions of Martin van Creveld's book.

In the first edition, published in 1988 under the auspices of the German Institute for Military Research, (*Militärgeschichtliches Forschungsamt*), Martin van Creveld states:

> Nothing in my study of the fighting power of the *Wehrmacht* should be construed as an acquittal of the *Wehrmacht* from its responsibility for the events of 1939-1945. On the contrary, the outstanding organisation of the *Wehrmacht*, particularly at the lower level, and the totally professional Officer Corps, made it possible for them to be used as an instrument of a ruthless policy of aggression, accompanied by many crimes against humanity. A great majority of its officers and its soldiers were ready to obey the most criminal orders, and to participate in their execution. Although the *Wehrmacht* did not start the war, did not create the concentration camps, and did not decide upon the extermination of the Jews, those crimes could not have been committed without its active assistance. What remains is a heavy guilt from which

---

54 M. van Creveld, *Kampfkraft. Militärische Organisation und Leistung der deutschen und amerikanischen Armee 1939-1945*. 1st edition Freiburg 1989, 2nd edition Graz 2005 (henceforth; Van Creveld). Van Creveld defines fighting power as the sum of the mental elements which cause armies to fight. Such elements are discipline, cohesion, morale, initiative, courage, toughness, will to fight and readiness to die in combat. In his view, even the best equipped army is a fragile instrument if it is not endowed with "fighting power". van Creveld, p.17.
A study published under the direction of Colonel N. Dupuy, USA (ret.) attempted to determine the fighting power of the *Wehrmacht* by means of mathematical analysis. In a first attempt, Dupuy constructs a mathematical model of a battle, based on factors like the numbers engaged on both sides, the weapons employed, the terrain, and the effect of air power. The conclusions of his study show that victory or defeat could only be predicted, if it was assumed that the German units were between 20% and 30% more effective than the British and the American units facing them. In another model, Dupuy compares the losses suffered by both sides and uses a series of formulae, where attack gets valued as 1 and defence in fortifications get valued as 1.6. Dupuy's conclusions are summarized by van Creveld: "The tables show that the Germans always remained superior to the Allied armies, which widely outnumbered and finally defeated them. As an average, the Germans inflicted in every instance 50% more casualties upon their opponents than the ones suffered by themselves. This figure remained constant, both in attack and in defence, in encounters where the German enjoyed superiority in numbers and equipments or, which was mostly the case, when they suffered inferiority, if they had superiority in the air or were outnumbered by the Allied air force." (van Creveld, p. 20).

there can be no acquittal. I can only hope that the Germans will never endeavour to acquit themselves.

In the foreword to the second edition, published in 2005 by Ares in Graz (Austria), Martin van Creveld emphasizes:

… In German speaking countries, some readers hate my book, others admire it. To my dismay, I have noted that the second group contains a large percentage of people who look at my work as an exoneration of the *Wehrmacht's* participation in many war crimes, in particular in the Shoah. Let me take this opportunity to send such readers a clear message. I want nothing to do with them, either as persons or with their interpretation. There is ample evidence that great military achievements on one side, and participation in the worst crimes that history can record on the other, do not necessarily exclude each other. This is a terrifying truth, which in importance exceeds both the *Wehrmacht* and World War II.[55] (Not surprisingly, some American critics accuse van Creveld of "America bashing").

Organization of this book

Major military operations under Model's command, are described in order to illustrate his leadership methods, and to show the results they achieved. These descriptions also show how he turned into one of the great commanders of World War II, in spite of his impossible behaviour. They likewise show the limits in his understanding of such duties of high commanders that were not strictly to do with the narrow field of military thinking.

Chapters 1, 2 and 3 summarize Model's life until assumption of command of 9th Army, beginning with his schooling and the preparation that led him to choose the military. They include the First World War years which had a decisive influence on the future *Wehrmacht* commanders. Primary sources are the documents in the Model private estate and the Freiburg archives. There are comments by eyewitnesses who told of their experiences with Model, during World War I and the subsequent *Generalstab* assignments. They then show Model's career in the *Reichswehr*, later in the *Wehrmacht*, and ends with Model's appointment as *OB* of 9th Army.

Chapters 4, 5 and 6 show Model as the commander of the *Wehrmacht's* largest units as OB of 9th Army and Commander of Army Groups in the East. They contain detailed descriptions of his leadership style, based on both favourable and unfavourable assessments by high-ranking officers who served with him. Model's attitude to the 20 July 1944 plot is analysed.

Chapter 7 deals with battles in the West in 1944/45 under Model's command, including the Ardennes offensive (Battle of the Bulge) and Model's final days in the *Ruhrkessel*.

Chapters 8, 9 and 10 are devoted to specific war crimes, and the extent of Model's involvement in them. A number of Model's orders of the day are analysed, and the courts martial that took place within his authority are described.

---

55 van Creveld, p. 11.

Annex: Paul Carell

Paul 'Carell' was the last pseudonym chosen by Dr Paul Karl Schmidt, the press chief in Ribbentrop's Ministry for Foreign Affairs. He decided upon pseudonyms to avoid confusion with the Ministry's chief interpreter, also named Paul Schmidt, and who published his memoirs before 'Carell' came out with his book.

"Carell" joined the SS in 1938 and rose to SS-*Obersturmbannführer*. He was heartily disliked by most foreign correspondents in Berlin, whom he regularly threatened with expulsion if they did not follow the reporting lines prescribed by him. Howard Smith, the UP representative in Berlin, describes him in his book *Last Train from Berlin*, New York 1942, (p.211 ff): "Dr Paul Schmidt, a fat, repulsive, ambitious individual, took over the leadership of the Nazi 'choir', and struggled hard to build himself up a reputation as the 'German-Specialist-on-questions-involving-Roosevelt'. Like a good holy-roller preacher, Schmidt was capable of working himself into an alarming fury and actually slobbering at the mouth with rage. His attacks grew filthier day by day, until on one occasion, when he was unable to find more relevant features of the American President to pour vitriol on, he spat forth a long vile essay on the President's physical affliction."

During the war, Carell became editor in chief of the bi-monthly illustrated *Wehrmacht* propaganda review *Signal*, which appeared in many languages and reached a circulation of over two million. *Signal* was not distributed in Germany and was not circulated to *Wehrmacht* soldiers.

In 1944, Carell had entered the Ministry for Foreign Affairs with the title of envoy and was posted to Budapest. The mass deportations of the Hungarian Jews had not yet began. Carell wrote a note for the Secretary of State in the Ministry, advocating the deportations. In it he suggested that they should be presented as an act of retaliation against preparations of Jewish sabotage in Budapest. Carell offered to place compromising documents and explosives in the Budapest synagogues and other Jewish institutions. The German Ambassador to Hungary, Edmund Veesenmayer, turned down the proposal because the synagogues and other Jewish institutions in Budapest had already been thoroughly searched and sealed. In the IMT trial of the senior members of the ministry, the document received the name *Notiz für den Herrn Staatssekretär*. At Nuremberg, Carell had turned state's evidence. The Secretary of State, Adolf Steengracht von Moyland, who had transmitted the *Notiz* to Veesenmayer, was sentenced to seven years' imprisonment.

After the IMT trials, Carell embarked on a career as a journalist. He published a series of articles on World War II, with special emphasis on the war in the East. His tendencies were of the extreme right. He became a major proponent of the theory of Germany's 'preventive wars'. His series, later turned into books, are a typical mixture of fiction, veterans' tales, inventions of purported traitors, and the "brave German soldier and his wonderful commanders" opposed to the "cruel enemy". Carell became the *protégé* of the important German publisher Axel Springer. He had serialized the first chapters of Carell's bestseller, *Unternehmen Barbarossa*, in the Springer magazine *Kristall*. In 1959, the "*Kristall* scandal" broke out. Four of the senior editors resigned because they considered the presence of an incorrigible Nazi as degrading for the reputation of their magazine. Springer had to dismiss Carell. However, he arranged for him to have a column in the influential weekly *Der Spiegel*, which at that time employed a number of former high-ranking *SD* members.

In 1965, the prosecutor's office in the city of Verden, turned to the central office for research into NS crimes at Ludwigsburg, questioning if there were sufficient elements to indict Paul Carell for murder. The Ludwigsburg office replied that they were conducting preliminary investigations. At his hearing, Paul Carell stated: "The *Notiz für den Herrn Staatssekretär* had been written by me. I regret that the written reaction to my *Notiz,* by envoy Veesenmayer, is not shown here. This document shows clearly that Veesenmayer rejected my proposal because of my unimportant position. Furthermore, my proposals were impractical. This shows that I had no part in the deportations. I find it incredible that the Verden prosecutor finds it possible to indict me for murder... I never had any part in steps taken against Jews, unless my *Notiz* is looked upon as a participation in the deportations of the Hungarian Jews." The prosecution against Carell was dropped on 2 June 1971, because the German penal law of 4 August 1953 removed 'unsuccessful attempts of abetting crimes' from criminal offences. Surprisingly, until he died, Paul Carell succeeded in keeping the investigations against him from public knowledge. His file was found at Ludwigsburg in August 2003, by his biographer, Wigbert Benz, among thousands of discarded files.[56]

The manner in which Paul Carell wrote on the events at Kursk, and thus Model's involvement, in the second volume of his history of the War in the East, *Verbrannte Erde,* is a typical example of immediate post-war German literature. It all began with *Feldmarschall* Erich von Manstein. After the formation of the Stalingrad *Kessel,* and the battles for its relief, Manstein was already being strongly criticized by senior officers of 6th Army for not having given clear directives to its *OB,* Friedrich Paulus, in spite of almost daily entreaties.

In his memoirs *Verlorene Siege,* Manstein endeavoured to defend himself. He wrote that he had given 6th Army a break-out order on 19 December 1942, which Paulus had not dared to follow. Matters came to a height when 6th Army's Chief of Staff, *Generalmajor* Arthur Schmidt, returned from captivity in 1955. He stated unreservedly that Manstein's purported order had never reached 6th Army. Schmidt's statement was corroborated by other senior officers, among them Manstein's former quartermaster at 11th army, General Friedrich-Wilhelm Hauck.

Before General Schmidt returned from captivity, Paul Carell had already written the first series of his articles in the magazine *Kristall,* in which he had depicted Manstein as a commander of undisputed genius. Obviously, Manstein found Carell's article to be "very good and written with great objectivity." More or less simultaneously, the historian Joachim Wieder, who had also fought at Stalingrad, came out with his book *Die Tragödie von Stalingrad, Erinnerungen eines Überlebenden,* published in Deggendorf, in 1955. It was highly critical of Manstein. Wieder's book had considerable success and Manstein began to worry that Carell might use Wieder's account in his forthcoming chapters about Stalingrad. He therefore turned to Carell, who was flattered by Manstein's interest in his work. His chapters about Stalingrad turned into a hymn of praise to Manstein.

Carell then wanted to make more of his relationship with Manstein. He turned to *Generaloberst* Hoth, with a request to ask Manstein if operation "Citadel" could have been turned into victory. Obviously Manstein replied in the affirmative, after all, he was the father of that plan, and so the chapter about Kursk became another hymn of

---

56 Criticism of Paul Carell has also found its way into works of fiction. In his worldwide bestseller *The Kindly Ones,* Jonathan Littell has his "hero", the SS murderer Max Aue pouring scorn upon Carell's boring language and the mendacious content of his books.

praise to Manstein. But Carell was faced with a dilemma. Since Manstein and Model represented opposite views, and events proved Model right, Carell preferred to invent the story of 'the mysterious traitor' responsible for the failure of the German offensive. Thus the remainder of his second book, which ended with the Russian *Bagration* offensive of 1944, later became another hymn of praise, this time to Model.

Carell died in 1997 after having accumulated considerable wealth from his books. His biography by Wigbert Benz, *Paul Carell, Ribbentrops Pressechef Paul Karl Schmidt vor und nach 1945* was published in 2005.

1

Youth, World War I, and the *Reichswehr*

Walter Model was born on 24 January 1891, in the Genthin district of Magdeburg. The ancestry of both his parents can be traced back to the 16th century. It shows a strong religious background without any military heritage. Both his grandfather and his great-grandfather were church organists. His father had first wanted to become a priest, but chose instead to become a teacher at the girls' school at Genthin. There he was organist and choirmaster, rising to Royal Music Director. His father's brother held a senior position at the German central bank, the *Reichsbank*. Walter's brother Otto, to whom he was strongly attached, was an attorney.

Model first attended a local public elementary school at Genthin. Then he entered a *Gymnasium* at Erfurt, and finally, the Humanistic *Domgymnasium* in Naumburg on the Saale. He took his *Abitur* in February 1909. His marks were reasonably good and underscored his knowledge of Latin and ancient Greek.

During his school years at Naumburg, Model was a member of the literary Körner Society.

Choice of profession

Walter Model first decided upon a military career during his last year in school. Model's parents were acquainted socially with a number of officers' families. In German society at that time, a military career was an attractive choice for young men and was associated with great prestige. The soldier was looked upon as *Der erste Mann im Staate*, (the "first man in the state"). This resulted in attitudes which today can be looked upon as simply ridiculous. When *Reichskanzler* Theobald von Bethmann-Hollweg addressed the *Reichstag* for the first time, in 1909, he wore a Major's uniform. Five years later he felt that he could no longer fulfil his duties if he was not given the honorary rank of *Generalleutnant*.[1]

Walter Model's parents were not wealthy, and a military career was burdened with considerable expense. At the time Model became an officer, monthly dues to the Regiment could rise to 200 Marks in the prestigious units. The fee for a Lieutenant's *Patent*, (commission), was around 75 Marks. The uniform and other equipment cost up to 700 Marks. At that time, a medium grade white-collar employee earned around 100 Marks a month.

County Judge Dahlmann, who was the father of one of Model's schoolmates, was reported to have said to a friend: "Among the nine graduates of the class of 1909, seven want to become active military officers. One of them has bad eyesight and a lop-sided shoulder. His choice makes little sense."[2] He was referring to Model. On 17 February 1909,

---

1   Van Creveld, p.32.
2   Estate, Leppa Documents.

three days after passing his *Abitur*, Model entered Infantry Regiment 52 at Cottbus as a *Fahnenjunker*,[3] (Officer Cadet). One of his friends there was the future *Generalleutnant* Wilhelm Bohnstedt, who later took a critical view of him.[4]

First years in the Army

Walter Model was unhappy during the first months of his military career. He was severely put through the mill by his sergeant who told him: "I wonder if you have chosen the right profession. You are not sufficiently tough to become an officer."[5] Fate had it that the man who would later become one of the most brutal German commanders, was himself subjected to constant bullying during his induction period. Model even considered leaving the military and pursuing a career in banking, a possibility because of the position his uncle held at the *Reichsbank*.

The next few years passed without any noteworthy incidents. In 1910, Model became a *Leutnant*. During the years preceding World War I, he received a number of favourable performance ratings. In 1910, Major *i.G.*, Dr Martin Reymann, at that time Adjutant of 1st Battalion of the Regiment wrote:

> Model was looked upon favourably because of his manner of service, the strength of his character and his social behaviour. As an aide to the Adjutant, he fulfilled all his duties in an exemplary manner, including the complicated measures required for mobilization. In 1913, when I was assigned to the *Kriegsakademie*, (the war academy), I recommended Model as my successor in the Battalion. The regimental commander, Colonel von Jacobi, was at first surprised and said, 'This is impossible. The guy is just a youngster.' I replied that I could guarantee that Model was up to the task. Model got the job and performed remarkably well. Long after the war, Jacobi told me that I had been right.[6]

General von Vierow recalls:

> I met Model for the first time in 1910. We had many discussions related to problems of infantry combat, resulting from the Russo–Japanese War. While most of us were convinced of the superiority of our tactics, Model was critical. He advanced some ideas which were then considered to be 'utopian', but which were proved to be correct during the hard truth of World War I.[7]

---

3   Graduates from a cadet school entered the Army as *Fähnrich* (Ensign).
4   Martin Reymann recalls that Bohnstedt complained to him that Model had displayed excessive ambition when both had been Company commanders in Infantry Regiment 6 in the immediate post World War One years. On 25 December 1941, Bohnstedt, at that time Division commander, wrote to Reymann: "Even Model will have to give up his calculated optimism, if one can still use this term. Unfortunately, one has to look at things as they are." (Estate, Reymann, 16 April 1956).
5   Estate, Letter from Leppa to Hansgeorg Model.
6   Estate, Reymann, 16 April 1956.
7   Estate, Vierow, 10 January 1955.

Von Vierow's statement refers to the military aspects of Model's knowledge. However, in his later orders of the day, and in his letters to his family, there are also historic and classical quotations. Years later, as a Major, he took part in a literary competition. His essay on Gneisenau became one of the 25 chapters in an anthology on leadership published by General Friedrich von Cochenhausen.[8] In his foreword, General von Cochenhausen emphasized that the book was particularly attractive because every officer would later try to emulate the personality of his hero as much as possible. Undoubtedly Model was not a *Kommisskopf* (a German military slang expression describing a soldier whose knowledge does not extend beyond military service matters). But neither did he rank among the intellectual German Generals.

World War I

Model was promoted to Lieutenant in 1915, and to Captain in 1917. During the First World War promotions came slowly. Even the most capable officers, such as Manstein, did not progress beyond Captain during the war years. Model fought almost exclusively on the Western Front. He was wounded several times and highly decorated. He received the Iron Cross, second and first class and also the Knight's Cross of the *Königlicher Hausorden von Hohenzollern* with swords, which was conferred for special bravery.[9]

Colonel Fromme, Model's regimental commander in 1914, valued him highly:

During 1914, he displayed a strong sense of duty, total reliability and untiring efforts. A courageous and fearless officer, he was a shining example to his subordinates.[10]

The performance ratings by his superiors remained favourable throughout the war. Major Speeman, a cavalry inspector, spoke of Model's performance as a Brigade Adjutant. That performance rating is the first testimony to Model's closeness to the front line:

An outstanding officer. After the hard days of fighting, he would continuously visit the Regiments, and they held him in high regard. Thanks to his brilliant capabilities,

---

8   F. von Cochenhausen, *Führertum, 25 Lebensbilder von Feldherrn aller Zeiten,* Berlin 1930, pp.280-307.

9   Diploma 16 February 1917 in facsimile, Model/Bradley, p. 10. This decoration can be compared to the *Deutsches Kreuz in Gold* of World War II, a somewhat hybrid decoration outside the Iron Crosses group, which was given for eight acts of bravery, which were judged insufficient for the Knight's Cross of the Iron Cross. Until 1939, the Iron Crosses, which had been the standard decorations of the German Army since the wars of liberation from the Napoleonic Empire, were given in two "classes", first and second class. After 1939, new groups of Iron Crosses were introduced, at first the Knight's Cross, then the oak leaves, the swords, the diamonds. Finally, there was the Knight's Cross with golden oak leaves, swords and diamonds which was limited to twelve recipients. It was awarded only once, to Colonel Hans-Ulrich Rudel, a fighter ace. The Grand Cross of the Iron Cross must be mentioned. During World War I it was worn by the Emperor and awarded by him to Hindenburg, Mackensen, Ludendorff and Prince Leopold of Bavaria. During World War II it was awarded to Göring.

10 BA–MA, NL. 6/1.

he soon established himself, and far exceeded the normal requirements of a Brigade Adjutant.[11]

Generalmajor von Possek wrote:

Tireless performance, while lacking support from a rather mediocre *Intendant* (Director), he was a most valuable aide to the first *Generalstab* officer. He performed remarkably in issuing tactical orders, showing foresight and vision for overall requirements. He was always ready and able to present practical proposals.[12]

Generalmajor Graf von Rantzau, Commander 36th Reserve Division:

A talent way above average, he was a tireless worker. One could always rely on him to cope easily with every task entrusted to him.[13]

An interesting opinion can be found in a later statement of Prince Oskar von Preussen. During World War I, as *Infanterieführer* of 5th Infantry Division he was one of Model's superiors, and in World War II his subordinate:

…To the point, brusque, always grasping the essentials of a problem. Certainly not an easy subordinate, I served again with him, in 1940, when he was a *Generalmajor* and chief of staff of Busch's 16th Army. Then it was my turn to be under his orders.[14]

Model's first experience with the *Generalstab* began in 1917. He was assigned as O 4 in the operational division, within the office of the Chief of Staff of the Field Combat Army.[15] During that time Model paid a short visit to Turkey. The purpose remains unknown. He also made a short visit to Italy, after being asked to investigate a claim raised by the future *Feldmarschall* Erwin Rommel. Lieutenant Ferdinand Schörner, who in 1945 would become the last *Wehrmacht Feldmarschall*, had been awarded the *Pour le Mérite* order on the Italian front. Rommel, who was in action at the same sector, had complained that the award had been due to him. Finally, the dispute was solved, by decorating Rommel likewise with the *Pour le Mérite*.[16]

---

11 Ibid.
12 Ibid.
13 Ibid.
14 Ibid.
15 The officers serving as O1, O2, O3, O4 were not members of the *Generalstab*. The O1 position was considered to be the springboard to formal *Generalstab* acceptance.
16 The *Pour le Mérite* was the highest German decoration of World War I. Awards were unfair. The *Pour le Mérite* was reserved for officers and was given nearly automatically to generals and to air aces. The order was awarded sparingly to lower ranks. The only two Second Lieutenants of infantry to receive this decoration were the future *Feldmarschall* Schörner and the writer Ernst Jünger, who died in 1998, aged 103. (At the time of the Schörner-Rommel dispute, Rommel was already a full Lieutenant). During World War II, orders were awarded in a much more democratic manner and high decorations were also given to soldiers and non-commissioned officers. Criteria for the awards were different, depending upon the grade of the recipient. On 14

Model's second staff service was as Ib with a Guards Replacement Division. That assignment came after he had attended the "Sedan Course," a short, one-month *Generalstab* course that took place at Sedan. In August 1918, Model became Ib on the staff of the 36th Reserve Division.

In 1917, Model had received a "good" performance rating and had been ranked 17 among the 39 Lieutenants who were promoted to Captain. Thereafter he received the following performance ratings:

Generalmajor von Rantzau, Commander of 36th Reserve Division:[17] "In view of his talent and his performance, Captain Model is certain to serve in high command positions in the future."

Major Baron von Falkenstein:[18]

Conscientious, totally aware of his duties, reliable, and at all times my best Company commander. He was an example to his subordinates and a good educator. He took selfless care of the needs of his subordinates. It would be regrettable if this outstanding officer were not to be allowed to remain in the Army. I consider Captain Model to be a man who can be employed successfully in any position.

Before being formally accepted into the *Reichswehr*, Model became a *Generalstab* officer with the XII Corps, at Danzig, which was part of the *Grenzschutz Ost*. The borders between Germany and Poland were still in dispute, since before the Treaty of Versailles, and Polish troops made repeated incursions into German territory. Such incursions were countered by two units of *Grenzschutz Ost*: North and South which consisted of former Regiments manned by volunteers. One can describe them as a particular type of Free Corps (*Freikorps*) in as much as they came under the command of Army Generals who were still on the active list.[19]

When Model joined the *Grenzschutz Ost,* Major Edwin von Stülpnagel wrote:

On 22 December 1918, Captain Model volunteered for duty with the *Grenzschutz Ost.* He is a very capable young *Generalstab* officer with a quick grasp of problems,

---

March 1945, *Feldmarschall* Ferdinand Schörner (at that date still a *Generaloberst)* turned down an application for the oak leaves to the Knight's Cross for a Lieutenant Colonel Mokros and wrote that it was "the self evident duty of a regiment commander to lead his soldiers in attack with a machine-gun and hand grenades." Had the same award been requested for a Lieutenant, the oak leaves would have been conferred. In the US Army, officers were strongly favoured for decorations. Their percentage of recipients of the highest decoration, the Congressional Medal of Honour was 32.4, Distinguished Service Cross 46.7 Silver Star 32.4 Distinguished Service Medal 99.9, Legion of Merit 84.6. The Air Medal was more or less automatically awarded to airmen who had flown a mission. Its equivalent for ground forces, the Bronze Star, was given more sparingly, which led to continued frictions between the two arms. The Purple Heart was distributed practically at random and often for wounds which were not obtained in battle. (van Creveld, p. 133).

17 BA-MA, NL 6/1.
18 Ibid.
19 The most recent book about the *Freikorps* is the Ph.D. thesis by Matthias Sprenger, *Landsknechte auf dem Weg ins Dritte Reich. Zur Genese und Wandel des Freikorpsmythos,* Paderborn 2008.

and a sharp and versatile intellect. Good qualities of organization, great application, good tactical understanding, and pleasant behaviour. He is tactful and modest."[20] If in 1918 Model was described as being tactful and modest, change was quick to come – *tempora mutantur.*

The *Reichswehr* after World War I

By 1919, Walter Model had still not finally decided whether he should remain in the Army. Among other possibilities, he thought of becoming a physician, and registered for one semester at the University of Halle.

After returning from the *Grenzschutz Ost*, Model joined the Hacketau *Freikorps* (Free Corps.) That unit was part of Baron von Sparre's 3rd Westphalian Infantry Regiment. The Free Corps were self-created military units. They had no central authority. In every Free Corps its leader exercised total command. Around 500,000 officers and soldiers of the Imperial Army had remained in the East and became soon embroiled in the fights of the Russian Civil War. They were brought back with the help of Free Corps, some of which remained in the Baltics and engaged in the civil wars raging there. In the German West, civil war-like situations arose in a number of areas. The Free Corps were the only military units available which could be engaged against them. Most Free Corps were permeated with a spirit of right wing Nazi violence and engaged in a series of *Putsches*, also in the murder of perceived political opponents (known as *Fememorde*). They gave rise to a Free Corps mentality which persisted after the Free Corps were officially dissolved. Many of the high-ranking Nazi officials had been Free Corps commanders. Curiously, Hitler always had contempt for the Free Corps, which he already criticized in *Mein Kampf*, for their lack of political ideology other than his own. Some Free Corps and their commanders were taken into the *Reichswehr*. The Hacketau unit was embroiled in the riots that plagued the Weimar Republic at the beginning of its existence. It was confronted by angry civilian mobs when entering the city of Elberfeld in 1920, and was forced to withdraw into the British zone of occupation. The Hacketau *Freikorps* was a small and short-lived unit, dissolving itself after entering the British zone of occupation. It is not mentioned in the voluminous *Freikorps* literature. Model wrote a detailed article on the Hacketau unit which was published in a local newspaper at Bückeburg on 17 April 1920.[21]

In Elberfeld Walter Model met his future wife, Herta Huyssen, a great-granddaughter of the poet Friedrich Rückert. During that time, the *Kapp Putsch* occurred in Berlin. No detailed comments on the *Putsch* by Model are known. However, one can assume that he viewed it with the guarded sympathy of most *Reichswehr* officers, while carefully abstaining from any personal involvement. (Typical was Hindenburg's reaction whose ambition to run for *Reichspräsident* was no secret: "My heart supports the *Kapp Putsch*, my brain knows that it is doomed to failure…how sad.")[22] In a letter to his parents, dated 21 October 1920, informing them of his engagement to Herta Huyssen, Model wrote: "Kapp could hardly have imagined that something good would come out of his attempt." His sarcasm tends to indicate that he viewed the chances of success by the *Kapp Putsch*

---

20 BA/MA, NL 6/1.
21 Ibid.
22 W. Pyta, *Hindenburg. Herrschaft zwischen Hohenzollern und Hitler*, Munich 2007, p.451.

with scepticism. The Huyssen family belonged to high society. The marriage of Walter Model and Herta Huyssen took place on 11 May 1921. Herta Model died in 1985.

Later, after the situation within Germany had stabilized, the influence of the new Army head, *Generaloberst* Hans von Seeckt, led to the rise of the "non-political" German officer. General Heinz Guderian was critical of Seeckt's ultimate results. "His wish to remove the Army from party politics was justified at that time. In the long run, however, for all officers it led to the lack of development in their political understanding, in particular, for those officers who were to become members of the *Generalstab*. This was the weakness of his system."[23]

Guderian's comments are typical of the arguments which many German officers used, after World War II, in order to exculpate themselves from their support of Hitler. Obviously, it does not ring true. Seeckt could have forbidden officers to vote, or to engage in any political activity, but he could not prevent them from thinking. National-Socialism rapidly gained ground among officers of all age groups, particularly in the lower ranks.

Troop Commander

Model's Commands in the *Reichswehr* alternated between service with troop units and duties with the *Truppenamt*. Officers who had qualified for the *Truppenamt* were named *Führergehilfen*. Traditionally, assignments that alternated between service with the troops, and service with the *Generalstab*, were instrumental in developing the high standards of German commanders. Many officers, who had spent a considerable amount of time on *Generalstab* duties, were eventually very successful high-ranking troop commanders. As a commander of Companies, Battalions and Regiments, Model emerged as a competent officer who insisted upon strict discipline, but also had a sense of humour.

After the War, Model's subordinates told stories of him overlooking their minor breaches of rules, and of playing practical jokes on them. However, Model's own performance ratings began to disclose some of the negative aspects of his character, such as his abrasive manner, his hot temper, his impatience and intolerance, all of which left distasteful memories. Those aspects continued to grow as he rose through the ranks.

Promotions in the *Reichswehr* were very slow. Few of the officers who did not belong to the *Generalstab* managed to pass the *Majorsecke*, which called for retirement upon reaching the rank of Major. By the end of the First World War, Model was a Captain. In 1933 he had been promoted to Lieutenant Colonel and had successfully overcome the *Majorsecke*.[24]

Model's troop commands in the *Reichswehr* were successively as follows: in 1919 the 3 Company of 14th Infantry Regiment, and in 1920, the *MG* (machine-gun) Company of Battalion II of 13th Infantry Regiment. In October 1920 he commanded the *MG* Company of 18th Infantry Regiment.

During World War I, Model had served under General Friedrich von Lossberg who was one of the German Army's foremost experts on defence. They met again in Münster in 1921, where General von Lossberg commanded the local *Wehrkreis*, one of the military divisions of the German homeland. Model participated in a number of war-games conducted by General von Lossberg and his Chief of Staff, Colonel Alexander von

---

23 Guderian, p.414.
24 An officer who had overcome the hurdle of the *Majorsecke* could look forward to regular future promotions.

Falkenhausen, who later became military commander in Belgium during World War II.[25] After *Generalstab* service as *Artillerieführer* VI in Münster, and attending a *Generalstab* course in tactics and employment of arms, Model received command of 9th Company of 8th Prussian Infantry Regiment in Görlitz.

Staff duties at the *Truppenamt*

Model took part in his first *Wehrkreis* exercise in 1927. In 1928 he joined the staff of 3 Division at *Wehrkreis* Command III in Berlin. In 1929 he participated in a number of *Übungsreisen,* literally a "training journey." In practice they were the equivalent of the "staff-ride" in the British Army, or a NATO Map exercise.

In October 1929, Major Model joined the technical training section (T4) at the Truppenamt. *Generaloberst* Wilhelm Adam was head of the Truppenamt between 1930 and 1932. In his unpublished memoirs, Adam wrote about an exercise at Jüterbog before the war: "The head of the technical department at the *Generalstab* was Colonel Model, whom I had described as an *Irrlicht,* (will-o'-the-wisp), in a report some years ago."[26]

Model taught military history within a curriculum designed to prepare future General Staff officers. Some of the students liked Model's lectures. Others came close to turning him into ridicule. In a conversation with Görlitz on 7 September 1970, General Hans Speidel was positive. "He was an outstanding teacher. I learned much from him. When reviewing tactical situations, Model demanded immediate understanding and a quick issuing of orders. If someone could not cope with this, he was made to feel Model's contempt."[27] Speidel was referring to the future General Winter.

General August Winter was more critical:

> His knowledge of literature, and his capacity for analysing sources, rendered his course particularly interesting. It removed the danger of judging matters in a one-sided or tendentious manner. But I have to say that the value of his lectures was impeded by two factors. To begin with, he simply offered too much, 'less would have been more', and he spoke too fast. We often found it difficult to remain attentive. Model also inhibited discussion. His intolerant temperament made it difficult for anybody to complete a reply. All in all, his course left us with mixed emotions. We valued his knowledge, but did not consider him to be an exemplar of the 'ideal' teacher.[28]

General Adolf Heusinger's comments are full of irony.

---

25 A detailed report about the war games by General von Vierow in the Estate.

26 General Adam refers to an exercise on 15 August 1938 of an attack against Czechoslovak fortifications and blames Model for having conducted it in a manner which favoured the attacker and thus conveyed an erroneously optimistic picture of the fighting power of the German infantry. Both General Adam and General Beck were very angry. General Maximilian von Weichs, who also attended, felt that Hitler showed considerable technical understanding on this occasion and that he gave valuable advice. (T. Taylor, *Munich – the Price of Peace*, New York 1980, p.702 ff.)

27 Estate, Letter from Speidel to Görlitz, 17 September 1970.

28 BA–MA, N 6/1, A. Winter, 18 January 1955.

The R-course could just as well have been called the Reinhardt course. His teaching of tactics was a delight, as was the possibility of learning his logical thoughts, and hearing his recollections of service in World War I. At quite the opposite, we had 'firecracker-head' Model as teacher of military history. He was totally unable to grasp scientific research. His temper always gained the upper hand. He 'modelled' matters as he liked to see them, with an obviously unintended result that the pupils were unable to take him seriously."[29] (Heusinger used the term 'modelled' intentionally, because Model frequently used the expression due to the similarity with his own name).

General Rasp was complimentary.

In view of the very intense training of future *Generalstab* officers in the small *Reichswehr*, it was obvious that only the best officers were appointed as instructors. In our class, there was little doubt that Reinhardt and Model were foremost. Model's lectures were of high value. Naturally he demanded much from us. He had the gift of training young officers in a manner which made them able to cope with the heavy duties of World War II, the extent of which could not have been foreseen at that time.[30]

If those comments are combined, a portrait of the future *Feldmarschall* begins to emerge. Beyond doubt, Model was very knowledgeable, but he was obviously unable to control his temper. "Can this not be done faster?" was often included in one of his frequent outbursts. Constant demands for immediate solutions were simply too much for many of his pupils. His abrasive manner, hardly suitable in an environment for future *Generalstab* officers, would leave distasteful memories that remained with the students for years. His temper had begun to impair his teaching.

Visit to the Soviet Union

The 1922 Treaty of Rapallo, between Germany and the Soviet Union, established a friendly co-operation between the *Reichswehr* and the Red Army. Recurring visits became routine. Interactions between the two armies enabled the Russians to acquaint themselves with German *Generalstab* concepts, and their methods of troop commands. The Germans had

---

29 G. Meyer, *Adolf Heusinger. Dienst eines deutschen Soldaten*, Hamburg 2001, p.206, (henceforth: Meyer, Heusinger). In the eyes of his biographer and admirer Dr Georg Meyer, Heusinger emerges at times as a paragon of virtue and as an example of the non-Nazi officer. This is however an exaggeration, Heusinger was just as much enamoured with Hitler and the regime as his fellow generals. He was briefly arrested after 20 July 1944, after he had been named by subordinates (*Generalmajor* Stieff and Lieutenant Colonel Smend) who had been part of the attempt. He was set free after a few days in prison. Heusinger had great admiration for Hans-Georg Reinhardt who became one of the important *Panzer* commanders. Hürter shows a number of examples that in his "adoration" of Hitler in letters to his wife, Reinhardt went further than many of his comrades, including Model. One such instance: When he was decorated with the oak leaves to his Knight's Cross, Reinhardt wrote to his wife that he was "almost speechless, very surprised and deeply moved. He would continue to do his duty as the *Führer* expected from him, regardless of all difficulties and setbacks." (Hürter, p. 145). Reinhardt was sentenced by the IMT to 15 years for war crimes (case 12).

30 Estate, Rasp, 11 April 1955.

the opportunity of training with weapons, including airplanes and *Panzer,* which were prohibited to them by the Treaty of Versailles.[31]

Walter Model's visit to the Soviet Union took place between 22 August and 1 October 1931. He paid a visit to 9th Infantry Rifle Division at Rostov on the Don. His trip coincided with a lengthy visit to Russia by General Adam, while he was head of the *Truppenamt.* Manstein was also a member of Adam's delegation.

Walter Model's notes pertaining to this visit were destroyed with his papers in 1945. Herta Model included her personal recollections of talks with her husband, in a letter she wrote after the war, to the de-Nazification commission. At that time she was seeking a pension based on Model's military service. Her description of Model's thoughts could either refer to his early visit to the Soviet Union, or to those from his later experience as a commander in the East. "After his experiences in the Soviet Union, my husband had become increasingly hostile to Bolshevism. He saw in it the greatest danger for Germany."[32]

Leppa quoted a letter, purported to be from Walter Model in October 1931, without indicating a source: "Unfortunately, the Communist danger is still strongly underestimated abroad. What a pity that the 'simpletons', who are unwilling to learn, could not get a personal impression of this subculture. They would soon be converted."[33]

Both quotations sound somewhat doubtful. Every visitor to the Soviet Union was constantly accompanied by Russian observers who kept them away from the civilian population. Personal interactions were only permitted with direct service contacts in the Red Army. Model possibly noticed the dilapidated streets and the many parentless children, the *bezprizornyi,* who roamed around the railway stations, but that was the limit of his personal contacts. Model's opposition to Bolshevism was more than likely a consequence of his personal experiences after the end of World War I.

The Red Army Officers who came in contact with their German visitors were both competent commanders, and also career politicians, such as Voroshilov. Model had met General Michail Tukhachevsky, who favoured an alliance with France, and was no friend of Germany. Model also saw other Red Army officers, many of whom would fall victim to the "Great Terror" of 1937.[34] Commanders in the Red Army who rose to high posts during World War II were, at that time, relatively junior officers, and had no contact with the German visitors. A number of them were arrested during the purges and spent time in the Gulag concentration camps, but they would become prominent in later years. Marshals of the Soviet Union, Konstantin Rokossovsky, Kyrill Meretskov and Army General Alexander Gorbatov were among those who survived the Gulag.

---

31 For details of the military cooperation between the two countries, M. Zeidler, *Reichswehr und Rote Armee 1920-1933. Wege und Stationen einer ungewöhnlichen Zusammenarbeit,* Munich 1993 (henceforth Zeidler).

32 Estate, Letter from Herta Model, 10 May 1950.

33 Leppa, p.68.

34 General Yona Yakir so impressed Hindenburg at a *Reichswehr* course which he attended in 1928/29 that Hindenburg made him a gift of a copy of Schlieffen's study of the battle of Cannae, with a personal dedication: "To Mr. [sic] Yakir, one of the most talented commanders of present times, in remembrance of his visit to Germany." Zeidler, p.224. The index in Zeidler's book shows that the death dates of a majority of the Russian officers described were 1937, 1938 and 1938. The implication is obvious.

Generaloberst Adam gave a lengthy account of his visit[35] expressing his high opinion of Voroshilov.[36] He gave detailed descriptions of sumptuous meals that were served to him and his officers at a time when there was a severe famine in Russia. Manstein, who was no less opposed to Bolshevism than Model, gave a lengthy and generally positive account of his visit.[37] He was less enthusiastic about Voroshilov than Adam. "He conveyed the impression of being a politician rather than a soldier, although he had commanded a cavalry division during the Civil War."[38]

Manstein's impressions were both positive and negative. He confirmed that he had no contact with the Russian population except for one instance. A German-speaking farmer had approached him at a railway station and complained that peasants were being transported arbitrarily from one place to another. Repression against the *Kulaks* had begun at that time. It is doubtful that Model gained more insight than either Adam or Manstein.

The *Kuratorium*

The *Reichskuratorium für Jugendertüchtigung*, literally the Board for Youth Efficiency Training, was established in 1931 under the leadership of *General der Infanterie* Edwin von Stülpnagel. Model became its chief of staff, and 50 officers were ordered to join it. The *Kuratorium* was the creation of two men, *Generaloberst* Kurt von Hammerstein-Equord, Commander in Chief of the *Reichswehr*, and General Kurt von Schleicher, the head of the ministerial office in the *Reichswehr* Ministry. A few years later he was the last Chancellor before Hitler's assumption of power. The *Kuratorium* was one of the steps the Germans took to circumvent stipulations by the Treaty of Versailles and, indirectly, to strengthen the country's defence capabilities. Courses administered by the *Kuratorium* lasted for up to eight weeks. They included sports, map-reading, marching exercises, and training in light calibre arms.

After the Nazis assumed power, the *Kuratorium* encountered the hostility of the SA. The head of the SA training division, SA *Gruppenführer* Hans Jüttner, perceived the *Kuratorium* to be his competition and pressed for its elimination.[39] Edwin von Stülpnagel died in 1932, and the *Kuratorium* was disbanded in 1933. Edwin von Stülpnagel and Model had been close friends. At the General's funeral, Model carried the cushion with his decorations.[40] Model remained with the *Kuratorium* until it was disbanded in 1933.

---

35 Adam, unpublished memoirs, p.100.

36 Ibid.

37 E. v. Manstein, *Aus einem Soldatenleben*, Bonn 1958, p.139 (henceforth *Soldatenleben*).

38 Ibid, p.147.

39 Jüttner joined the SS in 1935 and became one of the most influential *Obergruppenführer*. He was not tried by the Allies, however a German tribunal sentenced him to ten years in 1948. Jüttner died in 1965.

40 An interesting parallel to the *Kuratorium* were the French *Chantiers de Jeunesse*, which were established in 1941 by the Vichy government. Men were drafted into the *Chantiers* at the age of 20 and served for eight months. The *Chantiers* were under the command of General de la Porte du Theil and were led by career officers of the French Army. They undertook agricultural work, but the discipline was military. The real purpose of the *Chantiers* was to partially circumvent the reduction of the French Army to 100,000 by the Armistice agreement and to have a reservoir of military trained men, should France re-enter the war.

2

Third Reich, *Reichswehr* and *Wehrmacht*

World War I, to the start of the war against Russia

Model's attitude to Hitler's rise to power

Like most *Reichswehr* officers, Model welcomed Hitler's accession to power. Whatever opposition that was found among the military concerned Hitler as a person, but not his programme for the future.[1] Most of the remaining doubts about Hitler were dispelled after he accepted an invitation from *Generaloberst* von Hammerstein-Equord to his apartment. There, on 3 February 1933, he addressed a gathering of high-ranking *Reichswehr* officers. With his oratorical talent, Hitler always found it easy to adapt his addresses to the assemblies he was facing. In a speech lasting two hours, he told the Generals exactly what they wanted to hear. He would transform the *Reichswehr* into a *Wehrmacht,* with the re-introduction of compulsory military service at the earliest possible moment. He would build the Army into a modern force, and remove the limitations imposed by the Versailles Treaty.

At first the atmosphere was cool. Then the "bravos" increased, and in the last part of the speech applause made for repeated interruptions. A few Generals remained sceptical. Ritter von Leeb is supposed to have said that a salesman, who has good merchandise, does not have to praise it with the shouts of a vendor at a street market. General Beck found Hitler's speech so "normal that he did not recall any details which had disturbed him". *Admiral* Raeder remembered it as "most satisfactory".

Model understood next to nothing about politics; he may be described as a political 'simpleton'. Officers, who were regular guests at his home, were unanimous in stating that politics was never a subject of discussion. Model also disliked talking about his experiences from the First World War. Matters relating to their present service were also precluded. Herta Model told Görlitz that her husband used to tell young officers on their first visit: "When you come to visit us, wipe off all the service rubbish on the door mat, here you are at home."[2] But Model's wilful ignorance of politics is unforgivable. In that respect

---

1 *Generaloberst* von Hammerstein-Equord and some of his close friends who had belonged to the "Schleicher circle" looked upon Hitler as a *parvenu*. A curious example of initial strong rejection of Hitler was the future *Generaloberst* Alfred Jodl, at that time a Major, who had repeatedly referred to Hitler as a charlatan. Jodl fell increasingly under Hitler's spell as Hitler went from success to success and after the successful Austrian *Anschluss* in 1938 he became Hitler's unreserved admirer. Jodl was hanged at Nuremberg.

2 Herta Model, in a conversation with Görlitz, 18 September 1970: In its verdict of 28 December 1949, the de-Nazification commission at Düsseldorf stated that the *Feldmarschall* had never expressed National-Socialist opinions in public. It further stated that Ms Model had disapproved of National-Socialism. In a conversation with the author, Hansgeorg Model disputed this last

he must share the blame with many of the other German Generals of his time. Politics can be studied sufficiently to be understood. At that time, at least some understanding was called for, lest one wanted to be swept up by the maelstrom into complicity with the crimes of the regime. Means of information were easily available. Foreign newspapers could be bought freely in Germany until the outbreak of the war. The German-language Swiss daily papers, and weekly magazines, wrote in great detail about the Third Reich. Before 1939 there was no prohibition on listening to foreign broadcasts. Every German who wanted to know what was happening in Germany had no problem in finding out. The common saying was, "We lived under a dictatorship. We had no means of knowing." They were just a flimsy excuse.

German military memoir writers like to quote a sentence by Liddell Hart: "The German Generals of the Second World War were more the total products of their profession, than their rivals in other armies. They could have been even better, had they had a wider horizon and a more far-reaching understanding. But had they become philosophers, they would have ceased to be soldiers."[3] The following sentence of Liddell Hart's is conveniently ignored: "The German Generals were only technicians, fully occupied with their professional duties. Thus it is easy to understand how Hitler could pull the wool over their eyes and, increasingly, turn them into willing tools."[4]

Model's troop commands up to the outbreak of World War II

Model's promotion to Major had occurred in 1929. After rising to Lieutenant Colonel, he took over the command of Battalion II of the Infantry Regiment at Allenstein. In 1934, Model became a Colonel and Commander of the Allenstein Regiment. The increasing pace of those last promotions was due to the rapid growth of the Army, implemented further in 1935. In the latter part of the war, promotions of officers came close to being inflationary.

The first assignment at Allenstein was not a happy experience. Model did not get on with his regimental commander. Colonel Fritz Kühne was eight years older, and wanted to "put the skids under him". Kühne became a *Generalmajor* in 1934 and a *Generalleutnant* in 1936, but he was not promoted during World War II. Görlitz could never resist searching for a political background in Model's career. He advanced the opinion that the posting in Allenstein was due to a desire to remove a "particularly exposed" officer from Berlin, in order to spare him trouble.[5] "Particular exposure" implied either known opposition to the regime, which could have been an obstacle to his further career, or known National-Socialist tendencies, which would hardly have led to his removal from the capital city. There was no need to single out Model's motives or opinions on matters of state, especially during the interim period between the World Wars. At that time, Model was a relatively insignificant officer who was still somewhat far down the ranks. Görlitz also stated that

opinion and emphasized that his mother was totally apolitical and that her main interests were her home and her family. In her eyes, one of her important duties was to invite officers who felt insulted by her husband and endeavour to restore normal relations.

3   Quoted by Manstein, *Verlorene Siege*, Foreword (no page number). This distinction makes little sense; there is no closed border line between philosophy and military talent. In Ancient Greece and Rome, philosophers and men of letters assumed military commands whenever called for.

4   Liddell Hart, p.8.

5   Görlitz, p.48.

Kühne thought he had found certain National-Socialist leanings in Model's opinions to which he objected. At that time, Kühne would have found it hard to find a replacement for Model who did not possess "certain National-Socialist leanings". A simple and logical explanation is that the two officers did not see eye-to-eye, hardly an exceptional occurrence.

Regimental command at Allenstein

Model was promoted to Colonel in 1934, and succeeded Kühne as Commander of the Regiment. In his new command, Model developed many of the methods which he would use in higher commands. Both the positive and the darker aspects of his character began to emerge. He took particular care of his soldiers, his non-commissioned officers and his younger officers. He closely supervised their training and saw to their personal well-being. At the same time, frictions increased both with officers of equal rank and with direct subordinates. His temperamental outbursts and his exaggerated demands drew criticism. His lack of tact and his constant sarcastic comments caused many raised eyebrows.

The following comments reveal varied reactions to Model's performance while he was assigned to Allenstein:

General Erich Reuter:

He demanded far more from his officers and soldiers than the previous commanders. He introduced new ideas into the somewhat antiquated principles of commands in East Prussia. This led to conflicts, both with other Regimental Commanders in the region, and with his own Company Commanders. Being accustomed to traditional methods, they were simply unable to cope with his sometimes erratic and excitable temper. All of a sudden they were required to adapt themselves to new methods, to display creativity, and to reach instant decisions. When Model arrived from Berlin, he injected new ideas, many of which were his own inventions, first into his Battalion and then into the Regiment.[6]

General Friedrich Schulz:

He demanded much from his young officers and his non-coms. On top of practical training, we were burdened with weekly tactical problems which had to be solved at home. At times we had to groan. However, there was compensation in his liberal granting of leave, and absence of censorship of free-time activities.[7]

General Wilhelm Knüppel:

He probably demanded too much of his subordinates. In particular, he required the solution of tactical problems that went beyond the level of understanding of the non-coms.[8]

General Hans Wagner:

6　Leppa, p.61.
7　Ibid, p.61.
8　Ibid, p. 62.

Later, he would always remind me of former times. As Company Commander he was very ambitious and unscrupulous. He would avail himself of every possibility that put himself and the Company into the spotlight. At that time his character did not display any warmth. However, I noticed that he remained particularly close to his former comrades in Infantry Regiment 52, and often displayed his affection for their unit.[9]

General Theodor Busse:

Model's Company was one of the best, in spite of his exaggerated demands which tended to erode morale.[10]

Events of 30 June 1934

Some popular books describe the events of that day[11] as the result of a *Putsch* attempt by the SA. This was not the case. If there was a *Putsch*, it was the wilful murder of the SA leadership after increasingly strong prompting from the Army.[12] True, Ernst Röhm and the SA leadership had become dissatisfied with Hitler's policies after he became Chancellor. In their eyes, the assumption of power by the NSDAP was the result of a revolutionary movement. A growing number of Communists switched to the NSDAP during the years 1930-1933. They were convinced that Hitler would be best able to deal with both the economic crisis and the massive unemployment. Once in power, Hitler's attention turned increasingly to the economic and financial elite, many of whom had kept their distance from him. The support of the working classes remained assured to him, since he showed that he was able to rid Germany of unemployment. In fact, in less than three years after Hitler's accession to power, full employment had been restored to Germany.

The Army viewed the SA with growing suspicion, having become worried by their sheer numbers, and by the fact that SA units were armed. Pushed primarily by the ambitious General Walter von Reichenau, the Army increasingly urged the use of force against the SA. Hitler was happy to oblige, since he needed the support of the Army. At the same time, he wanted to get rid of the increasing pressure from the SA leadership. What the narrow-minded Generals failed to see was that by 'robbing Peter' they had 'paid Paul'.

---

9 Ibid.

10 Ibid.

11 In some literature, 30 June 1934 is also called the "night of the long knives". Disgruntled SA leaders had threatened that their conflict with the party leadership could result in a night of the long knives. In his speech of 13 July 1934, Hitler used this expression, to mock the SA leaders' purported plans. (Domarus, p. 418). In his speech, Hitler pretended hypocritically to have "recently" learned with disgust about the many homosexuals among the SA leaders. His faithful mouthpiece, Dr Joseph Goebbels, spoke of the "horror" experienced by the *Führer*, when he entered the bedroom of the SA leader Edmund Heines and found him in bed with a young boy. The presence of homosexuals among the upper ranks of the SA leadership had been known in Germany for many years. As long as he had use for the SA, Hitler could not care less about their sexual leanings.

12 Some sources have Röhm's sister Hilde saying to Hitler the day after her brother was murdered: 'Had my brother intended to stage a *Putsch* against you, you would not have survived the day'. (C. Haensel, *Der Nürnberger Prozess. Tagebuch eines Verteidigers*, Munich 1980, p.240.)

The SA was Peter, Paul was the SS which became the new power factor. In their obsession with an imaginary danger from the SA, the Generals were even prepared to accept the murder of Generals von Schleicher and von Bredow. General von Reichenau cabled enthusiastically to his friend *Kapitän zur See* Patzig: "All catched" [sic.] (Reichenau had a fancy of expressing himself in English, however his knowledge of the English language was insufficient to know that it should have been "caught".) Only *Generaloberst* von Hammerstein-Equord, who had already retired, appeared at the funeral of his old friend von Schleicher. All the other officers obeyed the order of the Minister of War, *Generaloberst* Werner von Blomberg, to stay away.[13]

Abroad, the events of 30 June 1934 were registered with a mixture of surprise and horror. It quickly became apparent that the new German regime would not shrink from the utmost brutality if it suited its policy. In Germany, there was a widespread feeling of satisfaction. The SA had become increasingly unpopular, with its rowdy behaviour and its street riots, molesting passers-by without any reason or provocation. At that time the slogan '*Wenn das der Führer wüsste*'(if only the *Führer* knew), was widespread. In this context, it implied that Hitler had been too busy to know of the behaviour of the SA. In his speech to the *Reichstag* on 13 July 1934, Hitler proclaimed that, "In this hour, I was responsible for the fate of the German nation and I was the supreme judge of the German people."[14] That proclamation was greeted with loud applause by the audience and was also received with satisfaction by the wider public.

The oath of allegiance to Hitler

Reichspräsident Paul von Hindenburg died on 2 August 1934. Unfortunately, he died years too late. During the last years of his presidency he was simply a puppet in the plotting hands of his advisers. His election to a second term, in 1932, was mainly due to the support of the Social Democrats and other opponents of Hitler. He betrayed them shamefully when he appointed Hitler as Chancellor. The NSDAP had not achieved a majority in the *Reichstag*.[15] Once Hitler had been appointed, Hindenburg disgraced himself by attending the farcical 'day of Potsdam'. It was cleverly orchestrated by Hitler. Hindenburg attended in his *Feldmarschall's* uniform, wearing the old-style spiked helmet, and waving his *Feldmarschall's* baton. Hindenburg sent Hitler a message of congratulations

---

13 In the end, the funeral did not take place, because von Schleicher's body had been 'removed' the night before. Later the Army engaged in meaningless efforts to obtain a formal rehabilitation of Generals von Schleicher and von Bredow, who were long forgotten. On 28 February 1935, the Army finally issued a lame statement that although 'Generals von Schleicher and von Bredow had engaged in activities hostile to the government, their personal honour had remained intact'. Manstein makes a semantic distinction: 'Röhm and his associates were shot, Generals von Schleicher and von Bredow were murdered'. *(Soldatenleben,* p.192).

14 The complete text of the speech in M. Domarus, *Hitler, Reden und Proklamationen 1932-1945. Kommentiert von einem deutschen Zeitgenossen.* vol. 1 1932-1934, Wiesbaden 1937, p. 421 (henceforth Domarus).

15 Even in the election of March 1933, after Hitler had already become chancellor, the NSDAP only received 44% of the votes. In the elections of November 1932, it had suffered a temporary defeat and lost two million votes.

and thanks, after 'the night of the long knives'. He thus allowed government-sponsored murder, using his faked reputation.[16]

A recent biography of Hindenburg by the historian Wolfram Pyta (W. Pyta, *Hindenburg. Herrschaft zwischen Hohenzollern und Hitler,* Munich 2007) sheds a new light on Hindenburg. While Pyta admits that Hindenburg had no military talent, he shows that he had political acumen and that after his second election as *Reichspräsident* he was aiming at the creation of an authoritarian extreme right-wing state. Pyta likewise shows that Hindenburg viewed Hitler with increasing sympathy and that a number of moves by him were dictated by his desire to secure Hitler's appointments as *Reichskanzler* after making continued efforts to remove all remaining obstacles.

One day before Hindenburg's death, Hitler merged the offices of the *Reichspräsident* and the *Reichskanzler*. This was a clear *coup d'état* – article 2 of the *Ermächtigungsgesetz* (the law which gave Hitler four years of absolute legislative power without having to have laws approved by the *Reichstag*) stated explicitly that it did not apply to the functions and the rights of the *Reichspräsident*.

Following the day of Hindenburg's death all members of the military were immediately required to swear a personal oath of allegiance to Hitler. The text of the oath was written by two associates of General Walter von Reichenau, Major Edgar Röhricht and Major Hermann Foertsch. At that time, Reichenau had become Schleicher's successor as head of the *Reichswehr* ministerial office. The final wording of the oath was: "I swear this holy oath, before the Almighty, that I will owe unconditional obedience to Adolf Hitler, the *Führer* of the German *Reich* and the German people, and the Supreme Commander of the *Wehrmacht*. As a brave soldier, I will always be ready to put my life at stake to remain faithful to this oath."[17]

Model's sarcastic comment pertaining to the oath, "a small *coup d'état*", has been reported by a number of witnesses and confirmed in post-war literature.[18] General Heinz Guderian writes in his memoirs that he was "beset by doubts". In a letter to his wife, on the day after Hindenburg's death, he wrote: "Tomorrow we will swear allegiance to Hitler. This is an oath which can lead to heavy consequences. Hopefully both parties will abide

---

16 Hindenburg's military glory was largely built on bluff. Colonel (later Generalmajor) Max Hoffmann, in 1914 and Ia of 8th Army wrote in his diary on 1 September 1915: "We put the name v. Hindenburg under the orders without bothering to show them to him. Ludendorff does everything alone". On 16 October 1915: "Hindenburg pays no attention to military matters. He spends most of his time hunting. There are many funny things in this world. If [only] the German people knew that the real name of their hero Hindenburg was Ludendorff." In 1924, General Moritz von Lyncker, the former head of the Emperor's military cabinet, wrote that in 1914 Hindeburg was no longer on the list of the Generals to be employed in war time, because he had become ponderous in spirit and in body. He was only dug out because we were sure that he would follow Ludendorff's proposals. Hindenburg had also been warned that he would be recalled if disagreements arose between him and Ludendorff. F. Uhle-Wettler, *Erich Ludendorff in seiner Zeit. Soldat. Stratege. Revolutionär. Eine Neubewertung.* Berg 1995, p. 174ff.

17 Rumours have it that either Röhricht or Foertsch asked Reichenau, why it was necessary to introduce the Almighty into the text of the oath. Reichenau is supposed to have replied: 'Without God, the dopes will not swear.' (*Ohne Gott schwören die Trottel nicht*).

18 K. Müller, *Das Heer und Hitler, Armee und Nationalsozialistisches Regime 1933-1940,* Stuttgart 1969, p.137, footnote.

by it. The Army has always kept faith in its oaths. Let us hope that it can continue to do so with honour."[19]

At least Model and Guderian were aware that the oath to Hitler had more significance than previous oaths. Only one officer, *Generalmajor* Konrad Stephanus, declined to swear the oath of allegiance. Nothing adverse happened to him. He was retired, but was recalled at the outbreak of war, and commanded Divisions until his final retirement in 1942.

Model as department head in the *Generalstab*

The *Truppenamt* was renamed *Generalstab* when nationwide military service was reintroduced in 1935. The new *Generalstab* differed from the *Grosser Generalstab* of the old Imperial Army. In the old army the Chief of the *Generalstab* was entitled to report directly to the Emperor, and outranked the Commander in Chief of the Army. The new *Generalstab* of the Army was relegated to a position on the same level as the other main Army departments and its chief was one of the many *primi inter pares*.

General Ludwig Beck, who had succeeded General Adam as head of the *Truppenamt* in 1933, was named Chief of the *Generalstab*. With the rapid pace of rearmament, the *Generalstab* grew in size, and a Department T8 in Technology was established in July 1935. Model became head of Department T8 on 15 October. It was a senior *Generalstab* position, the department being directly subordinate to the *Oberquartiermeister* III, General Carl-Heinrich von Stülpnagel.[20] The appointment of Model as Department head at the Generalstab is evidence that he was now considered to be part of the officers' corps elite. General Beck retired in 1938, in protest at Hitler's war plans. He was replaced by General Franz Halder, who in turn was succeeded by Generals Kurt Zeitzler, Heinz Guderian, and finally Hans Krebs.[21]

Model's contribution to the mechanization of the German Army

Model was not known to have any particular technical knowledge, so his appointment as head of a technical division caused surprise. His son, Hansgeorg, agreed that his father had little acumen for such matters.[22] General Jaschke commented: "I was very surprised that Model, of all people, was named head of a technical department. Since I knew him well from our time in Görlitz, I knew that technique was not his *forte*."[23]

However, Model must have learned rapidly. Whether his contribution to the *Panzer* arm was meaningful is an open question. Guderian does not mention him in this

19 Guderian, p. 28.

20 Model was recommended to this position by Colonel Hossbach, Schmundt's predecessor as Hitler's Army ADC. (Estate, Conversation Hossbach with Görlitz, November 20, 1970).

21 Generals Guderian and Krebs were never formally named chiefs of the *Generalstab*. Relations between Hitler and Zeitzler had gradually deteriorated and Hitler had decided to replace Zeitzler with General Buhle, who was considered a second-rater. This suited Hitler, who had an increasing dislike for the *Generalstab*. Buhle was incapacitated after 20 July 1944. Hitler then opted for Guderian who received the title: *"Mit der Wahrnehmung der Geschäfte betraut'* ("acting chief"). Krebs, who succeeded Guderian when Guderian had his last falling-out with Hitler in March 1945 received the same title.

22 Estate, Letter from Hansgeorg Model to Leppa, undated. Model was a hopeless driver and his family felt relieved when Hitler forbade Generals to drive their cars.

23 Estate, Jaschke, 10 March 1955.

connection. In Guderian's memoirs, Model's name appears for the first time as commanding 3 *Panzer* Division, in Guderian's *Panzergruppe* 2, at the beginning of *Barbarossa*. As head of the operational division of the *Generalstab*, Erich von Manstein had been the proponent of new mobile artillery weapons. He proposed a new assault gun, the *Sturmgeschütz*, which had the chassis of a *Panzer* with a 7.5cm calibre gun replacing the turret.[24] There was a contribution by Model to its development, which was emphasized by the *Gemeinschaft für Sturmartillerie* in 1970:

> The name of Model is of great importance in the development and use of assault artillery. Alongside *Generalfeldmarschall* von Manstein, *Generalfeldmarschall* Model was a commander who was able to take advantage of the capacity of the assault artillery, in both the defensive battles, and the retreats, of Army Group North Ukraine in 1944, especially in successful local counter-attacks. He was an important sponsor of this weapon.[25]

Not many opinions of Model's performance as head of T8 have been preserved. General Friedrich Hossbach recalled Model's performance as having been "very valuable".[26] General Heinz Ziegler disagreed:

> As usual, Model had quickly grasped the potential of a weapon in an area which up to then had been alien to him. But many of his proposals lacked realism, and occasionally tended to increase the already difficult tasks of the inspectors.[27]

General Hans Röttiger offered mixed criticism and praise:

> I had to put up with Model for two years. This was far from easy. You needed a solid backbone and a thick skin. In spite of his limited grasp of technical matters, he succeeded in advancing valuable suggestions for developing and improving different weaponry.[28]

---

24 Heavy motorized artillery was not permanently available at the combat units. It remained at *OKH*, which would put it at the disposal of Army Groups, Armies and Corps for specific operations. When they were completed, the artillery units reverted to *OKH*. Manstein had understood that the future mobile war would need the constant support of heavy artillery. Since at that time, the top level officers at *OKH* were artillerymen and anxious to preserve the status of their arm, Manstein had devised a hybrid solution. The assault artillery would remain part of the general artillery, but one assault artillery unit was to remain attached to every Infantry Division.

25 Letter from Colonel *Bundeswehr* Heinz Timpe, head of the Gemeinschaft, to Hansgeorg Model, 112, 1997, Estate.

26 Estate, Conversation between Hossbach and Görlitz, 20 November 1970.

27 Leppa, p.89.

28 General Röttiger had to weather stormy times after the war. During the Nuremberg trial of the *OKW* and the *Generalstab*, he had submitted an affidavit, stating that "the war we conducted against the partisans had the real purpose of serving as a model for the ruthless extermination of the Jews and other undesirable elements." (Krausnick H./Wilhelm H.: *Die Truppe des Weltanschauungskrieges – Die Einsatzgruppen der Sicherheitspolizei und des SD 1938-*

General Erich Jaschke:

Given his temperament, he would often require new ideas to be put into practice at a day's notice. But he was soon to realize that every development of new weaponry requires considerable time and effort. When he took over the department, there were a number of heated arguments between his unit and other divisions of the *Generalstab*, but they soon began to work together. He had a particular gift for finding out what was relevant for us in the pile of foreign literature.[29]

Manstein wrote with his customary mixture of veiled praise, obscured by drops of poison. In fact, Manstein never forgave Model's interventions against the follies of his own plans for the battles of Kursk, nor that Hitler had chosen Model as his successor when he was dismissed. "Model was an especially capable and talented *Generalstab* officer, with a clear capacity of judgement and a quick understanding. He often behaved like a pike in the carp pond."[30]

Manstein was here alluding to a propensity by Model to interfere in the work of other departments. However, Manstein himself did this constantly, and was soon unpopular among his comrades. Yet, Manstein's superiority over Model at that time was undeniable and while his meddling often led to positive consequences, Model caused mainly irritation.

Visit to Spain during the Spanish Civil War

In the summer of 1937, Model paid a visit to Spain. Görlitz labelled this mission "Top Secret." This is one of Görlitz' many inventions. Since German troops were taking part in the Civil War, an inspection visit by a high-ranking officer from the *Generalstab* would appear to be perfectly logical. Leppa reported on a conversation he had with a Major Wilhelmi, at that time German liaison officer to Franco, who told him that the purpose

---

1942, Stuttgart 1981, p.292, henceforth Krausnick). Röttiger was immediately subjected to a barrage by the five Generals who had prepared the defence, with *Feldmarschall* Erich von Manstein as their spokesman. After several days of unrelenting pressure, Röttiger withdrew his affidavit. This incident was to pursue Röttiger for more than ten years. In 1956, Röttiger found himself in competition with General Friedrich Schulz for the position of inspector of the *Bundeswehr* ground forces. General Schulz had been Manstein's chief of staff during the battles for Stalingrad. Prior to his assignment with Manstein, General Schulz had been Goebbels' liaison officer to *OKW*. In 1945, while German surrender talks of their remaining forces in Italy were proceeding, General Schulz was *OB* of Army Group South and strongly opposed to any form of surrender. Röttiger was Schulz' chief of staff and had placed Schulz temporarily under arrest. When the two officers were competing for the new Bundeswehr post, Manstein came out strongly in favour of Schulz, however Röttiger prevailed. (For details, O. von Wrochem, *Erich von Manstein. Vernichtungskrieg und Geschichtspolitik.* Paderborn 2006, p.336 ff. henceforth Wrochem).

29 Estate, Statement by Jaschke, 10 March 1955.
30 *Verlorene Siege,* p.489. Leppa purports Manstein to have written that Model was full of ideas and dynamic, but that many of his ideas could not be followed. Leppa, p.89. This sentence can be found neither in *Soldatenleben* nor in *Verlorene Siege.*

of Model's visit was to review the *Drohne* group that was in charge of training German *Panzer* units in Spain. Model did not meet Franco.[31]

The Mortar Incident

In 1938, Model had been promoted to *Generalmajor*. In the same year the "Mortar incident" took place. The incident deserves mention because it was apparently the first instance when Hitler and Model were together at the same event. However, they did not speak to each other. General Gerhard Engel, at that time a captain and Hitler's Army ADC, recalled:

> In November 1937, Blomberg had presented a report to Hitler on the Czech fortifications. Model's department was ordered to present a shelling demonstration. This took place at Jüterbog in August 1938. Hitler attended unexpectedly. Part of the exercise was to try out the new 'Mortar 18' in attacks on bunkers and other fortifications. Hitler was dissatisfied and instructed the head of the office of armament, General Professor Karl Becker, to improve the weapon and increase production.

> At the end of the demonstration, Hitler addressed the Generals who were present. Quite possibly, Model also attended. Hitler gave a speech about the political situation and emphasized clearly that he had decided to solve the problems with the Sudeten-German population in Czechoslovakia.[32]

It is hardly likely that Hitler paid attention to Model on that day. His first conversation with the General confirmed that when Model later assumed command of 9th Army. Hitler's criticisms were mainly directed against General Becker, who had often endured Hitler's displeasure, and who ended up taking his own life.[33]

The Blomberg-Fritsch affair and the *Revirement*

When Blomberg's marriage to a registered prostitute was discovered, his succession became an immediate topic. Blomberg was cashiered and struck off the Army seniority list.[34] General von Reichenau proposed himself as new Commander in Chief of the Army. He had already done so, when *Generaloberst* von Hammerstein-Equord was replaced by *Generaloberst* Werner Freiherr von Fritsch. In both instances, Reichenau was vetoed by General Gerd von Rundstedt, the number one on the Army seniority list who acted

---

31 Leppa, p.93.

32 Estate, Letter from Engel to Hansgeorg Model, 18 May 1955.

33 In a situation meeting on 1 February 1943, during which Hitler vented his rage that Paulus had not committed suicide at the end of the battle for Stalingrad, he suddenly referred to Becker: "…or Becker, who had gotten mixed up with this weapon's storeroom. He took the consequences and shot himself…" H. Heiber (editor). *Lagebesprechungen im Führerhauptquartier, Protokollfragmente aus Hitlers militärischen Konferenzen 1942-1943*, Munich 1963, p.73.

34 The contempt in which Blomberg was held by his comrades is shown by an entry by Jodl in his diary on 1 February 1938. The minister of justice Hans Frank, later as Governor of the Polish *Generalgouvernement* and known as the "King of Poland", had asked General Adam: "How do you feel about your *Feldmarschall*?" and Adam had cuttingly replied: "He is not our *Feldmarschall,* he is yours." Among the SA leaders, who had managed to escape the massacre of 30 June 1934, there was a good deal of gloating that it now was the Army's turn to suffer embarrassment.

as spokesman for his comrades.[35] Since a file reporting *Generaloberst* von Fritsch, the Commander in Chief of the Army, to be a homosexual had been discovered, Fritsch was no longer to be viewed as the successor to Blomberg.[36] Blomberg then proposed that Hitler himself should become the new supreme commander.[37] That was logical. Hitler was already Head of State and had assumed quasi-dictatorial power. According to the Weimar constitution, which had never been formally abolished, nor even replaced later by a NSDAP constitution, the President of the *Reich* was the Commander in Chief of the armed forces.[38]

Blomberg then suggested that Hitler take General Wilhelm Keitel as his military aide. Keitel's new office received the pompous name *Oberkommando der Wehrmacht, OKW*, literally Supreme Command of the Armed Forces. But at that time, it was simply Hitler's military secretariat.

The conflict between *OKH* and *OKW* began immediately. Officers of the *Generalstab* were formally forbidden by Beck to have any personal contact with officers of *OKW*. After Hitler had dismissed his ADC, Colonel Friedrich Hossbach, Keitel appointed Major Rudolf Schmundt as his successor. Until that day, Schmundt had been a glowing admirer

---

35 Whether the exclusion of von Reichenau was a positive turn of events is open to discussion. Reichenau is considered as having been pro-Nazi to the extremes and in the East he certainly justified such a designation by showing cruelty and actively participating in the worst crimes. However in the 1930s, it was somewhat different. Reichenau was far more intelligent than both von Fritsch and von Brauchitsch. Modern historians credit Reichenau with a great amount of pragmatism and see his attachment to the *NSDAP* as part of a policy by which he could strengthen the position of the Army. Reichenau died of a stroke on January 17, 1942. A number of historians view him as the only "political brain" among the Generals.

36 The many stories describing the Blomberg/Fritsch crisis as an intrigue orchestrated by Hitler to get rid of the two Generals whom he believed were opposed to his war aims, can be dismissed out of hand. Had Hitler wanted to get rid of Blomberg and Fritsch, simply dismissing them would have been the easiest way. Hitler could not care less about the sexual inclinations of his associates. In February 1938, in the middle of the Blomberg/Fritsch affair, Hitler had replaced the finance minister Hjalmar Schacht with Walter Funk, a known homosexual. But since the Blomberg affair had become known in many circles, Hitler feared a new scandal, if the suspicions around von Fritsch were to gain ground.

37 The file had been shown to Hitler some years earlier but Hitler had dismissed it and ordered it to be destroyed. When the Blomberg scandal broke out, Hitler remembered it and wanted to see it again. Whether the Gestapo had not destroyed the file or whether it had reconstituted it has never been established. After it was proved that the file rested upon mendacious reports by a known homosexual who was a police stool-pigeon. Fritsch's name was cleared, but he was not employed again. He followed his former Regiment to Poland in 1939 and was killed by a stray bullet close to Warsaw.

38 Some historians have a tendency of interpreting every step of Hitler as evidence of his megalomania. However Hitler's appointment was not different from what was practised in other countries. According to the American Constitution, the President of the United States is the Commander in Chief of the US armed forces. In World War II, Stalin had himself appointed as Supreme Commander and in the memoirs of his commanders he is referred to as *Vierchovyi*, (Commander in Chief). Churchill had no formal appointment but he acted like the Supreme Commander of British forces from the day of his appointment as Prime Minister until the German surrender.

of Beck. When he presented himself in his new functions, Beck barely greeted him and Hossbach refused to introduce him into his new duties. Such rude behaviour had a price. Schmundt's previous devotion to Beck was then transferred to Hitler. Given Schmundt's increasing influence, the *Generalstab* had lost a new battle.

After rejecting a Reichenau candidature, Rundstedt advanced the name of *Generaloberst* Walther von Brauchitsch as successor to Fritsch. Brauchitsch hesitated. He could look back upon a brilliant career. In 1932 he had become the Inspector General of the *Reichswehr* artillery and in 1933 he succeeded von Blomberg as Commander of the East Prussian *Wehrkreis*, at that time the most important *Wehrmacht* ground command. At the end, Brauchitsch agreed to his new command. Until his death, he would curse himself for this decision. Never before had a German commander in Chief of the Army been subjected to the constant humiliations which Brauchitsch had to endure. Until he was relieved in December 1941 there was hardly a meeting between Hitler and Brauchitsch from which Brauchitsch did not return in despair.

The *Revirement*

Revirement was the name given to a major shake-up within the officer corps, in the wake of the Blomberg-Fritsch affair. Hitler feared that the *Wehrmacht* would be open to ridicule abroad. Therefore he made massive changes, not only in the *Wehrmacht*, but also in the Foreign Service and Civil Service ranks. Removal of Blomberg and Fritsch would then appear to be only a coincidental part of a larger reorganization. The posts which became vacant were filled by officers according to their order on the seniority lists. Some of the officers affected by the *Revirement* were placed on the temporary retirement list, with z.V., *zur Verfügung*, (still at disposal), after their rank. A number of them were first recalled during the Sudeten crisis of 1938, and a year later at the outbreak of the war. Wilhelm Ritter von Leeb and Ewald von Kleist rose to *Feldmarschall*. Some officers were transferred to other commands, including Erich von Manstein. He was dismissed as *Oberquartiermeister I*, (deputy chief of the *Generalstab*), and General Halder took his place. General Viktor von Schwedler left his position as head of the Army's personnel department. Manstein was appointed commander of an infantry Division at Liegnitz, and von Schwedler received command of a Corps in Dresden. Model was appointed his chief of staff.

During Model's tenure as Chief of Staff of von Schwedler's IV Corps at Dresden, a number of distasteful incidents occurred between Model and other Corps officers. By that time, such altercations had become part of Model's standard behaviour. General Röhricht, who was Ia of the *Wehrkreis*, wrote that Model was simply insufferable.[39]

Von Schwedler's Corps was part of Group 3 of the *Wehrkreise*, commanded by General Blaskowitz. *Generaloberst* Johannes Blaskowitz, often referred to the "Christian" General, had encountered Hitler's displeasure during an exercise before the war. In the campaign against Poland, he was *OB* of 8th Army. During the battle at the river Bzura, the only major encounter of the Polish campaign, new disagreements and a sharp exchange occurred between Hitler and Blaskowitz. He had to endure strong criticism from Hitler

---

39 Estate, Röhricht, 10 March 1956. The organisation of the *Wekrkreise* and the peacetime *Heeresgruppen* are given in detail in chapter 4.

in the presence of his subordinates. Blaskowitz received the surrender of Warsaw and was appointed as the first and only military governor of Poland.

He next incurred Hitler's anger when he lodged a series of sharp protests, in writing, against the brutal treatment of Polish civilians and Jews by German police units. (Blaskowitz was careful not to mention the participation of the *Wehrmacht* in many such actions. In February 1940, in a memo to Brauchitsch he had described Poles and Jews as the arch-enemies of the German people. Thus Blaskowitz also accepted the "bogeyman", only the methods were objectionable.)[40] After some other *Wehrmacht* commanders joined in the protests, Hitler reacted angrily that wars were not conducted with Salvation Army methods and closed down the military government in Poland.

The only 'punishment' endured by Blaskowitz was that he was the only General already *Generaloberst* in 1939, who was never promoted to *Feldmarschall*. It was yet more evidence that contradicting Hitler, even over basic policies in occupied areas, carried no real risk for the officer involved. Apart from the absence of promotion, Blaskowitz retained active commands. He was decorated with the oak leaves and the swords to his Knight's Cross. Blaskowitz had no connection with the military resistance. In 1944, during Model's time as *Oberbefehlshaber West*, Blaskowitz became his subordinate. Blaskowitz was indicted for war crimes by the IMT (Case 12) and committed suicide in prison.

Anschluss and the Sudeten crisis

On 12 March 1938, the *Anschluss* of Austria was completed. Pressure on Czechoslovakia began, increasing almost by the day. Model's Department T8 was disbanded in the autumn of 1938. He was appointed Chief of Staff to IV Corps at Dresden, which was commanded by General von Schwedler. In the event of a war with Czechoslovakia, Model was expected to become Chief of Staff of the 7th Army, *OB* General Hans Seutter von Lötzen.[41] It was not one of the major units foreseen for an invasion of Czechoslovakia. 7th Army was to be kept in reserve for duties elsewhere.

Second Czech Crisis

Before Germany occupied the whole of Czechoslovakia in March 1939, Model paid a short two-day visit to Prague, which was obviously kept secret. Görlitz alleged that "Model, true to his nature, wanted to get a personal impression of the capital city of a potential enemy." This cannot be taken seriously, a personal initiative of this kind on the part of a relatively junior General would have been unthinkable.

Colonel Dr Wolf Boysen, who had served under Model in the Kuratorium, recalled that he had observed Model in civilian clothes, at Linz, in May 1938. He said that Model had been ordered to appraise marching orders into Czechoslovakia from the former Austrian territory.[42] Lieutenant Colonel Lange wrote that, in 1938, Model had

---

40 K.Mallmann/J.Böhler/L.Matthäus (ed). *Einsatzgruppen in Polen. Darstellungen und Dokumente,* Darmstadt 2008, p. 69.

41 General Seutter von Lötzen, born in 1875 had been retired in 1933 as *General der Infanterie.* During his short return to active duty in 1938, he was number one on the Army seniority list. He was not employed during World War II but he remained on the seniority list.

42 Estate, Undated letter from Hansgeorg Model to Leppa.

already been entrusted with some unspecified secret missions related to a possible war with Czechoslovakia.[43]

Both accounts are open to doubt. Lange was a most unreliable witness and a self-inflated man. We will meet him again in chapter 8 dealing with war crimes. His testimony at the trial of members of the Sonderkommando 7a of Einsatzgruppe B was particularly damaging to Model. Had Model been entrusted with a secret visit to Prague, he would hardly have mentioned it either to Dr. Boysen or to Lange.

Poland

On 22 August 1939, Hitler addressed a group of top *Wehrmacht* commanders at the Obersalzberg, his mountain residence at Berchtesgaden. The meeting was attended by Generals Keitel and von Brauchitsch, the *OB* of the two Army Groups foreseen for the campaign against Poland, *Generaloberst* Fedor von Bock and *Generaloberst* Gerd von Rundstedt. Also present were the *OBs* of the five Armies, General Günther von Kluge, General Georg von Küchler, General Johannes Blaskowitz, General Walter von Reichenau, *Generaloberst* Wilhelm List, and the *OB* of the two Air Fleets (*Luftflotte*), General Albert Kesselring and General Alexander Löhr.[44]

Hitler told the Generals how he wanted the war to be conducted in Poland and what he expected of them. The significant sentences of his address were: "No formal declaration of war. Begin hostilities following a propagandistic invention. [This was obviously an allusion to the faked attack, by Germans in Polish uniform, on the radio station in Gleiwitz.] Unimportant, if this is believable. Legal aspects have no importance, only victory counts. Destruction of Poland is to happen by all available means. Soldiers must close their hearts to pity. Right is always with the stronger. Enforce *Grösste Härte* (maximum harshness). Poland must be destroyed. The aim is not to reach a certain line, nor a new border, but the annihilation of the enemy. Means employed have no relevance. No one asks the victor if his means conform to recognized rights. Right is unimportant, only victory counts."[45]

Officers and soldiers of the *Wehrmacht* thus knew what the leadership expected of them. As soon as the Germans entered Poland, atrocities took place against Polish civilians, with Jews among the prime targets. SS, police and *Wehrmacht* units took part. For many years, before Hitler came to power, Germans had been subjected to vitriolic hate propaganda

---

43 Estate, Letter from Hansgeorg Model to Leppa, undated, referencing a letter from Lieutenant Colonel Lange.

44 General Löhr was an Austrian and had commanded the Austrian air force before the *Anschluss*. He was the only full time air force professional among the high *Luftwaffe* commanders. Many high ranking *Luftwaffe* commanders, among them *Feldmarschall* Albert Kesselring, had begun their service in the Army and were thus later qualified for high army commands. Their experience in both Army and *Luftwaffe* provided them with good understanding of combined air-ground operations. *Generaloberst* Bruno Loerzer and *Generaloberst* Ernst Udet were aces of the First World War, who had left the Army as Lieutenants or Captains and who were directly promoted to higher ranks when the new *Luftwaffe* was created. At the end of the War, Löhr was *OB* of Army Group E. He was sentenced to death in Yugoslavia and shot for having commanded the air raid upon Belgrade on the first day of the German attack upon Yugoslavia and Greece.

45 Halder, war diary, vol. 1, Stuttgart 1962, p.25.

against Poland and the Polish people. Already on 11 September 1920, *Generaloberst* von Seeckt had written in a memorandum: "Poland's existence as a state is intolerable, and not compatible with Germany's claims to life. Poland has to disappear. It will disappear through its internal weakness and through actions of Russia, with our help."[46]

In spite of Hitler's instructions, some *Wehrmacht* commanders protested. The memoranda of *Generaloberst* Blaskowitz have already been mentioned. Generals Friedrich von Cochenhausen and Wilhelm Ulex, to name only two, joined in the chorus. Brauchitsch wrote a note, warning officers that their behaviour in Poland would be taken into account in their promotions after the war.[47] Other Generals, such as *Generalmajor* Walter Braemer, commander of rear area 850, showed themselves more ruthless than many SS and police commanders. By the end of 1939, 7000 Polish Jews had been murdered.

General Viktor von Schwedler's IV Corps, with Model as chief of staff, was part of Reichenau's 10th Army. 10th Army took part in many cruelties, against both Polish civilians and Jews. Görlitz wrote that Model was unaware of the war crimes, and of the massacre of Jews which followed the end of the campaign.[48] However, that is inconsistent with the facts. Every high-ranking German officer knew what was happening in Poland. In a recent study, Dieter Pohl shows that at least half of the murders in Poland were committed by the *Wehrmacht*.[49] The war diaries of IV Corps mention many instances of beatings, summary executions, burning of villages, and other atrocities.[50] Among the wanton murders in the area of 10th Army, the massacre at Konskie must be mentioned. The well-known film producer, Leni Riefenstahl, happened to witness the massacre as she was on her way to visit General von Reichenau. The events at Konskie are also widely reported in literature. [51]

In a letter to his mother-in-law at the end of the campaign, Model wrote: "One has to feel pity for the Polish soldier and for the Polish people. Both have fine qualities, but leadership and organization were dreadful."[52] Hürter praises Model: "One of the rare instances of pity on the part of a German commander."[53] However, the remainder of Model's letter shows that he understood nothing about the structure of Polish society and its fate. He continued: "The fear of the wealthy population that the poor will now retaliate is remarkable. Therefore all simply run away, landowners, priests, etc, all these who should have remained in their positions." While the Polish government under the leadership of the Commander in Chief, Marshal Edward Rydz-Smigły had fled to Romania, the higher social strata, both the 'intelligentsia'

---

46 Seeckt's diatribe can be labelled as having been prophetic, except that the roles in the destruction of Poland were reversed. Poland "disappeared" through action of Germany and with Russia's help.

47 BA-MA- N 104/3.

48 Görlitz, p.71.

49 D. Pohl, *Die deutsche Militärbesatzung und die Eskalation der Gewalt in der Sowjetunion* in C. Hartmenn/ J.Hürter/ P. Lieb, D.Pohl (ed.) *Der deutsche Krieg im Osten 1941-1944. Facetten einer Grenzüberschreitung*, Munich 2009, p. 74.

50 War diary IV Corps 16.9.1939, 11.9 to 10.10.1939, to mention a few examples. A detailed list in Newton, p.77 ff.

51 For details about the crimes committed in Poland in 1939, .K. Mallmann/J. Böhler/J. Matthäus (ed.) *Einsatzgruppen in Polen. Darstellung und Dokumentation*, Darmstadt 2008.

52 Görlitz, p.52.

53 Hürter, p.191.

and the clergy remained in Poland.[54] The majority of them were murdered by the Germans during the years of the occupation."[55]

France

On 23 October 1939, Model was appointed chief of staff of 16th Army. On 1 April 1940, he was promoted to *Generalleutnant*. The staff of the newly formed 16th Army was originally the staff of Georg von Küchler's 3rd Army in Poland. The OB of 16th Army, which was part of von Rundstedt's Army Group A, was General Ernst Busch, who must be ranked at the bottom of the list of German high commanders. Every operation which he commanded during the war turned into a failure.

Model's assignment as chief of staff to 16th Army must be considered fortunate for Busch, who gained a chief of staff far superior to him, and who may have kept him from blundering. Busch had already incurred Guderian's wrath during a conference at the Reichskanzlei in Berlin on 15 March 1940, which was attended by all Army OB of Army Group A. Guderian had described his plans for crossing the Meuse and proceeding to the channel coast. Suddenly Busch said: "Well, I don't believe that you will be able to cross at all", whereupon the hot-tempered Guderian replied, "You are not the one who has to attempt doing it."[56]

OKH was well aware of Busch's weakness but since, at that time, he was among the commanders valued by Hitler, he had to be employed somewhere. Halder saw to it that it was not in one of the decisive areas of the German offensive. 16th Army did not participate in the decisive *Panzer* breakthrough. In the final phase of the battle for France, it joined forces with 1st Army, under *Generaloberst* Erwin von Witzleben, to mop up the remaining forts of the Maginot line. When Newton wrote: "In a very real sense, the fact that Busch and Model earned not even the slightest mention by historians of the campaign, is the best evidence of the success of their mission",[57] one is tempted to reply that even Busch could not avoid being successful against the French Army of 1940. Furthermore, the daily *Wehrmacht* communiqué made special mention of the success of individual units, down to companies, and even to individual officers and soldiers, until the very end.[58] Apparently Newton has not read some of the important books about the Battle of France. He would have found in them references to Busch's 16th Army albeit in a manner hardly flattering for Busch.[59]

---

54 A recent German source has Marshal Rydz-Smigły returning to Warsaw in 1941 and enlisting in the Polish underground army as a simple soldier. He is said to have died of heart failure before the outbreak of the Warsaw uprising. T. Urban, *Polen*, Munich 2009, p.20.

55 Modern statistics put the total number of Poles murdered during the war at over 6 million. 2.5 million of the victims were Jews.

56 Guderian, p.82.

57 Newton, p 90.

58 For instance, the *Wehrmacht* communiqué of 26 April 1945 stated: "...In the fighting in Silesia, *Panzer* Regiment 27 of 19th *Panzer* Division succeeded between 15 March and 10 April in destroying or capturing 103 *Panzer* and assault guns and 104 artillery guns. These successes are due to the first unit of the Regiment commanded by Captain Büche."

59 Karl-Heinz Frieser criticizes Busch for having refused to put part of his *Panzer* at Guderian's disposal, after Guderian had broken trough at Sedan. (K.-H. Frieser. *Blitzkrieg-Legende. Der Westfeldzug 1940*, Munich 1996, p. 128). Alistair Horne mocks Busch. He recalls the incident

Generalleutnant Georg von Sodenstern had succeeded Manstein as Rundstedt's Army Group A, Chief of Staff. He wrote to Leppa that Busch had sent a request to Rundstedt to report directly to him, with the assistance only of his Ia, but excluding his chief of staff, Model.[60] That scurrilous idea was immediately rejected by Generals von Manstein, Günther Blumentritt and Ludwig Crüwell, who referred to approved procedures in the chain of command in the *Wehrmacht*. It can be safely assumed that Model would never have accepted such a snub.

In a post-war statement, Manstein emphasized that Model had recommended sticking to the first OKH Plan Yellow. This was the first of several variations of Plan Yellow which had some superficial resemblance to the Schlieffen Plan of 1914, but which only foresaw a breakthrough to the channel coast. Manstein added that Model's preference for Yellow was a consequence of his optimistic nature and his belief in Hitler.[61] That does not stand up, because Hitler had been opposed to the first Plan Yellow from the very beginning. Manstein conveniently omitted to mention that his own plan *Sichelschnitt* was only adopted because Hitler forced it down the throats of the conservative-minded OKH Generals.

A statement by Görlitz that Model "practically commanded 16th Army" can be put aside.[62] The chief of staff cannot issue orders, he is the adviser to his commander. If he disagrees with a step taken by his commander, he has to put his objection in writing. Without doubt, Model's advice was instrumental in preventing Busch from committing his usual blunders. Serving under Busch may well have strengthened Model's belief in his own future. Perhaps he felt that if even a second rate commander like Busch could be promoted to *Generaloberst*, such a rank was also in his reach in a not too distant future.

19 July 1940 saw a plethora of promotions in keeping with the victory in France. Nine *Generaloberst* of the Army were promoted to *Feldmarschall*.[63] Three Luftwaffe Generals were permitted to jump over the rank of *Generaloberst* and were directly named *Feldmarschalls*.[64] Several Generals, including Halder, became *Generaloberst*, and Göring was made a *Reichsmarschall*, a new rank created especially for him.

Görlitz wrote that Model was kept out of the promotions of 19 July 1940, "probably because of his brusque character and the growing number of his enemies".[65] Newton joins him:

> Conspicuously not a recipient of these laurels was Walter Model. The problem appears to be the fact that his brusque and reckless style, as chief of staff, only cemented his existing image, as something less of a gentleman, among other *Generalstab* officers.[66]

---

during the preparation of the battle when Busch had said to Guderian that he did not believe Guderian would be able to cross the Meuse. After his successful crossing, Guderian sent a sardonic cable to Busch, telling him that he had successfully crossed. (A. Horne, *To lose a battle, France 1940*, Boston 1969, p.157 and 167).

60 Estate, Letter: Sodenstern to Leppa (undated).

61 Manstein, 16.2.1955.

62 Görlitz, p.73.

63 von Brauchitsch, von Bock, von Rundstedt, Ritter von Leeb, List, von Kluge, von Witzleben, von Reichenau and Keitel.

64 Kesselring, Sperrle and Milch.

65 Görlitz, p.71.

66 Newton, p.99.

Both statements can be dismissed out of hand. No *Wehrmacht* General was ever denied promotion on grounds of rude behaviour. There was simply too much 'fruit salad' on 19 July 1940.[67] The only chiefs of staff who were promoted on that day were Halder, who became a *Generaloberst* , and Jodl, who rose to *General der Artillerie*. The chiefs of staff of the three army groups, Generals Georg von Sodenstern, Hans von Salmuth, and Hans Felber, had to wait until 1 August 1940, before being promoted to higher rank. The Army Chiefs had to wait a few months longer. Model had no claim whatsoever to a special promotion. His performances as chief of staff of Corps in Poland, and to Army in France, were in no way superior to other officers in those positions. Members of his staff made laudatory statements about him, but so did officers at other staffs about their chiefs. Model rose above average only when he joined the highest ranks and commands.

Seelöwe

Operation *Seelöwe* was the code name for the planned German invasion of the British Isles. Model took part in the staff preparations for *Seelöwe*. It was to be carried out by Rundstedt's Army Group A, with its 9th Army under *Generaloberst* Adolf Strauss, and 16th Army under Busch. Leppa reported on a conversation with Major Ulrich von Busekist, an officer on the 16th Army staff, that Model was optimistic about the prospects of the landing.[68] That may indeed have been the case. Many of the other officers thought likewise. It demonstrates that Model had little insight into strategy, and that he understood logistics even less.

---

67 The flood of promotions recalls a poem *The Gondoliers,* Act II, by W. S. Gilbert:
  On ev'ry side Field Marshals gleam'd,
  Small beer were Lords Lieutenants deem'd,
  With Admirals the ocean teem'd
  Around his wide dominions...
  In short, whoever you may be,
  To this conclusion you'll agree,
  When ev'ry one is somebodee
  Then no one's anybody!
68 Leppa, p.117.

3

War against Russia to Model's appointment as *OB* of 9th Army

Comparative size of *Wehrmacht* and Red Army units

During a pre-war army reform, units of the Red Army were reduced in size. Before the war, the prescribed strength of a Red Army Division was 8,000 men, but by 1941 many of the Red Army Divisions consisted of only 2,500 to 3,000 men, corresponding in size to a German Regiment. Red Army Divisions were generally commanded by Colonels or Lieutenant Colonels. There were more than a hundred Russian armies, but most were equal in size to an average German Corps. At times, the Red Army abolished Corps and later re-established them.

Russian Armies were grouped into "Fronts". There were more than 50 of them at various times. The "Fronts" bore no numbers, their names were mostly geographical, such as Belorussian "Front", Don "Front", Ukrainian "Front".[1] They were disbanded at short notice, and sometimes regrouped under new names, with a constant shifting of their commanders. Red Army "Fronts" could not be compared with German Army Groups, their size was the equivalent of a German Army.

For purpose of individual operations, several "Fronts" would be put under the command of a representative of the Stavka, either Zhukov or Vasilevsky. Those *ad hoc* units were disbanded after the termination of a specific operation. In Russian military language these units were not given a name, in foreign literature they would be referred to as "Theatres" For simplicity's sake, "Theatre" will be used in this book. A Red Army "Theatre" can be compared to a German Army Group.

In their post-war memoirs, German Generals often listed the Russian units they opposed, in order to imply the numerical superiority of the Red Army. Such superiority did exist, but it cannot be expressed by listing individual Russian units as if they were equivalent in size to German units with the same designations. They had the same names as German units, but there the comparison ended.

3rd *Panzer* Division

On 13 November 1940 Model became commander of 3rd *Panzer* Division. It was to be his first troop command of World War II. The Division was part of XXIV Corps, commanded by General Leo Geyr von Schweppenburg. The Corps belonged to *Generaloberst* Guderian's *Panzer* Group 2, which in turn was part of Army Group Centre commanded by *Feldmarschall* von Bock. General Geyr von Schweppenburg had considerable knowledge of international affairs, acquired during his five years as military attaché in Britain, Belgium, and the Netherlands. He was regarded as one of the more conservative officers. As with

---

1 A complete list of all Red Army "Fronts" during the war is given in an annex to A. Seaton, *The Russo-German War 1941-45*, London 1971 (henceforth Seaton).

many *Wehrmacht* Generals, this aspect of his personality had its ups and downs. At the beginning of the Polish campaign he had congratulated his 3rd *Panzer* Division for its high motivation to finally *den Polen mit höchstem Schwung ans Leder zu gehen,* (rip the hide off' the Poles with greatest energy).

In 1950, during the first formal talks on German re-armament with the Allied High Commissioners, Geyr von Schweppenburg unexpectedly caused a scandal. Adenauer had asked him to accompany him to a press conference. Suddenly the General exclaimed: "The German soldier is being slandered. In the hell of Normandy, and in the Caucasus, he had done nothing except serve his fatherland." This drew an immediate response from the High Commissioners: "The people of the Federal Republic have to decide on whom they want to confer responsibility for the safety of their state. It will depend on them if the *Generalstab* officers of Hitler's war of aggression are once again to have matters under their control."[2] Later, in the debates about the appointments to high commands in the new *Bundeswehr,* Geyr von Schweppenburg sided with the reformers around General von Schwerin, and was against the "old guard", led by Generals Adolf Heusinger and Hans Speidel.[3]

In a statement about Model after the war, Geyr von Schweppenburg wrote:

Model was certainly a brilliant soldier. Our views differed radically. His personal bravery was exemplary. At times he was too careless. While I was military attaché in London, and Model worked at the Ministry, we often wrote and spoke to each other. I always appreciated his open-mindedness in everything related to new technical development. He is dead and I honour his memory by keeping silent about our disagreements[4]

When Model was assuming his new command, von Brauchitsch is reported to have told him: "I am giving you the most modern Division available to me." Perhaps this was meant to encourage the new commander, because in reality the Division was in no shape for combat. In March 1941, Model complained to Halder that the Division could not be engaged in its current condition. When Model took its command, many of its *Panzer* and other motorized equipment had been dispatched to North Africa. In fact, originally 3rd *Panzer* Division had been foreseen as a unit of Rommel's *Afrika Korps.*

The Divisional staff was surprised to learn that Model was entrusted with a *Panzer* Division. He had had no previous combat experience in the war, and he was known as having only limited understanding of armour. As could be expected, his command began with a stormy incident. When his Ia Major Heinz Pomtow, arrived, Model greeted him with the words: "So you are the new Ia. Why have you only arrived now? You should have been here long ago."[5]

This was not only unnecessarily rude, since Pomtow, if he really was late, may have had many valid reasons for his delay. But Model's outburst was simply unnecessary. The

---

2   B. Manig, *Die Politik der Ehre. Die Rehabilitierung der Berufssoldaten in der frühen Bundesrepublik,* Göttingen 2004, p. 216 ff.

3   Details in K. Naumann, *Generale der Demokratie. Generationsgeschichtliche Studien zur Bundeswehrelite,* Hamburg 2007, p.96-169.

4   Estate, Letter: Geyr von Schweppenburg to Leppa, 20 December 1954.

5   Estate, Pomtow, 11 April 1950 and 26 April 1955.

Ia was the most important officer of a Division. Since German Divisions had no staff, the Ia was an acting chief of staff of the Division and he replaced the commander in times of temporary absence. Pomtow must have been a very capable *Generalstab* officer. For those officers who had come out top of the *Generalstab* training, a position in *OKH* was the Mount Olympus, but the second most desirable appointment was Ia of a Division. If an officer of the *Generalstab* felt that he was slighted by his commander, he could complain directly to the chief of the *Generalstab*.[6]

There must have been further unpleasant confrontations. Pomtow's correspondence, which is contained in the estate, lists a number of other minor confrontations which, even after the war, caused him to remain frustrated. Later, co-operation with Pomtow apparently improved. Model did not ask for his relief and Pomtow did not request another assignment. When Pomtow was transferred to another Division, Model gave him a farewell dinner and said, "When all is said and done, he did turn out to be a good *Panzer* Ia."[7]

Model's first performance rating as Division commander, dated 14 February 1941, was written by General Heinrich von Vietinghoff. It stated that Model was probably fit for Corps command. *Generaloberst* Eugen Ritter von Schobert, *OB* of 11th Army, added, "An outstanding Division commander."[8] Since this rating was issued before the attack against Russia had started, and Model had had no previous combat experience as a commander of large units, his steps to put his Division into fighting shape had obviously impressed his superiors.[9]

---

6   The right to complain was firmly embodied in the German Army. It was formally introduced in 1895, modified in 1921 and put into final shape in 1936. If a soldier or an officer felt that they were treated unfairly, they had the right to complain, either in writing or verbally, within three days (soldiers and non-coms) to their immediate superior. For officers, this delay was seven days. If the complainant did not receive satisfaction, he could go step-by-step to higher authority, in the last instance even to Hitler personally. If the complaint was shown to have been unwarranted, the complainant was not punished if he had acted in good faith and in accordance with regulations. In the US Army, complaints had to be directed to the Inspector General of the arm concerned. However the Inspector had only advisory authority. According to US Army Regulation AR 20-30 of 1937, the Inspector General could draw conclusions and make recommendations, but he could not issue orders of redress, neither decide upon punishment. Van Creveld adds that it is doubtful whether a US complainant could ever expect quick and warranted redress. Van Creveld, p.138 ff.

7   Estate, Letter Hans Georg Model to Leppa. Estate, undated.

8   Facsimile in Model/Bradley, p.40 ff.

9   Performance ratings for German officers were written by their immediate superiors at least once a year. Contrary to foreign popular perceptions of German procedures, the *Wehrmacht* reduced paperwork to the strict minimum possible. The performance ratings were short – they seldom exceeded two pages. Every rating had to contain a standard formula, that the officer was a National-Socialist. Performance ratings for *Generalstab* officers had to mention in addition that "he transmits belief in National-Socialism to his subordinates". The main part of the rating was an evaluation of the performance of the officer, a mention of his strengths and his weaknesses, a recommendation for either promotion or a new and more important assignment. Finally, a conclusion: "outstanding", "above average", "average" or "below average". (In performance ratings for Generals these ratings were generally omitted). In peacetime, a rating "below average" led to retirement of the officer. The ratings were completed with brief

During the weeks preceding the attack in the east, the Division was carrying out map reconnaissance of bridges, on the Soviet side of the border. It had crossed the Koden bridge several times in the days preceding the German attack. Model's Division captured the bridge a few hours before the official start of hostilities.

On the eve of the German attack, Model asked a Lieutenant Mertens: "What are you going to tell your men when you inform them of the outbreak of hostilities?" Since the Lieutenant hesitated, Model came forward with a dumb suggestion: "Just tell them that we need food for our war against the British and we are going into Russia to fetch it."[10]

Model's 3rd *Panzer* Division was part of *Panzergruppe* 2, which was commanded by *Generaloberst* Guderian, and assigned to Army Group Centre. During the first phase of *Barbarossa,* 3rd *Panzer* Division was constantly deployed as one of the spearheads of Guderian's army group. Guderian mentioned the Division several times in his memoirs.[11]

The main thrust of the war in the east was first directed north, towards Leningrad and Moscow. But when Hitler decided to suspend the attack on Moscow, in favour of an advance to the south, 3rd *Panzer* Division took part in the closure of the Kiev *Kessel*. *Panzergruppe* 2 then reverted to the centre. The attack upon Moscow was resumed on 2 October 1941, ending in the first German disaster of World War II.

Many of the German commanders who survived World War II claimed that Hitler's decision to continue southward, and give preference to the capture of the Donbas with its raw materials, was the primary cause of the *Barbarossa* failure. *Generaloberst* Heinz Guderian raised the loudest outcry and maintained his views in his memoirs. Among the high commanders in Army Group Centre, *Generaloberst* Maximilian von Weichs supported Hitler's decision.[12]

---

comments by the superiors to the officer writing the rating, up to the very top of the chain of command, a precautionary measure, to keep personal opinions, particularly dislikes, from finding their way into the ratings. In the US Army little value was attached to performance ratings, since as of 1941, there was a large surplus of officers. Replacements were often arbitrary. Officers who were replacing troop commanders in combat, often arrived from home with higher ranks than the ones they had to replace. In practice, the routines in the US Army made it close to impossible to dismiss an incompetent officer. He was simply transferred elsewhere. (After the war, more severe systems were introduced in the US Army). Van Creveld, p. 171.

10 Leppa, p.131.

11 26 July 1941: "At lunch with 3rd Panzer Division, I congratulated Model for his well deserved Knight's Cross". Guderian, 164. On 1 July 1941, Guderian had already written to his wife: "Model has brilliantly proved himself, both as a person and as a commander." (Letter communicated to Hansgeorg Model, by Guderian's son, *Generalmajor (Bundeswehr)* Heinz Guderian).

12 In his memoirs, which remained unpublished because von Weichs died before he could put the finishing touches to them, he wrote: "We cannot judge if we would have even been able to continue a successful advance upon Moscow without the successful *Kesselschlacht* in the South. And even if we had been able to take Moscow, it is far from certain that this would have been decisive. Given the stubborn resistance of the Russians, it cannot be excluded that they would have continued to fight, even if Moscow had fallen. Napoleon's experience should have been a warning to us. Undoubtedly, the decision to fight in the South before attacking Moscow was strategically sound." BA-MA. N.19/9, Bl.23-34. Quoted by Hürter, p. 294 ff.

Red Army commanders stated in their memoirs that Hitler's decision was the correct choice. The strong Soviet reserves concentrated around Moscow, and the difficulties of street fighting in a large city, would have rendered its capture virtually impossible, even if weather conditions had been more favourable. Capturing Moscow would have paled into insignificance, compared with the value of the raw materials to be gained from a successful campaign south through the Ukraine. The Germans would have found it difficult, if not impossible, to continue the war without such materials. Before the start of hostilities, the Russian high command expected that the *Schwerpunkt* of the German advance would be in the South, and they had concentrated the majority of their units there. As a result, the German Army Group South made slow initial progress, while the two other Army Groups, North and Centre, initially outpaced each other.

Model assumes command of XXXXI *Panzer* Corps – promoted to General *der Panzertruppe*

On 3 October 1941, one day after the start of the final attempt to capture Moscow, Operation *Taifun*, Hitler proclaimed in a speech that "this enemy, the Soviets, is totally broken, and will never be able to rise again."[13] The crisis of the *Barbarossa* planning had begun to cast its shadow much earlier. *Generaloberst* Halder, who until the beginning of the war with Russia had been considered as the epitome of caution, had suddenly displayed an increasing hubris.[14] On day twelve of the Russian campaign, he wrote in his diary that the war had already been won, and that only the mopping up remained. He stuck to this opinion for several weeks. However already in July, the Russian resistance at Smolensk, which halted the German advance in that sector for almost a month, should have been an eye-opener.

By October 1942, the *Wehrmacht* had already suffered heavy losses. Many officers, including a number of Generals, had been killed in action. Others were quite simply exhausted. At Army Group Centre alone, 20 Generals were relieved and immediate replacements were called for.

The German catastrophe began with the *Taifun* operation. It was to be the last attempt to conquer Moscow. The main advocates of *Taifun* were Halder[15] and von Bock. Halder still clung to his illusion of rescuing his *Barbarossa* plan. Von Bock was driven by his ambition to be the architect of a victorious conclusion of the Russian war. He was still smarting over his disappointment at Hitler's earlier decision of suspending the advance on Moscow, and turning south towards Kiev. The *Reichspressechef*, Otto Dietrich, instructed

---

13 Domarus, p.1758 ff.

14 Halder's biographer Christian Hartmann writes that Halder was initially opposed to a war with Russia and that all his attention was concentrated upon the struggle with Great Britain. C. Hartmann, *Halder, Generalstabschef Hitlers 1938-1942*, Paderborn 1991, p.271 ff.

15 Some historians, mostly foreign authors, tend to underestimate the part played by Halder in the war, and to exaggerate the authority and actions of the much weaker von Brauchitsch. Von Brauchitsch was officially Commander in Chief of the Army, but this remained an empty title. Below Hitler, the daily authority was with Halder. It was Halder who had put the finishing touches to Manstein's plan for the battle for France and who effectively commanded the Army during the campaign in the West. Again, it was under Halder's supervision that the *Barbarossa* plan was developed by his *Oberquartiermeister* I *Generalleutnant* Friedrich Paulus. The leadership of the first German onslaught against Russia was likewise under Halder.

the newspapers to display bombastic headlines saying *Der Feldzug im Osten ist entschieden* (the war in the East is decided).

Taifun began with the two largest *Kessel* of 1941 at Bryansk and Vyazma. The Germans took close to 800,000 prisoners. On 9 October 1941, the *Wehrmacht* communiqué proclaimed that "Marshal Timoshenko had sacrificed the last battle-worthy Red Army Divisions." In reality, *Taifun* was an example of the old adage of Horace, *quidquid delirant reges, plectuntur Achivi*. The *Ostheer* was already exhausted by its losses. Supply was deficient, most of the equipment was in need of repair, and no adequate clothing for the cold to come was available to the troops. Even the cautious Ritter von Leeb had been gripped by offensive illusions. He wanted to continue an advance towards Leningrad, although all his *Panzer* units had been diverted to von Bock's Army Group Centre. Busch believed that he could link up with the Finnish Army at the Svir river. In full knowledge that their troops were no longer capable of large-scale offensives, a number of Army *OB* and Corps commanders objected.

On 26 October 1941, Model was given the command of XXXXI *Panzer* Corps and promoted to *General der Panzertruppe*. The promotion was backdated to 1 October, placing him higher in the seniority list. (Such backdating was common procedure in the *Wehrmacht*). *Generalmajor* Hermann Breith succeeded him as a commander of 3rd *Panzer* Division. *Generalleutnant* Friedrich Kirchner remained the Corps commander, during the short interim hand-over period, until Model formally assumed command on 15 November. During this period, all *Panzer* Groups were renamed *Panzer* Armies. *Generaloberst* Reinhardt's 3rd *Panzer* Group became 3rd *Panzer* Army. At first, Model's XXXXI *Panzer* Corps was part of Hoepner's 4th *Panzer* Group and was then transferred to *Generaloberst* Strauss' 9th Army.

Görlitz wrote, "Here began Model's breathtaking rise which led foreign historians to conclude that he had simply put himself at the party's disposal and was thus rewarded."[16] There was, however, no "breathtaking rise." According to *Wehrmacht* policy, a General should hold the rank that corresponds to his level of command. A promotion came immediately upon a new assignment, or after only a short probationary period, during which the new commander had to prove himself. Model's promotion dates were hardly "breathtaking." With the exception of the short lapse of four months between his promotion to *General der Panzertruppe,* and rising to *Generaloberst* on taking over 9th Army, there was never any extraordinary "breathtaking" speed in his appointments, especially when compared to promotions of other Generals:

	Generalleutnant	*"Vollgeneral"*	Time between promotions
Model	1 April 1940	1 October 1941	18 months
Reinhardt	1 October 1939	1 June 1940	8 months
Rommel	1 January 1941	2 July 1941	6 months
Friessner	1 October 1942	1 April 1941	6 months
Harpe	1 March 1942	1 June 1942	3 months
Weiss	1 August 1942	1 September 1942	1 month

16 Görlitz, p.96.

Model's further promotions were likewise not faster than those of other high commanders. Model became a *Generaloberst* on 28 February 1942. The period between *Vollgeneral* and *Generaloberst* was indeed short, but at that time most high command positions in the east were being reshuffled. Model was promoted to *Feldmarschall* on 31 March 1944, thus a "waiting period" of two years. In the case of other *Feldmarschalls*, List, von Kluge, von Reichenau, von Witzleben, von Küchler, Rommel, von Manstein and Schörner the "waiting period" was less than one year.[17] The "breathtaking rise" began when Model was promoted to *Generaloberst* and assumed command of 9th Army. Had Model's fellow commanders been asked about his future prospects before he was appointed *OB* of 9th Army, they would have probably replied: "A good commander of a Division like many others, perhaps even a Corps commander, if he can change his behaviour." None would have foreseen that only two years later, Model would have become a *Feldmarschall* and command the largest units in the East and later also in the West.

Not surprisingly, a first serious incident with the staff of the Corps occurred immediately after Model assumed his command. Unlike many of the Generals whom Model later replaced, Reinhardt had not been relieved because of his poor performance. Reinhardt had been an excellent Corps commander and he was now given an Army command. The XXXXI *Panzer* Corps staff, which Reinhardt left behind, was of very good quality, so it was totally inappropriate for Model to storm into his command like an ill wind.

The victim of Model's temper was his old acquaintance, General Röttiger, who was the chief of staff of the Corps. In a post-war statement, Röttiger said that Model demanded the impossible of the Corps' staff officers, and that he held them responsible for matters outside their authority and beyond their control. The XXXXI Corps quartermaster, and several other staff officers, immediately requested transfer out of Model's command.

Röttiger took Model aside and told him that it might be preferable to replace the entire staff, whereupon Model replied in a manner which was to become typical, "that he had not really meant what he had said." Röttiger added that Model did calm down, but that similar incidents had continued to occur. Model even accosted officers whom he appreciated and respected.

Transfer of XXXXI *Panzer* Corps to 9th Army

XXXXI *Panzer* Corps was first transferred to 4th *Panzer* Army, commanded by *Generaloberst* Hoepner, and then to 9th Army, commanded by *Generaloberst* Strauss who had commanded a Corps under Kluge in Poland. Strauss had been an effective Army commander in France and his army had been scheduled to be part of the invasion force of the British Isles.

At the beginning of the war against Russia, 9th Army had been relatively small, only 12 to 15 Divisions. In October 1941, von Bock was critical of Strauss because of his slow

---

17 Some promotions to *Feldmarschall* occurred in an atmosphere of moodiness by Hitler. One day after Hitler had bemoaned the surrender of Paulus and declared that there would be no more *Feldmarschalls* in this war, v. Kleist, v. Weichs and Busch were promoted to *Feldmarschall*. Also Model's promotion to this highest rank took place in a non-conventional manner. Hitler told Model that he was to replace Manstein as *OB* of Army Group North-Ukraine and gave him his instructions. Model prepared to leave and Hitler said suddenly: "By the way, I also promote you to *Generalfeldmarschall*." (Told to the author by Hansgeorg Model).

advance on Vyazma. When Strauss attempted to justify his actions, von Bock replied that he continued to hope for a good personal relationship, but that he was unable to change his assessment of Strauss' performance.

The war diaries of 9th Army tended to show that Strauss was far removed from reality. The diary entry for 2 November 1941 stated that

> the bulk of the Red Army and its equipment was either destroyed or had fallen into German hands. Obviously, the Russians are no longer capable of undertaking offensive operations. Winter clothing for our own forces is arriving in bulk.

On 24 November 1941, the war diary entry stated that the attack on Moscow was

> … making steady progress and that winter clothing would be available for every soldier within two weeks, at the utmost." Brett-Smith wrote that "Strauss could console himself with the fact that he had gone of his own volition, without having committed any major mistake.

In the light of the statements in 9th Army's war diaries, such an opinion should be doubted.[18]

XXXXI *Panzer* Corps took part in the final assault on Moscow. German advance units reached the outskirts of the Russian capital. They were halted by the Red Army's counter-offensive which began on 6 December 1941. At first, Model underestimated the strength of the Russian attack. When he realized his mistake, he managed to extricate his Corps, but still suffered heavy losses.

Nemesis – The Russian counter-offensive at Moscow – *Wehrmacht* panic

The first sign of a German rout was the Red Army recapture of Rostov in the south, and Tikhvin in the north, in the second half of November 1941. On 6 December 1941, the Red Army launched its first major counter-offensive on Moscow. The Germans had advanced to within a few kilometres from the suburbs of the capital. To this day, a monument stands on the road between Sheremetevo airport and the city centre, showing the furthest point of the German advance. They were shattered and thrown back 150 kilometres, at one point almost 300 kilometres from the capital. The Russian advance showed the final bankruptcy of the *Barbarossa* planning. It was evidence of what should have been clear from the very beginning, that with close to 200 million inhabitants, its vast spaces, and twice the production capacity of Germany, Russia was the stronger country and that Red Army would vanquish the *Wehrmacht* as soon as the shock of the first *Kesselschlachten* was absorbed and new and capable commanders had been appointed to the major units.

Panic set in at the *Wehrmacht* high command. It took only five months of the campaign to transform the bragging *Wehrmacht* Generals of 22 June 1941, into dispirited weaklings who implored the *Führer* to put them out of their self-inflicted misery. Relations between Hitler and Brauchitsch had reached their lowest point. On 12 December 1941, Halder wrote in his diary: "The experience of these last days is depressing and shameful. The

---

18 Brett-Smith, p.100.

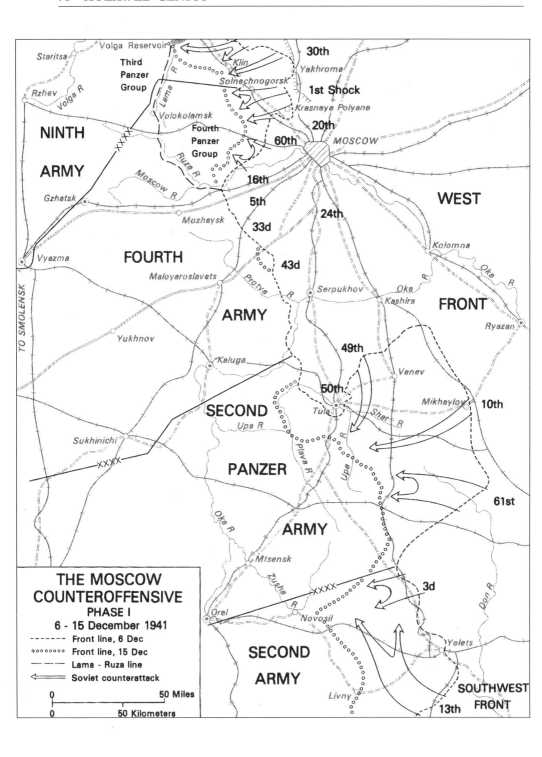

Staritsa

Rzhev

Volga R

NINTH

ARMY

Gzhatsk

TO SMOLENSK

Vyazma

Volga Reservoir

Third
Panzer
Group

Volokolamsk

Fourth
Panzer
Group

Moscow R

Mozhaysk

FOURTH

Maloyaroslavets

Yukhnov

Sukhinichi

Klin

Solnechnogorsk

Lama R

Ruza R

30th

Yakhroma

1st Shock

Krasnaya Polyana

20th

60th

16th

5th

33d

MOSCOW

24th

43d

Protva R

Kaluga

SECOND

Upa R

PANZER

Oka R

ARMY

Mtsensk

Serpukhov

Oka

Kashira

49th

50th

Tula

Plava R

Zusha R

Orel

Novosil

SECOND

ARMY

Livny

WEST

Kolomna

Oka R

FRONT

Ryazan

Venev

Mikhaylov   10th

Sha R

Upa R

61st

3d

Don R

Yelets

SOUTHWEST

13th   FRONT

**THE MOSCOW
COUNTEROFFENSIVE**
PHASE I
6 - 15 December 1941
- - - - - Front line, 6 Dec
ooooooooo Front line, 15 Dec
— · — Lama - Ruza line
⇐━━ Soviet counterattack

0 ———————— 50 Miles
0 ———————— 50 Kilometers

Commander in Chief of the Army is not even a mailman. The *Führer* simply ignores him and gives instructions directly to the Army Group *OB*."[19]

Feldmarschall von Bock, who had insisted on continuing the attack against Moscow, even after it became apparent that the capital was out of his reach, suddenly acted like a schoolboy. He refused to give up the idea of his offensive or to consider a retreat. He then bombarded Halder with demands for reserves which did not exist. On 9 December, he spoke to Halder, who tried to convince him that the crisis would be over by mid-December. Von Bock said: *"Dann ist aber unsere Armee kaputt."* (Then our Army will be destroyed). Halder replied: *"Der deutsche Soldat geht nicht kaputt."* (The German soldier will not be destroyed.) Von Bock insisted: *"Ich will nicht jammern und klagen, aber ich will Reserven haben,"* (I don't want to wail and complain but I must get reserves).[20] A few days later, Halder awoke to reality and admitted that the German Army was confronted with a major crisis, unprecedented in both World Wars.

Army commanders joined in the chorus. Hürter quotes from a number of their letters to their wives.[21] Almost daily, General Gotthard Heinrici wrote in a mood of despair to his wife, Hoepner: "Most of us have not yet known what real war looks like."[22] Reinhardt in a letter of 8 December to his wife: "We have to put up with everything, we are spared nothing."[23] In his diary on 9 December: "Everything fails. The soldiers have no strength left. Is everything now lost? No, this cannot be."[24]

Guderian to his wife, 16 December:

I can't recall ever having experienced such a tension in my career. I only hope that I will come through this. I cannot sleep. I torture myself with questions as to how we can help our poor soldiers who are exposed to this horrible winter. It is terrible, simply unimaginable."[25] Hoepner, again to his wife on 12 December: "Only terrible news. One shudders when the phone rings, and it does not stop ringing." On 17 December: "I am going through terrible days. At night, I am haunted by thoughts of 1918. But here, fighting the winter is much harder than facing the enemy in 1918.[26]

Heinrici to his wife, 17 December:

To sleep, to eat, to drink, all those belong in the past. Somehow the nervous system still functions. But can personal strength withstand the tension of daily having to run for one's life, not seeing any improvement, let alone any turn of events?" On 22 December: "I pray to the Lord for help. Only the Lord can give me advice.[27]

---

19 Halder, war diary, vol.III, Bl.332, quoted in Hartmann, p.302.
20 War diary Army Group Centre, KTB Ia, 9 December 1941, Bl. 66f, quoted in Hürter p.323.
21 All the following quotations are in Hürter, p.320 ff.
22 BA-MA, N 51/9, Bl.64.
23 BA-MA, N 245/2, Bl.13.
24 BA-MA, N 245/3, Bl. 16.
25 Guderian to his wife, 16. December 1941, IfZ, archives , ED 100/77.
26 BA-MA, N 51/9, Bl. 98.
27 Hürter, p.321.

Again Hoepner: "We are in the same situation as Napoleon in 1812." Heinrici, also with reference to Napoleon, wrote: "The retreat through ice and snow recalls Napoleon. And the losses are comparable."[28] On 1 January 1942, Heinrici said to General Felber: "The war is lost."[29] Even Hitler was conscious that victory was no longer in the cards. The diary of the *OKW Wehrmachtführungsstab* mentions: "When the winter campaign 1941/41 turned into a catastrophe, it became clear to the *Führer* that any thoughts of victory had to be abandoned."[30]

Quarrels arose amongst the Army *OB*. Guderian and von Kluge soon clashed. Guderian reported to Bock that no mutual trust remained between commanders. However, he did not mention names in that report. In his letters to his wife, he railed against *OKH, OKW* and von Bock for their "incompetence and absence of aim." Only Hitler was exempt from his criticism: "The people at *OKH* and *OKW*, who have never seen the front, have no idea of what is taking place. They issue orders which are impossible to follow, and refuse to take note of our complaints and requests. The feeling that one is not understood, and thus abandoned to events, is only destructive to the nervous system."[31] When von Kluge heard about Guderian's report to von Bock, he exploded: "It is absolutely necessary that Brauchitsch comes here, obviously *OKH* has not the faintest idea of the situation."[32]

A few days later, von Kluge took Hoepner to task. Hoepner's and Guderian's *Panzergruppen* had been temporarily subordinated to von Kluge's 4th Army. Kluge accused Hoepner of being too much of a pessimist. He ordered him to hold his line unflinchingly. Kluge threatened to turn directly to Hitler. Von Bock and Guderian felt likewise that Hitler's personal intervention was required.[33] Confidence in Hitler had remained unaltered throughout the chains of command. The Generals did not yet saddle him with the responsibility of the failure in the east. This would only come later, when they wrote their memoirs.

Therefore it came as no surprise that Hitler dismissed Brauchitsch on 19 December 1941, and personally took over the command of the Army, to the great relief of all his commanders. Finally they received messages and orders with undisputed authority behind them. Guderian wrote to his wife, that now "fast and energetic action could be expected and that Hitler would clean up the increased bureaucracy at *OKH* and *OKW*."[34] Reinhardt welcomed Hitler's *Haltebefehl*, (stay put order), and wrote in his diary: "Finally, a clear order by the *Führer*."[35]

A somewhat moderate first version of the *Haltebefehl* was issued on 15 December 1941.[36] Von Bock had apparently become more confused by the day. On 17 December,

---

28   Ibid.
29   Diary Felber, BA-MA, N 67/1, Bl. 9.
30   A. Kunz, *Wehrmacht und Niederlage. Die bewaffnete Macht in der Endphase der nationalsozialistischen Herrschaft 1944 bis 1955.* Munich 2007, p.56. Jodl testified at Nuremberg that Hitler was the first to understand that after the winter 1941/42 the war was lost. On January 21, 1942, Goebbels wrote in his diary that Germany may well lose the war.
31   Hürter, p.324.
32   BA-MA, RH 19 II/122, Bl. 69 ff.
33   Hürter, p.324.
34   Hürter, p.326, with reference to IfZ, ED 100/77.
35   BA-MA, N 245/3, Bl. 18.
36   BA-MA, RH 19 II/122, Bl. 129.

in a phone conversation with Hitler, he objected. He wrote in his diary that he had told Hitler that his Army Group could be torn to pieces at some point, at any moment. Hitler replied: *"Dies muss ich dann in Kauf nehmen,"* (I will have to live with this).[37] To erase any doubt, Hitler then put the *Haltebefehl* in writing, and in language that left no room for doubt: "Major retreat movements are forbidden. They would lead to total loss of heavy weaponry and other material. Commanders and officers have to order fanatical resistance, in their present positions, without consideration of enemy breakthroughs on their flanks or in their rear."[38]

After the war, the *Haltebefehl* became the subject of protracted discussions. However, there is little doubt that it was the only sensible measure that could be taken at that time. During the rapid advance in the first months of the Russian campaign, the *Wehrmacht* had neglected to erect support positions in the rear, which could be used if a retreat became necessary. The *Wehrmacht* command had not even taken into consideration such a possible turn of events. The *Haltebefehl* was not dictated by the stubbornness of Hitler. It was a necessary consequence of the failure of the *Wehrmacht* command to take any precautionary measures. Later it became a burden, since Hitler, who looked at his order as a *credo*, would increasingly forbid mobile warfare. Erich von Manstein, who was the master of the command of large mobile operations, would experience that burden repeatedly.

The turn of the year saw a massive re-shuffling of the *Wehrmacht* high command in the east. Ritter von Leeb, von Bock, and von Rundstedt were relieved. Von Bock and von Rundstedt would be employed again later. Ritter von Leeb remained retired until the end of the war. The three Army Groups received new commanders who were promoted from Amy Commands. Georg von Küchler became *OB* of Army Group North. Günther-Hans von Kluge took over Army Group Centre, upon the special recommendation of von Bock. Walter von Reichenau became *OB* of Army Group South. Among the Army *OB*, Guderian and Hoepner were dismissed. Hoepner was cashiered and forbidden to wear his uniform.[39] Corps commanders were promoted to Army *OB*. Gotthard Heinrici replaced von Kluge as *OB* 4th Army. Friedrich Paulus became *OB* 6th Army. Hermann Hoth had already replaced Carl-Heinrich von Stülpnagel as *OB* 17th Army. Georg Lindemann took over von Küchler's 18th Army. Guderian and Hoepner were replaced by Rudolf Schmidt and Richard Ruoff respectively. Finally, Walter Model replaced Strauss as *OB* of 9th Army.

---

37 Hürter, p.326.

38 Ibid, p.327, with mention of all the relevant archive documents.

39 Hoepner threatened to sue the state for protection of his accrued rights (*wohlerworbene Rechte*). Hitler's legal advisers told him that Hoepner would win this suit and Hitler had to call the *Reichstag* into session and require a vote that he could disregard any acquired rights. Hoepner was allowed to keep his luxurious service home and continued receiving full pay of a *Generaloberst*. After his execution following 20 July, his wife received her full pension.

4

Model's appointment as *OB* of 9th Army

Major units of *Wehrmacht* ground forces

In peacetime there were neither Armies nor Army Groups in the *Wehrmacht*. It was organized into a number of territorial units (*Wehrkreise*), which were commanded by a *Vollgeneral* and had a staff. The troops in every *Wehrkreis* were organized as Corps. At a later date, *Wehrkreise* were grouped together in *Gruppen* (Groups). Those Groups are not to be confused with *Heeresgruppen* (Army Groups). When mobilization occurred, Armies were formed. If mobilization was not followed by war, as with Austria and Czechoslovakia in 1938, the Armies were disbanded and their troops reverted to the *Wehrkreise*. The *Wehrkreise* exercised military authority over their troops until they were sent on combat duty. The Army (*Armee*) was the largest unit of the *Wehrmacht* in wartime. It included the complete arsenal of weaponry and men, along with their support services, food, maintenance, supply, transport, medical, judiciary etc. An Army had a large staff, with each department commanded by a senior officer. The Army Chief of Staff was at least a Colonel, but in many instances he was a *Generalmajor*. Most armies consisted of up to four Corps, and on average twenty-five Divisions, with a total of 200,000 – 250,000 men. The Army *OB* had executive power and judicial authority. The staff of an Army numbered a total of 1,900 of whom 60 were officers. A unit larger in size than the Army was the *Armeegruppe*. It is often referred to as an "Army Group" in literature outside Germany, but it was not. The *Armeegruppe* was a temporary *ad hoc* unit, often consisting of two armies, commanded by the *OB* of the larger. It had no staff of its own. Staff functions were assumed by the staff of the larger Army. In some instances an *Armeegruppe* would be formed by bundling together several Corps, without formally designating them as an Army. Such temporary organizations would be disbanded after completing the operation for which they were formed. The *Wehrmacht* made frequent use of *ad hoc* units. They were designated in different ways *Armeeabteilung, Kampfgruppe, Abteilung, Gruppe*. Such temporary units always bore the name of their *ad hoc* commander.

Army Groups (*Heeresgruppen*) were created in World War I, initially in the Imperial Russian Army, and then in the French Army. The Imperial German Army established them a short time later, but their span of authority and responsibility was not clearly defined. At first, they acted primarily as liaison between their armies, usually up to four in number. Their staff was smaller than Army staffs and was limited to operative functions. They had no quartermaster department.[1] The Commander of an Army Group held neither executive power nor judicial authority.

---

1   During the later stages of the war, some Army Groups were provided with quartermaster departments.

Territorially, the Eastern front was divided into three zones. The "combat zone" (*Armeegebiet*) was kept relatively small with an average depth of 20 kilometres behind the front lines. It consisted of all the Corps and Divisions directly engaged in combat. The staff of the *AOK* was located in the rear Army area (*Rückwärtiges Armeegebiet*) as were units charged with supply, administration, communication, medical services, the town commanders, prisoner of war camps and the military police units. The commander of the rear Army area was a General, the *Korück*, who was responsible for the enforcement of occupation authority, and in direct subordination to the Army *OB*. The *Korück* was either a *Vollgeneral* or a *Generalleutnant*. Finally, the rear areas of Army Groups were, geographically, the largest areas under military authority on the Eastern front. Their administrative authority was in the hands of a Corps commander, the *Berück,* who was subordinated to the Army Group commanders. The staffs of the Army Groups were located in those areas, as were the economic authorities (*Kommandos Wirtschaftsstab Ost*). They were also in charge of the feeding of the civilian population in the occupied areas.[2] Beyond the rear areas, command was in the hands of civilian authorities (*Reichskommissariate*).

Army Group Commanders were directly subordinated to Hitler. Depending upon the theatre of operations, their upward communication link could be either the *Oberkommando des Heeres* (*OKH*) or the *Oberkommando der Wehrmacht* (*OKW*).[3] In 1939 the Commanders of an Army Group were *Generaloberst*. After 1940, as promotions began to multiply, the *OB* of an Army Group was usually a *Feldmarschall*. During the last years of the war, Army Groups were also commanded by *Vollgenerale*. The *OB* of an Army Group could request the replacement of an Army commander, but he had not the authority to remove him.

Armies and Army Groups exercised "Operative Command", a term used in both the *Wehrmacht* and the Red Army. This can be defined as an intermediate command level, between strategy and tactics. A description has been made by Karl-Heinz Frieser in his classic work on the battle of France. Tactics involved the selection, and actual battlefield employment, of units with different weaponry and capabilities. Tactical commands were issued by a unit's immediate commanders, as relayed down the chain of command. Operative command was vested in senior commanders, who coordinated separate tactical actions within a larger operation. As a rule, operative command began at Army level. An exception was Rommel's *Afrika Korps*, which operated in a separate war theatre. Operative command is designed to achieve strategic goals. Strategic Command is the coordination of political, economic and military leadership of a country, in order to achieve the goal as defined by the government.[4]

The administration of conscription during the war, training of newly conscripted soldiers, replacement of material, and war material production came under the authority

---

2   Reality would have to define their duties as "withholding food from the civilian population", since the *Wirtschaftsstab Ost* units enforced a deliberate policy of famine in the occupied territories in the East, after the Army had delegated to them the part of its territorial authority.

3   "Supreme command of the armed forces" is the exact translation but it is a misnomer. When *OKW* was created, it was basically Hitler's military secretariat. Later, it became a second General Staff with responsibility for all theatres of war, except the Eastern front which was the responsibility of *OKH*. The *Generalstab* was part of *OKH*, its equivalent at *OKW* was the *Wehrmachtführungsstab* (*WFSt*). There was no separate training for *WFSt* officers, the senior ranks at *WFSt* were all officers of the *Generalstab*.

4   K-H. Frieser, *Blitzkriegs-Legende, Der Westfeldzug 1940*, Munich 1996, p.7 ff.

of the *Ersatzheer* (replacement Army). All *Wehrmacht* units stationed in Germany came under its authority. The commander of the *Ersatzheer* was an exceptionally capable officer, *Generaloberst* Friedrich Fromm.[5] The *Ersatzheer* was under the authority of the Commander in Chief of the Army. However, step by step the latter's authority was encroached upon by Keitel and *OKW*. After 20 July 1944, the *Ersatzheer* was placed under the command of Himmler. The presence of the *Ersatzheer* permitted *OKH* and *OKW* to concentrate their efforts exclusively on combat, since the *Ersatzheer* took care of all the problems of logistics in the rear.

Circumstances of Model's appointment to his new Command

Generaloberst Adolf Strauss had taken sick leave on 3 January 1942, and Model was appointed as acting *OB* on the same day. On 16 January he became *OB* formally, with promotion backdated to 1 January. He remained in that position until 3 November 1943, when Hitler relieved him and left him unemployed for three months. Command of 9th Army was Model's longest period in the same position and it was his personally preferred command of the entire war.

It would be surprising if Model's arrival had not started with an insult. Model did not find it necessary to pay the traditional call upon his predecessor. Obviously, *Generaloberst* Strauss felt slighted. He wrote: "During the morning of 16 January, *General der Panzertruppe* Model appeared at the headquarters of 9th Army, on his way to Army Group Centre and a meeting with Hitler. He met with my chief of staff, Colonel Krebs, and requested details about the general situation of the Army and the plans of its command. Hitler had appointed Model as my successor. Model agreed in a general manner to the immediate plans of the Army and proceeded to Army Group Centre, and to Hitler, without bothering to call upon me."[6]

Only six months had elapsed between Model's first troop command in World War II, as *Generalleutnant* and Commander of 3rd *Panzer* Division, and his taking over 9th Army and promotion to *Generaloberst*. Newton goes into a lengthy analysis in order to show that Model had sufficient seniority among the Corps commanders of 9th Army, to be chosen for the top job. This demonstration ignores the changes in *Wehrmacht* promotion practice which had taken place during 1942. Until then, seniority was the decisive factor in promotion. However, there was no rule that promotion from one high rank to another, in this instance from Corps commander to Army *OB*, had to be given

---

5   *Generaloberst* Fromm was one of the victims of 20 July 1944. He was not an active member of the plot, but he knew about it, after part of the staff of the *Ersatzheer*, with Colonel von Stauffenberg as its chief, had become the ultimate centre for the *Putsch*. When it became evident during the afternoon of 20 July that the plot had failed, Fromm had Stauffenberg, Stauffenberg's ADC Lieutenant von Haeften, General Olbricht and Colonel Mertz von Quirnheim shot. He allowed *Generaloberst* Beck to commit suicide and offered his personal friend Hoepner, who had taken his place during the hours of an apparent plot success, the same way out. Hoepner refused and was hanged. Fromm did his associates a favour, since he spared them the cruelty of Freisler's *Volksgerichtshof* and death by strangulation. Fromm was dismissed, later accused of cowardice and shot in March 1945. A recent comprehensive biography of him has been written by Professor Bernhard Kroener. (B. Kroener, *"Der starke Mann im Heimatkriegsgebiet". Generaloberst Friedrich Fromm. Eine Biographie,* Paderborn 2005.)

6   Estate, Letter by Strauss, 8.11. 1955.

to a Corps commander of the same Army. One example among many may be sufficient. When General von Manstein succeeded Ritter von Schobert as *OB* of 11th Army, he was transferred from command of LVI Motorized Corps in Busch's 16th Army, Army Group North, to 11th Army in Army Group South, although there were qualified Corps commanders in 11th Army.

At the end of 1942, Hitler had decided to introduce promotion by performance, to replace the exclusive seniority scheme. In November 1942 that idea was institutionalized by the Army's personnel department, after a direct order by Hitler: "The *Führer* has ordered that every officer, active, reserve or *z.V.*, who has successfully commanded a troop against the enemy, and who has shown the necessary professional qualifications, has to be promoted to the rank which conforms to his assignment. The *Führer* orders further, that officers with exceptional personalities and with performances which qualify for higher command, be recorded and correspondingly promoted, without considerations of seniority. Promotions according to seniority are in contradiction of the rule of performance and of leadership, to which the *Wehrmacht* has to adhere if it is to be victorious."[7]

The new rules strongly favoured front line officers, and reduced the chances of promotion for a *Generalstab* officer if he had not exercised successful troop command. By the second half of 1943, 79.5 % of officers' promotions had taken place according to the new rules, and only 20.5% according to seniority.[8]

The new system had not yet been formally institutionalized when Model was appointed *OB* of 9th Army. However, General Rudolf Schmundt, head of the Army's personnel division, had begun to implement it increasingly in individual instances. When Model was appointed, 9th Army was the most exposed of all Armies in the East as a result of its extended curving position. It invited Russian attempts to create a *Kessel*. Clearly, Schmundt had noted that Model had not panicked during the retreat from Moscow, that he had succeeded in maintaining his Corps in working order, and had brought it to its prescribed position. Commanders who kept their calm during the fateful weeks of December 1941 were obviously suited for higher responsibilities.

Model was mentioned, for the first time, in the daily *Wehrmacht* Communiqué on 21 February 1942:

> In the centre of the Eastern front, the Army commanded by *General der Panzertruppe* Model, operating under extremely adverse weather conditions, has succeeded after four weeks of hard battle, in encircling and destroying one Russian Army, and severely damaging a second. The enemy lost 27,000 killed in action, 5,000 prisoners of war, 187 *Panzer,* 615 artillery guns and 1500 machine guns and grenade launchers During the same period, his Army had successfully contained relief attacks by the enemy and inflicted heavy losses.

This communiqué reflects the pitiful state to which the *Ostheer* has been reduced. During the first weeks of the German advance in summer 1941 almost daily special communiqués mentioned the total destruction of a large number of Soviet armies and the capture of hundreds of thousands of prisoners of war. Now the destruction of one

---

7   Van Creveld, p.168.
8   Ibid, p.169.

Russian army and heavy damage inflicted upon another – together at best two medium size *Wehrmacht* corps – and a few thousands of prisoners of war and the loss of some equipment were deemed sufficient to deserve a special mention in the daily communiqué.

9th Army's Staff

Colonel Rudolf Hofmann, 9th Army's Chief of Staff under Strauss, had fallen severely ill. Colonel Hans Krebs replaced him. For once, Model had a chief of staff with whom he harmonized. During the later years of the war, Krebs served as Chief of Staff in Model's Army Group Centre, and finally in Army Group B. Krebs was not portrayed favourably in post-war military history. Judgements of him were influenced, to some extent, by his drunken orgies during the last weeks in the *Führer* Bunker, and by his ridiculous meeting with the Russian General Chuikov, after Hitler had committed suicide. In his last instructions before his suicide, Hitler had named Dr. Goebbels to be *Reichskanzler*, Krebs had been sent by Goebbels to Chuikov to try and negotiate an armistice with the Soviet troops in Berlin. Chuikov had shown him the door.

Until the beginning of *Barbarossa*, Krebs was deputy military *attaché* in Moscow. He had some knowledge of Russian. The German military *attaché* to the Soviet Union, General Ernst Köstring, described Krebs as witty, intelligent, and a man of clear judgment. However, Krebs' reports from Moscow certainly did not deserve this praise. In one report, he had written that it would take the Red Army more than twenty years to recover from the bloodletting of the years 1937-1939.

General Moritz von Faber du Faur writes about Krebs in his memoirs:

> When he was the junior pupil at the course for future *Generalstab* officers, nobody knew if one had to take him seriously, but all agreed that his sharp mind was able to find a credible answer to every problem and that he was capable of learning all that was required for his future task. He was a Rasputin-like type, who would have loved to heal mankind from all its woes but with means which made fools of everyone, including himself. He was certainly not a solid man but he had the courage to remove his artificial mask of the perpetual "No" which had been the standard expression of Ludendorff and his followers. Krebs never aspired to be the equivalent of Moltke and Schlieffen, he just wanted to be Krebs, a General who would always be able find a solution. When he shot himself in the *Führerbunker*, he had finally found his right solution. The *Generalstab* must be blamed for delaying the appointment of Krebs as its acting chief until a time when his power of inspiration had lost all meaning.[9]

Model's three performance ratings about Krebs during their time together at 9th Army were highly favourable:

> 17 April 1942: "Clear judgment, quick understanding, great agility, a 'doer'. Recommended for command of a Division, should become a good senior commander."

---

9   M. Faber du Faur: *Macht und Ohnmacht. Erinnerungen eines alten Offiziers,* Stuttgart 1953, p. 167 ff. (henceforth Faber du Faur) . When it became known that General Faber du Faur would publish his memoirs, many of his comrades were full of apprehension since they knew that he would attack the myth of the "clean" *Wehrmacht.*

31 January 1943: "A leader of men. Commanded a Division for a short time. Has proven himself an outstanding Army Chief of Staff. His strong feelings of comradeship have risked leading him to occasional exaggerations. Suitable for Chief of Staff of an Army Group or divisional commander."

18 February 1943: "Outstanding. Suitable for command of Corps or Army."[10]

Krebs was decorated with the oak leaves to the Knight's Cross, an usually high decoration for an officer who had never held major troop commands with the exception of the Division mentioned above, Reichhelm, who had been Id on 9th Army's staff under Strauss, remained with Model and rose to Ia in 1943. Lieutenant Colonel Georg Buntrock remained Ic during the entire time of Model's command.[11]

On 1 March 1943, Krebs became chief of staff of Army Group Centre. Colonel Harald von Elverfeldt succeeded him as Chief of Staff of 9th Army. Colonel von Elverfeldt had previously served as Chief of Staff of Manstein's LVI (Motorised) Corps during the first months of the Russian campaign. In *Verlorene Siege*, Manstein praised him highly.[12]

There was apparently some disharmony between Elverfeldt and Model. The relationship between the two is described by Görlitz, in his usual journalistic manner that repeatedly turned slanderous. He wrote that Elverfeldt was a somewhat timorous and sceptical man. "He feared Model more than the 'Ivans'. Model disliked him, but had to endure him."[13] Colonel Dr Hermann, a personal friend of Elverfeldt, who would later become a respected military historian, took strong exception to Görlitz's unflattering description. In a letter to Görlitz, he emphasized Elverfeldt's military qualifications. He said that, as a person, it was Elverfeldt who had to endure Model. In defending his friend, Hermann tended to become somewhat excessive. He contrasted Model's bad manners with Elverfeldt's tact, which he attributed to Elverfeldt's education as a cadet. Whether tact was learned at cadet schools is a moot point. In fact, neither had to "endure" the other. If Colonel von Elverfeldt had found it personally offensive to serve under Model, he could have requested a transfer.[14]

Hermann also contrasted the inborn courtesy of an aristocrat, with the behaviour of a man of common origin, such as Model. He overlooked the fact that a steadily decreasing

---

10 All three ratings in facsimile in the Estate.

11 Colonel Hermann Teske, who was in charge of transportation on 9th Army's staff, wrote in his recollections that Model understood next to nothing about railway problems and that his comments and instructions in this field were simply naive. H. Teske, *Die silbernen Spiegel, Generalstabsdienst unter der Lupe,* Heidelberg 1952, p.224 (henceforth Teske).

12 *Verlorene Siege,* p.204 ff.

13 Görlitz, p.135.

14 When *Generaloberst* Ferdinand Schörner took over command of Army Group *Südukraine*, *Generalleutnant* Walther Wenck was his chief of staff. After an altercation between the two, Wenck said to Schörner: "I am not your orderly. I am your chief of staff. If you don't want me as your chief of staff, I will phone *Generaloberst* Zeitzler and I am sure that I will get an equivalent assignment elsewhere." Schörner immediately retreated and said: "For Heaven's sake, forget about the incident." W. Paul, *Das Potsdamer Infanterie-Regiment 9, 1918-1945. Preussische Tradition in Krieg und Frieden,* Osnabrück 1985, p.593.

number of the *Wehrmacht* high commanders were born into the aristocracy.[15] Hermann added that Elverfeldt had requested a transfer, but before that, Model had him promoted to *Generalmajor*. Hermann added that Model never bore a grudge. He wrote later that Elverfeldt, as divisional commander in Army Groups under Model's command, was constantly given difficult assignments requiring leadership qualities. Such appointments would not have been possible without Model's consent. As to Elverfeldt's purported greater fear of Model than of the 'Ivan', Dr Hermann points out that Elverfeldt was mentioned by name in the *Wehrmacht* communiqué of 26 November 1944.[16] After Elverfeldt was killed in action, on 6 March 1945 in Cologne, he was posthumously awarded the oak leaves to his Knight's Cross.

The relationship between Model and Elverfeldt can be summarized. They simply did not see eye-to-eye in some areas. This was unusual at Army level. The number of areas of action which had to be divided between the *OB* and his chief of staff did not permit for any lengthy disharmony. The Army *OB* had to concentrate on the military actions of his Army. All other duties of his *AOK* were in the hands of his Chief of Staff, who decided what he had to submit to the Army commander personally, or what he could keep under his control. The ultimate authority remained under the Army *OB*.

This division of work, between *OB* and Chief of Staff, made it possible for Army Commanders to defend themselves in their post-war trials. Their argument was that they had not been sufficiently informed, by their Chiefs of Staff, of specific events that were charged against them. If the Chief of Staff was also indicted, he would claim that the incriminating events fell within the direct authority of the *OB* and that he had performed only advisory and informative functions. A strong disharmony between the *OB* and his Chief of Staff could seriously impair the efficiency of the Army command. Since 9th Army remained very efficient throughout the time of Model's command, the conflict, described in opposite ways by Görlitz and Herrmann, has obviously been exaggerated.

Görlitz's contention, that Model disliked Elverfeldt, is contradicted by entries in Herta Model's diaries: 24 November 1943: "Elverfeldt at our home for coffee". 23 December 1943: "General Elverfeldt and his wife our guests for tea". 16 May 1944: "Visit by General Elverfeldt and his wife". Model was present on all those occasions. In a letter of 24 March 1945, Model wrote to his wife: "Elverfeldt was killed in action near Cologne. A pity. He had performed outstandingly."[17] After the war, Elverfeldt's widow paid a call on Model's widow.

15　Only half of the Army *Feldmarschalls* were of aristocratic birth (von Bock, von Rundstedt, von Kleist, von Küchler, von Manstein, von Reichenau, von Weichs and von Witzleben). Ritter von Leeb received the personal and not hereditary "von" through the award of the Royal Bavarian Military Max-Joseph order during World War I. Von Kluge's father gained entry into the hereditary aristocracy during World War I through the award of the Prussian order of the Black Eagle. Among the 36 *Generaloberst*, only four were of aristocratic origin, von Arnim, von Falkenhorst, von Mackensen and von Vietinghoff. Ritter von Schobert had gained his "von" in the same manner as Ritter von Leeb.

16　"During the hard defensive combats in the area of Geilenkirchen, 9 *Panzer* Division, under the command of *Generalmajor* von Elverfeldt has shown exceptional bravery".

17　Model/Bradley, p.372 ff.

Relationship between Model and *Feldmarschall* von Kluge

The relationship was bad throughout the war. It is difficult to apportion the blame. Reichhelm's opinion that Kluge was personally unreliable, that he was always acting according to sudden moods, can be discounted, since Reichhelm simply repeated "His Master's Voice".

Model and Kluge shared a tragic destiny. Both committed suicide. Both had their papers destroyed. But Kluge's family never built up an estate comparable to the Model estate. Both were outstanding commanders. At later stages, Model outperformed Kluge. However, when Model took over 9th Army, Kluge was far more experienced. Kluge had already commanded an Army in Poland. After the Polish campaign he was promoted to *Generaloberst*. In France he acted again as Army commander. His performance was outstanding and, on 19 July 1940, he was promoted to *Feldmarschall*.

After the war, both were victims of an unfavourable press, but for different reasons. Basically, the background to the negative opinions of Model were the label "Nazi-General", and also his constant bad behaviour. Kluge is mentioned unfavourably several times in Guderian's memoirs. But Guderian's opinions express vitriolic hatred for Kluge, to the extent that they cannot be taken seriously. Whether the dismissal of Guderian, and also of Hoepner, were the result of a personal vendetta of Kluge's has always remained in doubt. Even at the beginning of the war in the east, Kluge had repeatedly turned to *OKH* with requests for separation from Guderian. He had offered to have his own Commands changed, if Guderian were to remain in his Army. Later, he offered to give up his Army Group Command, if Guderian's *Panzergruppe* remained subordinated to him. Furthermore, both Guderian and Hoepner had acted in contradiction of the *Haltebefehl*. Given the overriding importance which Hitler attached to the *Haltebefehl*, a contravention could not be overlooked. However, Kluge had no part in the punishment meted out to Hoepner.[18]

General von Faber du Faur writes about Kluge:

> I have just reported to *Generalfeldmarschall* von Kluge. The *kluge Hans* (clever Hans.) is presently in favour at highest level. ["*Kluger Hans*" was a sobriquet, a pun about the name Hans Günther von Kluge.] He is certainly clever and he is convinced that whatever he says reflect his true belief. But he believes in nothing except in the *gloire à tout prix* for himself. He knows what is possible and what is impossible but he keeps this knowledge to himself. He is a very courageous man of high intellectual military level. If he were given a free hand, he would find the right solution, but he is not given a free hand. He ordered me to look at his situation map and asked me: 'What is your opinion about this?' When I replied that I understood nothing, he

---

18   The respect accorded to Hoepner for his tragic end after 20 July 1944 should not overlook that Hoepner had issued one of the worst appeals for wanton murder at the beginning of the war against Russia, that he was among the ruthless executors of the Commissar-Order and that he had a close cooperation with his personal friend, Dr. Walther Stahlecker, the murderous head of *Einsatzgruppe* A. If one agrees with Ralph Giordano that Rommel's name should be stricken from *Bundeswehr* barracks, the name of Hoepner should likewise be removed from a Berlin *Gymnasium* which was named after him. (Hoepner's name was removed shortly before this book went to print.)

shrugged his shoulders and said: 'This map reflects present day's new tactics and you will have to get used to them.'[19]

An essay on Kluge by Professor Peter Steinbach, begins with the words: "History records only few names of high military commanders whose whole career and all their accomplishments are inextricably connected to a single event, and furthermore, one which turned into failure. *Generalfeldmarschall* Günther von Kluge is one such example."[20] Steinbach alludes to Kluge's part in the military resistance, and to the 20 July 1944 events.

The staff of Kluge's Army Group Centre, with Colonel von Tresckow as Ia, had become the centre of the military resistance movement, after initial plots by Halder had to be abandoned. Since the conspirators knew that they needed an active *Feldmarschall* at their head, Kluge was the only remaining choice. Other *Feldmarschalls* had been retired, or held commands in areas where no fighting took place. However, Kluge was unable to cope with a conspiratorial role. But he must be credited with having recognized the criminal nature of the regime earlier than his comrades of equal rank. He certainly realized it earlier than Model, who recognised it only a few days before he took his own life.[21]

Kluge's dislike of Model did not prevent him from giving Model two outstanding performance ratings:

10 April 1942: Very strong personality, at times obstinate. His urge for activity at times makes life difficult for his subordinates. But there is no doubt that he is a commander who, even in the most critical situation, will never cause disappointment. Great personal courage, ruthless towards himself. He expects the same of his troops who, after initial grumbling, quickly recognize who leads them and admire his outstanding personality. For his superiors he is a commander of invaluable qualities, in particular when an exceptionally strong will has to be enforced in perilous situations. Outstanding performance.[22]

17 March 1943: Strong elements: Healthy ambition, particularly strong will-power. Very high personal commitment. Particularly quick in reaching decisions. Weak elements: His constant craving for action is impossible to hold back, and can be a burden for his subordinates and his troops. Conclusions: In spite of the weak elements mentioned above, a commander far above average and of unique value. Suitability for

---

19 Faber du Faur, p. 263 ff.

20 P. Steinbach, *Hans-Günther von Kluge – ein Zauderer im Zwielicht*, in R. Smelser/E. Syring (ed.) *Die Militärelite des Dritten Reiches. 27 biographische Skizzen*, Berlin 1998, pp.288-324.

21 Kluge found the appropriate word about himself in his last talk with General von Gersdorff on 28 July 1944, after the plot against Hitler had failed. Gersdorff implored Kluge to make a new attempt to kill Hitler, adding that Kluge had to decide between being condemned by history, or being remembered as the saviour of last resort. All great men had faced a choice between such decisions. Kluge put his arm around Gersdorff's shoulder and said: "Gersdorff, *Feldmarschall* von Kluge is simply not a great man." (R. von Gersdorff, *Soldat im Untergang-Lebensbilder*, Frankfurt 1979, p.151 (henceforth Gersdorff).

22 Facsimile in Model/Bradley, p.56.

higher commands: Command of an Army Group. Recommendation for immediate future: Should remain in his present position.[23]

Their mutual dislike notwithstanding, both had to endure each other, and no personal clashes occurred. But at times Model turned personally to Hitler, without going through Kluge, when he was not sure that Kluge would support him. One could certainly say that it was Model who behaved badly – he would not have tolerated such behaviour from his subordinates. The first serious incident between the two occurred in the planning phase of Operation *Zitadelle*, the short-lived German offensive, in which the battle for the Kursk salient was strongly advocated by Kluge. But Model opposed the manner in which his 9th Army was to be engaged. Events proved Model to have been correct.

Model's first meetings with Hitler

The first personal encounter between the two occurred immediately after Model assumed command of 9th Army. General Schmundt told General Röhricht about this meeting:

> Model was the only General who did not complain about difficulties. He simply grabbed a scrap of paper, drew some lines with his pencil, and said: 'This is very simple.' Hitler was somewhat surprised and replied, 'Then just go ahead and do it.' After Model had departed, Hitler said to Schmundt, 'Did you see his eye? I believe that he can do it. But I would certainly not like to serve as his subordinate.'[24]

---

23 Ibid, p.63 ff. The recommendation: "should remain for the time being in his present position", could be interpreted as a sign of dislike of Model by Kluge and a desire to put obstacles to his further advance. In my view, the contrary is the case. Had Kluge wanted to get rid of Model, a recommendation to appoint him as commander of an Army Group without delay would have been his best opportunity. The recommendation can also be read in the sense that Kluge felt that in the particularly difficult situation on the date of the rating, Model was needed at the head of 9th Army. Obviously Kluge knew that an appointment by Model as Army Group commander would occur.

24 Estate, Röhricht, 10 March 1956. This statement by Hitler shows that he had not noticed Model on the few earlier occasions when Model happened to be in his presence. Had Hitler known Model before this day, he would have probably said to Schmundt something like: "Look at this man. I have known him for years, now I called upon him, because I feel that he will succeed". Another comment by Brett-Smith that Strauss was relieved by the convinced Nazi Model, who in 1939 had not even commanded a Division, (Brett-Smith, p.89) makes likewise little sense. Strauss was no less a Nazi than Model, and we will see in the chapter dealing with war crimes that he was as guilty as other high commanders in the wilful mistreatment of Russian prisoners of war and the murder of Jews by the *Einsatzgruppen*. Furthermore, a "convinced Nazi" can be an outstanding commander and a strong opponent of National-Socialism can be a failure. If an officer, who in 1939 had not yet commanded a Division, became one of the outstanding Army *OB* less than three years later, he was obviously a gifted commander. Brett-Smith also writes that Model had a strong influence upon von Kluge and that the latter always agreed with the commanders with whom he had spoken last. This statement is a strong underestimation of von Kluge's capacity. Furthermore Brett-Smith seems to ignore the strong hostility between von Kluge and Model.

The first real clash between Hitler and Model occurred on the day of Model's award of the oak leaves, which was often done by Hitler personally. The scene is recorded in almost every book dealing with the Russo-German war. Model's orderly, Lieutenant von Bonin und Ostau recalls:

> The subject was the introduction of a *Panzer* Corps to the Army reserve, and its positioning for eventual action. Hitler wanted to have the Corps in the Gzhatsk sector, Model preferred Rzhev. Both were obstinate and the tone became increasingly sharp. Model became more and more agitated, and suddenly there was an outbreak: '*Mein Führer*, are you commanding 9th Army, or is it me?' Hitler was shocked and said that he would put his opinion into an order. Model replied: 'I will not stand that.' All officers present appeared helpless, since nobody had previously dared to speak to Hitler in such a tone. But suddenly Hitler relented and said: 'All right Model, do it your way. But you will pay with your head if you don't succeed.' Relief on the faces of all officers present.[25]

Newton wrote that this was the first time that a German General had so bluntly contradicted Hitler – this is correct – and that the lesson was not lost on Model, which is problematic.[26] Model may have felt that he could go as far as he wanted in his many disputes with Hitler, but when he passed the limits of what Hitler considered tolerable, he was immediately relieved of his duties, and side-lined for three months.

---

25 Estate, von Bonin und Ostau, 1950.
26 Newton, p.182.

5

9th Army – the major battles

Section 1: Model's Operating Methods

Auftragstaktik (mission-type order)

In every army, commanders have to lead according to established general methods otherwise chaos would arise. However, *Auftragstaktik,* the general rule of command in the German army, which did not exist in other armies, gave German commanders more latitude in developing personal operating methods than commanders in any other Army. After the Napoleonic wars it had become the operative rule of the Prussian Army. Introduced by the Prussian Army's military reforms of Gerhard von Scharnhorst, *Auftragstaktik* was further developed by Ludendorff during the First World War, and finally became embodied in the Army Regulations (*HDV* 300) of 1936.

The Army rules, *Exerzierreglement* Number 2 of 1902, had already stated: "Combat requires commanders trained to act independently, and soldiers capable of acting under their own authority."[1] The rules of 1908, *Felddienstordnung* Number 37 went one step further and stated: "From the youngest soldier upward, independent thinking and independent physical effort, to the very limit of his potential, must always be required. Only in this way can fully satisfactory performance, in total cooperation, be expected."[2]

HDV 300 developed further …

36. Command is dictated by the *Auftrag* and the situation as known at the moment the *Auftrag* is given. Only seldom does the commander have an exact knowledge of the situation with the enemy. Every effort must be made to obtain as much clarification as possible, however to wait for information in a tense situation is not a sign of strong command and will often result in serious errors.

37. *Auftrag* and the general situation lead to decisions. If the original *Auftrag* has been overtaken by unforeseen developments, the commander's decisions may have to reach beyond or deviate partly from the original *Auftrag*. Such individual decisions have to be reported by the commander to the superior level, however the commander becomes solely responsible for his decision.

Decisions by the commander have to have a clear aim and must be followed up with utmost energy. The strong will of the commander is of decisive importance and will often lead to success. Once the commander has taken a decision, he may not deviate from it without compelling reason. However, rapidly changing conditions during

---

1   Quoted by van Creveld, p.51.
2   Ibid.

battles can turn remaining with a decision taken previously into a serious mistake. Early awareness of changing conditions is the prime element of the art of command."

The commander has to give maximum latitude to his subordinates as long as this does not endanger his decision. He is not allowed to delegate responsibility for his decisions to his subordinates ...

73. An order has to include everything which the subordinate must know to execute his *Auftrag* independently. The order has to be short, clear and complete. It must also be formulated in a manner which takes the individual capacities of every subordinate into account. The commander must always put himself in the position if his subordinates.

74. The order has to be worded in a clear and simple language. Clarity is more important than details. However brevity must not impair the subordinate's complete understanding.

75. Orders may not reach further than knowledge of the situation at a given moment. The situation will frequently demand to issue orders into the unknown.

76. Orders have to refrain from mentioning too many details if changes in the situation appear to be possible before the order can be executed. This is of prime importance in major operations where orders are issued for a number of days ahead. In such a case, the general operational aim becomes the decisive factor and this has to be clearly stated. For the execution of the order only general outlines may be given, the manner in which they are executed is at the commander's discretion ...

Lieutenant Colonel Walter von Lossow gives a summary of the doctrine.[3]

1.The *Auftrag* has to express the aim of the leadership in a manner totally devoid of ambiguity.

2. The aim is that procedures, like time limits, have to be totally clear and unambiguous, without reducing personal freedom of action more than is absolutely required. Above all, initiative by the individual officer and soldier, to whom the *Auftrag* is given, has to be the prime factor.

3. The way in which the *Auftrag* is executed may only have such limitations, set from above, as are required for coordination between several commanders.[4]

Martin van Creveld comments:

---

3   Walter von Lossow stated that the doctrine originated with troops from the German Hessen province which had taken part in the American War of Independence. Quoted by van Creveld p.52 from: Von Lossow, 'Mission- type tactics versus order-type tactics' in *Military Review* 57/6 (June 1977), p. 87-91.
4   Van Creveld, p.52.

In the *Auftragstaktik*, commanders have to give orders to their subordinates in what they have to do, but not how they have to do it. As long as the commanders do not deviate from the general framework of the order given to them, they have far reaching latitude in the planning and the execution of their procedures. Such a system obviously requires similar thinking and action, the result of thorough education, and the experience of many years. If those conditions are complied with, the system has strong advantages over measures taken by other Armies.[5]

Walter von Lossow sums up the advantages of the *Auftragstaktik*:

1. Commanders of all ranks are compelled to analyse their own position, as well as those of their immediate higher-level commanders.

2. The time for communication of orders is greatly reduced.

3. The measures which are finally taken are in conformity with the conditions which have arisen.[6]

After the winter of 1941/42 the *Auftragstaktik* gradually lost its meaning, as Hitler increasingly intervened in orders, by commanders at every level. In their inability to cope with the first real crisis of the war, the German Army Group and Army commanders had abandoned one of the cornerstones of their historic values. Gradually they became recipients of orders.

---

5   Ibid.
6   Van Creveld, p.53. The US Army's FM 100-5 has many requirements which the German HDV-300 warns strongly against. It attempts to foresee the many possible developments of a situation in great detail and says nothing about the independence of subordinates. In 1953, *Generaloberst* Halder was asked by the US Historical Division to give his comments to a new version of FM 100-5 which was in preparation. Halder emphasized that the German system required a high degree of independence at all levels of command. The *Auftragstaktik* is based on discipline by all concerned in their acting in conformity with the original *Auftrag*. The German system avoids any form of rigidity. It requires clear and unambiguous decisions and the quick establishment of *Schwerpunkt*. Care for the well-being of the troops and maintaining fighting power is a prime consideration.
Halder then criticized the American concept:
As opposed to the German system, the American rules show a tendency of forecasting various possible situations and determine in each case the action to be taken. This reduces the freedom of action of the commander and removes his possibility to react to unforeseen developments. The American rules do not give sufficient attention to the individual soldiers in modern warfare. Since the US Army always operated with considerable numerical superiority in equipment, the new rules have a clear tendency to underestimate the importance of surprise and improvisation. The intention to forecast every situation creates the danger of clichés.
The American rules tend to underestimate the physical and psychological aspects of war. Halder proposed finally to add the following sentence to FM 100-5: "In war, character is more important than intellect." van Creveld p.56 ff.

Generaloberst (Luftwaffe) Wolfram von Richthofen assisted at a meeting of Army Group Centre in April 1942. His comments were scathing:

> Level of a school teachers' conference. Undignified horse-trading about the relief of Divisions. Nobody takes responsibility. Kluge begins the meeting with the glorious sentence: 'Gentlemen, we are unfortunately compelled to take risks.' A great commander at war! When I was an Ensign at the war academy, I had a different view of Generals.[7]

By October 1941, von Richthofen had complained after a meeting with Strauss, where Strauss had told him that he had transmitted an order from above with which he disagreed: "I have one opinion only and I act accordingly. I am not used to pass on my responsibility. All these men have lost any trace of vigour. It is simply sickening."[8]

Model's methods of command[9]
In some instances Reichhelm is a qualified source, in others he let his devotion to Model lead him into exaggeration. In his capacity as Ia, Reichhelm had the responsibility of drawing up the plans for every operation. Obviously he followed Model's methods, which he described in the unpublished appendix to his recollections.[10] Reichhelm gives a general description of Model's guiding principles. The two general rules were *Vorhalten* and *Anschauen.*

Vorhalten has no connection with this word in everyday language, where it stands for "reproach" or "accused". There it was Model's invention, and was intended to mean the most careful preparation of every move. In practice, it meant that every officer should be able to gauge enemy intentions, even when no intelligence was available. Once those officers had assessed the enemy's capabilities and objectives, Model would require them to present three solutions.

Anschauen, (view), was likewise an invention of Model in that connection. It was intended to mean constant interaction between troop and *Generalstab* assignments. It implied that a staff officer could only perform efficiently in similar assignments to those he had experienced in combat.

Leading from the front
Model always attempted to lead from the front line. Whilst he was in command of Divisions, leading from the front was in line with German Army regulations. Those stated explicitly that the divisional commander had to station himself in his Division's combat area. Even at Corps level this method was acceptable, but with the command of large size units, such

---

7   BA-MA, N 671/ 9, Bl.14.

8   Ibid., Bl.61.

9   Newton writes at length about a *Schwert und Schild* method which he credits Model of having developed. There is no objection of affixing a name to a method, although the one chosen by Newton can not be found in any work of German military literature known to the author. Moreover, *Schwert und Schild* has an unpleasant connotation, since it was the motto of the secret service (*Staatssicherheit – Stasi*) of the German Democratic Republic. (*Die Stasi – Schwert und Schild der Partei*).

10   I have been privileged to receive one of the few typed copies as a gift.

as Armies and Army Groups, it became more questionable. As *OB* of 9th Army, and later of Army Groups, Model was fortunate in having competent staffs which remained devoted to him, in spite of his regular outbursts. However, with the vast areas controlled by Armies, not to speak of Army Groups, the commander leading from the front line seldom had an all-round view of his unit. If a crisis occurred in a sector from which he was absent, only his Chief of Staff could issue the immediate orders that were required.

Reichhelm emphasized that Model's proximity to the front line never resulted in his gaining popularity with the soldiers of his units.[11] In his Division and his Corps, where soldiers often were in direct contact with him, they trusted him and used to say, "somehow he will succeed in 'modelling' the situation", or "if the situation is difficult, Model will find a way out."[12]

Model used every available method of arriving speedily at an advanced position. He used *Storch* reconnaissance planes, cars, motorcycle side-cars, sledges and even horseback. A negative element, stressed by Reichhelm, was Model's constant distrust of his higher level subordinates, both Division and Corps commanders who were serving under him when he became commander of 9th Army and later of Army Groups. If a proposal on their part did not meet with his immediate approval, he would dismiss it rudely, issue his own order and supervise their compliance through his orderlies. He thus made many enemies among his higher level commanders.

Other principles of Model's methods:

- Carefully planned deepening of the defensive area by filling them with sufficient supply units. Reichhelm saw there the influence of General von Lossberg who had been Model's first teacher in defence tactics.
- Construction of an adequate road network, consisting of two roads at right angles to the front line, and a third road parallel to the front line, but at a distance of three to six kilometres, to permit rapid movements between front line positions.
- Personal supervision by Model of all repair and maintenance units.

Breaking up of units

This method, the transfer of units such as regiments, battalions, companies from one Division to another, was often used by Model. It was a serious infringement of one of the basic rules of the *Wehrmacht*.

All German units, from Divisions down, were recruited on a regional basis. The general rule was that all soldiers should come from the same region. If there were more

---

11 Search for popularity by high commanders can be a double-edged sword. Eisenhower always "kow-towed" to the GI. His popularity reached unprecedented heights when he inflicted an exaggerated punishment upon Patton, after the General had slapped a soldier in Sicily. If Patton was at fault, an apology to the soldier and the witnesses of the incident, which took place in a field hospital, would have been sufficient. The slapping incident cost Patton the overall command of the American ground forces after "Overlord". Instead of maintaining his most capable commander in this position, Eisenhower replaced him with the timorous and far less able Omar Bradley. Van Creveld expresses the opinion that, given the extensive tolerance of unwarranted battle fatigue in the US Army, Patton may well not have been wrong to slap a soldier who was unwilling to return to combat. Van Creveld, p.118.

12 At Armies and Army Groups, every *OB* was too remote, and separated from his soldiers by too many levels of command, for them to generate personal feelings.

than one dialect spoken in that region, recruitment saw to it that newly arrived troops were put into units where the same dialect was spoken. Replacement units were recruited on a similar basis. Soldiers, who had been wounded and put out of action for a lengthy period, would be returned to their previous units. The *Ersatzheer*, which was in charge of recruiting, saw to it that every large unit, from Division up, maintained a reserve battalion in every *Wehrkreis*. If that system led to a reduction of the prescribed manpower number (*Sollstärke*) of a Division, it was accepted. Effectual numbers (*Iststärke*) were given preference, in order to maintain regional coherence. Obviously, soldiers who fought alongside former comrades, in their own regional environment, performed better than hastily formed units without regional coherence.[13]

Given van Creveld's repeated unfavourable comparisons between the *Wehrmacht* and the US Army, the following paragraph in his book must be quoted: "But the fact remains that the American GI has won the Second World War. And furthermore he won it without inflicting personal wilful damage on many enemies, without committing serial rape and without molesting too many people. Wherever he came – even within Germany itself – he was received with relief, or at any rate without fear. To him no greater tribute than this is conceivable."[14] Revisionist German authors, who constantly refer to van Creveld, obviously never mention this paragraph.

In 1944, Model finally became aware of the disadvantages of his constant breaking up of units. On 8 April 1944 he sent a note to his Army Group *Nordukraine*:

> Mixing up of units: Defensive operations, over the past months, have shown a visible decrease in fighting power which has affected sectors of the front in an intolerable manner. This is due to the rapid bringing forward of reserves, in Company and Battalion strength, but taken from other Regiments and Divisions. This has resulted in an intolerable mixing of units.
>
> In major defensive actions, commanders must find more suitable methods of replacement. All efforts have to be directed to replace a Division weakened by losses, with a new Division, rather than sending into combat small numbers recruited from existing Divisions. On no occasion may parts of a Division, of less than regimental strength, be withdrawn and given to other Divisions as replacement.[15]

---

13 Recruitment in the US Army followed an opposite policy. After being drafted, soldiers were given their basic training in a replacement training centre. After going through basic training, soldiers were given between ten and twelve days' leave and were then sent to replacement depots – "repple depple" – in US embarkation ports. Upon arrival in Europe, they were sent to a theatre depot. In France, their main destination, the depot was in Le Havre. There they could be given additional training for periods of up to five weeks. From there they were sent to forward depots and finally to Divisions. Maintaining Divisions at prescribed strength was a prime consideration, in the US Army, regional background of the soldiers was not taken into account. As a result of the sticking to prescribed strength, the US Army had far fewer Divisions than the *Wehrmacht*. They were stronger in numbers but less efficient. The US Army had a total of 91 Divisions in Europe, out of which 89 were engaged in combat. Van Creveld, p. 97 ff. *The Wehrmacht* had several hundreds of Divisions.

14 van Creveld, p. 195.

15 Facsimile in Model/Bradley, p.117.

On 7 October 1944, as commander Army Group B in the West, Model sent the following order to *AOK 7*, *AOK 15*, 1st Airborne Army and to the *Wehrmacht* commander in the Netherlands:

> In view of obvious disadvantages in tactical, personal and material matters, I herewith order: I forbid the partition of Regiments into separate Battalions which are then to be employed in other Divisions. The basic structure of every Regiment must be preserved at all costs.
>
> I forbid their partition or the atomization of artillery, *Panzer* units and similar units. All have to be maintained in their original shape. Any infringement of this order has to be reported immediately by the Corps commander, with an indication of the measures taken against the guilty commander.[16]

In the summer of 1944, during the giant Russian offensive, against Army Group Centre (Operation *Bagration*), breaking up of units had resumed on a large scale.

Contradictions and direct approaches to Hitler, bypassing von Kluge
Both have already been mentioned. Görlitz gave a number of examples. However, it is unnecessary to repeat them. There is no disputing the fact that Model never hesitated to state his opinions directly to Hitler, and that he often disregarded von Kluge. That von Kluge did not view this with equanimity need hardly be emphasized.

Combat against partisans
In a letter to the author, Reichhelm attempted to describe Model's methods in partisan warfare. He wrote:

> If partisans were in action in the area of the front line, authority in combat with them was left to the respective Divisions. There were instances when Model ordered the burning of an entire village, after having issued warnings, and the partisans not having retreated from the village, nor surrendered. Shooting of captured partisans was only allowed if German soldiers had been killed. No individual commander was allowed to decide upon the fate of a captured partisan. A special court martial, presided over by an officer, assisted by a non-com and a soldier, had to issue a verdict in due form. I don't know if this rule was observed in most instances.[17]

Only the last sentence is true. The remainder is hogwash and Reichhelm knew it well, since he himself had been an early participant in a ruthless and totally unwarranted action against Russian purported partisans. Reichhelm wrote in his memoirs: "After we entered the town of Sychovka, 14 October 1941, 9th Army's Chief of Staff, Colonel Weckmann walked alone through the streets. In the market place he was beaten up by Soviet civilians." (In fact, the report to Army Group Centre states that Weckmann was beaten up by Soviet soldiers, perhaps by Commissars who had stayed in the town).[18] "Weckmann had to be

---

16 Ibid, p.317.
17 Letter from Reichhelm to author, 28 March 2000.
18 BA-MA, RH 20/913.

evacuated with a concussion. The commander of the staff headquarters, Major Stammler, ordered that two of the perpetrators be publicly hanged in the market place. This was the only possibility of restoring order."[19]

When the *Berück* of Army Group B, General Max von Schenkendorff, was told by *Feldmarschall* von Bock about this incident, he was overjoyed. He saw an active fight against partisans, real or imaginary, as his main concern, and was now given the opportunity to act with total ruthlessness.[20] Between June 1941 and May 1942, the Germans executed 80,000 partisans and innocent civilians suspected of being partisans. In the rear area of Army Group B, during the same period, in the fight against partisans, German losses came to 1,094 killed in action. At that time, the partisan movement was still too weak to cause the Germans meaningful losses. The combat against real and purported partisans led to a rapid increase in their number. Once again the Germans had dug their own grave.[21]

The cruelty of the *Wehrmacht* in treating partisans has been common knowledge for years. The term "partisan" was employed *ad libitum*. It often designated Jews, who were also murdered. There is not the slightest reason to believe that 9th Army under Model behaved differently from other Armies.

The fact that partisans were officially designated as "bandits" and partisan units as "gangs" speaks for itself. By 13 August 1941, Himmler had issued an order: "Psychological factors make it incumbent to avoid using the word 'partisan', which in Soviet terminology has a heroic connotation. In our view they are not soldiers, but bandits, hidden snipers and common criminals."[22] General Heinrici viewed partisans differently. On 6 November 1941 he wrote to his wife: "All admire the steadfastness of the partisans. None betray their comrades, all remain silent and expect their death."[23] But on the same day, Heinrici wrote in his diary: "I asked Beutelsbacher to see to it that partisans not be hanged within 100 metres from my window. It is not a pleasant sight."

Treatment of the civilian population

During the de-Nazification procedure, Model's Ic Lieutenant Colonel Georg Buntrock, stated:

> Model took greater care of the civilian population than his quartermaster could do within his own responsibility. Foodstuffs had to be regularly brought into the different areas under the control of 9th Army. Army surgeons had to take care of the civilian population. Model exceeded by far the rules of the Hague Convention. He took special care of local administration and the good functioning of the court

---

19 Reichhelm, p.122. Obviously the Russians who were hanged were chosen at random. Since Colonel Weckmann was alone on the market place when he was beaten up by Red Army soldiers, it would hardly have been possible to identify two perpetrators among the civilian population. Public and multiple executions by hanging were a popular form of *Wehrmacht* sadism and the many soldiers who attended rivalled in their eagerness to take photographs.

20 Hürter, p.420 ff.

21 Figures in Hürter, p.438 ff.

22 Order Nr. 65 by *Kommandostab Reichsführer-SS*, 13.8.1941.

23 J. Hürter, *Ein deutscher General an der Ostfront. Die Briefe und Tagebücher des Gotthard Heinrici 1941/42*, Erfurth 2001, p.107. (Henceforth Hürter Heinrici).

system. He even ordered foodstuffs and other goods to be brought from Germany to relieve local shortages.[24]

Even if one accepts that exaggerations could be made during the de-Nazification procedure, in order to help Model's widow and his son, Buntrock's statement is simply obscene. 9th Army was not an isolated island of humanity, detached from the cruelty of all other armies. Like other armies, it enforced a wilful policy of famine. It followed the *Barbarossa* order in disregarding legal pursuit of German soldiers for crimes committed against the civilian population. There is more on this order in the section of this book dealing with war crimes.

One can quote from a letter which the Ukrainian archbishop, Count Andreas Scheptycky, wrote to Pius XII on 29 August 1942:

When the German Army appeared to liberate us from the Bolshevik yoke, we experienced at first a feeling of some relief. But that lasted no more than one or two months. Step by step, the Germans introduced their regime of terrible cruelty and corruption. Today, the people feel that the German regime is even worse. In a devilish way, it is worse even than Bolshevism. It simply appears that a band of madmen, or of rabid dogs, have descended upon the poor population.[25]

Model's methods viewed by some of his comrades
Professor Percy Schramm, during the war chief editor of the *OKW* diary wrote: "A tireless officer, Model inspected every sector of his area without ceasing. He had no feeling of fear and disregarded any danger to himself. His methods enabled him to stabilize Army Groups North and Centre. Hitler's confidence in him increased and led to him being appointed Supreme Commander West. Once again a miracle occurred when optimists there had begun to give up hope. The Western Front was stabilized. He may have appeared unbearable at times, but his conduct was the result of a feeling of heavy personal responsibility. He never requested more from his subordinates than he demanded from himself. His energy was matched by high intelligence and logic. But he was more than simply a brilliant tactician. Even in the most critical situation he could find an idea."[26]

---

24 Estate, Buntrock, 1.6.1950.

25 F. Seidler, *Die Kollaboration 1939-1945. Zeitgeschichtliche Dokumentation in Biographien,* Munich 1999, p.488 ff.

26 P. Schramm, *Die Vorbereitungen der deutschen Offensive in den Ardennen,* September – December 1944, his report written for the US Historical Division, p.6. The German contributions to the US Historical Division are generally reliable in their description of military operations. However, the officers who wrote for the Historical Division were under orders by Halder and other high ranking commanders, among them von Küchler, to abstain from any negative word about the *Wehrmacht* Generals and to stay with the image of an "unblemished *Wehrmacht*" on the one side and the criminal dilettante Hitler on the other. Miracles do not occur in wartime. The Western Front was not stabilized by Model alone. Allied advances were slowed down by supply difficulties, primarily fuel, by disputes between US and British commanders, by the failure of Montgomery's airborne operation at Arnhem-Nijmegen and also by the cautious operational command of Eisenhower. But Model's defensive operations certainly deserve the highest compliments.

General Günther Blumentritt, Chief of Staff at *OB* West at the time of Model's appointment to that position, later Corps commander and Army *OB* in Model's Army Group B in the West, wrote:

> Army, Corps and Division commanders held him in high respect. Some feared him. He would appear unannounced at every sector of the front and would question the commanders in his usual cocky and abrasive manner. He always required information about the slightest detail. The specialists, Artillery Generals, Pioneers, and Intelligence officers were his favourite victims. He would constantly berate them, and one could see that he literally enjoyed putting them under pressure.[27]

General Erich Jaschke, Commander of LV Corps in 9th Army wrote:

> He always supported the troops. In his relations with officers, particularly with Division commanders, he could be very abrasive, and often say that they simply had no ideas, or were unable to cope. Such officers were quickly sent home. He was a master of improvisation, very agile and always finding a way out.[28]

General Hermann Balck, at that time commander of XXXXVIII *Panzer* Corps wrote:

> Model, Manstein's successor, visited us on 1 May 1944. Small size, has a clear view of the situation. He knows a lot. He is often erratic. He does not always follow a clear line. But he has much energy and will-power. My first impression of him is that he is above average. His frequent visits to the front line cause much unnecessary trouble. Some of his orders become contradictory at very short notice. In his talks to his commanders, he often does not find the right tone. Officers and soldiers were simply not up to this behaviour.
>
> I requested a personal talk with Model. I told him to his face that things could not continue in this manner. If his behaviour caused the troops to become nervous before the battle, they will fail when going into combat. My Divisions were good, all had performed above average and they will continue to do so. His constant stirring up trouble and irritation will lead to the opposite. Model heard me out quietly. He said that he agreed to a number of points raised by me. As of this day, he left my corps alone.
>
> His staying away from my Corps was a relief for the soldiers. I wrote in my diary that it is certainly not easy to work with him. He does not care for good relations with subordinate commanders. A bad psychologist, his Stakhanovism prevents the rise of personalities. Thankfully, he leaves my Corps alone after I had bared my teeth. For the troops, he is unbearable.[29]

---

27 Estate, Blumentritt, 26 May 1955.
28 Estate, Jaschke, 10 March 1955.
29 H. Balck, *Ordnung im Chaos. Erinnerungen 1893-1948*, Osnabrück 1981, p.515 ff. At the end of the war, General Balck was *OB* of *Armeegruppe* Balck (6th German Army and 1st and 3rd Hungarian armies). He was decorated with the diamonds to his Knight's Cross.

General Siegfried Rasp, was one of Model's pupils at the *Truppenamt* course. Later, as a colonel, he served as Model's Chief of staff of 9th Army's XXIII Corps. He wrote:

> He never lost sight of the overall situation. A brilliant operational and tactical commander, his heart was always with his soldiers. His demands made coping difficult for many Corps and Division commanders and their staffs. During a period of 14 months, I had no fewer than four Corps commanders.[30]

General Rasp added that Model had later relieved him of his command after a disagreement during Operation *Zitadelle*.

General August Winter, also one of Model's former pupils, became Model's Chief of Staff of 2nd *Panzer* Army during the retreat from Orel. He was critical:

> Certainly a master of tactical defence. Beyond doubt, a very courageous soldier going to the very limit of physical endurance. He had a singular capability in foreseeing enemy activities. But there were negative aspects. In summer 1943, his nerves began to show signs of exhaustion and this had an adverse effect upon the clarity of his leadership. His outbursts of temper did not create a healthy atmosphere in his relationships with his staff. His methods would at times make it difficult for him to keep an overall view of his army, particularly when he was caught in the middle of a tactical crisis at a Division or a Regiment. He would then issue orders based upon his impression of what he had witnessed. The personal bravery of the *Generaloberst* could result in fluctuations of his orders. His edginess led him to treat higher officers and staff members as lightning-rods for his temper. In my opinion, the *Feldmarschall* cannot be included among the great commanders.[31]

General Peter von der Groeben, Ia of 86th Division in 9th Army, and later Ia of Army Group Centre, acknowledged Model's success. But he echoed General Winter's assessment of Model's character:

> Without doubt, it was due to him that 9th Army was not destroyed in the Rzhev area. He showed clear tactical conception, unbending energy, and disregard for personal danger. His troops had an unlimited respect for him. He would ruthlessly break up units and, at times, take personal command of battalions. His command in the front line was appreciated, but it also carried the disadvantage that his instructions, delivered while visiting a front unit, ignored the global situation that had developed in the meantime. Certainly not a pleasant person. Towards men who did not know how to stand up to him, his behaviour and his tone were often rude, to the point of becoming outrageous. He was a good tactician with an understanding of technical problems. We were never able to understand how an officer who had been brought up in the old Army, and who had become an outstanding commander, could have such bad manners.[32]

---

30 Estate, Rasp, 11 April 1950 .
31 Estate, Winter, Letter to Leppa, 18 January 1970.
32 Estate, von der Groeben letter to Görlitz, 24 November 1970.

Generaloberst Johannes Friessner:

A master of operative planning. His personal preparations of all actions were of the highest *Generalstab* calibre. The *Büffel* operation south of Rzhev, and the retreat from Orel, were both conducted with clockwork precision. He was a highly uncomfortable superior who was widely feared. His remarks could come close to personal insult.[33]

General Edmund von Glaise-Horstenau:

I had a talk with General Mickl. He says that during one year in the East, Model is the only General whom he has ever seen in the front line. All the others remain in their comfortable shelters … Model is one of the most brutal *Wehrmacht* Generals. Only the loudmouthed Ferdinand Schörner is worse. Until 1934 he professed to be an opponent of National-Socialism, but he changed shirts at the right moment for his career. Now he is promoted over the heads of many and was recently given command of an Army Group …[34]

General Edgar Röhricht recalled incidents with Model before the war, but he emphasized that Model saved his Corps:

Not a commander of great conceptions. He was a remarkable improviser, but liable to turn temporary expedients into a norm. Physically he was tireless, full of inventions and without personal needs. At times he would treat subordinates like dirt. His temperament often got the better of his understanding. Basically, a naive personality.[35]

Colonel Dr Hermann, in his criticism of Görlitz's description of General von Elverfeldt:

In spite of Model's repeated successes, Elverfeldt was in disagreement with his methods. The ruthless interventions in the actions of his subordinates inclined the latter, in turn, to pass on their frustrations to their own subordinates.[36]

Section 2: The battles for Rzhev

The *Wehrmacht* had taken Rzhev during the summer months of 1941. After the defeat at Moscow, 9th Army's situation became particularly precarious. Rzhev was in the centre of a large salient toward the east that was vulnerable to Russian attacks. 9th Army was connected to its neighbouring German units only by a narrow corridor. In several of the sectors, front lines were reversed with the Germans facing west and the Russians facing east. General Friessner's XXIII Corps was entirely cut off.

Before being relieved and going on sick leave, Strauss had several times proposed a retreat to a defensive position. Von Bock, who wanted to pursue his attack on Moscow at all costs, disagreed at first. Later, after a new request for retreat from Strauss, Hitler forbade

---

33 Estate, Friessner, undated.
34 P. Broucek, *Ein General im Zwielicht. Die Erinnerungen Edmund Glaises vomn Horstenau,* Vienna 1999, vol.3. p.349, 391.
35 Estate, Röhricht, 10 March 1956.
36 Estate, Letter Hermann to Görlitz, August 1975.

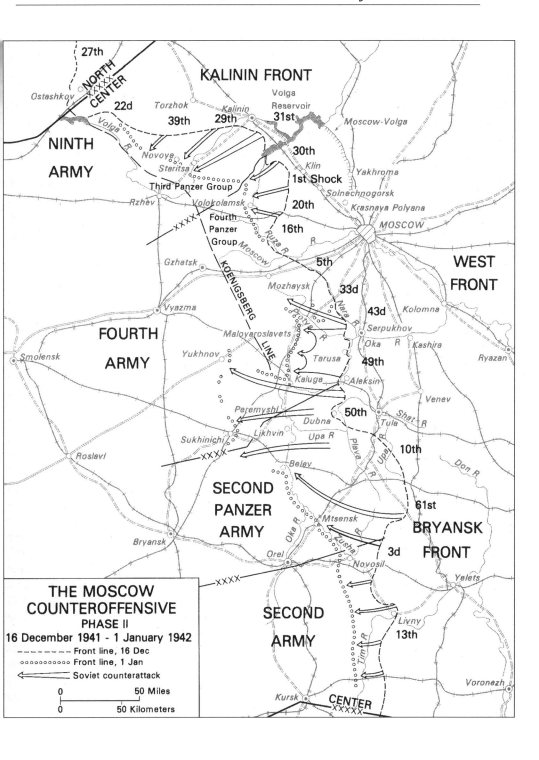

27th

NORTH
CENTER

Ostashkov

KALININ FRONT

Volga
Reservoir

Moscow-Volga

22d

Torzhok

Kalinin

31st

39th

29th

30th

NINTH

Volga R

Novoye

Klin

Yakhroma

ARMY

Staritsa

1st Shock

Third Panzer Group

Solnechnogorsk

Rzhev

Volokolamsk

20th

Krasnaya Polyana

Fourth
Panzer
Group

16th

Ruza R

MOSCOW

Moscow R

Gzhatsk

KOENIGSBERG

5th

WEST

Mozhaysk

33d

FRONT

Vyazma

43d

Kolomna

Nara R

Maloyaroslavets

Serpukhov

DON LINE

Oka   R

Kashira

FOURTH

Yukhnov

Ryazan

ARMY

Tarusa

49th

Smolensk

Kaluga

Aleksin

Venev

Peremyshl

50th

Shat R

Dubna

Tula

Likhvin

Upa R

Sukhinichi

10th

Roslavl

Belev

Plava R

Upa R

Don R

SECOND

61st

PANZER

Oka R

Mtsensk

BRYANSK

ARMY

Susha R

3d

FRONT

Bryansk

Orel

Novosil

Yelets

CENTER

Livny

SECOND

13th

ARMY

Tim R

Voronezh

**THE MOSCOW
COUNTEROFFENSIVE**
PHASE II
16 December 1941 - 1 January 1942

– – – – – – – Front line, 16 Dec
ooooooooooo Front line, 1 Jan
⇐―――――― Soviet counterattack

0	50 Miles
0	50 Kilometers

Kursk

it, with reference to the *Haltebefehl*. When Model took over 9th Army, he suggested a retreat to a position similar to the one advocated by Strauss.[37] However, he proposed to follow that movement with an immediate counter-offensive. In the atmosphere of the winter of 1941/42, suggestions for offensive operations from Army commanders were exceptional. Therefore Hitler was favourably surprised, particularly since Model requested no reinforcements, nor any combat support, except for *Luftwaffe* transport planes to airlift the units he constantly repositioned.

First battle

9th Army's defensive lines encompassed the areas of Sychovka, Belyi, Olenin and Rzhev. The area was successfully defended by 9th Army during all the battles for Rzhev. Rzhev was the keystone. The city was invested by the Red Army. Troops and supplies had to be flown in. The main centre of supply, Sychovka, was also in danger of encirclement, but reserves and supplies could still reach it by road. The Russians attacked Rzhev from three directions, almost encircling the city. After repulsing attacks by two Russian Armies, Model seized the initiative and launched an attack of his own, breaking up the ring around Friessner's XXIII Corps. Any Russian breakthroughs were countered by concentric circle tactics that completely enclosed them. One of the two Russian armies was completely surrounded and destroyed. The other was so extensively damaged that it was no longer fit for combat.

Model then shifted his tactics to a new concept, the "Snail Offensive" which Reichhelm described in some detail in a letter to the author: "The two main supply routes, at Rzhev and Olenin, were still dangerously exposed. In the north and the east, the front had been stabilized by a system of deep trenches. Supply lines had to be protected by mobile operations directed inward. 9th Army's troop strengths were insufficient to stabilize the line of defence throughout the whole area of its responsibility.

"The 'Snail Offensive' concept was based upon an understanding that the Red Army leadership still lacked coordination. Model ordered every Division to execute a series of daily pin-point attacks. The objectives of those individual actions varied. Some would retake a village. Others would dislodge partisans. At times, they were simply diversionary tactics designed to keep the enemy unaware of further German intentions. A secondary objective was to prevent the troops from remaining in place, and inactive, during the extreme cold weather. New trenches were dug continuously. This proved to be very difficult, since the earth was frozen for the most part, but heavy snowfalls made it possible."[38]

The concept of the "Snail Offensive" was developed by *Generalmajor,* later *Generaloberst* Erhard Raus, commander of 6th *Panzer* Division. In a performance rating of Raus, dated

---

37 In a statement of 5 November 1955, in the Estate, Strauss complained that Model had advocated the same measures which he himself had proposed several times and that his relief was unjustified.

38 While I was writing my book about the former Austrian Generals in the Wehrmacht, I asked Reichhelm about his opinion of Raus: "In my opinion, Raus was not part of the elite among the German commanders, but among the divisional commanders in 9th Army, he was one of the very best. He was well liked by his soldiers and always gave good advice in difficult situations. I would say that Raus performed better in the command of a Division than when he was in command of a Corps and later of an Army. He stood up to Model whenever he disagreed with him and was never intimidated by his insults." Letter from Reichhelm, 13 June 2000.

19 April 1942, Model wrote: "He had the specific merit of having brought his *Panzer Division* back into shape in spite of it having suffered heavy losses during the winter battles. This enabled him to develop the 'Snail Offensive' and to implement it successfully." The first battle came to an end on 10 February 1942.

Second battle

The logical course of action would have been to conduct a series of immediate troop evacuations and to shorten the defensive lines. Those actions would have freed more units for the offensive towards Stalingrad and the Caucasus. Kluge and Model made several such requests to Hitler, but Hitler insisted upon obedience to the *Haltebefehl*. Reichhelm was of the opinion that Hitler may have considered those positions as a point of departure for a new offensive towards Moscow. That view can be discarded. Hitler was no military dilettante. The *Ostheer* had suffered over one million casualties during the first six months of the Russian campaign, one third of its original strength. Hitler knew that, in 1942, the *Wehrmacht* had to concentrate offensive actions on only one sector of the front, namely the South. The second battle for Rzhev consisted of a series of failed local Russian attacks. On 2 July, those were followed by a counter-offensive of 9th Army, Operation *Seydlitz*.[39]

Third battle

The Red Army had brought in strong reinforcements and had regrouped. Some of its units were then posted in the rear of 9th Army, forcing it to fight on two fronts. On 23 May 1942, Model was wounded during a reconnaissance flight. He remained out of action for a few weeks. General von Vietinghoff replaced him.

9th Army, with Model at its helm once more, commenced a major concentric offensive on 2 July 1942. Model had obtained early knowledge of the Russian plans. He succeeded in preventing breakthroughs, surrounded the Red Army units, and annihilated them. 9th Army had by that time become a coherent unit. Renewed evacuation requests to Hitler were again denied. A major Russian attack was launched at the end of July. There were partial successes and partial failures on both sides. In the end, 9th Army succeeded in throwing back the enemy. The "Rzhev fighter" had gradually become a household name.[40]

---

39 Newton describes the second battle for Rhzev as Zhukov's worst defeat during the course of the war. (p. 209). This is "Model hero worship" pushed to the extreme. In autumn and winter 1941, Zhukov was in charge of the defence of Moscow, and the *Kesselschlachten* at Bryansk and Vyazma during the first weeks of *Taifun* cost the Russians close to one million POW. The Red Army units during these battles were under the command of Zhukov. The four battles for Rhzev were of a much smaller size than the first German offensives during summer/autumn 1941 and the second battle was one of four episodes. Had Newton written that the second battle for Rhzev was a local setback for Zhukov he would have remained within the limits of realities. Zhukov, like all Red Army commanders, suffered many setbacks of comparable size. Incidentally Zhukov's last setback occurred during the first week of the battle for Berlin, when his clumsy attempt to cature the Seelow heights delayed the offensive for several days and thwarted the Russian ambition to finish the capture of Berlin on May 1, 1945.

40 In his revolting speech of 30 January 1943, just before the end of the fighting at Stalingrad, Göring had stated that it was indifferent to the German soldier if he was killed at Stalingrad, at Rzhev or in Africa.

Fourth battle

On 15 November 1942, the Red Army launched a new major offensive. It was mainly directed against Sychovka, Rzhev, Olenin and Belyi. The Germans succeeded in holding all the cities, and the Russian attack came to an end on 9 December. Model then proposed a limited offensive, *Sevastopol 502*. By then, Hitler had removed *Generaloberst* Franz Halder as head of the *Generalstab,* and General Kurt Zeitzler had been appointed as Halder's successor. Hitler opposed Model's plan because he felt the objective was too broad for the available forces. General Zeitzler agreed with Hitler. Stalingrad had already become encircled, and Manstein's attempted relief operations were given priority. Hitler issued a formal order on 15 January 1943, prohibiting *Sevastopol 502*. Model then made new requests to evacuate the area. Again, they were denied.

The *Büffel* retreat

By the end of January 1943, Hitler finally consented to a partial evacuation of Model's troops. This was not a cancellation of the *Haltebefehl*. More troops were needed for the projected offensive against Kursk which was in its first planning phase.

Operation *Büffel* was conducted in cooperation with 4th Army, commanded by *Generaloberst* Gotthard Heinrici. Its scope exceeded the massive retreat to the Hindenburg Line in 1917. 9th Army had to retreat more than 100 kilometres in four weeks, and then prepare new lines of defence. 200 kilometres of new roads for motorized transport, and 600 kilometres of smaller roads for sledges and horse-drawn equipment, were constructed. More than 200 trains and large-size transport units moved military and industrial equipment. Operation *Büffel* came to a successful end on 22 March 1943.

In his recollections, Reichhelm credited Model solely for its success. But this is unfair to von Kluge, who coordinated the actions of 4th and 9th Armies, and who had the overall direction of the retreat.[41] Reichhelm also fails to mention Heinrici's part in *Büffel*. Reichhelm states further that more than 60,000 Russian civilians were evacuated of their 'own free will' during Operation *Büffel* . Not only was Reichhelm's figure on the low side, but 'own free will' is divorced from reality. Russian officials, in occupied cities and townships, had collaborated with the Germans. More than a million Russians served as *Hiwi* (voluntary helpers) with the *Wehrmacht*. Another half million served as local policemen, were taken into SS units and acted as guards in concentration camps. They had every reason to fear Soviet reprisals and would certainly have agreed to leave with the Germans. But the bulk of the Russian civilians were deported by the Germans in their retreat. They were sent to Germany to work in the war production industry, where they worked as slave-labour, in unspeakable conditions. Gerlach's analysis shows

---

41 Teske compares the figures of *Büffel* with the retreat to the Hindenburg Line in 1917 (Operation *Siegfried*).
Length of front line prior to the retreats: *Siegfried* 175 kilometres, *Büffel* 754 kilometres.
Length of front line after the retreats: *Siegfried* 120 kilometres, *Büffel* 280 kilometres.
Largest single retreat: *Siegfried* 45 kilometres, *Büffel* 160 kilometres.
Period of time of the two operations: *Siegfried* 3 days, *Büffel* 22 days.
Divisions engaged prior to the retreats: *Siegfried* 29, *Büffel* 30.
Divisions engaged after the retreats: *Siegfried* 21, *Büffel* 16.
Abandoned space by the retreats: *Siegfried* 3,000 square kilometres, *Büffel* 24,000 square kilometres. Teske p.170 ff.

that Reichhelm's figures are wide off the mark. Not 70,000 but 130,000 civilians were evacuated, 41.3% of the area's civilian population.[42]

After his success at Rzhev, Walter Model became known as the 'Lion of defence'. The holding of Rzhev against heavy odds, and the orderly *Büffel* retreat, may well be regarded as the most outstanding *Wehrmacht* achievement in 1942. It certainly surpassed 11th Army's capture of Sevastopol. Manstein's faulty planning had turned the battle on the Crimean peninsula into a graveyard of soldiers killed in action. Manstein's operational talent played no part in the capture of Sevastopol. The city was practically shot to pieces by the heaviest artillery deployment of the war. The two 'Dora' guns, which had been designed for use against the heaviest fortresses of the Maginot line, had a calibre of 80cm and a barrel 30 metres long. 60 trains were needed to bring them from France to the outskirts of Sevastopol.[43] Rommel's ephemeral successes in North Africa do not belong in the same league as Model's achievements in the east. They were obtained in a theatre of secondary importance. The same can be said of the German conquest of Crete. It was a skilful operation but it had no impact on the developments on a major theatre. Churchill labelled it correctly "a Pyrrhic victory".

From then on, Hitler was to entrust Model with every command where immediate defensive skills were required. His choice was limited. The German *Generalstab* training was still dominated by the "Schlieffen school". Traditionally, it had concentrated on offensive operations. Defensive operations and tactics had been looked upon as trivialities.

The battles for Rzhev viewed by the Russians
The high command of the Red Army had greatly improved in quality after the disasters of the *Kessel* in the summer and autumn of 1942. Many of the new Front commanders showed themselves equal to the *Wehrmacht* Army OB. The appointment of Army General Alexei Antonov as Deputy Chief of the General Staff, *Stavka*, led to a rapid improvement of the *Stavka*.

One question remains. Why did the Red Army not put the *Schwerpunkt* of its winter offensives 1941/42 to the Rzhev region? The curve of the Rzhev salient was almost an invitation to create a *Kessel*. It may well have succeeded, and could have marked the end of Model's career. But at that time, the concept of *Schwerpunkt* had not yet gained ground with the Red Army. After his success at Moscow, Stalin felt that he could attack everywhere.[44] However, Stalin was a quick learner and did not repeat that mistake.

Red Army units in the battles for Rzhev
Russian military history does not treat the battles for Rzhev in an isolated manner, but includes them in the general review of operations in the Centre. Rzhev was at first attacked

---

42 Gerlach, p.500.
43 The real victor of Sevastopol was the artillery expert General Robert Martinek. General Martinek was an Austrian. Before the Anschluss he had been the inspector of artillery in the Austrian *Bundesheer*. He was taken into the *Wehrmacht* as a Colonel. During the Second World War, he rose to *General der Artillerie*. He became a Corps commander and was killed in action during the Russian offensive against Army Group Centre in summer 1944.
44 G. Zhukov, *Vospominania i Razmyshlenya* Moscow 1967, p.379 ff (henceforth Zhukov). Zhukov adds that Stalin said at a *Stavka* meeting on 5 January 1942 that he did not want to listen to any contradiction.

by three "Fronts", the North-West Front under General Kurochkin, the Kalinin Front under General Konev, and the West Front under General Zhukov. At first, the three "Fronts" were grouped into a "Theatre", likewise commanded by Zhukov. But the Theatre was soon disbanded. During the first battles, the strongest Front was Konev's Kalinin Front.

On 11 January 1942, Stalin sent his order 17007 to Konev:

> On 11 January, and in no instance later than 12 January, the city of Rzhev has to be taken. *Stavka* recommends using all material available, in particular artillery, rockets and aircraft. Attack in full strength, and without consideration of destruction of the city's infrastructure. Receipt of this order has to be confirmed and execution reported.[45]

During the first battle for Rzhev, the two main Red Army units were 39th Army, under the NKVD General Maslennikov,[46] and 29th Army under General Shvetsov. Initially, the 1st Shock Army under General Kusnetzov, and 16th Army under General Rokossovsky, held the area, but they were removed.[47] After the first battle, Shvetsov's Army was destroyed, with only 5,000 men remaining.[48] Maslennikov's Army had to be disbanded after being decimated in a *Kessel*.

By the end of March 1942, the idea of *Schwerpunkt* was brought up for the first time at a meeting of the *GKO* (the State Committee of Defence), the highest military body during the war. At a meeting presided over by Stalin, Generals Zhukov, Voroshilov, Timoshenko, Shaposhnikov, Vasilevsky and Bagramyan, proposed to concentrate all efforts on Rzhev. Stalin disagreed and decided on an offensive against Kharkov. It ended in disaster.[49]

On 27 February 1943, Konev was dismissed from the command of the West Front, which he had taken over from Zhukov: "The commander of West Front, Colonel General Konev, is to be dismissed, since he did not succeed in leading his front. He is put at *Stavka* disposal for future assignments."[50]

---

45   Volkogonov, p.619.

46   Before the war, Maslennikov was commander in chief of all NKVD troops. After the war, during which he later commanded a number of "fronts", he returned to the NKVD.

47   General Kusnetzov happened to be a protégé of Zhukov who objected to *Stavka* against the removal of Kusnetzov's army. Marshal Shaposhnikov replied to him: "Nothing to do, *golubka* (little pigeon), it is a personal order of Comrade Stalin." – Zhukov, p.383.

48   *IVOVSS*, vol.2, p.328.

49   General Friedrich Paulus, who had just taken over as *OB* of 6th Army, commanded the bulk of the German troops during the counter-offensive. To his later misfortune at Stalingrad, he was now viewed as a capable Army *OB*.

50   *Stavka* order 0045, 27 February 1943. Konev was later promoted to Marshal of the Soviet Union and given increasingly higher commands. The mutual dislike between Zhukov and Konev permitted Stalin to spur both commanders to their maximum level of performance in carefully chosen neighbouring areas. During the battle for Berlin, Zhukov and Konev competed for the laurels of being the Red Army Marshal to take Berlin. The race between the two led several times to confusion with units of Red Army fighting each other, with dust from gunfire and from buildings shot into rubble preventing them from recognizing each other at a distance.

"The chapter on Rzhev has to be re-written" – March 2000

A German "Rzhev *Kuratorium*" was established in 1992 by Ernst-Martin Rhein. It immediately started an exchange of letters with authorities at Rzhev. In March 2000, the city's mayor, Galina Meshkova, invited the members of the *Kuratorium* to a memorial meeting. It was attended by the former Commander in Chief of the Warsaw Pact armed forces, Marshal Kulikov, and a number of Russian veterans of the battle. The Russian participants at the meeting complained that Soviet military history had given only brief and erroneous accounts of the fighting. However, according to the veterans, it equalled the fighting at Stalingrad in intensity.

After the meeting with the *Kuratorium*, the Russian historian, Oleg Kondratev, published the first genuine Russian version of the battles.[51] Kondratev is highly critical of earlier Soviet accounts which were primarily concerned with hiding the mistakes made by Stalin. As a result, no Red Army commander at Rzhev was awarded the top decoration, "Hero of the Soviet Union". The term "Battles for Rzhev" was not used by *IVOVSS*. It reported only isolated combats of various units. The Soviet losses sustained at Rzhev were published, for the first time, in 2000, in articles in the papers of the region's capital city Tver. They amounted to 362,664 killed in action, and 746,485 severely wounded and unfit for further combat service.

Section 3: Kursk and the "Hagen" position

Much has been written in British, American and French literature on Model's part in the successive postponements of the *Zitadelle* attack. The German initiative in the battles for Kursk turned into a complete fiasco. Some authors, including Newton, look at Model's objections to the battle, and his intervention which led to several postponements, as one of the major causes for the ultimate failure of the operation. Such opinions require correction:

- Model had no part in the first plans for attacking the Kursk salient. As one of the Army commanders foreseen for the operation, he dealt exclusively with the problems of his 9th Army, which he considered to be in unacceptable condition for the task it would be given.
- Model presented his objections directly to Hitler, without going through von Kluge. He thus increased Hitler's doubts, which led to successive postponements.
- Even without Model's objections, the operation was doomed from the very first planning onwards. Had Model not caused the attack to be postponed, the fiasco would have been worse in terms of casualties. The break-up of a major operation, after only one week, was unprecedented in World War II. Undoubtedly, it would have been preferable if Model's repeated objections had led to a complete cancellation of an offensive which infringed every established principle of strategy.

Zitadelle or the Battles for Kursk

German historians tend to treat *Zitadelle* as a separate operation. Russian historians see the *Zitadelle* phase, more correctly, as only the first part of the battle for Kursk, (*Kurskaya bitva*). It was followed by the Russian counter-offensive at Orel, between 12 and 18 of August, then by a counter-offensive at Kharkov, up to 28 August, and finally by the fall of Kiev to the Red Army, in November 1943.

---

51 O. Kondratev, *Die Schlacht um Rzhev – ein halbes Jahrhundert Schweigen*, Munich 2000.

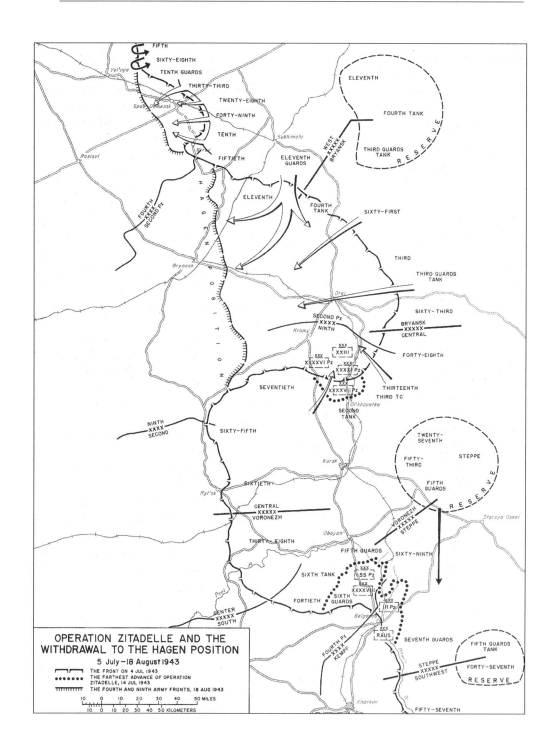

OPERATION ZITADELLE AND THE
WITHDRAWAL TO THE HAGEN POSITION
5 July – 18 August 1943

THE FRONT ON 4 JUL 1943
THE FARTHEST ADVANCE OF OPERATION
ZITADELLE, 14 JUL 1943
THE FOURTH AND NINTH ARMY FRONTS, 18 AUG 1943

10   0   10   20   30   40   50 MILES
10   0   10   20   30   40   50 KILOMETERS

Russian historians continue to see the battles of Moscow and of Kursk as the two decisive encounters of the Russo-German war. German historians tend to attach more weight to the battles of Stalingrad, and the Russian offensive against Army Group Centre in the summer of 1944. Stalingrad was the greatest loss of prestige to the *Wehrmacht*. But no Russian operation wrought more havoc than the *Bagration* offensive. It began on 22 June 1944, exactly three years after the German attack on Russia. Logic is on the side of the Russian opinion. Moscow marked the end of the German possibilities of action on the whole of the Eastern front. After the failure of the *Zitadelle* offensive, the Germans lost their last capacity for initiative. Thereafter, they were continuously pushed back until the Red Army captured Berlin. The ideological overtones, which in former times always used to accompany Russian victories, came close to exaggeration after the victory at Kursk.[52]

In their memoirs, German historians and Generals could be expected to distance themselves from Soviet accounts. However, in that instance they would concur, without adopting any ideological overtones. Given the disaster of the battle, the German Generals were eager to distance themselves from it, in particular those who had opposed the German offensive from the beginning. As usual, the blame was laid at the footsteps of the 'bungler' Hitler.

But the real culprit was neither Hitler, nor the new chief of the *Generalstab*, General Kurt Zeitzler, but the great brain of the German Army, *Feldmarschall* Erich von Manstein. He had made the first proposal of a major offensive on 10 March 1943.[53] The salient at Kursk, with a front length of 500 kilometres, had developed into a strong Russian *Schwerpunkt*. Manstein's plan was based on the cardinal offence of an attack on a *Schwerpunkt*, which had always been rejected by all strategists. The only explanation of Manstein's folly is that his hubris had reached such dimensions that he would recommend almost any operation, provided it took place under his command. If the operation turned into a failure, he was always quick to shift the blame to other commanders and register another "lost victory".

Hitler had never been an enthusiastic supporter of the Kursk operation. During the winter of 1942, Hitler had issued an operational directive (*Weisung*) Number 5. It was for a limited operation in spring 1943, with the purpose of keeping the initiative in German

---

52 Two examples: Marshal Vasilevsky saw Kursk as the final proof of the superiority of the Red Army command. (A. Vasilevsky, *Sache des ganzen Lebens*, East Berlin 1977, p.310). The historian Boris Solovev went further: "The battles of Kursk were evidence of the indisputable superiority of the military and economic elements of socialism that would turn the Red Army's victories at Kursk into an iron-clad law of world history." (B. Solovev, *Wendepunkt des Zweiten Weltkrieges-Die Schlacht bei Kursk*, Cologne 1984, p.13 ff.) Since the collapse of the Soviet Union, Russian historians have distanced themselves from such ideological elements. At a meeting of military historians from various countries on the battlefield of Prokhorovka, the historian Grigoryi Koltunov admitted: "I have committed forgeries and lies. I was ordered to exaggerate German losses and to minimise Red Army casualties well below genuine figures. My works cannot be taken seriously." (Article in the daily *Berliner Morgenpost*. 20/21 July 1996, supplement, p.2.) However none of the post-Soviet corrections dispute the impact of the Russian victory on the remaining years of the war in the East. The first artillery salute of the war was fired in Moscow after the Russian capture of Orel. Thereafter salutes were fired after the retaking of every major city.

53 *Verlorene Siege*, p.484.

hands. During the increasingly violent discussions about *Zitadelle*, Hitler kept a cool head. Although he finally did agree to the operation, he was quick to understand that it had been a failure from the outset. He broke it off after one week. He overrode Manstein's objection who saw in the defeat of *Zitadelle* another "lost victory".

A book on Model need only concern itself with his part in the preparation of the battle, in his performance during the week that *Zitadelle* lasted, and in the successful retreat by him to the "Hagen position". There, Model gave up Orel in disobedience to orders by von Kluge. After the end of the *Hagen* retreat, Model was relieved of his command of 9th Army and dispatched into the doldrums for three months.

German major units at *Zitadelle*
The attack was to be conducted by two Army Groups, Army Group Centre (*OB Feldmarschall* von Kluge) and Army Group South (*OB Feldmarschall* von Manstein). Army Group Centre consisted of five Armies, 9th Army (*Generaloberst* Walter Model*)*, 2nd Army (*Generaloberst* Walter Weiss), 4th Army (*Generaloberst* Heinrici), 2nd *Panzer* Army (*Generaloberst* Rudolf Schmidt) and 3rd *Panzer* Army (*Generaloberst* Reinhardt). 9th Army was the largest unit of Army Group Centre and was designed to spearhead the offensive.

Army Group South consisted of 1st *Panzer* Army (*Generaloberst* von Mackensen), 4th *Panzer* Army (*Generaloberst* Hermann Hoth), 6th Army (*Generaloberst* Karl Hollidt)[54] and the *Armeeabteilung* Kempf (*General der Panzertruppe* Werner Kempf).[55] The largest unit of Army Group South was Hoth's 4th *Panzer* Army.

Model's preparations and objections
Model began immediately with a thorough and critical examination of his own strength, the main constituents of his Army, and the capacities of his opponents. Contrary to Manstein, Model never underestimated the Red Army. In fact, Manstein's contempt for the Red Army was to prove to be his Achilles' heel, as the war in the east moved increasingly to Germany's disadvantage. 9th Army was given two code names during the preparatory phase of the battle, first *"Festungsstab 11"* and then *"Gruppe Weiss"*. At first, *OKH* had foreseen only two further limited operations – Operation *Habicht* and Operation *Panther*, in the area later to become the battlefield to *Zitadelle*. While those two operations were being discussed, Manstein was in hospital, where he had undergone a tonsil operation to delay his growing cataracts. During his absence, Model replaced him as *OB* of Army Group South. On 4 April 1943, Model spoke to *Generaloberst* Hoth, who told him that there were not sufficient German forces for *Panther*. (If Army Group South's strength was insufficient for the limited *Panther*, one may well ask how Manstein could view it as sufficient for the much larger *Zitadelle*).[56] On the following day, Model spoke with

---

54 After the destruction of 6th Army at Stalingrad, Hitler had decided to create a new 6th Army.

55 The *Armeeabteilung* was an increased Corps, intended to become an Army.

56 The French historian Pierre Masson, who had written a comprehensive history of the *Wehrmacht* (*Die deutsche Armee. Geschichte der Wehrmacht 1935-1945*, Munich 1996, henceforth Masson) wrote: "*OKH* had been guilty of grievous miscalculations in its overconfidence of its own forces and in its inexcusable underestimation of the enemy's reserves." (p.269). *Bundeswehr* four-star General von Kielmansegg, who wrote the comments to the German edition of Masson's book, strongly disagreed. He wrote in his footnote on the same page: "This statement is not correct. Hitler's objections concerned mainly the equipment available, but not the operative

General Kempf and his staff, who confirmed Hoth's sceptical views. Model then made a series of aerial reconnaissance flights which revealed that the Red Army had built up an enormous net-work of defensive positions, stretching over 20 kilometres to the rear.

In Model's first formal position, in writing about *Zitadelle*, on 8 April 1943, the sentence "available forces would be only just sufficient" appeared for the first time.[57] On 15 April 1943, 9th Army reported to Army Group Centre that there were insufficient qualified non-coms with the Divisions and that reserves in general were not available in sufficient quantity.[58] On 17 April 1943, Model wrote to Army Group Centre, that the operational capacity of his Army was insufficient and that he was unable to proceed with the attack at the date foreseen.[59] After 9th Army received only a fraction of the reserves Model had requested, a new message was sent to Army Group Centre, with the additional sentence: "I request an immediate decision by the *Führer*."[60] On 18 April 1943, Model wrote directly to Hitler, stressing the strength of the Russian defence system, adding that the German *Panzer* had insufficient strength to cope with the new Soviet anti-tank artillery.[61] Brett-Smith, no admirer of Model, wrote: "Model's objections should have been taken seriously, for Model was not the man to complain idly."[62]

On 20 April 1943, a heated discussion took place between Model and General Krebs, who had become Chief of Staff of Kluge's Army Group. Krebs said that 9th Army had never been in better shape. Model's reply to this assertion stressed that the troops were in weakened condition and that additional time for training was imperative. One can assume that Model had better knowledge of the state of his Army than Krebs, who was obviously forced to defend Kluge's views.

Model then instructed Reichhelm to prepare a comprehensive assessment. It turned out to be seven pages in length. When it was completed, and for greater emphasis, Model

---

idea. Insufficiency of equipment caused him to postpone the original *OKH* plan that called for a date in early May. Zeitzler was in favour of the offensive only until mid-June. After that date, he began to oppose it and voiced his objections with the strong support of Heusinger. It was Manstein and Kluge who insisted going forward with the original plan. They were the ones whom Masson labelled the 'sinners' and who were guilty of over-confidence in their own strength and the inexcusable underestimation of the enemy's strength."Another somewhat curious comment by Masson must be mentioned: "Kursk was forced upon a reluctant Hitler by Zeitzler, Manstein and Model." Again, Kielmansegg contradicts: "This is totally wrong. Hitler had finally come round to accepting the concept of *Zitadelle*. No one could ever force anything upon him. In June, Zeitzler wanted to cancel the whole operation. Strongly prodded by Manstein and Kluge, Hitler refused. He felt that he was bound to take the initiative and that the increasingly unfavourable war situation made it incumbent on him to score at least some success." Liddell Hart, to whom every word by Manstein comes close to gospel, wrote that *Zitadelle* failed because Model had requested its postponement. Newton advances a similar opinion. (Newton, p.219).

57 AOK 9, Ia, KTB Nr.8., Anlagen IV, Bd. I, Befehle und Meldungen des AOK, 30. March-2 May 1943(35939/12).
58 Ibid, Sonderanlage Nr.1. 31 March-12 July 1943 (35939/18).
59 Ibid, Anlagenband IV, Band I, Anlage IV, 9 f (35939/18).
60 Ibid, Anlagenband V (34890/1).
61 Ibid.
62 Brett-Smith, p.199.

had it signed by his four Corps commanders, Generals Friessner, Gollnick, Harpe and Lemelsen. The presentation was totally factual and void of any emotion. It ended with a statement that Model's forces might be sufficient, provided he was given two additional Divisions, and the general situation was favourable.[63]

By now, Model had reached the limit of his patience and felt that he had to turn to Hitler directly. He did not trust von Kluge to present his views in a satisfactory manner. In that instance his distrust was justified. Model therefore, took advantage of the occasion of his award of the swords to the oak leaves of his Knight's Cross. He had a long talk with Hitler, who was strongly impressed. He had already considered a delay of the attack until 10 June. But first Hitler decided to call a meeting at Munich of the Army Group *OB* who were fronting the attack. Generals Zeitzler, Guderian, and Jeschonnek, Chief of Staff of the *Luftwaffe* were likewise invited.[64] Model did not participate in the meeting.

Munich meeting – 4 May 1943

The only reliable accounts of what was said at Munich are the stenographic minutes of Manstein's chief of staff, *Generalmajor* Theodor Busse. They will be reproduced in full. The memoirs and verbal accounts of the other participants serve mainly to show how right they were in their objections, while casting aspersions on those who did not share their view. Thus Guderian wrote that Manstein, as usual, was not 'at his best' when confronting Hitler.[65] Coming from Guderian, such a statement makes strange reading, since it would be difficult to find an occasion when Guderian was at his best when facing Hitler.

Some historians' accounts contain contentions as facts. For example, David Irving quotes *Generaloberst* Jeschonnek as having advanced the opinion that Manstein and Kluge had initially agreed to a postponement. When they heard that this was also Hitler's view, they suddenly urged an immediate launching of the offensive, to avoid later blame.[66] Any statement by David Irving must be viewed with caution. Irving has amassed one of the most extensive archives about Hitler in private possession. However, he often manipulates his documents to adapt them to his views. In this case, he contends that his statement was taken from a page from Jeschonnek's diary which Richthofen had then pasted into his own. But Irving gives no clear identification of either. Jeschonnek was already depressed, since he had been shouldered with the blame for the insufficient air supply at Stalingrad. In August 1943 he shot himself. Irving also writes that no minutes from the conference exist, although Busse's account was available to him at the BA-MA.

The following is the complete text of Busse's minutes. The stenographic style remains unaltered:

Discussion between *OB* [Manstein] and Chief *Generalstab*:

Chief *Generalstab* informs *OB* about the matters to be discussed and develops his views. *Führer* has become hesitant after having listened to the report by *Generaloberst* Model. He is no longer convinced that the attack will break through. *Führer* is mainly

---

63 Facsimile in Model/Bradley, p. 65 ff. Reichhelm's initials "R" are clearly visible.

64 *Generaloberst* Jeschonnek shot himself on 18 August 1943. He had become the victim of increased depression after the *Luftwaffe*'s failure to supply 6th Army at Stalingrad.

65 Guderian, p.278.

66 D. Irving, *Hitler's War 1942-1945*, London 1977, p.501.

impressed by maps showing a Russian defensive system, with a depth exceeding 20 kilometres, and very close firing positions. *Generaloberst* Model has submitted a six-day plan for an attempt at breakthrough. *Führer* has reached the conviction:

1. that it is doubtful if 9th Army's Infantry can succeed if *Panzer* are held back.

2. that it is more than questionable if a *Kessel* can be established. He feels that the enemy, supported by his large size defensive system, will have sufficient time to withdraw from any encirclement.

Since *Führer* feels that, given the overall military and political situation, this first offensive of the year has to result in a conclusive success, he has the opinion that, in particular, Army Group Centre has to be strengthened with additional *Panzer* and anti-tank weaponry. This should be done by means of more '*Tiger*' *Panzer*, strengthened armour of *Panzer 4, Hornissen, Ferdinand,* an extra heavy *Porsche-Panzer*, and anti-tank guns. Since all this can only be available on 10 June at the earliest, *Führer* intends to postpone the date of attack accordingly. *Führer* is supported in his views by *Generaloberst* Guderian."

Chief *Generalstab* then developed his view: He is against a postponement, since preparations are already advanced. The troops are mentally ready for battle and look forward to it with optimism. Therefore any postponement will be to the enemy's advantage. We will only lose the advantage of striking against an enemy not yet fully prepared, beat him and thus become able to build up new reserves for other purposes. He doubts if the additional *Panzer* and other equipment will arrive in good time, recent experience points to the contrary. The new *Ferdinand* still suffers from 'teething troubles', even *Generaloberst* Guderian doubts if they can become combat-ready in June.

[Guderian wrote about the *Ferdinand Panzer*:

They were a variation of the '*Tiger*', designed by Professor Porsche, equipped with electric propulsion and a 1.70 metre long 8.8 cm calibre gun, similar to an assault gun. Apart from this gun, the *Ferdinand* had no other weapons and was thus useless in close combat, in spite of its heavy armour and the good quality of the gun. Since production had already begun and 90 *Ferdinand* were available, I had to use them although I could not share Hitler's enthusiasm for the latest 'toy' from his favourite constructor Porsche.][67]

Chief *Generalstab* has therefore asked *OB* and *Feldmarschall* von Kluge to come to Munich, to get their views about *Führer's* opinion and to assist him in his presentation to *Führer*. *Generalfeldmarschall* von Manstein said that he was in basic agreement with the views of Chief *Generalstab*. He was concerned with the increasing risks at the Eastern and Donets sectors facing his army group. While he did not dispute that additional reserves had to be brought to the battle, he doubted if they could

---

67 Guderian, p.271.

compensate against corresponding increases by the enemy and a further strengthening of Russian defensive positions. As far as he was concerned, the only advantage of a postponement would consist in not limiting reinforcements to equipment, but also bringing in additional infantry Divisions. He was unable to judge if this was possible, since his overall view of available troop reserves was not sufficient. [When this was reported to Hitler, he was happy to throw one of his usual barbs at Manstein, that he always asked for more troops than were available.]

All participants then went into Hitler's situation room. *Führer* gave a lengthy outline of the reasons that led him to consider a postponement. He insisted on the following points:

1. He had been impressed by the maps of enemy defensive positions given to him by *Generaloberst* Model.

2. He increasingly doubted if he had sufficient strength available.

3. The failed attack at Novorossiysk had shown that, without strong *Panzer* support, the infantry could not penetrate a strong defensive position that was doggedly defended."

He had the same fear for 'Citadel', where Model's 9th Army was to attack with infantry only, but with its *Panzer* kept in reserve. Meanwhile, Army Group South had only few Infantry Divisions and had already used its *Panzer* during the first attempt. Since Army Group South's Infantry was not sufficient, its *Panzer* would already be decimated during the first breakthrough attempt, and would then be unable to force the final breakthrough. *Führer* then explained at some length that reinforcements could be made available by 10 June. In particular, the *Ferdinand* would reduce casualties in attacks of enemy fortified positions. He then requested the *OB* of the two Army Groups to present their views about a postponement.

Generalfeldmarschall von Manstein commented: He could not judge the extent to which an early success in the East was necessary, even desirable, against the overall political and military situation. His Army group was too weak for the assault, in particular the infantry. Success was only possible if he was given additional Infantry Divisions. In particular:

1. I feel that a success in the East must be obtained before the fall of Tunis, and before the establishment of a new front by the Western Allies. [Tunis had fallen two months earlier !]

2. To wait means an increased risk at the front at Mius-Donets. At present, the Russians are not ready to attack there, in June they will certainly be ready.

3. It is doubtful whether our reinforcements will be able to compensate for the additional units that the Russians will bring forward. There has been one additional month of Russian tank production, new defence lines, and their recovery from the first mortal blow of German success.

Führer replied that additional Infantry Divisions for Army Group South are out of the question, and that *OB* had to keep in mind that additional *Panzer* would more than compensate for insufficient infantry.

Generalfeldmarschall von Kluge strongly objects to any postponement. The information given by *Generaloberst* Model about the strength of enemy position is grossly exaggerated. His maps show a number of former positions that had remained from previous battles, but which were no longer manned. He fears that we will be relegated into the rear. We will be compelled to withdraw forces from the attack Divisions, and become unable to offer any further offensive actions during the remainder of the year.

Führer replied that *Generaloberst* Model was quite optimistic during his presentation, it was he himself who was the pessimist.

Generaloberst Guderian emphasized that no efforts should be spared in attempting to reduce human loss of life by bringing forward as much equipment as possible. He felt that all available *Panzer* had to be given either to Army Group Centre, or to Army Group South, to be totally powerful at any one point.

Generaloberst Jeschonnek agreed with the views of *Generaloberst* Guderian. The attack should concentrate on one single point, and all available air force be likewise concentrated there. Russian air concentration shows that they intend to direct their attack against Army Group South. Sizeable German air reinforcements are not available, but two additional *Stuka* groups could be put at their disposal.

Führer closed the meeting without having reached a final decision. It is however apparent that he has already decided on a postponement.[68]

On the day following the conference Hitler decided to postpone 'Citadel' until 12 June. General von Mellenthin wrote: "Had *Zitadelle* been launched in April or May, it would have yielded a rich harvest. By June all favourable elements had vanished."[69] Such words belong to the typical post-war wisdom of German memoir writers. An attack in April was never on the cards, because in April the muddy period still prevailed. The operational order Number 6 is unambiguous: "All units of both Army groups have to make the necessary preparations far in the rear of the lines earmarked for the launching of the offensive, and under cover of every measure of camouflage and deceit, so as to enable *OKH* to issue the final order six days after 28 April. Earliest possible date, 3 May".[70]

Further postponements

On 10 May, Guderian attended a meeting at the *Reich* Chancellery in Berlin. Hitler had ordered a review of delays in *Panzer* production and set new targets with higher numbers. After the meeting ended, Guderian requested a personal talk with Hitler. He asked him: "Why do you want to attack in the East at all this year?" Keitel said that there were political reasons and Guderian replied: "Do you really think that any person world-wide knows where Kursk is? It is totally indifferent to the world if we have Kursk or not. I repeat my question. Why attack at all in the East?" Hitler replied: "You are entirely right. The whole idea gives me an increasingly funny feeling in the pit of my stomach." Guderian said: "Then you have the right feeling. Simply keep your hands off the whole idea." Hitler assured him that he had not reached a final decision.[71]

Even lower ranks began to grumble. At a meeting at *OKH*, Colonel Helmut Staedtke, chief of staff of XXXV Corps, said to Colonel Heinz Brandt, the Ia at *OKH*'s operational

---

68 BA-MA, RH 19-VI/95.
69 Mellenthin, p.146.
70 *Führer* operational order Nr.6, item 3.
71 Guderian, p.218.

department: "What is the purpose of the offensive? To conquer some more square kilometres of Russian territory? Surely we have enough of them already."

Manstein kept his illusions:

> At Army Group South, we remained convinced that the offensive would be difficult, but end in success. We had some doubt if we could beat back a simultaneous enemy offensive in the Donets region, but we were convinced that, after a victory at Kursk, we could overcome any crisis in the Donets region and turn it into a great victory.[72]

Finally, 5 July 1943 was decided upon. Hitler issued an order of the day:

> The German forces have to strike a decisive blow and bring about a turn-round of the war. The operation has to be the final battle for German victory. A new severe Russian defeat will compound the breakdown of the already shaky Russian hopes of a final victory of Bolshevism.[73]

The battle itself requires no detailed description. Hitler ordered it terminated after a week. Model had advanced some 10 kilometres, his Army had suffered 20,000 casualties. Manstein had advanced a little further, 35 kilometres. On 13 March 1943, Hitler called Manstein and Kluge to the *Führerhauptquartier* and informed them of his decision to terminate *Zitadelle*. The Allies had landed on Sicily and the massive counter-offensives of the Red Army in the Orel region had already begun. Model presented a final report in which he stressed that the new Russian defence measures against German *Panzer* had not been overcome.[74]

German accounts tend to exaggerate the overall importance of the *Zitadelle* failure, since it marked the end of any German initiative in the East. But in the total war context, the Allied landing at Sicily was far more important. It brought the overwhelming American industrial might on to the European continent. By the same token, El Alamein had far greater significance than Stalingrad.

Zitadelle viewed by the Russians

Stavka planning

After the victory at Stalingrad, where the last phase of the Russian offensive (*Koltso*) was placed under Rokossovsky's command, the future Marshal was ordered to transfer his Front without delay to the region between Bryansk and Voronezh. *Stavka* had planned a major attack in the Kursk region, which was scheduled to begin on 15 February 1943. Rokossovsky considered this date to be premature, because he was unable to regroup his units in such a short period. However, his complaints were turned down.[75] He argued that there was only one single railway line, that railway time-tables led to confusion, that there were not enough trains and that the lorries were unsuitable for the region. The only

---

72 *Verlorene Siege,* p.494.

73 BA-MA, RH 20 – 9/138.

74 Facsimile in Model/Bradley, p.73.

75 Rokossovsky p.175 ff.

result he obtained was a dispatch of a larger number of *NKVD* units, who were ordered to see to it that the work of railway workers improved. They mainly caused fear and confusion. The rear area had no quarters for the additional troops required. The offensive was delayed until 25 February 1943.

Rokossovsky writes that in spite of some initial success, *Stavka* had miscalculated. He added that he also bore part of the responsibility, because he had given in to *Stavka*, and had not paid sufficient attention to the preparation of his troops for the new operation. In connection with this operation, the name of General Ivan Chernyakhovsky appears for the first time. He was in command of 60th Army on Rokossovsky's front. In a short time he became one of the foremost Red Army commanders.[76]

The Russian offensive was brought to a halt by Manstein's counter-offensive against Kharkov and Belgorod. Rokossovsky emphasizes that the *Wehrmacht* had often succeeded in breaking through Russian defence lines with relative ease, because the Red Army had paid insufficient attention to their depth.[77]

Russian preparations for *Zitadelle*

German intentions to attack in the Kursk region had been quickly detected. Discussions arose between acting from the "forehand", (taking the initiative of an attack), and from the "backhand", (awaiting the German onslaught, and then counter-attacking). Similar discussions had taken place within the *Wehrmacht*, during the preparation for *Zitadelle*. Zhukov wrote that Stalin hesitated at first and was inclined to give preference to the "forehand", because he was not convinced that the Red Army was yet able to withstand a major German attack.[78] General Vatutin supported Stalin's view. Zhukov could not resist the temptation of a side-swipe against Khrushchev, who was head of the Southern political directorate, where Vatutin's Front operated.[79] Zhukov, Vasilevsky, Antonov and Rokossovsky had several meetings with Stalin, and finally succeeded in convincing him to give preference to "backhand". The Red Army command also prepared for the possibility of evacuating the Kursk salient, if the danger of a German *Kessel* were to arise.

Rokossovsky began with the construction of an in-depth system of defensive lines which extended over an area of more than 20 kilometres. Model had recognized it through aerial reconnaissance, but von Kluge felt the figures were exaggerated. The Red Army knew that the *Wehrmacht* planned to employ some of its new *Panzer*. Therefore, special training was put in place against the new *Tiger* and *Panther Panzer,* as well as new types of assault guns. Nevertheless, the *Tiger Panzer* caused initial surprise.

The local political authorities in the provinces around Kursk expressed the desire to evacuate the civilian population. Rokossovsky and the other Red Army commanders voiced strong opposition, since they wanted to avoid any feeling that a Russian retreat

---

76 In a number of works, Chernyakovsky is described as a Jew. However, this is an error. His name is typically Ukrainian. There were no Jews among the highest ranks of Red Army Commanders during World War II. The most senior Jewish General was Lieutenant General Kreiser, who rose to Army General under Khrushchev.

77 Rokossovsky, p.182.

78 Zhukov, p.483 ff.

79 Vatutin was one of the "Southern Generals" who were passed over for promotion during the war, as Stalin's relations with Khrushchev began to deteriorate. He served both at Stavka and as Front commander. Vatutin was killed by Ukrainian partisans after the recapture of Kiev.

was in the offing. Rokossovsky emphasized that there was never any doubt in his mind that the Red Army would win the battle. Their commanders had become the equals of the German opponents and they had much larger reserves to fall back on. The somewhat further advance of Manstein's Army Group was attributed by Rokossovsky to mistakes made by General Vatutin. It is always customary to search for a scapegoat. Rokossovsky came out in favour of commanding from the front line, but emphasized that it could not be turned into a method in every situation.[80]

Massive Russian counter-offensive

The Russian counter-offensive began on 12 July 1943. It was at first directed against 9th Army. On 10 July, *Generaloberst* Rudolf Schmidt had been suddenly relieved of his command, and placed under arrest.[81] Model assumed the additional command of 2nd *Panzer* Army. The police had discovered letters, from Schmidt to his family, which were said to have contained violent criticism of Hitler.[82] Schmidt was arrested and indicted at the *Reichskriegsgericht*. The head of the military justice body, Dr Karl Sack, had succeeded in quashing the indictment, stating that medical examination of Schmidt had established that he had fallen into depression and was no longer in control of his free will. After his release from prison, *Generaloberst* Schmidt made frantic efforts to be reinstated. He even turned to Himmler, in a personal letter, asking for his support. Himmler replied that he should prove his devotion to the *Führer*. If he was convincing, a new command was possible. In 1944 Schmidt was even considered as a candidate for replacing Zeitzler as chief of the *Generalstab*.[83] The lenient treatment of *Generaloberst* Schmidt was yet more evidence that contradicting Hitler was not fraught with major danger.[84] In Schmidt's case it was even worse than simply contradiction.

The Russian offensive gained increased power on 15 July, with its main effort directed against 9th Army and 2nd *Panzer* Army. A number of Red Army Divisions had been returned to their prescribed strength of 8,000 men.[85]

---

80 Rokossovsky, p.202.

81 Model maintained the two Armies as separate units with their respective staffs. This was certainly an organizational error on his part. A sensible solution would have been to set up an Armeegruppe with 9th Army's staff.

82 The letters by *Generaloberst* Schmidt could never be found, their content is therefore open to speculation. Hürter, p.602.

83 Details in D. Bradley/R. Schulze-Kossens, *Tätigkeitsbericht des Chefs des Heerespersonalamtes General der Infanterie Rudolf Schmundt, fortgeführt von General der Infanterie Wilhelm Burgdorf.* 1 October 1942-29 October 1944, Osnabrück 1984 and Goebbels, Diary entry 15 July 1944.

84 After the war, Schmidt paid a visit to his native city Weimar in the Russian zone of occupation. He was recognized and arrested. He remained in prison until 1955, and was then allowed to return to West Germany where he died in 1957.

85 In his memoirs, Rokossovsky mentions Model by name: "With the aim of boosting army morale, the Nazi command had brought the troops of the 2nd Panzer and 9th armies holding the Orel salient together under the command of Colonel-General Model, who enjoyed the special confidence of Hitler and was regarded as an unsurpassed master of defence, especially after the protracted fighting on the Rzhev-Vyazma sector." This General's order of the day, announcing his assumption of command, fell into our hands. It started with the words: "Soldiers, I am with you". (Rokossovsky, p. 204).

Model spent most of his time at the command post of 2nd *Panzer* Army. Hitler had issued his usual *Haltebefehl*, but in a less decisive manner than before. New theatres of operations had arisen in the Mediterranean. Partisan warfare was rapidly gaining strength in the Balkans. Manstein's Army Group South needed reserves, in order to face a threatening Russian offensive against Kharkov and the Donets basin.

In a situation meeting at the *Führerhauptquartier,* on 26 July 1943, a sharp exchange of views occurred between Hitler and von Kluge. Hitler demanded an evacuation of the Orel salient. Kluge objected. He felt that the retreat of Model's Armies had to be delayed because the "Hagen" line, which was foreseen as the rallying point for Model's two armies, and the positions around Karachev, were not yet sufficiently equipped.

Model withdrew 9th Army to its position before the beginning of *Zitadelle*, thus making six additional Divisions available to 2nd *Panzer* Army. Thereafter, he succeeded in bringing his two Armies back to the "Hagen" position.[86]

Rokossovsky wrote positively about Model's defensive tactics: "Stubborn resistance of the Nazis, who ably used their well-fortified lines. They battered through one position after another. The enemy resorted to mobile defence tactics. While some units held the defence, others occupied a new line, five to eight kilometres away. Time and again he counterattacked with *Panzer,* which he still possessed in adequate numbers. He also made wide use of manpower and material, manoeuvring within the inner line of his defences."[87]

Rokossovsky was critical of parts of the Red Army's performance during the offensive. He felt that a number of units were not sufficiently deployed in depth. In his opinion, it would have been preferable to attack on two separate lines, north and south of Bryansk. He was likewise critical of *Stavka's* continued pressure for urgency, which led to the neglect of attempting to form a *Kessel*.

The Russian Fronts participating in the offensive were Rokossovsky's Centre, which was the strongest, Bryansk under Popov, Voronezh under Vatutin, West commanded by Sokolovsky, and Steppe commanded by Konev.

Orel was taken by the Russians on 5 August. In spite of his disputes with von Kluge, Hitler had finally sided with him and issued an order forbidding him to give up the city. Von Kluge transmitted this order to Model under his own authority. Model refused to obey and replied to von Kluge that he would not sacrifice his troops for such nonsense. Von Kluge should inform Hitler accordingly.[88] Von Kluge persisted in his order and Model

---

86 Masson writes that the Hagen line was basically a "fiction" (Masson, p.275). Rokossovsky describes it as having been very strong. (Rokossovsky, p.210). One has to assume that the Russian General had a better view of the positions which were opposed to him than Masson. In the unpublished appendix to his recollections, Reichhelm's conclusions about the Hagen retreat make little sense. He writes that 9th Army and 2nd Panzer armies had severely weakened Red Army's offensive capacity. (p.46) Given the accelerated Russian advance until Winter 1943, this is one more example of his Model hero worship.

87 Rokossovsky, p.205.

88 This exchange of opinions between Kluge and Model is reported by Görlitz, p.155. As mentioned several times, accounts of word by word exchanges by Görlitz cannot be taken at face value. According to his sources at the end of the relevant chapter, he may have heard this from Major i.G. Gerd Niepold, Ia of 12 *Panzer* Division. The fact that Model evacuated Orel in direct contradiction to orders by Hitler and Kluge is not under dispute.

gave up Orel under his own responsibility. As a result, he was relieved as commander of 9th Army and replaced by General Harpe.

Model's dismissal as commander of 9th Army

On 5 November 1943 Model was suddenly relieved of his command and placed in the *Führerreserve OKH*.[89] The reasons for this sudden dismissal have never been clarified. It is conceivable that Hitler saw Model's evacuation of Orel, against his own orders, and the order by von Kluge, as the last straw. He may also have grown tired of the increasing impertinence in Model's contradictions and he may have felt that the General needed "a rap on the knuckles". He obviously knew that he would employ him again. At that time it was difficult to find a suitable replacement for a commander of Model's quality. Model's son told the author that his father made repeated attempts through personal friends to find out the cause for Hitler's sudden displeasure.[90]

Model's worries were clearly expressed in a number of his letters. On 8 December 1943 he wrote to General Friessner:

In spite of my hope for a quick clarification, nothing positive has occurred. A Condor plane landed here during an alert exercise, but it was not intended for me.[91]

On 30 December 1943 he wrote to General Gollnick:

I can't tell anything new about me, since after my quick relief the foreseen redress did not occur. I can thus enjoy a lengthy vacation. As a change, this is also pleasant.[92]

On 23 December 1943 Model wrote to General Wiese:

Unfortunately I have to accept that the original intention of my new assignment did not materialize. Instead I am now enjoying a lengthy vacation. Art of war knows sudden changes, one has to accept them and eventually they have their positive sides."[93]

This would appear to have been wishful thinking. Model had no idea of any 'original' intention. Had he known about it, he would have specified it.

On 27 December 1943 he wrote to Lieutenant Colonel Filbig: "I now have an agreeable vacation and I await the call to other duties."[94]

---

89 *Führerreserve* was a pool at *OKH*, *OKL* and *OKM* which contained all officers on the active list who at a given moment did not have an active command. If an officer were transferred to another command, he stayed in the *Führerreserve* for the day or the number of days taken by the transfer. If he was not given another command, he remained in the *Führerreserve* until his eventual removal from the active list.

90 Winrich Behr told the author that Model was always anxious to learn what was said about him in the *Führerhauptquartier*.

91 Estate, Letter to Friessner, 8 December 1943.

92 Estate, Letter to Gollnick, 30 December 1943.

93 Estate, Letter to Wiese, 20 December 1943.

94 Estate, Letter to Filbig, 27 December 1943.

Conceivably, Hitler did not know at first what he should do with Model. He let him 'stew' for two months in his home at Dresden. Rumour had it that there were thoughts of having Model replacing Fromm as commander of the *Ersatzheer*. That would have been a grievous mistake. Model's military comrades had to put up with his manner. The many top managers of industry and finance, with whom the *Ersatzheer* was in daily contact, would not have tolerated it.

After two months of 'welcome vacation', Model was called to the *Führerhauptquartier*, where he stayed for one month. He took part in the daily situation meetings. On 1 January 1944 Model was appointed *OB* of Army Group North.

6

OB of Army Groups North, *Nordukraine* and Centre

M odel's successive commands of the three Army Groups in the East lasted six months. During the first five months, events followed the general pattern of the Eastern front, after the battles for Kursk – continued advances by the Red Army in the Centre and the South, with short interruptions due to logistical necessities. Three momentous events occurred during the last month of Model's presence in the East, the Russian offensive, *Bagration* with the destruction of Army Group Centre, the failed attempt to kill Hitler on 20 July 1944, and the Warsaw Uprising.

Section 1: Army Group North

Developments at Army Group North
On 9 January 1944, Model replaced *Generalfeldmarschall* Georg von Küchler as *OB* of Army Group North. Hitler's original intention had been to relieve *Feldmarschall* Erich von Manstein and appoint Model as his successor. But a sudden crisis had developed in the North, after the Russians succeeded in breaking through the German blockade of Leningrad. Hitler apparently felt that a new and more energetic commander of the Army Group was needed. At this point in the war, there was always an immediate search for a scapegoat after every set-back.

Generalfeldmarschall Georg von Küchler
Georg von Küchler had succeeded *Feldmarschall* Ritter von Leeb at the first major reshuffling of the high command positions, in the East, after the catastrophe in the winter of 1941/42. During the battle for France, Küchler had commanded 18th Army. It had entered Paris after the French capital had been declared an open city. Hitler's decision to attack Russia was taken immediately after the victory over France. Küchler's Army was the first major unit transferred to the East in summer 1940. Conceivably, Küchler was considered the best man available for that first build up. Before the war he had commanded I Corps in East Prussia, at that time the most important *Wehrmacht* ground command. The assault upon Leningrad was to be launched from East Prussia.

By 5 August 1940, 18th Army's Chief of Staff, *Generalmajor* Erich Marcks, had submitted the first detailed plan for an invasion of Russia. Parts of it were then included in the final *Barbarossa* plan of 18 December 1940.[1] Both German and foreign historians described Küchler as a somewhat blurred personality. Brett-Smith wrote: "Of all Hitler's

---

1   General Marcks was killed in action at St. Lô in June 1944, a few days after the beginning of *Overlord*.

Field-Marshals, the one who seems to us most shadowy today is Georg von Küchler."[2] To this date, the most comprehensive attempt of an analysis of Küchler is an essay by Johannes Hürter.[3] But even Hürter's study contains a number of question marks. "How was it possible?" "Who was that General?" etc.

Küchler's personality is indeed difficult to gauge. In Poland he was *OB* of 3rd Army. He was among the commanders who had voiced the strongest protests against the first German excesses. He had attracted Himmler's ire when he described the SS as the shame of Germany. As a result, Küchler was the only Army *OB* in Poland who was not promoted to *Generaloberst* after the campaign. A year later, he made a complete turn around and after his arrival in East Prussia he issued increasingly strange orders.[4] At first, he admonished his commanders and soldiers "to abstain from any criticism of the treatment of the Polish minorities [sic], Jews and clerics."[5] On 22 June 1940 followed another order: "The ethnic struggle, *Volkstumskampf,* that has gone on over centuries on our Eastern borders, will require a final solution with sharp measures. The soldier has to stay clear of their activities, which he is not allowed to criticize.[6] Special bodies of the state, and the party [Küchler refers to the *Einsatzgruppen*], have been entrusted with the conduct of this ethnic war."

Throughout the war, Küchler was very popular with his soldiers.[7] For cruelty in Russia he yielded to none. He was a ruthless executor of the "Commissar-order". A typical entry in his war diary read: "Nothing special to report. 18 commissars were shot."[8] He intensified the brutal famine policy against Leningrad which had been initiated by Ritter von Leeb. He co-operated actively with *Einsatzgruppe* A. In his trial before the IMT (Case 12) he was indicted for the massacre of 240 female inmates in an asylum for mentally deranged at Makeyevka.[9] He was sentenced to 20 years. He was released after a few years.

With more than 40 divisions, Army Group North was the strongest of the three Army groups in the East. Fighting in the North had been stationary after the initial assault against Leningrad had failed. However, the Army Group stood close to the East Prussian border. The fear of seeing Red Army units penetrate the German homeland caused it to be retained stronger than immediate military necessities required.

---

2   Brett-Smith, p.94.

3   J. Hürter, ,Konservative Mentalität, militärischer Pragmatismus, ideologisierte Kriegführung: Das Beispiel des Generals Georg von Küchler', in G. Hirschfeld/T. Jersak (ed.) *Karrieren im Nationalsozialismus. Funktionseliten zwischen Mitwirkung und Distanz,* Frankfurt 2004, p. 239-255.

4   Hürter feels that Küchler, like many German Generals, fell to the euphoria of the rapid victory over France.

5   NOKW 1531.

6   Ibid.

7   Brett-Smith recalls a talk with one of Küchler's subordinates: "The men in his army speak in the most glowing terms of his fatherly care for his soldiers – how he would stand by a wounded man while shots were popping all around him, until the first aid could arrive. They told me with pride how he ventured out to the front lines day after day, sitting in the side-car of a motorcycle." Brett-Smith, p.95.

8   Küchler, Diary, 18 July 1941.

9   Entry in the diary of XXVIII Corps, 25 December 1941, with the mention: The *Herr Oberbefehlshaber* has agreed to the solution of the problem. [sic]

After Küchler assumed command of his army group, frictions arose between him and his Army commanders, *Generaloberst* Georg Lindemann and *Generaloberst* Ernst Busch. Küchler was on friendly personal terms with Lindemann, but disagreed with some of his operational views. He had no respect for Busch, and made several unsuccessful attempts to have him relieved. By the end of 1943 Küchler began showing signs of ageing. Disagreements between him and *Generaloberst* Lindemann increased.

After Kluge was incapacitated by a car accident in summer 1943, Busch replaced him as *OB* of Army Group Centre. General Christian Hansen became *OB* of 16th Army. During Model's command of Army Group North, his relations with Hansen were very good,[10] but with Lindemann they were less so. Lindemann, in spite of his disagreements with Küchler, had remained attached to his former commander and resented his replacement by Model.

After the Russians had broken through the blockade around Leningrad, Küchler proposed to Hitler a retreat to the "Panther" position. The Ia of 18th Army, Colonel Friedrich Foertsch, was present. He felt that Küchler's presentation was somewhat less than propitious.[11]

Incidents on Model's assumption of command

No reader will be surprised that unpleasant incidents took place. However, it has never been established what happened between Küchler and Model on that day. After the war, Küchler refused to comment. When questioned by Leppa, his reply was very elegantly phrased: "With regard to your query of 21 October 1955, I am unwilling to say anything about what occurred in January 1944, when *Feldmarschall* Model relieved me, but to remain true to the maxim, *De mortuis nihil nisi bonum*".[12] A few days later, Army Group's Chief of Staff, *Generalleutnant* Eberhard Kinzel, appeared at *OKH*. General Heusinger related Kinzel's talk with General Zeitzler:

Kinzel:

I request a new assignment as soon as possible. I find it impossible to continue working with Model.

Zeitzler:

I have heard this many times. But I can't appoint new Chiefs of Staff every time Model appears somewhere. The *Führer* always sends him to places which are burning.

Kinzel:

Our differences simply can't be bridged. I can't say one thing today and the opposite on the next. I have always agreed with old man Küchler, who more than once told the *Führer* that the edge of the front line, stretching from the Volkhov river to the gates of Leningrad can't be defended. He repeatedly asked for permission to withdraw. I

---

10 Model had proposed Hansen for promotion to *Generaloberst*. Hitler refused.

11 After the war, General Friedrich Foertsch became Heusinger's successor as inspector general of the *Bundeswehr*.

12 BA-MA, N6/1.

am glad that he remained stubborn and preferred to be relieved. Then Model arrives with orders to keep the front line intact. Not surprisingly the Russians have broken through at a number of points.

Zeitzler:

You are now living through the same experience which we had in the South. We are fighting 'windmills'. I hope that you will somehow succeed in retreating to the Peipus line. Perhaps matters will improve then. But until that occurs, you have to stay where you are. However, I promise you that you will not have to stay with Model for ever.

Kinzel:

At least I am satisfied as far as my own future is concerned.[13]

Model spent close to three months at Army Group North. Kinzel remained with him during the whole period and altercations with Model continued. On one such occasion in March 1944, Model phoned Kinzel during the early morning hours and requested his presence. Kinzel replied that he had barely gone to bed and that a Chief of Staff was also entitled to some sleep. Model insisted, and Kinzel appeared in pyjamas and a bathrobe. Model snorted at him: "Impossible clothing! An impertinence!" Model was so furious that, while preparing to fly to the front line, he climbed up on a wing of his plane and dictated an order about "rules of sleeping at Army Group North."[14] Kinzel phoned Krebs, at that time Chief of Staff of Army Group Centre, and said: "He is completely insane, but he is the only one who has not noticed it."[15]

(Kinzel was one of the Generals who took part in the partial surrender to Montgomery, a few days before Germany's unconditional surrender. He committed suicide in 1945).

Model then had a talk with Friedrich Foertsch and told him that he had to restore the trust of troops in their commanders. Foertsch replied testily that such trust had never been impaired and that no further encouragements by Model were necessary.[16]

The *Waffen*-SS orderly

When Model took over his new command, he requested Schmundt to provide him with an orderly. Schmundt told him that army regulations did not authorize the commander of an Army Group to have an orderly. On the following day, Model paid a visit to Hitler's headquarters and vented his anger on SS *Gruppenführer* Hermann Fegelein whom he met

---

13 A Heusinger, *Befehl im Widerstreit. Schicksalsstunden der deutschen Armee 1923-1945*, Tübingen 1950, p.293 ff. Quotations from Heusinger's book require careful examination since a number of chapters serve the purpose by Heusinger to paint himself and commanders whom he respected as opponents of NS policy and blame Hitler's stubbornness for all reversals. However this scene is typical for the reactions of chiefs of staff who found themselves suddenly under Model's authority.

14 Told by Model's *Waffen-SS* orderly, SS-*Hauptsturmführer* Rudolph Maeker. Estate, 26 April 1963.

15 Told by General Peter von der Groeben, 24 November 1970, Estate.

16 Foertsch letter to Görlitz, 19 July 1975.

by chance. Fegelein was a shady figure. In 1941, he had commanded a Cavalry Division of the SS that assisted the *Einsatzgruppen* in the massacre of Jews. He would play a major role in quashing the 1944 Warsaw Uprising.[17]

Fegelein was elated when he heard of Model's request for an orderly and immediately reported this to Himmler, who saw an opportunity to have a *Waffen* SS officer placed close to a high-ranking Army commander. Himmler assigned SS *Hauptsturmführer* Rudolph Maeker as Model's orderly. In his statements made after the war, Maeker always insisted that he never considered his post as a liaison between the Army Group and the *Waffen* SS. However, things are seldom as idyllic as memoir writers want them to look. In 1941, Maeker had been an assistant to Fegelein and had been present at the massacre of the Jews in the Pripet swamps.[18] Maeker was severely wounded on 22 July 1944, and replaced by SS *Sturmbannführer* Heinrich Springer. Springer's memoirs show him to have remained an incorrigible Nazi.[19]

After the war, Model's decision to employ an orderly from the *Waffen* SS was strongly criticized. There must also have been some grumblings at that time. General Hermann Balck came to Model's defence. After describing a violent incident with Model, hardly an unusual experience, he added:

> General Raus, my *OB*, talked with me about Model. We both agreed that he causes much unnecessary trouble. On the other side, he is often successful. In times of peace, his behaviour would not be tolerated, but now he bears the weight of tremendous responsibilities and that has to be taken into account. Model's strong side was that he had good relations with Hitler. He always showed his political orientation. One such step was that he took a *Waffen-SS* officer as orderly, a decision that was criticized by a number of fools. That Model succeeded in obtaining much from Hitler, and thus helped the troops, was apparently indifferent to them. Finally, there was a commander not subject to Hitler's permanent mistrust.[20]

17　Later Fegelein married the sister of Eva Braun and became Hitler's brother-in-law. During the last week of the battle for Berlin, he deserted from the Bunker. Hitler gave orders to find him and he was discovered in his apartment in Berlin. He was brought back to the Bunker and summarily shot.

18　M. Cüppers, *Wegbereiter der Shoah. Die Waffen-SS, der Kommandostab Reichsführer-SS und die Judenvernichtung 1939-1945*, Darmstadt 2005, p.318.(henceforth Cüppers). After the war, Maeker was accepted in the *Bundeswehr* and rose to Lieutenant Colonel.

19　H. Springer, *Stationen eines Lebens in Krieg und Frieden – Zeitgeschichtliches Zeugnis des SS-Sturmbannführers und Ritterkreuzträgers der Leibstandarte-SS 'Adolf Hitler'*, Berlin 1996, p.119-131.

20　H. Balck, *Ordnung im Chaos. Erinnerungen 1893-1948*, p.514. Newton must have used an incorrect translation of Balck's book when he writes that Balck castigated Model for inappropriate comments of his SS aide. (Newton, p.282) The only reference to Model's *Waffen* SS orderly, (not aide), is in the passage quoted above. Furthermore Balck could hardly castigate Model. Model was a *Generaloberst* and *OB* of an Army Group. Balck had only recently been promoted from *Generalleutnant* to *General der Panzertruppe* and had received a corps command more or less at the same time Model took over Army Group North.

Baltic 'volunteer' fantasy

Sometime early in 1944, Model toyed with the idea of creating Baltic volunteer units, and he issued a "general mobilization" order to Estonia and Latvia. When the *Wehrmacht* had attacked the USSR in 1941, the Lithuanians, the Latvians and the Estonians had welcomed the Germans. The Lithuanians and the Latvians had taken an active part in the atrocities against the Jews. A number of them had served as guards in the extermination camps. Baltic SS units were created. There were only a few Jews in Estonia, but all were murdered.

Model's ideas are a typical example of a political ignoramus who suddenly feels an urge to dabble in matters with a complicated political horizon. Model knew that the Baltic nations had been forcibly incorporated into the USSR, and he felt that they would therefore be prepared to fight alongside the *Wehrmacht* as the Red Army came closer to their borders. But like all *Wehrmacht* commanders, Model never understood the national problems of the Soviet Union. Hatred of the Soviet Union had prevailed in the Baltic provinces, but in 1944, when it was clear that Germany was losing the war, new concerns arose. The intelligentsia in the Baltic nations understood that the Third *Reich* was no longer a viable alternative. Neither, of course, was the Soviet Union. Their only hope was that the Western Allies would bring Soviet expansion to a halt. The United States had never recognized the annexation of the three Baltic States and had not closed their legations in Washington DC. That was their single ray of hope. No attention was paid to Model's pipe dream.

Treuegelöbnis – The 'pledge of faith' of the Field Marshals

Many of the senior German officers who were taken prisoner of war at Stalingrad, joined two bodies established by the Russians: the *Nationalkomitee Freies Deutschland-NKFD* (National Committee for a Free Germany) and the *Bund Deutscher Offiziere-BDO* (Association of German Officers). The most prominent officer in the *BDO* was General von Seydlitz-Kurzbach, the scion of a famous Prussian military family.

The captured officers began writing letters to former comrades, imploring them to lay down their arms. General von Seydlitz-Kurzbach wrote to Model, whom he had known well before the war. The letters were to no avail because the German Generals discarded appeals to common sense and continued to live under the illusion that they were fighting out of duty to the fatherland. Nevertheless, there was increasing concern at the *Führerhauptquartier* that the appeals, which were also broadcast over loudspeakers at the front line, might influence some of the troops. Schmundt was motivated to draft a "pledge of faith". The document was signed by all *Feldmarschalls* who held active troop command, and by Model, even though he was still a *Generaloberst*.

The signed pledge was then handed to Hitler on 30 March 1944, not surprisingly by the servile Rundstedt. The document was a product of the worst Nazi propaganda jargon. It contained expressions such as "contemptuous treason of our holy cause by General von Seydlitz-Kurzbach;" "heinous attitude;" "knowledge that you, *mein Führer*, remain close to your officers and soldiers and that you are convinced that this is just a case of isolated treason," "we feel the need to assure you that we have cut all ties with these cowardly traitors who have trodden upon the holiest principles of the German officers," and so forth. The document was signed by von Rundstedt, Rommel, von Kleist, Busch, von Kluge, von Manstein, von Weichs and Model.

Manstein strongly criticized the document in *Verlorene Siege*. Given his dislike of Model, he made a special point of Model not yet being a *Feldmarschall*.[21] However, no officer in his right mind would have refused to sign such a paper. One cannot exclude that Model was flattered by the request to have himself singled out as a *Generaloberst* among the signatories.

Model was informed of his promotion to *Feldmarschall* one day after he had signed the document. Hitler apparently attached considerable weight to Model's name being on it. He may have feared that the appeals could influence some troops and he knew that Model was particularly close to front line units.

Retreat of Army Group North

The only major operation of Army Group North under Model was the retreat to the "Panther" line. Hitler had turned down a similar proposal from Küchler, but finally acceded to Model's arguments. Apparently a "Panther-psychosis" arose in Army Group North, which led Model to forbid any further use of the words "Panther line". Model wrote Lindemann a conciliatory message, in which he appealed for trust, and reminded Lindemann of their former cooperation.[22] At a later stage, *"Armeegruppe Narva"* under Friessner was added, in order to halt the Russian advance along the Baltic seacoast. Friessner had commanded a Corps at 9th Army under Model. Model held him in high regard but, at times, Friessner could also become victim of Model's temper. He recalled that on one occasion Model intended to 'finish him off' during the fighting at Rzhev. On a later occasion, Model gave Friessner a dressing-down in the presence of his subordinates because some Alsatian soldiers had deserted, and he held Friessner responsible for their actions. Friessner requested immediate transfer but, as so often, the incidents ended in reconciliation.[23]

Model made several attempts to acquire officers from his former staffs whom he knew and respected. He requested Reichhelm as Ia. Reichhelm joined Army Group North staff in March 1944. Eight days after his arrival, Schmundt appeared and informed Model that he had to take over Army Group *Nordukraine*. When Model left, Kinzel issued a message to the troops, "Schweinfurt". It was not a reference to the city of Schweinfurt. Kinzel chose the name to imply *"Schwein fort,"* meaning the swine is gone.

---

21 *Verlorene Siege*, p.607.
22 NOKW 141.
23 After the war, Friessner became President of the "Association of German Soldiers". (*VDS = Verband deutscher Soldaten*). Friessner showed himself to have remained an incorrigible Nazi, both in his statements in Germany and also in interviews with foreign newspapers. He was increasingly criticized abroad, also in such major newspapers as the *New York Times*, *The (London) Times*, the French *Le Monde* and the Swiss *Basler Nationalzeitung*. A reporter of *The (London) Times* asked him if the German soldiers had known in 1939 why they had attacked Poland and Friessner replied: "Yes, of course the German soldier knew. The red flood had to be stopped and the border population had to be protected from the squabbling and chicanery of the Poles." *Times*, 22 September 1951. In 1952, the "Friessner crisis" led to his removal. For details, B. O. Manig, *Die Politik der Ehre. Die Rehabilitierung der Berufssoldaten in der frühen Bundesrepublik*, Göttingen 2004, p.401-447.

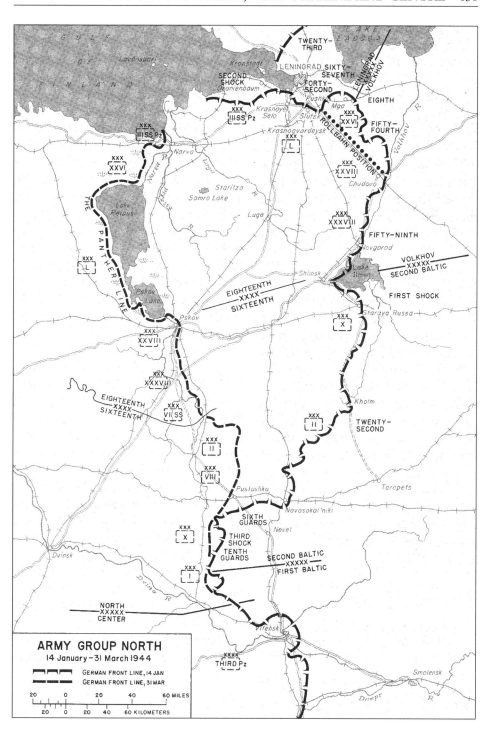

ARMY GROUP NORTH
14 January – 31 March 1944

GERMAN FRONT LINE, 14 JAN
GERMAN FRONT LINE, 31 MAR

Incidents between Model and Lindemann after Model's appointment as *OB* of Army Group *Nordukraine*

Generaloberst Georg Lindemann succeeded Model as *OB* of Army Group North. Apparently Model was under the illusion that he could still issue orders to his former Army Group. On 30 May 1944, Model was at Berchtesgaden to receive Hitler's instructions for his new command and to be informed of his promotion to *Feldmarschall*. He asked Reichhelm to phone Lindemann with an order to withdraw five Divisions from Army Group North and send them to his new Army Group.[24] On the same day a heated exchange occurred between Model and Lindemann over the telex:

Model:

The position taken by Army Group North is diametrically opposed to what I reported to the Führer.

Lindemann:

I have only repeated what General Hansen has told me.

Model:

Now the Army Group says that the Divisions can only be transferred on 20 April. Only yesterday, the date was 5 April. It is impossible that the judgment of Army Group has changed to such an extent.

Lindemann:

The judgment of Army Group has not changed. We must abide by the premises which I described in my telex. This is what General Hansen has always said.

Model:

20 April is impossible. I appeal to your understanding and to your *esprit de corps*.

Lindemann:

15 April is the earliest possible. Furthermore OKH has ordered that nothing can be transferred without permission by the Führer.

Model:

I never ordered you to release any Divisions, I was only taking preparatory measures. I don't know who began to meddle between us, but I will find out. But I have to report to the Führer about all possibilities. Then he can give an order, but he must have full knowledge before reaching a decision.

---

24 BA-MA, RH 19 III/ 277 a.

Lindemann:

I will see to it that 15 April is possible.

Model:

But everything must be ready at that date. The situation may also require an earlier one. There is no sense in holding the position in the North if this results in the loss of the war in the South. I will report to the Führer in this spirit.

Lindemann:

But the premises outlined by me remain. I am expecting an order from the Führer, before this nothing will be done.

Model:

Obviously, such an order is required. You will have to accept whatever disadvantages may arise. The Führer has to decide. We remain with the date of 15 April.

Lindemann:

Yes and I will be waiting for an order by the Führer.[25]

At that point Zeitzler lost patience and told Lindemann to simply disregard Model's messages.

Lindemann was relieved after two months and replaced by Friessner. A few weeks later, Friessner was relieved by Schörner, who was in turn replaced by Hilpert. Hilpert remained *OB* of the remainders of the Army Group until Germany's surrender. During the last months of the war, new Army Groups were created, existing Army Groups were dissolved and commanders were moved at short intervals.

Section 2: Army Group *Nordukraine*

On 31 March 1944, *Feldmarschall* von Manstein was relieved as commander of Army Group South, which was renamed Army Group *Nordukraine*. On the same day, *Feldmarschall* von Kleist was dismissed as *OB* of Army Group A. It was renamed Army Group *Südukraine* and placed under the command of General Ferdinand Schörner, who was promoted to *Generaloberst*. Manstein and Model met briefly. Their encounter was cool, but without altercation. Upon learning from Hitler that Model was to succeed him, Manstein had made some condescending remarks. Model displayed better manners. Model had led a successful operation that broke through the *Kessel* of *Generaloberst* Hube's 1st *Panzer* Army. Hitler congratulated him and Model replied that he had only completed an operation his predecessor had planned and initiated.

---

25 Facsimile in Model/Bradley, p.162 ff.

Manstein's staff officers were exceptionally devoted to him, and requested reassignments when Model took command. General Theodor Busse, the Chief of Staff, who had served under Model in the *Reichswehr* in a junior command, had to remain, since uninterrupted staff work was a requirement. The Ia, Colonel Georg Schulze-Büttger, asked for a transfer which Model refused, because he felt that he could not dispense with an Ia who was familiar with the needs of his new Army Group. Schulze-Büttger became one of the victims of 20 July 1944.

There was never any doubt that major Russian offensives would be launched in the summer of 1944. Nevertheless, Hitler issued the following directive (*Weisung*) on 2 April 1944: "The Russian offensive in the southern area of the front has already passed its climax. The Russians have worn out their units and dispersed them. The time has come to halt the Russian advance. I have already taken the measures required."[26]

After taking a more realistic overall view, *OKH* believed that a Russian offensive would first be directed toward Galicia and Lvov. Model wanted to launch a preventive attack. He obtained the transfer of LVI *Panzer* Corps from Army Group Centre to his own command. Busch was obviously annoyed and complained to Hitler. By that time, every German commander was in need of additional units. Since no reserves were available, they requested troops from other formations whose commanders strongly objected.

The Red Army was a master in disguising its movements. That made the task of German intelligence increasingly difficult. During the whole war, German intelligence was deficient. During the first days of June, both Busch and Model had begun to realize that there was movement against Army Group Centre. Their reports to *OKH* and to Hitler proved to be useless. When the intentions of the Red Army became clear, it was too late to prepare counter-measures.

Model released a series of instructions. Basically he simply repeated similar orders of his own when he assumed any new major command.[27] General Reuter commented on the difference between Manstein's and Model's methods of command: "I feel that I cannot voice a definite opinion as to the value of both methods. As long as conditions did not get out of control, Manstein's method of leading from behind was certainly preferable. When total confusion arose, Model's leading from the front line cannot be dismissed out of hand."[28]

Section 3: Army Group Centre

Bagration rout, 20 July 1944 – The Warsaw Uprising

No operations of major importance took place at Army Group *Nordukraine*, before Model was given the additional command of Army Group Centre on 28 June 1944. On 22 June, the Russians had launched the massive *Bagration* offensive. A hybrid situation developed which lasted until Model was sent to the West on 17 August. *Generaloberst* Harpe formally became commander of Army Group *Nordukraine*, but since Model knew that Harpe was not up to a command of an Army Group, he had *OKH* issue an order: "All reports by

---

26 Estate, War diary entry of Army Group Centre, 2 April 1944.
27 Positioning of Infantry Divisions in defence, optimal utilization of *Panzer* units, systems of counter-attacks, replacement of lost individual arms. All these instructions in facsimile in Model/Bradley p.169-180.
28 Estate, Reuter on tape, undated.

Army Group *Nordukraine* have to be sent to *Feldmarschall* Model. *Feldmarschall* Model has to agree to every order by Army Group *Nordukraine* before compliance. In the event *Feldmarschall* Model cannot be reached, any order issued by *Generaloberst* Harpe has to state this explicitly. *Feldmarschall* Model has then to report to *OKH* is he is in agreement with such orders."[29]

A more absurd system would be difficult to imagine. Harpe had a very good Chief of Staff in *Generalmajor* Rudolf Ritter von Xylander,[30] and Reichhelm remained as Ia of Army Group *Nordukraine* until he joined Model in the West. Even an outstanding staff cannot replace a commander. Perhaps Model had fallen victim to some early megalomania. Model knew that *Bagration* would tax his capacities to the limit and that he would have no time for simultaneous supervision of Army Group *Nordukraine*. There were sufficient good Army *OB* who could have taken over *Nordukraine*. Harpe's limitations as a commander were no secret and by the *OKH* order, Model had them come into the open in an official document. (Model may have felt that *Bagration* could spill over to the area controlled by Army Group *Nordukraine* and that the two Army Groups, Centre and *Nordukraine*, would become one entity).[31]

Model had also to oversee the co-ordination of his movements with Army Group North. After the start of the *Bagration* offensive, Army Group North was attacked by the Front of General Bagramyan, and came under an increasing threat of being separated from Army Group Centre. During his remaining time in the East, Model in practice became Supreme Commander East, a position that Manstein had repeatedly endeavoured to obtain for himself.

Hans Krebs had remained Chief of Staff of Army Group Centre. It consisted of four armies: 3rd *Panzer* Army (*Generaloberst* Reinhardt), 4th Army (at first *Generaloberst* Heinrici, then General Kurt von Tippelskirch, and finally General Hossbach), 9th Army (first General Hans Jordan, and after the dismissal of General Jordan on 27 June 1944, General Nikolaus von Vormann), and 2nd Army (*Generaloberst* Walter Weiss). Hungarian troops were part of the Army Group's reserve.

At a meeting with Hitler on 20 May, Busch had recommended shortening his front line. He received the angry reply that he had "apparently joined the generals who would always look backwards." After this dressing-down, Busch became totally passive. He simply referred to Hitler's orders when responding to objections voiced by his Army commanders. In his memoirs, Zhukov criticized Busch's leadership: "While we observed the German command and their troops during the offensive, we were surprised by their serious mistakes. Instead of quickly retreating to rear lines, and bringing strong covering units to their flanks, the Germans allowed themselves to become embroiled in long battles, both east and northeast of Minsk."[32] Albert Seaton wrote that Zhukov's criticism was undoubtedly justified, but added that Zhukov had to know why Busch acted as he did,

---

29 Facsimile in Model/Bradley, p.195 ff.

30 General von Xylander was promoted to *Generalleutnant* on 1 December 1944. He died in an airplane crash on 15 February 1945.

31 In January 1945, Harpe was demoted as army goup *OB* and given command of 5th *Panzer* Army.

32 Zhukov, p.561.

since in 1941, Zhukov himself had been repeatedly forced to obey illogical orders from the stubborn Stalin.[33]

Feste Plätze – The stronghold scheme

On 8 March 1944, Hitler had introduced a new variation of the *Haltebefehl*, known as the *Feste Plätze* (singular *Fester Platz*. The term carries connotations of fortresses or strongholds.) His order stated that *Feste Plätze* had to be assimilated into fortresses. If surrounded, they were to pin down the attackers, and later become the starting point for a counter-offensive. Every *Fester Platz* was to be commanded by a specially selected and tough General who would be responsible upon his soldier's honour, for the successful accomplishment of his duty until the very end. The commander of a *Fester Platz* was equal in authority to a Corps Commander. A *Fester Platz* could only be evacuated upon an order from the *OB* of the Army Group, and the *OB* was required to obtain permission from Hitler in each instance.

The concept was of questionable value since it was based upon the assumption that the Red Army would direct its main attacks against the *Feste Plätze*. If the Soviets would not do Hitler this favour, the *Feste Plätze* would become an encumbrance. Within Army Group Centre, the cities of Bobruisk, Mogilev, Orsha, Vitebsk, Slutsk, and Minsk were initially turned into *Feste Plätze*. In due course, other cities would also be added to the list, including Baranovichi, Brest and Vilna.

Model's arrival at Army Group Centre was greeted with mixed reactions. In the war diary of 9th Army, there is a short mention: "The news of the assumption of command by *Feldmarschall* Model is received with confidence."[34]

General Peter von der Groeben, Ia of Army Group Centre, disagreed in part: "We knew Model, in particular from his command of Army Group North. We were confident that he would be able to obtain support from 'above'. Immediately after his arrival, Army Group Centre received two or three additional Divisions which Busch had requested several times in vain." [In fact, it was four Divisions, two transferred from Army Group North, and an activated *Panzer* Division, which was part of the reserve of Army Group Centre.][35] "But our main criticism was that he avoided arguments with Hitler."[36]

That last statement is unfair to Model. General von der Groeben refers to one specific instance. He had accompanied Model and Friessner to Hitler, in their attempt to obtain permission to evacuate the Courland peninsula. Hitler refused and Model told von der Groeben: "Stop getting excited, you can see that he simply does not want it."[37] One thing Model never avoided were arguments with Hitler. However, given the disastrous situation of Army Group Centre after the beginning of Operation *Bagration,* and the speed of the Russian advance, there was simply no time for protracted discussions at the *Führerhauptquartier.* Furthermore *Grossadmiral* Dönitz attended the meeting and Hitler probably did not want to yield to Model's entreaties in Dönitz's presence.

---

33 A. Seaton, *The Russo-German War 1941-1945*, New York 1962, p.459. (Henceforth Seaton).

34 G. Niepold, *Mittlere Ostfront Juni ,44. Darstellung, Beurteilung, Lehren,* Bonn 1987, p.149. (Henceforth Niepold).

35 Ibid, p.142 ff.

36 Estate, von der Groeben 24 November 1970.

37 Ibid.

Professor Hermann Gackenholz, a historian, who as a reserve Captain kept the diary of Army Group Centre, wrote after the war: "The esteem in which Hitler held our new commander resulted in his immediate agreement with measures taken by Model. At the staff of the Army Group this caused some surprise, given our past experience with his predecessor."[38]

Busch was upset at his dismissal, since he felt that he had only obeyed Hitler's order. It is not established if he met with Model when the command of the Army Group was transferred. Görlitz purports that a "friendly conversation" took place between the two.[39] Gackenholz, who was present, wrote that Busch had received advice from Zeitzler to meet with Model, but that he avoided it by departing before Model's arrival.[40]

The *Bagration* rout

The *Bagration* offensive was initially a fulfilment of Churchill's request for a major offensive in the East that would coincide with the Allied Operation *Overlord*. However, the situation had developed to the Red Army's advantage to such an extent that the offensive would have been launched anyway. The Russians chose the name of *Bagration*, because a General Bagration had defeated Napoleon on some of the same battlefields. The Soviet offensive began on 22 June 1944, exactly three years to the day after Germany had invaded Russia.

The offensive was preceded by a massive partisan strike. According to Soviet sources, some 240,000 partisans were concentrated in the area of Army Group Centre. On the night of June 19, more than 10,000 railroad communications towers were destroyed. When Model arrived, there was practically no connection between the Armies of the Army Group Centre. On 23 June, *Generaloberst* Reinhardt had administered a dressing-down to his Corps commanders. He said that "it was a scandal to talk about the loss of defensive power after only two days."[41]

Many of the *Feste Plätze* had already been captured, including Bobruisk, Vitebsk, Orsha and Mogilev. The subsequent surrender of Vilna was preceded by long discussions between Hitler and Model. Model finally convinced Hitler by telling him that the troops at Vilna had run out of drinking water. Hitler always remembered his experiences as a soldier in the front line during World War I and Model's argument must have impressed him. Hitler also knew that the town Commander whom he had appointed, *Luftwaffe*

---

38 H. Gackenholz, ,Der Zusammenbruch der Heeresgruppe Mitte 1944' in H. Jacobsen/J. Rohwer (ed.) *Entscheidungsschlachten des Zweiten Weltkrieges*, Frankfurt 1960, p.445-478, here p. 467. (Henceforth Gackenholz).

39 Görlitz , p.179.

40 Gackenholz, p.467. Busch became increasingly depressed after his dismissal. On 10 September 1944, Reinhardt wrote to Guderian that there were many rumours about Busch – some mention that he had taken his life, others that he had run over to the Russians. Reinhardt asked Guderian to have Hitler give a sign that Busch continued to enjoy his trust. When General Schmundt died of the wounds sustained on 20 July, Busch was asked to deliver the eulogy at his funeral. (S. Micham, 'Generalfeldmarschall Ernst Busch', in G. Ueberschär (ed): *Hitlers militärische Elite. Vom Kriegsbeginn bis zum Weltkriegsende*, Darmstadt 1998, p.25).

41 Niepold, p.76.

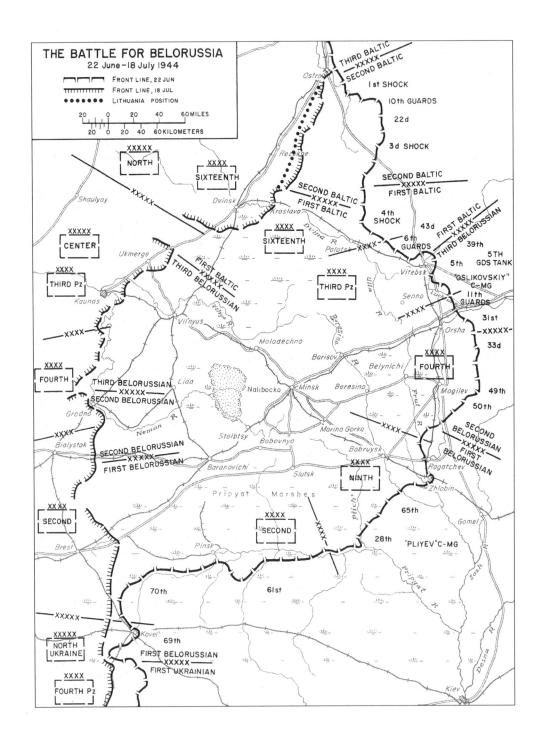

THE BATTLE FOR BELORUSSIA
22 June–18 July 1944

FRONT LINE, 22 JUN
FRONT LINE, 18 JUL
LITHUANIA POSITION

20   0   20   40   60 MILES

20   0   20   40   60 KILOMETERS

General Rainer Stahel, was known as a particularly tough commander and that he would not advise a retreat if it was avoidable.[42]

Chaos increased rapidly. 4th Army and 9th Army were no longer coherent units. There were no lines of communication between them. The Chief of Staff of 4th Army noted on 27 June that the front consisted of only disorganized masses. "Combat is conducted by officers with small assault parties without artillery support."[43] A report from the 134th Infantry Division, about the fighting near Bobruisk, stated that "no trace of order remained. Vehicles and heavy armour were simply blown up and troops escaped *en masse* over the remaining bridges."[44] Zhukov wrote that, "the German soldiers were running around like madmen. Either they gave themselves up or they were simply mown down."[45]

General Vincenz Müller, who had been a close associate of Schleicher in the 1920s, commanded XII Corps. He ordered his Corps to lay down their arms. When that was completed, he drove to the headquarters of the Russian General Boldin, told him that he wished to surrender and asked how to do this. General Boldin was surprised and replied: "This is very simple. Your soldiers lay down their arms and become prisoners of war. I guarantee treatment in accordance with international conventions."[46] *Bagration* resulted in the total loss of 20 German divisions. More than 250,000 German officers and soldiers were taken prisoner. Eight Corps and Division commanders were killed in action, or committed suicide. 17 Generals were taken prisoner, and a number joined the *BDO*.

Major Red Army offensives had developed on other fronts. In the north, the Red Army approached the borders of East Prussia. The Balkans were overrun. Romania and Bulgaria switched sides and declared war on Germany. Finland had concluded an armistice with the Soviet Union. The Red Army had progressed to the outskirts of Warsaw. A lull in the fighting around Warsaw followed, until 18 January 1945. Red Army offensives had swept the *Wehrmacht* out of Russian territory in less than two months, had driven them back into the centre of Poland and into parts of the Baltic States. It was the worst rout the *Wehrmacht* had ever experienced.

Model's Staff

Neither Krebs nor Model bore grudges against each other, even though they had been on opposite sides of their altercations while planning the Operation *Zitadelle* offensive. In spite of what he may have thought at the time, Krebs had been Kluge's Chief of Staff and had to support his commander's opinions. Model was obviously aware of this and did not hold it against him. But Krebs was not spared Model's occasional outbursts. Colonel Hermann Teske wrote in his memoirs that he complained to Krebs on one occasion about Model's personal insults and that Krebs replied: "What do you want? Only yesterday he threatened me, his old Chief of Staff, with court-martial. But the man has unbelievable

---

42 Prior to his appointment at Vilna, General Stahel had been town commander of Rome. He died 1955 in the Russian POW camp at Voikovo.

43 Niepold, p.122.

44 Ibid, p.129.

45 Zhukov, p.580.

46 General Vincenz Müller immediately joined the East German Army (the *NVA*). After the war, he became Chief of the General Staff *(Hauptstab)* of the *NVA*. In 1961 he committed suicide. In 1941/42 he was chief of staff of 17th Army and cooperated actively with *Einsatzgruppe* C.

capability and here he is our sole hope."[47] (Model constantly threatened with courts-martial, however most of the threats remained empty.)

Model's methods during *Bagration*

Model remained true to his habit of leading from the front. It could not be avoided, given the panic which had gripped many troops. But it likewise had a negative consequence. Model's outbursts against his already strained subordinate commander conveyed the impression that he simply accepted Hitler's orders without contradiction.

Generalleutnant (*Bundeswehr*) Gerd Niepold, during *Bagration* Ia of 12th *Panzer* Division, wrote:

> How are the opinions of Hitler and *Generalfeldmarschall* Model to be judged, when they proposed to attack eastward of the Niemen river in the direction of Minsk? One can hardly assume that Model really believed that he could achieve more than a delaying action, with only three *Panzer* Divisions on a front of 100 kilometres. Model was much too knowledgeable not to see the situation as it really was, and also how it would be judged by the Army *OB* and the Corps and Division commanders. Perhaps the intention of his repeated orders to attack was to give the appearance of accommodating Hitler, in order to be able to prepare the later retreats. He may also have felt that limited, short, offensive actions would keep the troops in active shape, and therefore, in order to save what could be saved, capable of meeting the first units of attack from the Red Army. *Feldmarschall* Model thus showed himself as a most meritorious commander in balancing between the utopian visions of Hitler and the objections of his subordinate commanders. Displaying great capacity of judgment and energy, he always found the best solution. But saving his Army Group and the Eastern Front was beyond his means.[48]

General Peter von der Groeben is again critical:

> Leading from the front line had some advantages, but the orders given by Model often did not take the overall situation into account. He flew to the front line every day at 8 am and returned to his staff late in the afternoon. Turbulent meetings at his staff followed, and he went to sleep around 10 pm. His behaviour, and his tone towards subordinates who were unable to react, was rude and personally insulting, both with officers of his staff and with troop commanders who had arrived for reporting. All this was unnecessary. When he encountered resistance, he resorted to cheap behaviour.[49]

The British historian Albert Seaton joined in that opinion:

> Model kept up a display of energy as he toured the battle area, livening up his divisions. He often left a trail of disorder behind him, losing some of the confidence

---

47 Teske, p.217.

48 G. Niepold, *Mittlere Ostfront Juni '44. Darstellung. Beurteilung. Lehren*, Herford 1985, p.194.

49 Estate, von der Groeben, 24 November 1970.

and the respect of his subordinates, by wanton interference in details which were not his concern.[50]

This is unfair to Model. Since no coherent command structure under him had remained in place, every detail was certainly his concern.

Model resorted again to the breaking up of units. He withdrew individual battalions from their regiments. Then he used them for isolated counter-attacks, in order to maintain some cohesion between larger units, while preventing another collapse of the front line. In this situation he had no choice. *Generalleutnant (Bundeswehr)* Gerd Niepold was complimentary:

> *Feldmarschall* Model was a matchless master of such operations. Always personally at the focal points, his method of command was tough, ruthless and full of high risk, but it had a stroke of genius. He removed battalions from sectors which were not under immediate threat, used them to plug holes in sectors which had been partially overrun, and followed on with short counter-attacks. This allowed restoration of continuity at the front, and prevented a new breakdown of the Army Group. Breaking up of units was now a lesser evil. Unlike his predecessor, *Feldmarschall* Busch, *Feldmarschall* Model enjoyed Hitler's trust, to the extent that Hitler was now able to trust anyone. Model refrained from endless requests. He often acted on his own and thereafter reported his decisions.[51]

General Peter von der Groeben wrote:

> He was totally ruthless in breaking up units, and would personally supervise bringing battalions into new positions. He usually flew the battalions' commanders to their new positions, in his plane, and saw that their units rapidly followed on.[52]

Zhukov praised Model's actions:

> I have to admit that the commander of Army Group Centre found the right way to deal with this very critical situation. Since the Germans no longer had a continuous front line, and lacked the units necessary for the establishment of a new one, the Army Group commander decided to slow down our progress by means of short counter-blows. Under their cover, troops in rear areas were able to organize a new defensive line, by means of units withdrawn from other sectors of the Eastern front and from the German homeland.[53]

Undoubtedly, Model's final stabilization of the chaos, and re-establishment of a coherent front line, must rank among the greatest performances by German commanders during World War II. The award of the diamonds to his Knight's Cross on 17 August was

---

50 Seaton, p.444.
51 Niepold, p.257.
52 Estate, von der Groeben letter to Görlitz, 24 November 1970.
53 Zhukov, p.587.

well deserved. Hitler made the point, in a situation meeting on 31 August 1944, when he stated: "When *Feldmarschall* Model arrived, Army Group Centre was only a 'hole'. There were more 'holes' than front lines, now there are more front lines than 'holes'."[54]

Coordination with Army Group North

On 9 July, Model and Friessner reported jointly to Hitler and proposed to evacuate Estonia. Hitler refused. He was supported by *Grossadmiral* Dönitz, Supreme Commander of the German *Kriegsmarine* who felt that he needed the Estonian harbours. A month earlier, on 12 June, prior to the onslaught of the *Bagration* offensive, Friessner had made a personal appeal to Hitler. Hitler had viewed this as a hidden threat and decided that Friessner should soon be relieved.[55] (Friessner's statement is one more typical example of a German memoir writer's bragging. No German General could ever threaten Hitler, the opposite was true).

After the situation worsened, Model and Friessner again went to Hitler. Friessner became outraged when Model requested that his Army Group North should close a gap that had formed within Army Group Centre in Lithuania. Army Group Centre simply did not have sufficient troops for that purpose. On 11 July, Model had sent a note to *OKH*, with a personal copy to Hitler, complaining that Friessner's Army Group North had been inactive at the boundary between their two Army Groups.[56] On 23 July, Friessner was relieved by Schörner, and took over the latter's former Army Group *Südukraine* which was renamed Army Group *Südost*. As a "consolation", Friessner was promoted to *Generaloberst*. At that time, his new Army Group was considered to be of less importance, but this changed when the Russians entered the Balkans. Friessner's Army Group was destroyed – in his memoirs it became a *Verratene Schlacht* (battle lost through treason).[57]

The connection between Schörner's Army Group North and Model's Army Group Centre was re-established during Operation *Doppelkopf*, and then broken again. Army Group North, later renamed Army Group *Kurland*, remained surrounded until the end of the war.

Apart from the statement by Zhukov mentioned above, Russian military historians do not pay attention to Model's Command. The fourth volume of *IVOVSS* only mentions that Model had replaced Busch. Rokossovsky wrote that when he told his officers that Model had assumed command, they replied, "Model? We can take on Model too."[58]

Bagration Operations from the Russian point of view

Some of the Russian commanders, including Zhukov and Rokossovsky, devoted little space to *Bagration* in their memoirs. Zhukov's 570 page work mentions *Bagration* on only 32 pages. Rokossovsky covered the topic in 20 pages out of his 340 page total. General Gorbatov, who commanded an army during the battle, did not mention *Bagration* at all.

Russian and German accounts of *Bagration* do not differ on technical matters. Rokossovsky emphasized that he had encountered critical logistical problems, which forced

---

54 H. Heiber (ed.) *Hitlers Lagebesprechungen – Die Protokollfragmente seiner militärischen Konferenzen 1942-1945*, Munich 1963, p.276.
55 J. Friessner, *Verratene Schlachten,* Hamburg 1956, p.18 ff. (Henceforth Friessner).
56 Facsimile in Model/Bradley, p.211.
57 *Verratene Schlachten* is the title of Friessner's memoirs.
58 Rokossovsky, p.249.

him to halt his advance at the outskirts of Warsaw, and to remain in place there. His account has obvious political implications. Rokossovsky's behaviour during the Warsaw uprising became the subject of fierce post-war discussions which were compounded by his Polish origin. Although he wrote extensively about the Warsaw uprising, political constraints limited what he could say in public and write in his memoirs.

Stavka planning for Bagration

The first meetings at *Stavka* took place in the spring of 1944, under the chairmanship of Army General Antonov, and with the participation of his deputy, General Sergey Shtemenko. Zhukov and Vasilevsky also attended, both had been earmarked as Theatre commanders. A destruction of German Army Group Centre was on the cards from the very beginning. However, the first plans went no further than creating a *Kessel* around Minsk. On 22 April Zhukov, after consulting with Rokossovsky, had suggested proceeding further to Brest. However, *Stavka* objected, feeling that additional units were required which *Stavka* preferred to keep in reserve. The final plan was adopted by *Stavka* on 23 May and came close to Zhukov's proposal. It did not, however, foresee progress beyond 200 kilometres for a first phase. The Russians did not believe that Army Group Centre would simply fall apart.

Four Fronts were foreseen. The largest was Rokossovsky's First Belorussian Front, which grouped 10 Armies. The Third Belorussian Front, which included the largest number of tanks, was placed under the command of Colonel General Chernyakhovsky. The Third Baltic Front was commanded by Army General Bagramyan. The Fourth Baltic Front, the smallest of the four, was originally placed under the command of General Petrov, who was relieved after some political trouble and replaced by Army General Zakharov. Rokossovsky's and Zakharov's Fronts were placed under Zhukov, the two others under Vasilevsky. Some units of the Polish *Armja Ludowa*, which had remained in Russia and was communist-oriented, also took part in the battle. It did not fight as a separate unit and its troops were integrated in the Russian Fronts.[59]

---

59 The personalities of the Russian Front commanders reflect the changes which had taken place in the Red Army's leadership after the Great Terror and the first phases of the war. General Rokossovsky was of Polish origin. In 1937 he was a Corps commander (*Komkor*; at that time Generals' ranks had not yet been introduced in the Red Army.) He was arrested and accused of having conspired with another officer. This officer had however been killed in action twenty years earlier in the civil war and Rokossovsky said to his interrogator: "Can dead men testify?" (Quoted by R. Conquest, *The Great Terror – A Reassessment,* New York 1990, p.429). Such arguments carried little weight with the NKVD and Rokossovsky remained in prison until 1940. All his teeth were knocked out and he was later fitted with a steel denture. During the war he rose to the highest ranks and became a Marshal of the Soviet Union. Vasilevsky was a Major General at the beginning of the war and deputy chief of the operational division at the Ministry of Defence. During the war he became Chief of the General Staff, but was mainly employed as commander of Fronts and "Theatres". He rose to Marshal of the Soviet Union. At 36, Chernyakovsky was the youngest Army General in Red Army. He was killed in action in 1945 during the combats in East Prussia. Bagramyan was a Colonel at the beginning of the war. During the Great Terror he was suspected of an affiliation with the nationalist Armenian Dashnak movement and excluded from the party. This was usually followed by immediate arrest. His Armenian compatriot Mikoyan, a member of the Politburo, intervened in his favour and

After the general plan for *Bagration* was adopted, the Front commanders, their chiefs of staff, and their highest-ranking Commissars, were separately called to Moscow and requested to state their opinions. Thereafter, they met in turn with their Army commanders and instructed them about their respective assignment. Finally, all Front and Army commanders, again accompanied by their chiefs of staff and their Commissars, were called to a general meeting and briefed about all the aspects of the forthcoming operations.

During Rokossovsky's first meeting with Stalin, a difference of opinion arose between the two. Stalin favoured one single attack. Rokossovsky insisted that two separate simultaneous attacks were needed. Stalin was irritated by a contradiction in the presence of a large forum. Twice he asked Rokossovsky to leave the room and think the matter over. During one of the breaks, Molotov and Malenkov went to Rokossovsky and asked him angrily how he dared to contradict Stalin in that manner. Rokossovsky remained steadfast and in the end Stalin agreed to his proposal.[60]

Parade of German prisoners of war through Moscow

On 17 July, Stalin ordered 57,000 German captured soldiers, preceded by their Generals, to be marched through the streets of Moscow. His purpose was to show the Russian people that there was no longer any organized German retreat and, at the same time, vividly display the Red Army's might. The British author, Alexander Werth, witnessed the parade and recalled that there was no hostile reaction by the crowd. Some youngsters had begun to jeer and throw stones at the soldiers, but they were quickly restrained by their elders.

20 July 1944

Model's attitude to the military resistance movement and the events of 20 July 1944 can be summed up in two words, totally negative. Some of the letters, which he sent home after the attempt had failed, are frightening in their lack of understanding and sensitivity. On 5 August 1944 he wrote to his son: "What a terrible meanness that Korten had to become one of the victims. Let us hope that the motto 'Faith is the core of Honour' will now be strengthened.[61] For us the bitter fact remains that this could be done by soldiers."[62] Model wrote regularly to his son. Their father-son relationship was particularly close. While Model refrained from writing about military operations, many of his letters were lessons in morality, behaviour and planning for the future. To associate his rejection of 20 July with a peripheral incident, such as the death of a *Luftwaffe* General, betrays an appalling naiveté of judgment. Also the words, "The bitter fact remains that this could be done by soldiers," show a lack of understanding. When he wrote his letter to his son, Model already knew who was implicated in the plot. A number of the 'soldiers' were comrades

---

he was spared further consequences and reinstated. During the war, he had his ups and downs as a commander, but he rose to Army General. As one of the "Southern" Generals, he had to wait until 1955 before being promoted to Marshal of the Soviet Union. General Zakharov is described as a mediocrity. He was a Commissar during the major part of his career. Under Khrushchev he became Chief of the Red Army's General Staff.

60 Rokossovsky, p.250 ff.

61 Here Model used the SS slogan "faith is the core of honour".

62 Letter in the Estate. Model had known General Korten during his time in the *Reichswehr*. Korten died of his wounds sustained during the explosion on July 22 and was promoted to *Generaloberst* on the same day.

of his, whom he had known and respected during his career. One of the officers who was hanged was Colonel Schultze-Büttger, who had remained on Model's staff, at Model's request, when taking over Army Group *Nordukraine.*

A few days later Model wrote to his aunt Magda:

> The total effort, after the criminal attempt, which in its baseness is totally incomprehensible to any soldier, will help us in overcoming the present climax in the war. In this spirit, forward march![63]

Even this letter shows blindness. Given the number of officers of high standing who had participated in the plot, the words "totally incomprehensible to any soldier" strike one as being divorced from reality. At this date Model could not know that more soldiers would be killed in action between 20 July 1944 and the German unconditional surrender in May 1945, than in all the years of the war up to 20 July 1944. But he obviously knew that the war was long since lost for Germany. Such sentences as "overcoming the present climax in the war", and "in this spirit, forward march", could not have been uttered in good faith.

Was Model ever approached?

Soliciting Model's participation in, or endorsement of, a plot against Hitler would have been useless. General Röhricht recalled a conversation with Tresckow during which Model's name was mentioned. Tresckow had known that Röhricht had become opposed to the regime, and had tried in vain to convince him to take an active part in the resistance. Tresckow was supposed to have said:

> I understand that *Feldmarschall* Model wants to call upon you. Until now, he has never shown any agreement with our opinions. You have known him for years, and you are one of the few who can speak candidly with him.[64]

There is reason to doubt that account. The extremely cautious Tresckow would never have thought of approaching Model, either directly or through a third party.

Colonel von Gersdorff's attempt

Chance had it that Model could have become the victim of one attempt on Hitler's life. On 21 March 1943, Colonel von Gersdorff, at that time Ic at Army Group Centre, attempted to assassinate Hitler. Hitler had visited the *Zeughaus* (Arsenal) Army Museum in Berlin, on Heroes Remembrance Day (*Heldengedenktag*), to inspect Russian arms and equipment that had been captured by the Army Group. After speaking with Tresckow, Gersdorff had agreed to carry two British 'clam' grenades in his pockets and blow himself up together with Hitler. British explosives were known to be more effective than German ones. Hitler had requested Kluge and his wife to accompany him. Since Tresckow and Gersdorff felt that Kluge would be indispensable if the attempt succeeded, they were able

---

63 Estate, Letter 7 August 1944.
64 Röhricht, p.201 ff.

to convince Kluge to let Model attend the ceremony instead. Model was, in Gersdorff's words, a 'willing vassal of Hitler' and did not need to be spared.

On 20 March, Model and Gersdorff flew to Berlin and met with Schmundt. Schmundt told Model that Hitler had ordered the number of visitors to be strictly limited, and that Gersdorff would not be permitted to attend. Model objected, because he did not have Gersdorff's knowledge of the exhibits, and did not wish to be embarrassed if he was unable to answer Hitler's questions. Schmundt reluctantly agreed to Gersdorff's presence.

An additional problem arose because the hour of the presentation was to be kept strictly secret. Model had planned to be at home with his family in Dresden, rush to Berlin, and then return to Dresden as soon as the show was over. He insisted upon knowing the exact time of the ceremony. Schmundt refused to tell him at first, but Model pressed him. Finally, Schmundt relented, after pledging Model to total secrecy.

Gersdorff had ignited the 'clams' as soon as he had entered the exhibition hall. Hitler was supposed to remain between fifteen and twenty minutes, but he simply hurried through, and left after no more than two or three minutes. Gersdorff did not succeed in approaching him, so he defused the 'clams' and flushed them down a toilet. Had Gersdorff succeeded in his attempt, Model would have been blown up with all the others present. The success of Gersdorff's attempt would have been a blessing for the world, and also for Model. Death as a soldier killed in action had certainly been one of his dreams for a proper end in war, and he would have been spared his suicide.

There is little doubt that Model, like most *Wehrmacht* Generals abhorred the manner in which the officers implicated in 20 July had been executed. SS *Obergruppenführer* Wilhelm Bittrich, who commanded a Corps under Model in the West, had 'exploded' when he heard that his former Army commander, *Generaloberst* Erich Hoepner, had been hanged. He shouted in front of his staff, "This is the end of the German Army. Never before has a German officer been hanged for high treason. He was shot." His chief of staff warned him not to make such comments in public, but Bittrich simply waved him away.

When Himmler heard of Bittrich's outburst, he ordered Bittrich's Army commander, General Heinrich Eberbach, to relieve him, but General Eberbach refused. Himmler insisted and requested that Bittrich report to him in person during Operation *Market Garden*, the Allied airborne assault on Arnhem and Nijmegen. Model told Bittrich to ignore Himmler and retained him in his command until the end.[65]

"The day" at Army Group Centre

The headquarters of the Army Group were in the area of Vilna, which was very close to the *Führerhauptquartier* at Rastenburg in East Prussia. Model often attended Hitler's daily situation meetings. On 20 July he did not. He had gone on one of his usual visits to the front line. *Generalmajor* Otto Heidkämper, chief of staff of Reinhardt's 3rd *Panzer* Army, wrote that Model had visited the headquarters of 2nd and 4th Army.[66] At some time, late in the afternoon, Model heard of the attempt. He returned to his headquarters after nightfall and his congratulatory cable to Hitler was sent at 9:00 pm when he was

---

65 H. Mühleisen, 'Wilhelm Bittrich, Ritterlicher Gegner und Rebell', in R. Smelser/E. Syring (ed.) *Die SS. Elite unter dem Totenkopf. 30 Lebensläufe,* Paderborn 2000, p. 81.

66 O. Heidkämper, *Vitebsk*, Heidelberg 1954, p.158 ff. (Henceforth Heidkämper).

still *en route*. The text of the cable was transmitted by wire to all the staff headquarters of the units of his Army Group.[67]

Stauffenberg's bomb had exploded at 12:50 pm. From the headquarters of the *Putsch*, in the offices of the *Ersatzheer* at the Bendler street complex in Berlin, the telex messages to the *Wehrkreise* had been sent between 5:35 pm and 8:03 pm.[68] The first messages from the *Führerhauptquartier* were sent out at 5:00 pm but they were not yet broadcast.[69] The first broadcast message came out at 5:42 pm and was continuously repeated thereafter. Model must have listened at around 9:00 pm. His cable to Hitler began with the words: "At this moment we have learned…" Somewhat later, the exact hour is unknown, Model returned to his headquarters. Colonel Teske wrote that he told Model that he was on friendly terms with some of the conspirators and that Model told him to stay at Army Group headquarters overnight, "no one knows how fast the *SD* will act."[70]

Hitler's address to the nation was broadcast on 21 July, at 1:00 am. Teske wrote that he saw a 'sarcastic smile' on Model's face and that he had heard comments by him such as "even worse prepared than the Kapp-*Putsch*" and "greatest disgrace (*Blamage*) ever in the history of the German *Generalstab*."

During the afternoon, strong edginess prevailed at all *Wehrkreis* headquarters. Tension also reigned at the headquarters of Army Group Centre. Heidkämper recalls that he received a phone call from Krebs, in the afternoon, asking him if his Army had received any order, from any authority, during the day. Should such an order arrive, he should immediately ask Krebs if the order should be executed, even if the document received by Heidkämper bore the signature of Krebs, or of any other staff officer of the Army Group. At that stage, Krebs could not give further details. At 10:30 pm Krebs phoned again and inquired repeatedly if any order had arrived. When Heidkämper replied in the negative, Krebs asked him if he told the truth.[71]

Model's purported first cable to Hitler

On 20 July, 9:00 pm, Model sent the following cable to Hitler:

> *Mein Führer!* We, the soldiers of Army Group Centre and Army Group *Nordukraine* have just heard with outrage and hatred of the criminal attempt against your life. We all thank the Almighty that he kept you, and all of Germany through you, from unimaginable disaster. We look upon this as a confirmation of our just cause! Our wishes to you are extended with total confidence in our final success, and with the extreme readiness for combat of your old fighters in the East.
>
> *Heil mein Führer!*
> Model, *Generalfeldmarschall*, Commander in Chief of Army Groups Centre and *Nordukraine*.[72]

---

67 Model/Bradley, p. 220.
68 P. Hoffmann, *Widerstand, Staatsstreich, Attentat. Der Kampf der Opposition gegen Hitler*, Munich 1973, p.473. (Henceforth Hoffmann).
69 Ibid, p 491.
70 Teske, p.226.
71 Heidkämper, p.179.
72 Facsimile in Model/Bradley, p.220.

Many post-war accounts claim that this was the first cable sent to Hitler after the failed 20 July attempt on his life. Liddell Hart made a somewhat abstruse statement that this telegram strengthened Hitler's confidence in Model's military capacity. Other authors followed suit, including Brett-Smith, who emphasized that this was the first telegram received by Hitler. But he did not add Liddell Hart's curious assessment about garnering confidence.[73] Other historians wrote accounts similar to Brett-Smith's.[74]

Whether Model's cable really was the first message cannot be ascertained. Probably Model would have been quite happy had that been the case. But on 20 July, and the days following, many commanders sent messages of congratulation to Hitler.

At 9:00 pm *Generaloberst* Friessner sent a cable to Hitler: "My *Führer*, Army Group North will now fight all the more."[75]

Generaloberst Weiss, Commander of 2nd Army, sent a telegram to Hitler during the evening and repeated its wording in an order of the day of 20 July:

> While we were engaged in heavy fighting, news reached us about the contemptible attempt on the *Führer's* life. We feel disgust about this cowardly action, and hatred and contempt for the traitors. At the same time, we experience the deepest gratitude to fate which has spared us the *Führer*. Our guidance is now even more: Fight until the end for our people, our fatherland, and our *Führer*. Long live the *Führer*.[76]

Kluge cabled Hitler during the evening of 20 July:

> Providence succeeded in foiling the wicked attempt, by hand of murder, against your life, my *Führer*. All *Wehrmacht* units under my command join me in my congratulations and assure you of our unchanging loyalty, come whatever may be.[77]

In the witch-hunt that ensued after 20 July, the absence of a congratulatory cable would have immediately aroused suspicion. Even the retired *Feldmarschall* Ritter von Leeb, sent a letter to Hitler on 24 July, thanking him for granting his repeated requests for additional sizeable monetary gifts, and added words of congratulation.[78]

Undoubtedly, Model's message reflected his opinion about the plot, but in this he was not alone.[79]

---

73 Brett-Smith, p.200.
74 Carlo d'Este: "Model was the first high commander who assured Hitler of his devotion after 20 July" (C. d'Este, 'Field Marshal Model', in C. Barnett, *Hitler's Generals*, London 1989, p.322). J. Ludewig: "The first congratulatory message from the Eastern front was sent to Hitler by *Feldmarschall* Model". J. Ludewig, 'Model – Hitlers bester Feldmarschall'? in R. Smelser/E. Syring (ed.) *Die Militärelite des Dritten Reiches – 27 biographische Skizzen*, Berlin 1995, S. 379.
75 BA-MA, RH 19/III-313.
76 BA-MA, RH 20 – 2/937
77 Facsimile in Model/Bradley, p.220.
78 Facsimile in G. Ueberschär/W. Vogel *Dienen und Verdienen. Hitlers Geschenke an seine Eliten*, Frankfurt 1999, p.257 "…I am taking this opportunity to congratulate you for your miraculous escape from the wicked attempt on your life. Victory to the German Army. *Heil Hitler!*"
79 When the German Generals wrote their memoirs, 20 July 1944 was still viewed in a negative light by a majority of the population. It is therefore no surprise that most memoirs rival in their

The "Speidel case"

Generalleutnant Hans Speidel was chief of staff of Army Group B in the West when Model assumed its command. Speidel's part in the military resistance movement is still subject to discussion. His opponents hold him responsible for a testimony at the *Ehrenhof* which damaged Rommel, and finally led to Rommel's suicide. (The *Ehrenhof,* presided by the servile von Rundstedt, was established after 20 July 1944 with authority to decide expulsion from the *Wehrmacht* of officers implicated in the plot. In his unpublished memoirs *Generaloberst* Adam wrote that Rundstedt, after accepting to preside the *Ehrenhof,* had forever forfeited his honour.) After expulsion, they were tried by Freisler's *Volksgerichtshof.* Rumours have it that *Generalleutnant* Heinrich Kirchheim, a member of the *Ehrenhof* and personally hostile to Rommel, was happy at Speidel's testimony, and saw to it that Speidel was not expelled from the *Wehrmacht.* However, Speidel was arrested on 5 September 1944. At that time Model was already in the West.

Model was informed that Speidel was under suspicion and that he would be replaced as chief of staff. Captain Maisch, O1 of Army Group B, overheard a sharply worded telephone conversation between Model and *Generalleutnant* Wilhelm Burgdorf, who had succeeded Schmundt as head of the Army's personnel division. Schmundt had been severely wounded by Stauffenberg's bomb and died a few weeks later.

Burgdorf:

Herr Feldmarschall, General Speidel must be replaced as your Chief of Staff.

Model:

What do you mean? That is nonsense.

Burgdorf:

Speidel is strongly suspected to have been involved on 20 July. I want to ask *Herr Feldmarschall* whom he desires to have as a successor.

Model:

But this is nonsense. I cannot now part with my Chief of Staff away and I demand that this is taken into account. Tell this to the *Führer*! Suspicion? Have you any proof? I repeat, this is all nonsense!

Burgdorf:

But *Herr Feldmarschall* …

---

condemnation of the plot. Had the plot succeeded, the same Generals would have been the first to boast that they had recognized the criminal nature of the regime from the beginning and that they had assisted the plotters up to the limit of their possibilities.

Model:

Does not interest me! Finished![80]

In another conversation with Keitel on the same issue, Model stated that he had better things to do in the West than to follow up events concerning 20 July, and that he was not willing to part with his Chief of Staff.[81] Following that conversation, Model told his Ia Colonel Freyberg: "He was absolutely crazy. Speidel should leave? Something about 20 July? Political nonsense."

Model was unable to prevent Speidel's removal. However, on 3 September he gave a farewell dinner for him, at which he made a short speech that Speidel himself described as a most cordial endorsement.[82] During a subsequent discussion with Freyberg, concerning a performance rating of Speidel, Model told him that this would have to be written very carefully in order not to harm Speidel.[83]

After Speidel was arrested, he sent a personal letter to Model with the request to intercede on his behalf. Model supported the efforts of Lieutenant von Metzsch, O4 on Army Group B staff, to give Speidel some reassurance after he was arrested. When von Metzsch informed Model that he wanted to visit Speidel in the prison at Moabit, Model granted him leave and made a car available for him. Lieutenant von Metzsch confirmed this in a conversation with Hansgeorg Model on 4 December 1954:

All efforts to get Speidel released from custody were tolerated by the *Feldmarschall*. For instance, Model paid a visit to Speidel's wife at Christmas 1944. He also intervened with Speer and with Hitler.[84]

Model's selfless efforts on Speidel's behalf – any assistance to a suspect in the July 20 plot was fraught with danger – did not prevent Speidel from maligning Model in his memoirs.[85]

At times there is a balance of justice in history. Speidel could later not escape his own fate and was destroyed by a stronger personality. He met his doom in General de Gaulle. (Of course, there was no connection to Model. Probably de Gaulle had never heard of Model – if, by chance, he had, he would have felt the same contempt for him as for

---

80 Estate, Maisch, 25 April 1950.
81 Estate, General Blumentritt, 16 May 1955.
82 Estate, Conversation between Speidel and Görlitz.
83 Estate, Conversation between Hansgeorg Model and Freyberg, 19 August 1955.
84 Estate, Letters from Hansgeorg Model to Speidel, 30 June 1954.
85 Some extracts: "…Model had an exaggerated opinion of himself… he tended to curry favour with the soldiers at the expense of their officers…although he knew better, he had totally bowed to Hitler's ideology…I had several talks with him. He was aware that the situation was desperate, but he refused to confront Hitler…all appeals to his responsibility for the reputation of the German soldier and for the German people were laid beside…No decisions of principle could be expected from him, he contented himself to execute orders against his better judgment… *Minima non curat praetor* was alien to him." (Extracts from H. Speidel, *Invasion 1944 – Ein Beitrag zu Rommel und des Reiches Schicksal,* Tübingen 1949). Given Speidel's influence in Western Germany, his book led to a first refusal to grant a pension to Model's widow.

almost all Generals, including his French compatriots.) Speidel had become commander in chief of NATO ground forces in Central Europe and held court in Fontainebleau like a "*Roi Soleil*". De Gaulle considered Speidel's presence in France to be intolerable. A close woman relative of his, who had been deported, told him that Speidel had had a part in the deportations of Jews from France during the occupation. When Hitler paid a visit of a few hours to Paris after the armistice with France, Speidel acted as his guide through the city. Speidel's record during his commands in Russia was likewise not unblemished. De Gaulle requested the recall of Speidel on several occasions. Adenauer would have sacrificed any General for the sake of de Gaulle's friendship, however his Minister of Defence, Franz Joseph Strauss objected. In his exaggerated opinion of himself, Strauss felt that he could have the better of de Gaulle. Charles de Gaulle then finished Speidel off with one of his typical gestures. On 2 July 1962, Adenauer visited Paris. General de Gaulle greeted him at the airport. All German officers serving with NATO lined the red carpet, accompanied by their spouses. General de Gaulle shook the hands of all Germans present, however when he came to Speidel, he ignored the General's outstretched hand and passed him by without giving him a look. He then made a point of greeting Ms Speidel with demonstrative courtesy and talked for some minutes with a German colonel, standing next to Ms Speidel. Speidel was shattered and his NATO career was soon finished. Shortly after, de Gaulle advised Adenauer that he would have Speidel declared *persona non grata* in France, if Adenauer would not recall him without delay. This threat was sufficient to lead to a recall of Speidel from his NATO command.

The lack of a reply to the widow of Colonel Schultze-Büttger

In October 1944, Ms Schultze-Büttger, whose husband had already been hanged, wrote to Model, asking about her husband's fate. Neither his trial nor his execution had been reported in the press. In the first weeks after 20 July, the newspapers had reported on every arrest and trial, but when the growing number of participants became known, the coverage became more restrained. Colonel Freyberg reported that Model had mentioned the letter from Ms Schultze-Büttger to him and had said: "I am staying out of this. I want nothing to do with this." Model had then ordered Freyberg to simply forward the letter to the Army's personnel division and to inform Ms Schultze-Büttger accordingly.

There had been some irritation between Model and Schultze-Büttger, who wanted to leave the staff of Army Group Centre after Manstein was dismissed. Model refused and some unpleasant words were apparently exchanged between the two.

Nevertheless, Model's behaviour was outrageous. He was in no personal danger and he knew about the fate of Schultze-Büttger. A letter to the widow under those tragic circumstances would have been elementary courtesy.[86]

The Warsaw Uprising

1 August 1944 saw the beginning of an uprising in Warsaw that lasted for two months until it was crushed on 2 October. Massive civilian executions and the complete destruction of

---

86 *Generaloberst* Heinrici who was opposed to the attempt of 20 July nevertheless made an effort on behalf of Schultze-Büttger. He was turned down, but at least he showed more courage than Model. BA-MA, N 265/35, Bl.54, letter from General Hermann Reinecke to Heinrici, 24.10.1944. Quoted in J. Hürter, *Ein deutscher General an der Ostfront. Die Briefe und Tagebücher des Gotthard Heinrici 1941/2*, Erfurth 2001, p.48.

the city followed. Teske described the Warsaw uprising as a landmark: "Here, and nowhere else, the 'cold war' between East and West was to start."[87] Much has been written about the Warsaw Uprising, but access to this information had been restricted for many years behind the Iron Curtain.

In the early 1990s, following the dissolution of the Soviet Union, the Russian and Polish archives became accessible to scholars, and provided additional information and records that led to revised accounts. An anthology was published, in 1999, by Polish and German historians under the auspices of the Polish Academy of Historical Science and the German University at Freiburg.[88]

Opinions about responsibility for the uprising are varied, and some are misleading. An unequivocal explanation has yet to be established. The Red Army did urge a Polish uprising, but that was a typical Soviet tactic prior to invading a major city. The Soviets were actually dismayed by this event. The Red Army had become exhausted and its supplies had not caught up.

The situation was complex, due to political factors. Had the uprising succeeded, Russian politicians would have found themselves in a quandary. Such a victory would have made the Polish Underground Army (*Armja Krajowa*) powerful enough to compete with the future Polish communist government that had been formed at Lublin. The *Armja Krajowa* was under the authority of the Polish government in exile in London. As the insurrection progressed, the Red Army chose to become passive observers. Landing rights to British and American planes that were attempting to support the beleaguered Poles were refused.

The Polish government in exile in London was cautious at first, and then opposed a military uprising.[89] After the accidental death of General Władisław Sikorski, the structure of the Polish government was altered. According to Polish tradition, Sikorski had been both Head of the Government and Supreme Commander of the armed forces. Following Sikorski's death, Stanislaw Mikołajczyk became prime minister and was more inclined to compromise. The extreme nationalistic and uncompromising General Kasimierz Sosnkowski became Commander in Chief of the Army. When this split occurred within the Polish government in London, it no longer had complete control over *Armja Krajowa*, which launched the uprising on its own initiative.

Diplomatic relations between the USSR and Poland had been renewed in the aftermath of the German attack upon Russia. A new Polish Army was set up in Russia. There, thousands of Polish officers and soldiers languished in POW camps, after the Russians had grabbed half of Poland in 1939. Recruitment of officers was very difficult, since thousands of Polish officers had been massacred by the Russians at Katyn. Most of the Polish troops who had remained in Russia, joined an Army commanded by General Władisław Anders.

---

87 Teske, p.228.

88 *Der Warschauer Aufstand,* Warsaw 1999. (Henceforth Warsaw).

89 "The government demands sabotage and other local actions against the Germans. Such steps should only have a political aspect of demonstration. The march into the city by Soviet troops must be preceded by an armed uprising against the Germans." Order by the Polish government, Nr. 5989, 27.10.1943, quoted by H. von Krannhals, *Der Warschauer Aufstand 1944,* Frankfurt 1962, p.68. (Henceforth Krannhals).

It left for Persia and put itself under the authority of the Polish government in London.[90] Smaller groups remained and became the *Armja Ludowa* (Polish People's Army).

The participants

On 1 August 1944, the city of Warsaw was within the area of responsibility of Army Group Centre. Territorial authority was vested in 9th Army under General Nikolaus von Vormann. *Luftwaffe* General Rainer Stahel had been appointed military commander of Warsaw on 27 July. Units of the police and the SS had been engaged, under the orders of SS *Gruppenführer* Erich von dem Bach-Zelewski and SS *Gruppenführer* Heinz Reinefarth. Some of the SS and police brigades, such as the ones commanded by Bronislaw Kaminski and Dr Oskar Dirlewanger, consisted of common criminals. Before the war, Dr Dirlewanger had been sentenced to two years' imprisonment for rape. Some of the men in Kaminski's unit had raped German women who had remained in Warsaw. Kaminski was a native of Azerbaijan who had volunteered for the SS. Several of his men spoke no German. In the end, von dem Bach-Zelewski, himself hardly an innocent bystander, had Kaminski shot.

The *Armja Krajowa* (*AK*) had remained strongly anti-Semitic and during the Warsaw Ghetto Rising the Jews had found it difficult to buy weapons from them. When they did manage to purchase a few, they had to pay exorbitant prices.[91] But, in fairness to Poland, it must be emphasized that the Polish government in London was the first to alert the Allies about the wholesale murder of Jews in Poland. More Poles than other nationals are honoured with monuments in the remembrance gardens of the Yad Vashem memorial in Jerusalem. They had hidden Jews, and assisted them in many ways, although any aid given to Jews by Poles led to the execution of the saviours and of all the members of their families.[92]

AK was at first commanded by General Stefan Rowecki. When General Rowecki was shot by the Germans, General Count Tadeusz Komorowski succeeded him and adopted the name of Bór. Before the war, General Komorowski had at times been a professional tournament horse-rider and had made friends with Fegelein and the German *Generalleutnant* Hans Kaellner. General Kaellner did his best to assist Bór in a soldierly surrender.

The Red Army Front facing Model at Warsaw was commanded by Marshal Rokossovsky. It contained elements of the *Armja Ludowa*, under the command of General Zygmunt Berling. The Soviet Union and Poland had resumed diplomatic relations, which had been broken off by the Russians, after the discovery of the Katyn graves, and the request by the Polish government for an investigation by a neutral commission.

---

90 General Anders is on record with a statement that the uprising was a crime and that its leader, General Bór Komorowski, should be brought before a court martial. Warsaw, p.105.

91 *Armja Ludowa* was no less anti-Semitic and Jewish soldiers in its units were exposed to mockery and at times to physical violence. For a detailed study of Polish anti-Semitism, an important source is the book by Agnieszka Pufelska, *Die "Judäo-Kommune". Ein Feindbild in Polen. Das polnische Selbstverständnis im Schatten des Antisemitismus 1939-1948,* Paderborn 2007. (For *Armja Ludowa*, p.164 ff).

92 Many Poles likewise turned Jews over to the Germans. But in this they were not alone. Jewish arrests and deportations in the West were carried out with massive assistance by the local authorities. The Dutch police were particularly ruthless.

Model's actions

Model is said to have remarked to Teske: All these who have led to this, through their corruption and their shameless treatment of the Polish people, should now clean up the mess. This is not a job for my troops."[93] On the other hand, SS *Gruppenführer* Heinz Reinefarth quoted Model as having told him on 3 August 1944: "Simply burn down the city. 1,000 metres on both sides of the road. Show no consideration. Otherwise we will be unable to fight our way through.[94]

Army Group Centre's war diary stated on 1 August 1944:

> Chief of Staff is requested by *Feldmarschall* Model to inform General Wenck that *OKH* should see to it that civilians and equipment are removed from a zone of 30 kilometres behind the front line. Military considerations make this unavoidable.[95]

On August 3, *Generaloberst* Guderian, who had become acting Chief of the *Generalstab* after the 20 July assassination attempt, wrote to the governor of Poland, Hans Frank: "An exemplary punishment should be inflicted upon Warsaw."[96]

Model's statement to Teske is reminiscent of his first comments after the end of the Polish campaign in 1939. Whatever he may have said would have been of no consequence, since Himmler had made an addition to an order by Hitler:

> The city must be razed, every street, every house, and everything to be found there must be destroyed."[97] That order was passed on to 9th Army, which added that those additional stipulations had also emanated from Himmler: "Himmler has ordered the evacuation of the city. Raze it.[98]

The Red Army then resumed its offensive, and all German units, *Wehrmacht*, SS, and police, were heavily engaged. By that time, Model was already in the West.

Newton advances the opinion that Model's transfer to the West was due to an intrigue by Guderian, who wanted his friend Reinhardt to take over Model's commands on the Eastern Front. The relevant paragraph ends with the words: "In the background hovered Guderian, smiling triumphantly". (Newton, p. 302) It would be interesting to know from which source Newton obtained this account, which is inconsistent both with facts and with the personalities mentioned by him. After 20 July 1944, the prestige of the *Generalstab* had reached its nadir. Guderian had not succeeded Zeitzler as Chief of the *Generalstab*, but he was *"mit der Wahrnehmung der Geschäfte betraut"*, meaning at best "acting chief". Seaton writes that Hitler had eroded the status of Guderian's appointment to that of an executive who acted as the intermediary and telephonist between Hitler and the Army Group Commanders. There remained to the Chief of the *Generalstab* not a vestige of authority or initiative.[99] Moreover, the Chief of the *Generalstab* never held authority

---

93　H. Teske, *Die silbernen Spiegel, Generalstabsdienst unter der Lupe*, Heidelberg 1952, p.228.

94　BA-MA, H 12 – 9/9.

95　Ibid.

96　H. Frank, *Dziennik Hansa Franka* (Diary of Hans Frank), Warsaw, 1957, p.525.

97　BA-MA RW/vol. 912.

98　Krannhals, p. 437

99　Seaton, p. 452.

over the appointment of Army Group and Army commanders. But even more important, *OKH*'s domain was restricted to the Eastern Front only. Guderian made increasingly desperate appeals to Hitler to move more troops from other theatres to the East, since he was convinced of impending major Russian offensives. Hitler paid no attention to him. In this situation it would hardly have been logical for Guderian to seek the removal of Model, at a time when Model had become the foremost *Wehrmacht* commander in the East and have him replaced by Reinhardt, who was a good commander but who did not come up to Model's level. Finally, Guderian knew that Hitler listened to Model, while Hitler seldom paid attention to Guderian. In Hitler's eyes, Reinhardt was just one of many *OB* whom he dismissed in January 1945 and never employed again.

The West

Führer Order 51 assigning priority to the West

On 3 November 1943 Hitler issued his Order Number 51:

The heavy combats against Bolshevism over the past two and a half years, with their heavy losses, have made extreme demands on our military potential. This was due to the size of the danger which we faced. But the situation has now changed. The danger in the East remains. But a greater danger begins to loom in the West, a landing by the Anglo-Saxons. In the East, distances allow for retreats of a major size which are not deadly to the fate of our nation.

Things are different in the West! If the enemy succeeds in breaching our defences on a broad front, future developments will soon become impossible to assess. All available intelligence shows that the enemy will attack in the West, at the very latest next spring, perhaps even earlier.

I can no longer allow the West to be further weakened by strengthening other war theatres. I have therefore decided to strengthen it, particularly in such areas where we will later be able to launch attacks against the British Isles. These are the locations where the enemy will attack. There the decisive landing operation will take place.

Attacks on other fronts in the West can also be expected. An offensive against Denmark cannot be excluded. Technically such an attack is more difficult, but if it succeeds, its operative and political consequences will be enormous…" (Then follow several pages of detailed orders).[1]

The command structure

The West came under the authority of *OKW*. Only the Eastern Front had remained under *OKH*. At *OKW* the equivalent of the *OKH Generalstab* was the *Wehrmachtführungsstab* (*WFSt*).[2] A literal translation would be, "Staff of the *Wehrmacht* leadership", but it was simply a name chosen to distinguish it from the *OKH Generalstab*. All senior commanders at the *WFSt* were *Generalstab* officers. The *WFSt* was headed by *Generaloberst* Alfred Jodl.[3] As a staff officer Jodl was superior to both Zeitzler and Guderian. He wielded more

---

1 War diary *OKW*, vol. IV, 2, p. 1530 ff.

2 In September 1941, Stauffenberg had said in his course for future *Generalstab* officers: "The structure of our high command is even more stupid than the most capable *Generalstab* officers could imagine, had they been given the task of finding the most nonsensical construction." G. Megargee: *Hitler und die Generäle. Das Ringen um die Führung der Wehrmacht 1933-1945*, Paderborn 2006, p. XV.

3 Nominally Jodl was subordinated to the head of *OKW*, *Feldmarschall* Keitel, but Keitel was busy playing a political game of his own. He was instrumental in creating the "unholy alliance" with Martin Bormann, the most powerful of Hitler's satraps, and Hans Lammers, the head

power than either, since *OKH* could only act in the East, while *OKW* and Jodl's *WFSt* could move any *Wehrmacht* unit from one theatre to another outside the East. We have already seen that Jodl had been opposed to Hitler in 1933, but that after 1938 he became subservient to him.[4] In June 1943, Guderian had a talk with Jodl in which he referred to the need for a genuine Chief of the *Generalstab* having the authority the position had had in former times. Jodl cut him off and said: "Do you know a better Commander in Chief than Adolf Hitler?"[5]

Prior to the Allied landings in North Africa and in Sicily, the West had seen only a few isolated operations, such as the aborted Allied landing attempt at Dieppe on 19 August 1942. The Supreme Commander West (*OB* West) was *Feldmarschall* Gerd von Rundstedt. He had been recalled after his dismissal as Commander of Army Group South in the East in December 1941. *OB* West had authority over all the Western theatres, extending from the Netherlands down to Italy. He had two Army Groups assigned to him, Army Group B under Rommel in northern France and *Armeegruppe G*, later Army Group G, under Blaskowitz in southern France. *OB* West's headquarters were located near Paris, at St. Germain. The headquarters of Army Group B were at La Roche-Guyon. General Blumentritt was Chief of Staff at *OB* West, and General Speidel was Chief of Staff of Army Group B. *OB* West also maintained liaison with the Navy and the *Luftwaffe*, but he had no command over either. He had authority over the military Governors of the occupied territories and their administrations. Before *Overlord*, such extended responsibility presented few problems. However, after the success of *Overlord*, Rundstedt's staff could no longer cope with the command of both Army Groups. Although the post of *OB* West was maintained, operations came under the command of the Army Groups that reported directly to *WFSt*.

Curiously, the Allies were not aware that Rundstedt was no longer the 'Rundstedt of old'. In their memoirs, Bradley and other Allied Commanders, wrote of "Rundstedt Offensives" at a time when Rundstedt had become increasingly lethargic and limited most of his activities to signing papers submitted to him by his Chief of Staff.

---

of Hitler's chancellery. The main concern of this trio was to reduce the influence of Göring and Goebbels. Keitel has been maligned and ridiculed in many post-war accounts and also in the memoirs of German Generals. The American historian Gene Mueller recalls a talk with an ADC of Halder, Burkhart Müller-Hildebrandt, who told him that he had once come to the *Führerhauptquartier* and simply walked past Keitel, without recognizing him and without saluting him. He nervously turned to Halder and asked him who this obviously very senior officer was. Halder turned around, recognized Keitel and told the ADC "Don't worry, it is only Keitel." G. Mueller, 'Wilhelm Keitel-Der gehorsame Soldat' in E. Smelser/E. Syring (ed.): *Die Militärelite des Dritten Reiches. 27 biographische Skizzen*, Berlin 1998, p.262. However Keitel was likewise a very competent *Generalstab* officer. With all the scorn and mockery which his fellow Generals poured upon him in their memoirs, one can wonder how such a purported zero reached high positions. Keitel was sentenced to death at Nuremberg and hanged. He defended himself with dignity and frankly admitted his failures. None of the Generals who mocked him in their memoirs emulated him.

4   Jodl's dictum "The whole *Generalstab* should be disbanded" occurred during a dispute between him and Guderian – Guderian, p.318.
5   Guderian , p.294.

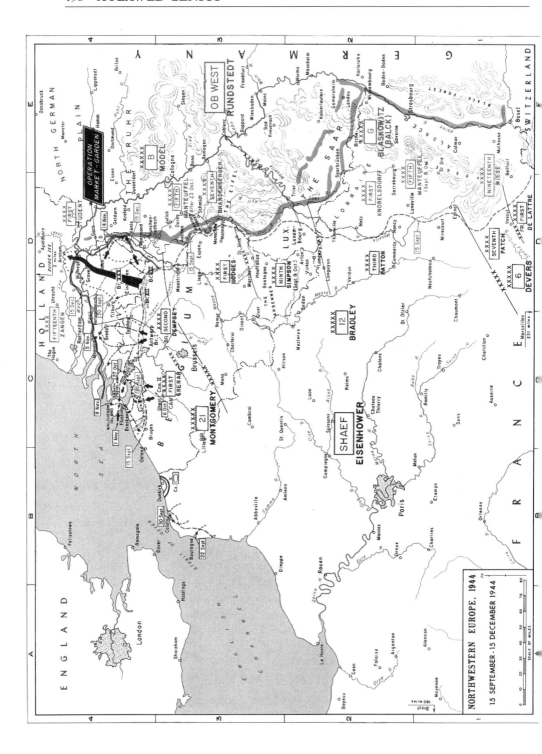

NORTHWESTERN EUROPE, 1944
15 SEPTEMBER - 15 DECEMBER 1944

Following the successful Allied landing in Normandy, Hitler had stepped up his practice of relieving commanders, in the belief that new names would lead to improvements. On 7 July 1944, one month after the Allied invasion, von Rundstedt was dismissed, and replaced by *Feldmarschall* von Kluge. After his car accident in 1943, Kluge had remained in the *Führerreserve* for close to one year. Prior to taking over his new command, Kluge was subjected to Hitler's customary indoctrination about the failures of his predecessor, and the staff and subordinates they had left behind.

Hitler was particularly scathing about Rommel. Rommel had begun to fall from grace after his defeat at El Alamein. From then on he became more and more pessimistic. At Kluge's first meeting with Rommel, Kluge insulted him to his face and told him that he had to start obeying orders.[6] Rommel replied angrily that he was of equal rank and that Kluge better watch his language. After two days, Kluge realized that Hitler's criticism of Rommel was unjustified. On 17 July 1944, Rommel's command car had been fired upon by two British planes and he was severely wounded. Kluge then assumed Rommel's command of Army Group B, in addition to the post of *OB* West. After the failed 20 July plot, Kluge's position became precarious. He had been aware of the strong body of military resistance in his staff, at Army Group Centre in the East. He had spoken with several leaders of the civilian resistance movement, without ever entirely committing himself.

Paris was the only place where Operation *Walküre*, the code name for the actions to be taken after Hitler's death, was successfully carried out. General Carl-Heinrich von Stülpnagel, military governor of France, had the top SS commanders and party officials arrested. When it became apparent that the plot had failed, General Blumentritt attempted to save Stülpnagel. He arranged a dinner for him and the SS officers who by then had been released. Kluge had reported Stülpnagel's actions to *OKW*. After relieving him of his command, he told him to don civilian clothes and to "disappear somewhere". Stülpnagel refused. He attempted to commit suicide near the 1916 battlefields of Verdun. He had fought at Verdun during World War I, and he wanted to end his life on his former battlefield. The shot failed to kill him, but it permanently blinded him. He was later tried and hanged.

On 15 August 1944, Kluge had driven into the Falaise Pocket to meet General Eberbach, commander of 5th *Panzer* Army. His communications car was attacked by Allied fighter planes and disabled. When Hitler heard that Kluge could not be reached, he assumed he had simply gone over to the Allies. Hitler ordered his dismissal. During subsequent interrogations by the Gestapo, Kluge's name was mentioned several times by his own staff officers, and also by officers on Stülpnagel's staff.

Supreme Commander West and Commander of Army Group B

Before Model's arrival, Army Group B was placed under the interim command of SS *Oberstgruppenführer* Hausser. Apparently there was some debate as to who was to become the new *OB* West. *Feldmarschall* Albert Kesselring's name was mentioned. Finally, preference was given to Model, who was considered to be the master of crisis situations.

Model had mixed emotions about his new assignments. He regarded himself as an expert on the East. His only service in the West had been in 1940 when he was Chief of Staff of Busch's 16th Army. Prior to arriving at his new post, Model was subjected to the usual indoctrination. Hitler told him that he would be inheriting two staffs which were

---

6   B. Liddell Hart (ed.) *The Rommel Papers,* London 1953, p.480 ff.

"contaminated", because Kluge had been implicated in the 20 July plot. Model appeared at Kluge's headquarters on 17 August 1944, and personally handed him the written order relieving him from command. The order contained the sentence: "*Feldmarschall* von Kluge must report immediately where he intends to go in Germany." Kluge knew that this meant that he would be arrested upon his arrival. Liddell Hart wrote that Kluge remained with Model for a day and a half, to present his successor with a detailed overview of the positions.[7] That was not the case. The two Generals, who shared a mutual strong dislike, met only briefly.[8] Kluge then drove away and took poison.

Due to the heavy fighting in the West, it soon became apparent that the two commands could not be effectively held by a single General. General Blumentritt suggested to *OKW* that Rundstedt be recalled as *OB* West.[9] Hitler requested Model's agreement before deciding. Model, aware that Army Group B would require his full attention, raised no objection.[10]

Model's relations with Rundstedt have been described as correct but lacking in mutual warmth.[11] The usual forms of courtesy were kept by both and Model always addressed his reports to Rundstedt.[12] In the case of a direct report to Hitler, he saw to it that Rundstedt received a copy.[13]

Command structure of Army Group B

On the day Model arrived at his new headquarters, typical incidents occurred with his new chiefs of staff, Generals Günther Blumentritt and Hans Speidel. Neither of those men mentioned these altercations in their memoirs, probably because they attached little importance to what both knew was typical of Model. Personal relations remained acceptable. Blumentritt recalled, with some amusement, that Model immediately requested the transfer of 30 divisions from the Eastern Front to the West, since "there were already far too many Divisions in the East". Blumentritt wrote that this was simply impertinence, adding that Model must have had no illusions that any attention would be paid to his request.[14]

---

7   Liddell Hart, p.99 ff.
8   Colonel Freyberg stated that they had a quick breakfast together. Letter Freyberg, 19.8.1955, Estate.
9   Facsimile in Model/Bradley p.272.
10 Ibid.
11 The following volumes of *United States Army in World War II*, Office of the Chief of Military History, Department of the Army, Washington, D.C. (Henceforth US Army) will be frequently quoted in this part. The volumes treating the war in Europe are grouped under the title *The European Theatre of Operations*. Separate volumes *The Ardennes – Battle of the Bulge*, Washington 1956 (henceforth *Bulge*), *The Supreme Command*, Washington 1954 (henceforth Supreme Command).
12 A series of reports to Rundstedt are in facsimile in Model/Bradley, pp.277, 292, 295, 296, 297, 298, 302, 310, 311, 312, 313, 315, 319, 320, 321, 328, 329, 330, 331, 332, 355, 358, 359.
13 Facsimile of direct reports to Hitler in Model/Bradley, pp.284, 285, 287, 288. Apparently Model did not trust Jodl – in his review of enemy positions and expected actions he emphasized that his report be submitted to Hitler.
14 Estate, General Blumentritt, 16 May 1955.

Allied Command structure (SHAEF)

On 15 August 1944, after the second Allied landing in Southern France, Operation *Anvil*, the structure of command at SHAEF remained basically unchanged until the end of the war. The exception was a short period during the Ardennes offensive, when 1st and 9th American Armies were temporarily placed under Montgomery's command. Eisenhower was Supreme Commander, and his deputy was the British Air Chief Marshal Sir Arthur Tedder. His Chief of Staff was the US Army Lieutenant General Walter Bedell-Smith. SHAEF had three Army Groups. 21st Army Group under Montgomery, contained 2nd British Army under General Miles Dempsey, 1st Canadian Army under General Henry Crerar, and 1st Allied Airborne Army under General Lewis Brereton. General Omar Bradley's 12th Army Group consisted of 1st US Army under General Courtney Hodges, 3rd US Army under General George Patton, 9th US Army under General William Simpson, and 15th US Army under General Leonard Gerow.[15] 6th Army Group, under US General Jacob Devers, consisted of 7th US Army under General Alexander Patch, and 1st French Army under General Jean de Lattre de Tassigny.

Command structure of the German Army Group B

The German command structure in the field began to look like a 'carousel'. Commanders of Army Groups and Armies were relieved and replaced at ever shorter intervals. They were moved like chess pieces from one command to another. Army commanders were relieved at intervals so short that often no working relationships could be established between them and their Army Group commanders. Some Armies simply consisted of staffs. In many instances, communications between Armies and their Corps were so unreliable that Army Group headquarters bypassed the Armies and issued orders directly to Corps.

After 20 July, Hitler's distrust of his Generals had reached a point where all proposals put forward by any commander were regarded with suspicion. That could have led to chaos, but a number of very capable German commanders, with outstanding staffs, were still able to maintain some cohesion

List of the Army Commanders in Army Group B:

AOK 7:

SS *Oberstgruppenführer* Hausser until 21 August 1944.
General Eberbach until his capture on 31 August 1944.
General Brandenberger until 20 February 1945.
General Felber until 26 March 1945.
General von Obstfelder until the German surrender.

AOK 15:

Generaloberst von Salmuth until 22 August 1944.
General von Zangen until the German surrender.

AOK F:

Generaloberst (*Luftwaffe*) Student.
General (*Luftwaffe*) Schlemm until 20 March 1945.

---

15 Until March 1945, 15th US Army was a reserve unit. It was then activated with responsibility for the military administration of the occupied German provinces. Prior to that, General Gerow had commanded a Corps. When Patton was relieved of his command of 3rd Army, he received command of 15th Army.

General Blumentritt until 10/15 April 1945.
Generaloberst Student again until the German surrender.
AOK 5 Panzer Army:
General Eberbach until 23 August 1944.
SS *Oberstgruppenführer* Dietrich until 12 September 1944.
General von Manteuffel until 6 March 1945.
Generaloberst Harpe until end April 1945.
AOK 6 Panzer Army, set up on 26 October 1944:
SS *Oberstgruppenführer* Dietrich until the German surrender.
AOK 12
General Wenck until the German surender. The subordination to Army Group B was theoretical. AOK 12 was set up anew on 10 April 1945. At that date, the *Ruhrkessel* was already closed. 12th Army was engaged in the Battle for Berlin.

Netherlands: The units under the command of General (*Luftwaffe*) Christiansen, came under Model's order when fighting spread to the Netherlands. However they were not part of Amy Group B. At a later stage they were named "*Festung Holland*" and became part of *Generaloberst* Blaskowitz's Army Group H until the German surrender.

Relations with the Army Commanders

This section is limited to the six *OB* who were subordinated to Army Group B for any appreciable length of time: *Generaloberst* von Salmuth, General von Zangen, *Generaloberst* Student, General von Manteuffel, SS *Oberstgruppenführer* Sepp Dietrich and General Brandenberger.

Generaloberst Hans von Salmuth

General von Salmuth did not belong to the elite of Army commanders. In a performance rating of 1942, Manstein had reluctantly declared him fit for command of an Army, adding however, that he was "not a rousing personality". During their first meeting, Model rejected Salmuth's assessment of the situation.

Salmuth recalled:

After a talk with Sepp Dietrich, I requested a meeting with Model. I told him that I considered myself capable of judging the situation, since I had been in action here from the very first day of *Overlord*. I strongly emphasized that the small partial attacks Model suggested would turn out to be futile. I suggested that he should withdraw his whole Army Group to the eastern bank of the Seine, and attempt to set up a new line of defence there. Model was taken aback and replied that I was obviously too much of a pessimist. His orders had to remain unchanged.[16]

Salmuth was retired on 27 August. He did not believe that Model had any part in his dismissal, and stated that the information which Hitler and *OKW* had given to Model was erroneous. After the war, Salmuth was sentenced by the IMT to twenty years' imprisonment. He was released from prison after only a few years.

---

16 Estate, von Salmuth, 19 November 1955.

General Gustav-Adolf von Zangen
The Model and von Zangen relationship was very poor. Reichhelm recalled that after Model had directed a mass of accusations against General von Zangen, the latter told Reichhelm that there were only two practical solutions. He would either shoot Model or shoot himself. Model had dispatched Reichhelm to von Zangen to "take a look and attempt to restore some order."[17] After receiving Reichhelm's report, Model did not follow his usual habit of admitting that he had gone too far. In a conversation with the author in May 2000, Reichhelm added that no further incidents occurred.

Generaloberst (Luftwaffe) Kurt von Student
Model's meetings with *Generaloberst* Student were only sporadic and the two Generals hardly understood each other. Student had a very slow and halting way of expressing himself.

General Hasso von Manteuffel
The relationship was very good. Manteuffel was a scion of a famous Prussian Army family. He had been mentioned five times in the daily *Wehrmacht* Communiqué and been decorated with the diamonds to the Knight's Cross. He rose directly from command of a Division, to Army commander, without having gone through *Generalstab* training. Professor Percy Schramm wrote that Manteuffel was a very different person to Model, but that he respected him as a man and as a commander. During the Ardennes offensive, Manteuffel was the most capable of the three German Army commanders. Model had intended to place him at the spearhead of the attack, but Hitler, motivated by political considerations, gave preference to Dietrich's 6th SS *Panzer* Army.

In a performance rating of Manteuffel, 13 March 1945, Model wrote:

> An outstanding leader, strong personality, great mental and physical vigour. Ruthless and untiring in his personal commitment, great military talent, with a clear view of the essential. Communicates successfully his own energy to his subordinates. Has repeatedly proved himself as Army commander and leader of *Panzer* units, both in attack and in defence.[18]

During the last weeks of the war, Manteuffel's Army took part in the battles around Berlin.

After the war, Manteuffel was elected to the *Bundestag* for the liberal *FDP*. His speeches, inspired by Nazi ideology, became an embarrassment to his party. In the elections of 1957, he lost his seat in the *Bundestag*. In the same year, he was indicted for the wanton murder of a soldier during the war. A corporal had been sentenced to two years by a court martial for cowardice.[19] Manteuffel disregarded the sentence and had the corporal shot. It was in accordance with the *Führerbefehl* Number 7, of 24 February 1943, which authorized superiors, including non-coms, and in certain specific instances even ordinary soldiers, to have any disobedient soldier shot without waiting for a court decision. Manteuffel was sentenced to 18 months. Until 1971, he was forbidden to use his former rank of *General*

---

17 Conversation between Reichhelm and Görlitz, 13 October 1970.
18 *NOKW* 141.
19 The corporal had seen a non-com of his unit desert to the Russians, but had not reported him.

der Panzertruppe a. D. (retired). The right was restored to him by act of clemency by the *Bundeswehr* Inspector General. The prison sentence remained on his record.[20]

SS *Oberstgruppenführer* Sepp Dietrich

Dietrich was perhaps the most interesting of the Army commanders. He was one of only three SS officers who reached the rank of *Oberstgruppenführer*, corresponding to the Army rank of *Generaloberst*. The two other were Hausser, and the police General, Kurt Daluege, who was hanged in Prague after the war. Dietrich was decorated with the diamonds to his Knight's Cross. (The only other *Waffen-SS* commander to receive that decoration was *SS Obergruppenführer* Herbert Gille). Dietrich had been a member of the SS before transferring to the *Waffen* SS. On 30 June 1934, he had commanded the execution squad of the SA leaders. He was nicknamed "the butcher" in the years between the two wars, perhaps an allusion to his former profession.

Dietrich had served as a non-commissioned officer in World War I and never received higher military training. One of his subordinates, SS *Obergruppenführer* Wilhelm Bittrich, recalled: "On one occasion, I spent one and a half hours trying to explain to Dietrich the situation on a map. It was useless. He did not understand a word."[21]

Gradually, over the war years, Dietrich did develop into a good troop commander. However, he was not up to Army command and he was aware of this. On 23 August 1944, he asked Model to have him relieved because he did not feel up to the job. The war diary of Army Group B of that day mentions: "*OB Pz AOK 5* requests to be relieved of his command, since his performance of Army commander does not come up to expectations. He is being given tasks which he is unable to fulfil. *OB* of Army Group declines."[22] During their talk, Model told Dietrich to forget about his request and to stay in his command.

General Erich Brandenberger

Model and General Brandenberger never had a satisfactory working relationship. Professor Schramm described Brandenberger as an outstanding *Generalstab* officer. He was a very courageous man, decorated with the oak leaves to his Knight's Cross, and highly respected by his staff. Görlitz wrote that "General Brandenberger was more afraid of Model than of the Commander of US 1st Army, Lieutenant General Courtney Hodges, whose troops were facing him".[23] This was one of Görlitz's many slanders. Later, at the trial of General von Schwerin, it was clear that General Brandenberger was far from afraid of Model. He stood up to him face to face, during Model's unwarranted attempts to squash Schwerin's acquittal. Schramm added that the Army's personnel department should have realized that he was a mismatch for a personality such as Model. General Brandenberger may have had an unimpressive personality, but it had been a mistake to put him under Model's

---

20 Four of the Generals decorated with diamonds were sentenced to prison by German courts after the war for wanton murder of subordinates, Ferdinand Schörner, Hasso von Manteuffel, Hermann Balck and Theodor Tolsdorff. When Newton writes: "There might be a place in the next Germany for Hasso von Manteuffel" (p. 365), he could have added: "In jail and with loss of rank".

21 H. Höhne, *Der Orden unter dem Totenkopf – die Geschichte der SS*, Munich 1978, p.407.

22 Facsimile in Model/Bradley, p.263.

23 Görlitz, p.216.

command.[24] During the Ardennes offensive, Brandenberger's 7th Army had only supporting assignments. After being relieved at 7th Army, by General Felber, Brandenberger became commander of 19th Army and remained in that post until the end of the war.

The Staffs

On 9 September 1944, General Siegfried Westphal replaced General Blumentritt as Chief of Staff *OB* West. Rundstedt was content to allow Westphal to do most of the work without interference. He effectively relinquished command of the day-to-day operations of *OB* West to Westphal. During the planning for the Ardennes offensive, Westphal tried to induce Rundstedt to issue a last warning to Hitler, but Rundstedt preferred to remain silent.[25]

On 5 September 1944, General Krebs succeeded General Speidel as Chief of Staff of Army Group B. Krebs had now to serve Model, for the third time, as Chief of staff. He received news of this assignment with mixed emotions. He had been led to believe that he would receive a Corps Command, and knew that serving under Model was not going to be a pleasant experience. Furthermore, he was not eager to become the Chief of a staff that Hitler had described to him as being 'a total mess.'[26] Model, who had always held Krebs in high esteem, did not object. Krebs remained as Model's Chief of Staff until 17 February 1945, when he was transferred to *OKH* as Guderian's successor as acting Chief of the *Generalstab*.

Generalmajor Carl Wagener was then assigned as Chief of Staff of Army Group B and he remained in that position until the end of the war. Wagener had previously been General Manteuffel's Chief of Staff. The official US history of World War II described Manteuffel's staff as having possibly been the best in the West.[27] Wagener served Model without incidents, but the two men would never be close. Wagener wrote later that his relations with his commander never reached a level that could be described as undisturbed. "Our natures had little in common."[28]

Allied capture of Paris and the German rout

In the first two months after the Allied landing in Normandy, Allied progress had been slow. Fierce combat raged in a countryside favourable only for defensive operations. After the Allies had broken through at Avranches in the first week of August 1944, strong American forces were converging upon Paris. Hitler had issued an order to defend Paris at all costs. He appointed *Generalleutnant* Dietrich von Choltitz, who commanded LXXXIV Corps in Normandy, as commander of Paris. He was given the authority of a fortress commander.[29]

General von Choltitz is a typical example of the Jekyll-Hyde personality of a number of German Generals in World War II. He refused to carry out Hitler's intention of destroying Paris, and surrendered an intact city to the French General Leclerc. Leclerc's Armoured Division had been given the privilege of being the first Allied unit to enter

---

24 Schramm, op.cit.
25 *Bulge*, p.29.
26 Freyberg, 19 August 1955, BA-MA N6/1.
27 *Bulge*, p.173.
28 BA-MA, ZA 1/1252, p.1.
29 D. v. Choltitz, *Soldaten unter Soldaten*, Zürich 1951, p.224 ff. (Henceforth Choltitz).

the city. After the war, the French authorities decorated General von Choltitz with the *Légion d'Honneur*. The luxury Hotel Meurice, where he had his headquarters in 1944, offered him a suite, free of charge, any time he visited Paris. On the other hand, in talks with comrades in the British POW camp at Trent Park, he boasted that as a regimental commander in Manstein's 11th Army, he had ruthlessly participated in the murder of Jews in the Crimea, in 1941. On 29 August 1944, only four days after he had surrendered Paris and was taken to Trent Park, he told General Wilhelm Ritter von Thoma: "The most difficult assignment ever given to me was the liquidation of Jews. I carried out that order to the utmost limit."[30]

On 18 August 1944, Model ordered General von Choltitz to report directly to him:

The Commander of '*Gross-Paris*', General von Choltitz is personally and directly subordinated to me as of 17.8, at 12 am.

The foreseen measures of destruction, which were discussed on 17 August, at 9 am, may only be carried out by an order from myself.[31]

In a message to *OKW* on 21 August, Model showed some scepticism of Hitler's destruction order:

Paris remains a major problem. If the Allied attack is accompanied by an uprising, 20,000 German troops are insufficient. I have therefore ordered planning for a new line of defence north and east of the city.[32]

The following day, Hitler gave an additional order,

The city must be turned into a heap of rubble. The commander fights to the last bullet and will let himself be buried under the ruins.[33]

The war diary of Army Group B contains the following passage on 23 August:

OB Army Group takes a very serious view of the situation in Paris. One has to be prepared for the possibility that things will turn out to be different from those foreseen. Should this occur, *OB* requests clear instructions for eventual fighting within Paris. Chief of *OKW/WFSt.*, Jodl, has replied that Paris must be held 'for the time being'. *OB* stated that he is not prepared to receive provisional orders. He requires a clear directive for the possibility that the situation in Paris is no longer under control. In reply to Chief *OKW/WFSt*, that reinforcements are under way to *OB* West, *OB* Army Group states that one assault gun unit, or other weak units, are unable to defend a city, with millions of inhabitants, against attacks both from the

---

30 Neitzel, p.258. General von Choltitz's admission was an additional nail in the coffin of Manstein's repeated mendacious statements that 11th Army had nothing to do with the slaughter of Jews and that he was not even aware of it

31 Model/Bradley, Facsimile p. 249.

32 Ibid.

33 Choltitz, p.256.

outside or within the city. *OB* Army Group requests Chief *OKW/WFSt.* to transmit his opinion directly to the *Führer*.[34]

In his memoirs, General von Choltitz recalled his last phone conversation with Speidel on 24 August:

Choltitz: "Please let me speak to the *Feldmarschall*."

Speidel: "The *Feldmarschall* is listening in."

Choltitz: "Please let me talk to him."

Speidel: "The *Feldmarschall* is shaking his head. He has no more orders to issue."

The resistance groups in Paris could not have coped with organized German troops. General von Choltitz had commanded the air raid upon Rotterdam, in 1940, which had resulted in numerous civilian casualties, so his assumption of command in Paris caused some initial fears.

On 14 August, a demolition squad arrived in Paris. On the following day, General von Choltitz received a written order to blow up the bridges over the Seine. He ordered the commander of the demolition squad to remain in place, to make preparations to carry out the orders, and to await instructions. A few days later he simply sent the men away.

General von Choltitz then entered into negotiations with the Paris representatives of the Vichy government, about maintaining order, and supplying the civilian population with foodstuffs. Raoul Nordling, Swedish Consul General in Paris, whose mother was French, and Roger Naville, the Swiss delegate of the International Red Cross in France, joined in General von Choltitz's efforts.[35]

Local French resistance groups did not take part in the negotiations. General von Choltitz did however receive representatives of de Gaulle, who had come to Paris, but he had to be careful because he could not trust his own officers. When Minister Alexandre Parodi and two more of de Gaulle's representatives arrived in the city, they were arrested. General von Choltitz received a phone call from the officer who had made the arrest. The officer boasted of a "wonderful capture" and asked him if the de Gaulle representatives should be shot. General von Choltitz replied that he would want so speak to them first. In his memoirs he recalled, with some humour, that the first question one member of Parodi's group put to him was, "Do you speak German?" to which he replied, "Probably better than you." Parodi warned him about the lack of discipline in the various resistance groups.

On 19 August, General von Choltitz received his last order from *OKW*. It was signed by Hitler. It ordered him to turn the city into rubble and, if required, to die in the fighting. He refused to comply and surrendered the city.

---

34 Facsimile in Model/Bradley, p.264.
35 Choltitz, p.248.

Rout, disintegration, and re-establishing a line of defence

After the fall of Paris, the German retreat turned into a rout and units began to disintegrate. In places, roads recalled the images of the French soldiers' flight in 1940. Model succeeded in stabilizing the situation within a few weeks. That accomplishment must rank among his major successes of the war. Most of his direct messages to Hitler remained unanswered. Model understood that the new situation compelled him to act upon his own initiative, without waiting for orders from Hitler. An entry in the war diary of Army Group B, on 31 August, stated tersely: "The situation has developed as *OB* had foreseen. The British and the Americans have broken through and there are no forces capable of opposing them."[36]

A leaflet that Model had air-dropped to his troops in the field, stated clearly that Germany had lost a battle.[37] Troops were encouraged not to wait for orders from their local units or assembly centres, but to act on their own, and join any fighting unit they could find. An order issued that same month forbade any transfer of units to Germany.[38] Direct operational orders were then issued to the Armies. 5th *Panzer* Army was directed to display more resolve.[39] Reserves were brought in, including a strong Infantry Division with 14,800 men. At the beginning of September, the Allied command still had expectations that a rapid end to the war was in sight. Bradley wrote in his memoirs that the restoration of a stabilized front line was "nearly miraculous".[40] Bradley, as do a number of British and American writers, credits Rundstedt.[41] But the official US history emphasized that the "miracle" that had occurred in the West "was mainly due to the capable, energetic, and fanatical commander, Walter Model."[42]

Failure of Operation *Market Garden* – the Allied airborne assault on Arnhem

A number of books have been written about *Market Garden*. Two of those books became bestsellers, namely Cornelius Ryan's *A Bridge Too Far*, and Alexander McKee's *The Race for the Rhine bridges*.[43] The books appeared more than forty years ago and their sources are outdated.

In 2001, the British historian, Dr Arnold Harvey, published a detailed and seriously researched book, *Arnhem*.[44] This chapter follows Harvey's analysis without repeatedly mentioning the source in footnotes.

---

36   Model/Bradley, p.267.

37   Ibid, p.282.

38   Ibid, Facsimile 259 ff.

39   Ibid, p.261.

40   O. Bradley, *A General's Life*, New York 1983, p. 349 (henceforth Bradley).

41   "When we started our November offensive, we knew that the experienced professional Rundstedt had taken over supreme command in the West. We could there expect a 'text book' defence." Ibid, p.350.

42   US Army, Volume: *Siegfried Line Campaign*, p.392.

43   C. Ryan, *A Bridge too Far*, London 1974, and A. McKee, *The race for the Rhine Bridges 1940 and 1944-45*, London 1971.

44   A. Harvey, *Arnhem*, London 2001. A German translation of Harvey's book appeared in 2004 as the second part of a book *Kreta und Arnhem. Die grössten Luftlandeoperationen des*

Market Garden was the largest airborne operation ever. Three Allied Divisions of paratroopers, carried by gliders and transport planes, were intended to occupy the region around the city of Arnhem, and to secure the bridges for XXX British Corps. The first wave consisted of 360 British and 1,174 US transport planes, 419 gliders and 910 fighter planes. The attack was preceded by an attack of 1,113 bombers, accompanied by 330 fighter planes.

The final objective was to cut through the Netherlands, leaving it divided in two parts, thus opening the way to Germany, and bypassing the *Westwall* fortifications. General Montgomery had insisted that the final assault was to be conducted by 2nd British Army. He wrote in his memoirs that the British troops would show themselves to be the equals of troops from other countries in mobile operations. (The prestige rivalry between the US and British Armies was one of the major problems besetting Eisenhower). Furthermore, V2 rockets were launched against British objectives from Belgium and the Netherlands. Churchill pressed for a capture of their launching pads. But Montgomery had not paid sufficient attention to logistics, which showed that a victorious final offensive before the end of 1944 simply was not in the cards.

The Allied plans were further compromised by the presence of two *Waffen-SS Panzer* Divisions, *Hohenstaufen* and *Frundsberg*. Their arrival had escaped the attention of Allied intelligence. Two elite *Waffen-SS Panzer* Divisions could have played a major factor in tipping the scales in German favour. However, neither *Hohenstaufen* nor *Frundsberg* were outstanding units. Both had been decimated in previous fighting. Of the two divisions only 7,000 men and a handful of *Panzer* remained. Neither of the two divisions had distinguished themselves in previous encounters. Both were awarded the smallest number of Knight's Crosses among all *Waffen-SS* Divisions.

Most of the German high commanders and units during *Market Garden* were from the *Waffen-SS*.

Harvey was critical of a programme on Channel 4, on 24 February 2000, that described Market Garden as one of the "greatest stupidities of World War II". He advanced the opinion that the far-reaching strategic goal was questionable, but that the immediate aims could well have succeeded if the detailed planning had been better.

For some years after the war, rumours persisted that the operation plans had been betrayed to the Germans by a Dutch informer, Christian Lindemans, known as 'King-Kong'. Like all popular tales about espionage and treason, that has been proved pure fiction. Generally speaking, the importance of espionage during the war has been widely exaggerated by journalistic authors.[45] The Germans knew, by means of intelligence, that the Allies had one Airborne Division and two Infantry Divisions brought in from Normandy. They had taken part in the battles after D-Day and later, been put into reserve for other operations. Apparently the Germans believed that they were to be used as support for a future Dutch uprising, similar to the Warsaw uprising.[46]

Zweiten Weltkrieges, Graz 2004. The part of the book about Crete is written by *Bundeswehr Generalleutnant* (ret.) Dr. Franz Uhle-Wettler.

45 More than half a century after the events, a German TV program had Prince Bernhard, the German-born husband of Queen Juliana of the Netherlands, responsible for leaking the secrets of the operation to the Germans. This has likewise been established as pure nonsense.

46 Harvey, p.155-160.

The first Allied units landed barely two kilometres away from Model's command post. Model had to run to safety. He is reported to have said to *SS Obergruppenführer* Wilhelm Bittrich: "They nearly got me. They were after my headquarters. Just imagine! They nearly got me." Bittrich was at some pains to tell Model that he should not overrate his own importance. The operation was far too sizeable for the Allies to bother about one German commander, even if he was as important as Model.

A few hours later Model, once more in control of himself, organized the defensive actions. He withdrew troops from positions which were not attacked, used them as mobile units, and attacked the narrow corridor between Eindhoven and Arnhem on both flanks. The Allied troops now faced the danger that the German pincers could close and create a *Kessel*. However, Harvey felt that Model failed to understand the strategic thoughts behind the operation. He was of the opinion that the landings mainly served the purpose of preventing him from utilizing the bridges at Nijmegen and Arnhem in actions by Army Group B. For that reason, Model overrode Bittrich's advice to blow up the bridges. If they had to be blown up, he did not want to do the Allies' work, but wanted to leave it to them to blow up the bridges when they reached them.

Allied progress was hampered by masses of jubilant Dutch. They felt that their hour of liberation had come, and streamed into the streets of the cities in the zone of combat. On 24 September, the battle turned in German favour, and on the night of 25 September the Allied troops were withdrawn.

The operation ended in failure and led to the usual complaints between the Allies. Officers of the US airborne units felt "cheated" when the British tanks did not progress to capture Arnhem and secure the remaining bridges. The Polish General, Stanisław Sosabowski, Commander of the 1st Polish Airborne Brigade, was accused by a British officer of being "recalcitrant and disinclined to engage with full strength in the fighting". That was slander, because the Polish troops fought hard and Sosabowski had an established reputation as a particularly tough commander. Sosabowski, and the commander of the 4th British Airborne Brigade, shared the opinion that the whole operation had not taken sufficient account of the Germans' fighting power.[47]

10,200 British soldiers had landed at Arnhem. 1,440 were killed in action or died later of wounds, 6,000 were taken prisoner. 105 Allied planes were shot down. 450 Dutch civilians were killed. German casualties, taken from a report by *SS Obergruppenführer* Bittrich's staff, showed 1,300 killed in action, and 2,000 wounded. Harvey feels that their losses must have been higher. In his view, many of the German soldiers at Arnhem had not finished their training, and a number of their junior officers were not up to their task. The main asset of the German senior commanders was their flexibility, and their power of quick reaction to unforeseen circumstances. In Harvey's eyes, *Market Garden* was no real success for either side. Even if the Allies had reached their goals, Montgomery's idea of using the battle as a stepping-stone for a successful invasion of Germany was simply not

---

47 Harvey writes that Sosabowski's qualities were better appreciated by his British civilian employers after the war than by his British comrades in arms. Sosabowski had found employment in a plant producing electronic equipment. His performance was judged to be of such quality that the firm kept him until the age of 75, well beyond retirement age, Harvey, p. 269 (the page numbers refer to the German edition, in which Harvey's part was preceded by Uhle-Wettler's account of the battle for Crete).

on the cards. The local success scored by the Germans was likewise meaningless. At that stage of the war, most German officers knew that the war was lost and their continued fighting was a "flight from reality and not even a realistic one".[48] Harvey emphasized that the main reason for the German success was the actions of the three most senior German commanders. *Feldmarschall* Walter Model, *Generaloberst* Kurt Student and *SS Obergruppenführer* Wilhelm Bittrich hardly ever took a wrong step, while their opponents, Lieutenant General Frederick Browning, Lieutenant General Brian Horrocks, and Major General Robert Urquhart, were never able to do the right thing and were afraid to take risks. In Harvey's opinion it was not the British soldiers who failed. They were among the very best British units, while many of their German opponents were a mixture of tired and insufficiently trained soldiers. The responsibility for the Allied failure had to be searched for higher up, not only at the local commanders' level, but up to Montgomery.

Operation *Market Garden* was followed by particularly hard fighting around Aachen and in the Hürtgen Wald, with heavy losses on both sides. Bradley described them as one of the bloodiest "butcheries" during the whole of World War II. Model succeeded in beating an orderly retreat to the *Westwall*.

The Ardennes offensive[49]

The Ardennes offensive was the last major *Wehrmacht* offensive in World War II. It ended in fiasco. During its planning phase, Model favoured a "small solution," as opposed to Hitler's "grand solution." Although Allied intelligence generally had a clear view of German intentions, the plans and preparations for an offensive in the Ardennes went undetected. Such an intelligence failure by the Allies was a rare occurrence in World War II. As a consequence, there was some initial panic on the Allied side when the offensive began.

The main sources for this section are an unpublished report by Professor Percy Schramm, the unpublished recollections of Colonel Günther Reichhelm, who was the Ia at Army Group B,[50] and the official US History of World War II, a volume entitled *The Ardennes – Ardennes offensive*. The memoirs of British and American commanders are of little value. The official British history, *Victory in the West*, published in 1974, is likewise somewhat unreliable. Many of the British archives had not yet been made available at that time.[51]

Preparations

In an appendix to his unpublished memoirs, Reichhelm, the Ia of Army Group B, described the concealment measures adopted by the *Wehrmacht*. Troop concentrations were designated by the code name "Defensive Battle." No telephone conversations about

---

48 Ibid, p.259.

49 Although the German term is more appropriate, "Battle of the Bulge" will also be used since it is the accepted name in British and US terminology.

50 Reichhelm's account was part of a study completed for the US Army's historical division. Since it deals with operations only, his account is reliable.

51 The memoirs of Bradley and Montgomery recall a comment by Alistair Horne about the battle for France: "They [General Gamelin and General Georges] are so busy making war on each other that they have no time to make war on the Germans." A. Horne, *To lose a battle – France 1940*, Boston 1969, p.113 ff.

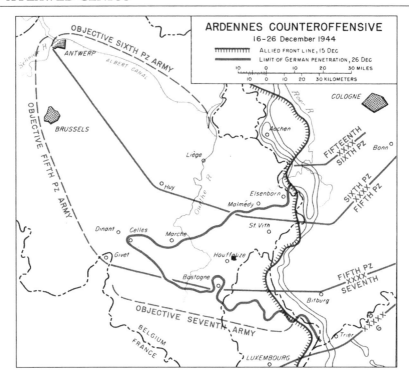

the impending offensive were allowed. The Divisions were to conduct their training in isolated companies, at widely separated locations. The front line had to remain unchanged and no replacements were permitted. Supply to the front line was carried out by horse-drawn vehicles only, and the hooves of the horses were muffled with straw. Fictitious operation names were used. Maps were given to the commanders only three days before the offensive was launched.

Model had intended to use Manteuffel's 5th *Panzer* Army as the spearhead, but had to accede to Hitler's order to leave that assignment to Dietrich's 6th *Panzer* Army. For once, there were no altercations between Model and his army commanders. Manteuffel agreed with his opinions. Dietrich had little understanding about operational matters, but he showed discipline, and carried out every order. Because of his distrust of General Brandenberger, Model relegated his army to operations in the rear.

"Grand solution" and "Small solution"

Such "solutions" may be summarized as follows: The "grand solution" called for the German Army to encircle the American and British troops north of Bastogne, Brussels, and Antwerp, then destroy them. It was to consist of two successive phases. The initial phase would involve an attack towards the Meuse River, to establish bridgeheads. The second phase called for an advance towards Antwerp, and the capture of the Allied main supply centre.[52] The ultimate objective was then to entrap the Allied forces, surround them, and systematically crush them.

The "small solution" was restricted to an advance towards the Meuse River and the occupation of Liège. This tactic was designed to separate the Allies in the Aachen area from the rest of the Allied forces. The main objective was to prevent an Allied advance toward Cologne and the Rhine area. When questioned by Model, Manteuffel had replied that the "small solution" was feasible as long as all available reserves were committed, and would not be diverted to other parts of the front.

Model's warnings in Autumn 1944

After being appointed *OB* West and *OB* of Army Group B, on 17 August 1944, Model issued a series of warnings directly to Hitler and *OKW*. He emphasized the enormous Allied superiority in manpower and equipment. Model also pointed out that his own troop strength was weakening: "My soldiers are burnt out."[53] A report on 24 August stressed that the Allies enjoyed total air supremacy.[54] On 27 August, with a request for communication to Hitler, Model made a demand for reserves which, "given the weakened units of Army Group B, are indispensable".[55] A message of 29 August, with request for communication to Hitler, emphasized the insufficient equipment in small arms.[56] On 1 September and again on 3 September, Model complained that anti-tank artillery was not available and repeated that his troops were exhausted.[57] Requests for new armoured units were denied because Hitler was already toying with the idea of a large-scale offensive in the West.

On 11 September, Model reported that he could not guarantee his troops could hold the *Westwall* fortifications and that the door to *Reich* territory would be thrown open.[58] On 15 September, a general situation review to *OB* West stated that the situation was becoming more critical by the day, that the fighting power of 7th Army was reduced to an unsustainable level, that the *Westwall* had been breached on several points and that the pressure on Aachen had increased.[59] On the same date, he complained that many of his subordinate unit commanders had become exhausted and had to be replaced.[60] The American book about the Ardennes Offensive stated that Rundstedt's and Model's appeals were becoming increasingly desperate.[61]

---

52 The city and the port of Antwerp had been taken by the Allies, but the Schelde estuary could not be used for Allied shipping because the Walcheren peninsula was still in German hands. The definition of Antwerp as the main supply centre calls for some restriction.
53 Model/Bradley, facsimile, p.265 ff.
54 Ibid, p.250.
55 Ibid, p.271.
56 Ibid, p.277 ff.
57 Ibid, p.287.
58 Ibid, p.292.
59 Ibid, p. 296 ff.
60 Ibid, p. 302.
61 *Bulge,* p. 15 – There were no direct complaints or requests from Rundstedt. Rundstedt only forwarded Model's reports and complaints addressed to *OB* West to Hitler.

Fight for the "small solution"

Hitler began to plan for an offensive after the Allied Operation *Anvil* landing, in the south of France, in August. At first, he only thought in general terms, without focusing on a firm goal. US official military history recorded that Hitler had agreed to an "orderly retreat" in order to make forces available for the forthcoming offensive.[62] That was obviously not the case. After the Allied breakthrough at Avranches, there were no orderly German retreats. The troops panicked and units began to disintegrate.

On 19 August, a conference took place at Hitler's headquarters. Hitler ordered Albert Speer and General Walter Buhle, head of the Army staff at *OKW*, to make large troop units available together with corresponding quantities of equipment. According to official US military history accounts, a meeting took place between Hitler and Jodl on 6 September.[63] The exact date of that meeting has not been verified. At that meeting, Hitler told Jodl that reports from Rundstedt had led him to fear the *Westwall* could not be held, so he intended to launch a major offensive on 1 November. That account is doubtful, since in September, the Allies were still some distance from the *Westwall*.

Rundstedt and Model were informed of Hitler's plans on 28 October. Official US military history accounts state erroneously that they had already been informed in September.[64] Details of Hitler's plans had been kept secret until then, but rumours had obviously reached the commanders. The two Chiefs of Staff, Westphal and Krebs, represented Rundstedt and Model at the meeting of 28 October when Hitler outlined his basic plans. Both Westphal and Krebs expressed scepticism, but Hitler assured them forcefully that sufficient reserves would be made available. According to US military history accounts, Keitel pledged his word of honour as an officer that enough fuel was on hand.[65] No formal orders were issued on that occasion. Instead, the commanders were directed to scrutinize the plans and to state their own opinions.

Westphal reported his sceptical views to Rundstedt, and Krebs did likewise with Model. US military accounts quoted Model as having said, "This plan does not have a damned leg to stand on."[66] The only point on which Rundstedt and Model were in total agreement was the impossibility of taking Antwerp. Rundstedt developed his *"Martin Plan"*, which called for a two-pronged attack. Model proposed his own *"Herbstnebel Plan"*, which called for one single point of main effort. Both plans were made within the framework of the "small solution." From that point on, Model received no further support from Rundstedt, and the pressure for the "small solution" was left to Model alone. Model presented his proposals to *OKW* on 2 November.

Meanwhile, Hitler and Jodl had differences of opinion. Jodl had submitted his own plan to Hitler on 24 October. It suggested two alternatives, either an attack on Antwerp from Venlo which corresponded to the "grand solution," or an encirclement of Liège which was the "small solution." Jodl expressed his strong conviction that the capture of Antwerp

62 US Army, Volume: *U.S. Army in World War II, the Ardennes – Battle of the Bulge,* henceforth: US Army, *Bulge* p.15.
63 Ibid.
64 Ibid.
65 Ibid.
66 Ibid., p.6.

was only possible if all available troops, down to boys of school age, were mobilized.[67] Moreover, he felt that the front commanders had to be given some flexibility of command.

Hitler rejected Jodl's proposals, and said that the "small solution" was ridiculous. He directed Jodl to combine his two ideas into one. But he did not agree to authorize a total mobilization, nor to transfer troops from the East. When Jodl realized that he could not convince Hitler, he sent Rundstedt a formal order, signed by Hitler, which emphasized that Hitler was irrevocably committed to the "grand solution."

Since Jodl wanted to distance himself from Hitler's decision, he appended a letter of his own. It emphasized that the forces available were not sufficient, but that all bets had to be placed 'on one horse.'[68] Rundstedt sent a somewhat meaningless reply on 3 November. US official military accounts described it as an example of the Prussian military tradition to always keep a written record of disagreements.[69] From that time on, Rundstedt participated in no further meetings, choosing instead to be represented by Westphal.

Model then informed Rundstedt of his opposition to Rundstedt's "*Martin* Plan," particularly the proposed attack by XII Corps which Model considered too weak.[70] Rundstedt replied that, in his view, XII Corps had to proceed as he himself had suggested.[71] There was further confusion when Hitler issued an order on 11 November rejecting the "*Martin* Plan".

Rundstedt then completely revised his opinion in an 18 November letter to Jodl which supported Model's views.[72] On 20 November, Model submitted a compromise proposal to Jodl which had Rundstedt's agreement. Model's compromise proposed to try the "small solution" first, and if it succeeded, then try Hitler's "grand solution." Hitler did not send Model a personal reply. Instead, he dictated Jodl's reply, that no alterations or improvisations were permitted.[73]

On 26 November, Jodl went to Rundstedt's headquarters where he met Rundstedt and Model. Both Rundstedt and Model pleaded again for the "small solution". In reply, they were informed that there could be no change in Hitler's plans.[74] The language between Model and Jodl became increasingly abrasive, and Jodl returned without an agreement. Manteuffel reported that he had listened in on a telephone conversation between the two and that Model had said to Jodl: "You can tell your *Führer* that Model will not carry out such an order."[75] If those words were really said, they were empty talk, since Model did eventually carry out "such an order".

On 2 December, Model was ordered to present himself at the chancellery offices in Berlin. He was accompanied by his Army commanders Manteuffel and Dietrich. Reichhelm also attended that meeting as the Army Group's Ia. In his memoirs, Reichhelm wrote

---

67 This would indeed happen during the last days of the war.
68 Letter Jodl to Westphal, 1 November 1944, KTB *OB* West, Anl.50, Vol.1, p.67-70. Also quoted in *Bulge,* p.28.
69 *Bulge,* p.28.
70 Ibid. p.29.
71 Ibid.
72 Ibid, p.30.
73 Ibid.
74 Ibid, p.31.
75 Estate, Testimonial by Manteuffel at the Model de-Nazification hearing, 21 March 1950.

that Model was close to physical exhaustion when he made his final plea for the "small solution." Hitler simply refused to listen. Reichhelm wrote that when the officers left the meeting, Manteuffel and Dietrich spontaneously gripped Model's hand and thanked him for his uncompromising stance.

I feel that no handshake and no thanks were in order. On the contrary, Model had hardly distinguished himself at that meeting. The only worthy course which was open to him, would have been to say to Hitler: "*Mein Führer*, I have given you all the reasons for my opposition to the operation, based on my knowledge and experience. If you refuse to take my objections into account, you will have to appoint another *OB* for this battle. I cannot live with the responsibility of sending my troops into a battle where I know that they will be destroyed." Had Model acted in that manner, not only the handshakes and the thanks would have been in order, but history would have applauded him. But he behaved no better than a sergeant and the kick which he received with Hitler's message of December 15 was well deserved.

Hitler's order to Model on 15 December 1944

Fearing that Model might act on his own initiative, Hitler issued a direct order containing language that was unusual for a communication to a *Feldmarschall*. Hitler's orders included very detailed instructions as to the limits of Model's authority for every step of the operation.

> I have reached my final decision. All prerequisites for a successful operation are in hand. The size and the dimensions of the success rest solely upon the operational steps to be taken.
>
> I make it incumbent upon you to carry out every order from supreme command, unconditionally, and to see to it that obedience will be observed down to the smallest unit.
>
> I forbid any turning of armoured units east of the Meuse to the north.
>
> I order *Panzer* units of 6th *Panzer* Army to be removed far enough from XII Corps to prevent them from being engaged in the actions of the Corps.
>
> All roads within the area of 5th *Panzer* Army, if required up to Namur, have to be put at the sole disposal of 6th *Panzer* Army, if it appears that crossing the river in and around Liège will not succeed.
>
> I hold you personally responsible that no concentration of tank units will occur in the Liège area since this will lead to their becoming engaged east of the Meuse.
>
> The advance upon Antwerp on its eastern flank will have the natural cover of the Meuse channel, and no further defensive positions are allowed to be set up further west.
>
> The left wing of 15th Army has to be strengthened to the point that it will make it unnecessary to have Infantry Divisions of 6th *Panzer* Army involved in the combats around Simmerath, and thus weaken the defensive flank between Monschau and Liège.
>
> If all these instructions are obeyed, a great success is assured.
>
> Adolf Hitler[76]

---

76 Facsimile in Model/Bradley, p.338 ff.

In his reply to *OKW* and to Rundstedt, on 16 December, Model stated that Hitler's orders had been passed on without alterations to his army commanders and that "the goal of Army Group is and remains Antwerp," followed by an exclamation mark.[77] Rundstedt released an order of the day containing Hitler's orders *verbatim*, but Model appended a short order of the day of his own. Model's order of the day ended with the words which he often used: "No soldier worldwide may be better than the soldier of the Eifel and of Aachen."[78] In a curious exchange of letters between Rundstedt and Model, Model had repeatedly complained to Rundstedt that sufficient fuel was not available. On 19 December, three days after the battle had begun, and failure was already apparent, Rundstedt admonished Model to be careful with fuel, and ended with the absurd words: "Whatever additional fuel we need, we will grab from the enemy."[79]

Rundstedt remained as *OB* West until 11 March 1945, when he was retired for the last time. *Feldmarschall* Kesselring replaced him. Kesselring had begun his military career in the Army. When the *Luftwaffe* had been created, Kesselring had been one of several army officers who had "changed uniforms". As head of one of the *Luftflotten* in France, Kesselring had become a *Feldmarschall* on 19 July 1940. Later he became head of the Mediterranean Theatre of Operations. He was a capable officer, although he was not Brett-Smith's "great commander". His assessments were blurred by excessive optimism, and he always attempted to present views which would ingratiate him with Hitler.[80]

Kesselring and Model never developed a close personal affinity, and their interactions were strictly limited to necessary military matters. By that time, Model had become fully aware that the situation had become desperate, and he found it difficult to reconcile his assessments with Kesselring's optimism. During the few remaining months of the war, Kesselring issued a number of orders of the day which bore no relation to the true situation, and included simply atrocious insults to officers serving under him.

Was the "small solution" likewise doomed?

In Reichhelm's opinion, the "small solution" alternative was likewise doomed to failure, and he gave the following reasons:

- Preparations were not complete.
- The troops available were too weak in combat strength and equipment, and their number was far from the numbers required to meet the objective.
- Supplies were not adequate.
- Promised air support bore no relation to reality.
- Allied air supremacy would have paralyzed operations and supply.

After the failure of the Ardennes offensive, Hitler was looking for a scapegoat. When the young Colonel Hellmuth Mäder was promoted to *Generalmajor* at the age of 36, he reported personally to Hitler, on 5 February 1945, for the award of the swords to the oak leaves of his Knight's Cross. Hitler asked him why he felt that the battle had failed. Mäder had taken part in the battle, and tried to answer with standard military arguments, but

---

77 Ibid, p.338.
78 Ibid, p.339.
79 Ibid, p.342 ff.
80 Kesselring's nickname was "smiling Albert".

Hitler cut him short. Hitler complained that he had planned a large size operation while Model had insisted on a smaller one, "Model simply flattened me."[81]

At Nuremberg, Keitel told the American prosecutor:

> After the failure of the Ardennes offensive, Hitler told me that Rundstedt was too old. He did not have the right understanding and had insufficient influence over his generals. 'I cannot ask a man of his age to run around daily from one command post to another. We need a new and more active man'. I replied, 'Why don't you take Model? He knows the whole front and he is always on the move.' I received no reply. I was convinced that Hitler needed to have a scapegoat to avoid history shouldering him with the responsibility.[82]

But can the Ardennes offensive be analyzed with military logic? The answer must probably be in the negative. All the discussions about the various aspects of the "grand" and "small" solutions were an exercise in futility. The whole operation was Hitler's sole decision, far more so than the attack on France 1940. At that time, Hitler had the support of commanders who belonged to the "teams" of Manstein and Guderian. In 1944, every high commander of the *Wehrmacht*, when asked to give his opinion about the Ardennes plan, vehemently opposed it. Hitler was no military novice and he was obviously aware that the operation was doomed from the very beginning. He did not need Model's advice that the plan did not have a leg to stand on, he knew it himself. He also knew that his last order to Model, with "a great success assured", was empty talk, as were his previous replies to the objections made by all commanders and chiefs of staff involved.

Hitler had obviously not foreseen that the offensive would catch SHAEF by surprise and lead to initial panic. But even this lasted barely a week. On 24 December, the offensive had already collapsed. Sebastian Haffner advances the opinion that Hitler knew from the beginning that the offensive was doomed. But Hitler was following his own political views which tied the fate of the German people to his person. In his probably unique analysis of Hitler's character and motives, Haffner feels that one basis for Hitler's weakening the Eastern Front, in favour of a hopeless operation in the West, may have been his growing admiration for Stalin and his increasingly pathological hatred of Roosevelt and Churchill.

Most of the German people were tired of the war. Their last hope was that the Western Allied Armies would advance quickly and, as far as possible, before the Red Army arrived. By launching an offensive which perhaps could delay the Allied advance in the West, Hitler intended at least to spoil that hope. At that time, he already knew that he would issue the "Nero" order, calling for a destruction of the remaining German infrastructure.[83] It has already been mentioned that the *Wehrmachtführungsstab* diaries, which were kept by Jodl, reveal that already in December 1941, Hitler no longer believed that the war could

---

81 Mäder was one of the youngest *Wehrmacht* Generals. In the *Bundeswehr* he rose to three-star General. On 19 October 1976 he was indicted in Cologne for fraud and corruption and was sentenced to two years without probation.

82 Office of the United States Chief Counsel for Prosecution of Axis Criminality, *Nazi Conspiracy and Aggression,* US Government Printing Office, Washington, 1948.

83 Haffner, p.193 ff.

be won.[84] On 27 November 1941, before the beginning of the Russian counter-offensive at Moscow, Hitler said to the Danish foreign minister Scavenius and the Croatian foreign minister Lorković, "I am always ice cold.[85] If, at some time in the future, the German people will not show themselves to be strong, and ready to sacrifice their blood to assure their existence, they deserve to perish and be destroyed by a stronger nation. I will shed no tears about their fate."[86]

In his "table talk" of 26 January 1942, Hitler said: "I see things with the coldest objectivity. If the German people lost their faith, if the German people were no longer inclined to give themselves body and soul in order to survive, then the German people would have nothing to do but disappear!"[87]

In his last talk with Speer, on 18 March 1945, Hitler said, "If the war is lost, so are the German people. There is no need for consideration of the fundamentals which are needed for continuing their most basic existence. On the contrary, it is preferable to destroy them ourselves. The German people have shown themselves to be weaklings, and the future only belongs to the stronger Eastern nation. Anyhow, only weaklings remain, all the brave have fallen".[88] Deep down, Hitler had probably laughed when Model, Manteuffel, Dietrich and Reichhelm came to him with their "last, desperate plea".

The Remagen tragedy

The Ludendorff Bridge at Remagen was seized by the Americans on 7 March 1945. The capture was of little military significance. It did not shorten the war by a single day. A few days later the Rhine was crossed at many other locations. Rivers were never major obstacles during World War II, but the bridge at Remagen had a tremendous psychological impact. The capture of an intact bridge was a source of great satisfaction to the Americans. They had crossed the Rhine before Montgomery's British forces.

At first, *Wehrmacht* communiqués were ambiguous and refrained from mentioning the capture of the bridge by name. The name "Remagen" appeared for the first time on 12 March, five days after it had fallen into the hands of the Americans: "East of Remagen, hard fighting takes place. The enemy did not succeed in widening his narrow bridgehead."

The communiqués of 13 to 17 March simply described continued hard fighting around Remagen. The communiqué of 18 March included the following: "A summary court martial

---

84 "…in particular, it became evident to the *Führer* and to *Generaloberst* Jodl that after the winter of 1941/42 no more victory was possible…" Jodl stated at Nuremberg: "Hitler was the first to understand during winter 1941/42 that the war was lost".

85 Ice cold (*eiskalt*) and lightning speed (*blitzschnell*) were two favourite expressions of Hitler.

86 Ibid, p.152.

87 H. Trevor-Roper (ed.), *Hitler's table talks 1941-1944,* London 1953, p.257.

88 Speer, p.446. Any statement by Speer has to be viewed with extreme caution after the historian and movie producer Heinrich Breloer exposed his lies in 2005. (H. Breloer, *Speer und Er. Hitlers Architekt und Rüstungsminister,* Berlin 2005). Speer's biographer Joachim Fest and the publisher of his recollections, Wolf Jobst Siedler, admitted that Speer had fooled them. (*Er hat uns allen eine Nase gedreht*). Gitta Sereny's 800 page book about Speer has likewise been unable to uncover Speer's active part in the Shoah. (G. Sereny, *Albert Speer. Das Ringen mit der Wahrheit und das deutsche Trauma,* Munich 1997). Breloer does not contradict Speer's account of the Nero order, therefore here Speer's recollections can safely be followed here.

has sentenced Major Strobel, officer at an Engineer Battalion, Major Scheller, Adjutant of a Corps, Major Kraft, officer of an Engineer Battalion, Lieutenant Peters, in charge of anti-aircraft defence of the Rhine bridge and, *in absentia*, Captain Bratge, commander of the Remagen combat, zone to death, on grounds of cowardliness and criminal neglect of their duties. They had carelessly neglected to blow up the Remagen Bridge and did not defend it decisively. The sentences against Strobel, Scheller, Kraft, and Peters have been carried out immediately."

Captain Wilhelm Bratge was fortunate enough to have been taken prisoner by the Allies. His account is the primary source of the events which occurred at the bridge.

German and Allied forces at Remagen

Remagen was in the area of the German 15th Army commanded by General von Zangen. The bridge itself was in the area of LXVII Corps, commanded by General Otto Hitzfeld. On 2 March, a special staff under General Joachim von Kortzfleisch was established to prepare for the defence of the bridge. The officers responsible for the details were those named in the *Wehrmacht* communiqué of 18 March The bridge itself was commanded by a company assigned to an Engineer Battalion under Captain Karl Friesenhahn.

On the Allied side, Remagen was within the area of the 1st US Army under Lieutenant General Courtney Hodges. The capture was made by parts of 277th Mechanized Infantry Battalion commanded by 2nd Lieutenant Timmermann which was part of Major General John Leonard's 9th US Armoured Division. The Division belonged to the US III Corps commanded by Major General John Milliken.

Major Scheller's actions

Major Hans Scheller arrived at Remagen on 7 March, between 10 and 11 am. He accompanied Captain Wilhelm Bratge to General Otto Hitzfeld and told him that he intended to defend the bridge on the left bank. Scheller was made Commander of the Remagen Combat Area. A reinforcement company was dispatched but was taken prisoner before reaching its destination.

Five soldiers with a machine-gun were placed on the road leading to the bridge, but they soon disappeared. Major Scheller had remained on the west bank to wait for the arrival of an artillery unit. Approximately 45 critical minutes were then lost. Captain Karl Friesenhahn searched for Captain Bratge, who in turn was trying to find Major Scheller. The demolition order was given at 3:20 pm, but the explosives failed to detonate. During the preparations, Major Scheller was in a tunnel in the vicinity of the bridge. A second attempt to blow up the bridge also failed, and the American crossings began. Major Scheller had left in the direction of Unkel, and Captain Bratge took over.

Model appeared at Remagen in the early hours of 8 March. At first, he paid little attention to the loss of the bridge. He knew that the bridge had little military importance. Perhaps he felt that Hitler's refusal to establish a line of defence on the eastern Rhine bank, had precipitated the catastrophe.

During the days between 7 March and 12 March, Major Scheller could not be located. General Hitzfeld and Captain Bratge both criticized him for having left for Unkel. In their opinion, Scheller was a very brave front line officer who was exhausted and did not possess the technical knowledge required for his mission.

On the night of 8 March, Major Scheller made a brief appearance at General von Kortzfleisch's headquarters. He appeared to be totally exhausted. His report did not mention that he had failed to take action to blow up the bridge, nor that he had not defended it. Lieutenant Colonel Warning, General Hitzfeld's Chief of Staff, remembered that Major Scheller was so tired that he had to lie down for a few hours' sleep. Warning was horrified by Major Scheller's return. He had hoped that Major Scheller had been taken prisoner. He told Major Scheller that he would certainly be court-martialled, but that he could be assured of General Hitzfeld's support.

On the following day, Major Scheller went to another command post, and dictated a report to *OKW* in the presence of four superior officers. The secretary who took his dictation said he appeared calm and relaxed. She knew that he was in danger, and advised him to don civilian clothes and to disappear. Major Scheller had fears for his family, so he returned to General Hitzfeld's headquarters.

The Flying Courts Martial and *Generalleutnant* Hübner

An order from Hitler arrived on 9 March 1945, announcing the establishment of the Flying Summary Courts Martial which were directly subordinated to him. Their jurisdiction extended to every offence committed by members of the *Wehrmacht* and the *Waffen* SS. Summary Courts Martial were also allowed to intervene in procedures which had been initiated against civilians. No appeal or pardon was permitted. Execution of a death sentence had to take place immediately after the verdict.

Generalleutnant Dr Rudolf Hübner was appointed Chief Judge. He was a most repulsive person. He had served in World War I and had risen to the rank of Reserve Lieutenant. Thereafter he became a dentist. In 1935, he was integrated into the active officer corps of the *Wehrmacht* with the rank of Captain. He began World War II as a Company commander and never commanded more than a Battalion. He had no legal knowledge. Eyewitnesses describe him as a sadist, and he conducted his court sessions in such manner.

The loss of the Remagen Bridge brought about a final end to Rundstedt's command. On 10 March, *Feldmarschall* Albert Kesselring was appointed *OB* West, and Hübner was among the guests who attended the farewell dinner for Rundstedt on that same date. Kesselring fuelled Hübner's rage by telling him that Remagen was a disgrace and could lead to the collapse of the whole front.

Model orders Scheller's arrest

Model arrived at General Hitzfeld's headquarters on 12 March at 8:50 am accompanied by his IIa, Colonel Theodor Pilling. Model was strongly critical of General Hitzfeld, who defended himself, and introduced Major Scheller to Model as the officer who had done everything possible to defend the bridge. Hitzfeld added that he would propose Scheller for a high award.

Model was already aware of what had occurred at Remagen. His chief legal advisor, the military judge Felix Janert, had attended a court martial of some soldiers of an engineering unit who had been with Scheller in the tunnel. Prior to his visit to General Hitzfeld, General von Kortzfleisch had reported his conversations with Scheller to Model, and had emphasized the discrepancies in Scheller's report.

Model had already learned of the excitement which the fall of the bridge had caused in Berlin. He knew that Hitler had initiated the first of his recently established Flying Summary Courts Martial immediately after the capture of the bridge, and that it was on its way. Model ignored the jurisdiction of that new court. Scheller took full responsibility for his actions. Model said: "Here we have the "rabbit" (*Karnickel*) [sic]," and placed Scheller under arrest.

The court martial against the four officers took place on 13 and 14 March. The hearings were conducted without a prosecutor, without a defence attorney, and without a stenographer. The death sentences were immediately carried out.

Model questioned by the Flying Summary Court Martial

Görlitz quoted Reichhelm: "Colonel Reichhelm later expressed his astonishment that Model simply accepted matters stoically, instead of having the court martial thrown out. Maybe this was a sign of resignation. Possibly it was also part of his usual policy to avoid any confrontation with party organisations."[89] After first denying his statement at one of our first meetings, Reichhelm told the author some years later that he did indeed say this to Görlitz.

Model himself was subjected to lengthy questioning by the court. The court also had intended to question Reichhelm as Ia of the Army Group. But Model interceded and told the court that it was unnecessary. Reichhelm said to this author that he did not understand why Model had agreed to be questioned by the court in the first place.

Model's responsibility for the fate of the executed officers

The execution of the four officers was an act of cold-blooded murder. Model was aware of that, since he had told Speer on the day of the Flying Summary Court Martial that the accused were totally innocent.[90] Model had not been compelled to order the arrest of Major Scheller. Scheller had already presented his report to Generals von Kortzfleisch and Hitzfeld, before Model appeared at General Hitzfeld's headquarters. While the report failed to mention some details of his actions preceding the capture of the bridge, the two Generals had already received that information from other witnesses. Neither had seen fit to order Scheller's arrest.

Under normal circumstances the arrest would have been in order. Scheller had also failed to perform some of his other duties, and those charges could have been brought before a court martial. There, Scheller would have had the assistance of a defence attorney and would have been subjected to standard military court procedures. All four of the officers were posthumously reinstated by a German court which indicated that the standard military court ruling would probably have been favourable to the defendants, and their lives would have been spared. General Hübner was sentenced to 4½ years in prison by a German court after the war.

Circumstances were not normal when the bridge was lost on 7 March. Model obviously knew that the bridge had no military value, and Hitler must have known that too. But the capture of a Rhine bridge had symbolic significance which led to a widespread feeling of panic in Berlin. Also, Model knew likewise that a summary courts martial was on

---

89 Görlitz, p. 247.
90 A. Speer, *Erinnerungen*, Berlin, 1976, p.450.

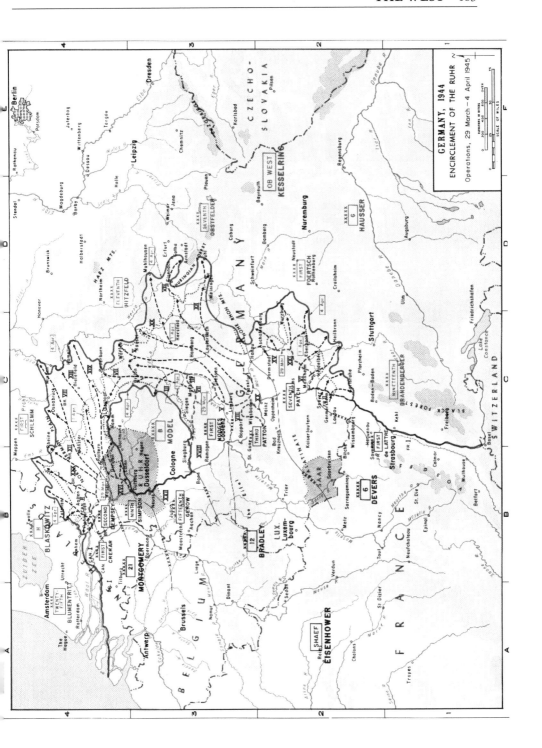

GERMANY, 1944
ENCIRCLEMENT OF THE RUHR
Operations, 29 March – 4 April 1945

SCALE OF MILES

its way and, given the prevailing sentiments, he must have known that death sentences would have been likely.

Model could have acted as Kluge did on 20 July, when he advised Stülpnagel to don civilian clothes and to "disappear somewhere." The female secretary to whom Scheller had dictated his report had the fortitude to advise him to do just that. In the widespread chaos, Scheller could have easily disappeared.

Model's submission to an eight hour questioning by Hübner is likewise incomprehensible. He could have broken off the discussions after a few minutes by referring to his rank and claiming he had other urgent duties to attend to. He could then have flown to Berlin and requested a personal meeting with Hitler. Flight connections with Berlin existed until the last days of Model's command in the Ruhr Pocket.

Model then added insult to injury by jointly signing with Kesselring the infamous order of the day which stated, "He who does not live in honour dies in shame." The *Feldmarschall* certainly did not heap honour upon himself on that day.

The *Ruhrkessel* and the "last bullet"
After the crossing of the Rhine by the Allies it became obvious that Army Group B would be drawn into a *Kessel*. The Allied troops surrounding Army Group B linked up during the first weeks of April. Model had stopped sending recriminations to Hitler after he received no reply to his repeated requests for more reserves of men and equipment. The only reply Hitler could give him during the last part of 1944 was that Model's requirements were simply not available. Model had not yet given up his trust in Hitler. His final awakening came in the last days of his life.

In March 1945 Model was still looked upon favourably by Hitler and Goebbels. Goebbels wrote on 28 March 1945: "Model is an outstanding commander, although a little too intellectual. But he remains fanatically devoted to the *Führer* and a genuine National Socialist."[91] On the same day, Hitler had told Goebbels that Keitel and Jodl had become 'old daddies' (*Papis*), who were tired and exhausted. Goebbels wrote in his diary: "The only commanders who respond to the claims of popular war are Model and Schörner. Model is more of an intellectual. Schörner speaks more through his heart and his feelings. But these two are the only great commanders remaining. The SS has not been able to generate strategists."[92] Another entry on 31 March: "Model is obviously a man who can be relied upon. But now he faces a nearly impossible task, since the troops which he needs are simply not available."[93] And finally, on 8 April: "The situation in the Ruhr area is somewhat more favourable since Model's Army Group performs in an outstanding manner."[94]

The *Nero* order
On 18 March 1945, Kesselring had complained to Hitler that civilians who had remained in their towns and villages had become an obstacle to his operations. They implored officers to avoid entering their villages in order not to expose them to destruction. Hitler

---

91 Joseph Goebbels, *Tagebücher 1945. Die letzten Aufzeichnungen,* Berlin 1977, p.411.
92 Ibid, p.412.
93 Ibid, p.467.
94 Ibid, p.528.

immediately ordered the evacuation of the entire population in the combat areas. One General who was present objected that it was impossible to evacuate hundreds of thousands civilians. There were no trains left. Hitler remained unmoved. "Then they have to walk". The General continued to object. There were no food reserves available and likewise no shoes. Hitler simply turned away, after stating that there was no room for any consideration of the population.[95]

On 19 March 1945, Hitler issued the following order:

> To *Reichsminister* Speer
> The struggle for the existence of our people compels us to use every possible means, in the areas still under our control, to weaken the enemy and to prevent his further advance. Every possibility has to be used to weaken the strength of the enemy. It would be an error to believe that means of communication, production, supply, which are not yet destroyed, could be used again to our advantage, after we retake the area. When he retreats, the enemy will leave behind him only scorched earth and will show no consideration for the population.
>
> I therefore order: All military installations, industrial plants, means of communication and supply, and every installation located in such areas as the enemy will be able to his advantage must be destroyed. The *Gauleiters* and the *Reichskommissare* have the responsibility of carrying out this order. The Army has to give them all assistance required.
>
> This order has to be communicated without delay to all commanders. Contrary orders are not valid.
> Adolf Hitler[96]

Speer had had a meeting with Model during the first week of March. He had obtained Model's promise that he would do his utmost to avoid any damage to the chemical plants of Bayer-Leverkusen and also that he would inform the Allies accordingly. On that day, Model was irritated. He had received an order to retake the Remagen bridge with two Divisions which had even less equipment than two companies. Model said to Speer: "In the *Führerhauptquartier* they have not the faintest idea. But I will be designated as responsible for the failure."[97]

After his meeting with Hitler on 18 March, Speer visited the Army commanders in the West, in the hope of obtaining their agreement to spare all industrial plants in their respective areas. Kesselring refused outright.[98] SS *Oberstgruppenführer* Paul Hausser was positive. *Generaloberst* Lothar Rendulic said to Speer that he was not going to participate in "a sabotage of a *Führer* order". Erich von Manstein, who had been dismissed a year earlier, was visited by two young Majors who asked him to give them a written power

---

95 Speer, p.444 ff.
96 Minutes of the Nuremberg trial against the major Nazi criminals – file Speer, No. 25.
97 Speer, p.442.
98 Speer, p.444.

of attorney, enabling them to oppose any destruction in his area of residence. Manstein refused and told them that he was personally still bound in loyalty to the *Führer*.[99]

When Speer visited Model, he hoped that the *Feldmarschall* was going to show common sense. But when he met Model, Kesselring had just communicated to Model an order to obey Hitler's instructions. Speer wrote that he saw an immediate change in Model's behaviour and that Model wanted to avoid any further discussion on the subject.[100] However, on 11 April, Model issued an order to *AOK* 15, to *Panzer AOK* 5, to the *Gruppe* Heinrich von Lüttwitz, to the Army Group's quartermaster, *Gauleiter* Hoffmann and personally to *Generaloberst* Karl Hollidt:[101]

> Only the troops are permitted to destroy military installations.
>
> The destruction of economic installation is under the sole authority of *Reichsminister* Speer, in cooperation with the Defence Commissar in the area controlled by Army Group.
>
> Bridges which carry cables, water pipes, etc, may not be destroyed, nor prepared for destruction.
>
> Dams may not be destroyed.[102]

The battle that never was

No actual battles occurred in the Ruhr Pocket. The Allies saw no reason to incur losses, since they knew that the entire valley would inevitably fall to them.[103] They were eager to capture the Ruhr industries intact, and to avoid taking any actions that might damage the plants. German troops had lost cohesion. Goebbels had written in a 31 March entry in his diary, that Allied tanks were driving around unhindered. More and more German soldiers simply abandoned their units. If they lived close by, they headed home. They were assisted by the civilian population. The battle staffs no longer had control. Winrich Behr told the author that on one day he drove past an anti-aircraft battery that was firing toward the east. The commanding officer told him that he had received an order to continue firing until he had no ammunition left, but since no targets had been specified, he simply let his guns fire at random.

General Wagener wrote that Army Group B succeeded in containing up to twenty American divisions. That makes little sense. A division can only be contained if it is engaged. Had the Allies found it necessary to engage those divisions against the Germans, they could have wiped out the *Kessel* within a few days.

---

99 K. von Hammerstein, *Spähtrupp*, Stuttgart 1963, p.194. This conversation was confirmed to the author by the late Clemens Graf von Kageneck, who was one of the Majors.

100 Speer, p.448.

101 *Generaloberst* Hollidt was already in the *Führerreserve*. On 1 March 1945 he had been appointed military adviser to the Commissars of Defence of the Ruhr area.

102 BA-MA, N 6/4.

103 General Wagener wrote that the US Army carefully advanced in a sector by sector tactic. Their almost schematic thinking, paired with a realistic understanding of aims and an eagerness to avoid unnecessary casualties were typical elements of their operations. However the Americans always knew when they had to begin large scale operations. Estate, Wagener, 13 February 1949.

Model came closer to a personal breakdown by the day. He took no measures against subordinates who wanted to convince him to end all resistance but, true to his habits, he threatened them. General Heinrich von Lüttwitz wrote that he had sent such a letter to Model. Model replied by scolding him, and admonishing him to limit himself to military duties within his command, otherwise he would take measures against him.[104]

The *Wehrmacht Communiqué* of 19 April 1945 is beyond comprehension:

> The combats between Rhine and Ruhr have come to an end. In weeks of uninterrupted heavy fighting, troops of all arms under the command of *Generalfeldmarschall* Model, have succeeded in containing the superior forces of two American Armies, and have fulfilled their duties in an exemplary manner to the last breath, inflicting heavy losses in men and equipment upon the enemy.

The final breakdown came on 19 April. Model listened to Goebbels' traditional speech on the eve of Hitler's birthday. Görlitz wrote that the speech contained the words "treacherous Army of the Ruhr"[105] and Newton repeats that statement.[106] Newton may perhaps not be blamed for taking a statement by Görlitz at face value, but Görlitz's account is simple forgery. The speech was broadcast and published in all newspapers still appearing in Germany, and in many works of post-war literature. The words "treacherous Army of the Ruhr" were not uttered. The text of the speech is given in Appendix I.

But the speech was sufficiently damning to lead to an outbreak by Model. Winrich Behr, who was with Model at that moment, wrote to the author:

> Model was sitting in a forest, repeatedly stung by mosquitoes. He had no longer any authority, since he had dissolved his Army Group. He had no more communication with the outside. We heard the speech by Goebbels over a portable radio. Suddenly Model exploded. I can't recall all the words, but I definitely remember that he said: "And those are the men one has trusted, blindly trusted, closing one's eyes to retain their trust. I had blindly taken the responsibility for compliance with soldierly duty in a just war. A just war led by those frauds? And how many sacrifices have I demanded from my soldiers only to serve these swine?"[107]

The shot which ended Model's life came on the following day, 21 April 1945.

American attempts to obtain Model's surrender

On 16 April, Major General Matthew B. Ridgway, Commander of US XVIII Corps sent Captain Frank Brandstetter, one of his staff officers, as a go-between to try to obtain Model's surrender. Model turned him down.

After receiving Model's reply, General Ridgway drafted a personal letter to Model:

---

104 General Heinrich von Lüttwitz had the nickname "the horse trader". He should not be confused with his namesake, General Smilo von Lüttwitz, who rose to three-star General in the *Bundeswehr*.

105 Görlitz, p.266.

106 Newton, p.357.

107 Letter from Behr to the author, 20 March 2000.

16 April 1945

To the General Officer Commanding Army Group B:

Sir:

Powerful Allied forces are today deep in the very heart of Germany. Its complete and rapid conquest is now beyond Germany's power to avert.

Of the encircled forces under your command, more than 180,000 have been taken prisoner. Your forces are completely surrounded by overwhelming United States forces. Their fate is irrevocably sealed. The alternatives are death or honourable submission.

Neither history nor the military profession records any nobler character, any more brilliant master of warfare, any more dutiful subordinate to the State than the American General, Robert E. Lee. Eighty years ago this month, his loyal command, reduced in numbers, stripped of its means of effective fighting, and completely surrounded by overwhelming forces, chose an honourable capitulation.

This same choice is now yours. In the light of a soldier's honour, for the reputation of the German Officer Corps, for the sake of your nation's future, I ask the immediate unconditional surrender of your forces. The German lives you will save are sorely needed to restore your people to their proper place in society. The German cities you will preserve are irreplaceable necessities for your people's welfare.

The bearer of this communication, an Officer of my Staff, is authorized to conduct your emissary to my Headquarters.

M. B. Ridgway

Major General, U.S. Army

The letter was again carried to Model by Captain Brandstetter who was turned down for the second time. General Wagener accompanied Captain Brandstetter back to General Ridgway, who offered General Wagener the opportunity to simply stay as a prisoner of war. General Wagener wrote that he declined and was taken prisoner a few days later.

General Ridgway must have been more than naive if he felt that he could impress Model at such a time with the example of a General of the American Civil War. Furthermore, Model was well versed in military history and he knew that Ridgway's eulogy of Lee was, mildly speaking, somewhat exaggerated.

Also, Model was very conscious of his rank and may well have felt insulted that he was addressed by a Major General, who was only a Corps commander. Protocol would have called for the letter to be signed by General Omar Bradley or, at least, by Lieutenant General Courtney Hodges, commander of 1st US Army. It should have been carried by a more senior officer, probably Ridgway's chief of staff.

When did Model understand that the war was lost?

Given his military knowledge, it is obvious that this must have been clear to him after Stalingrad at the latest. Here Model must share the blame with all other German Generals for having pursued a war which had become totally void of sense and which they could have prevented.

Surrender or dissolution of the Army Group?

In 1945, this question was legitimate. *Generalmajor* Wagener, Army Group's last chief of staff wrote about the situation on April 5: "…As long as Army Group could continue resisting, an eventual surrender had to be postponed. Both *OB* of Army Group and I myself agreed that any decision must be taken by us and responsibility could not be delegated to individual units."[108]

On 5 April Army Group B had requested permission to break out which was refused by *OKW*. Wagner asked Model to request permission to surrender. Model refused. Wagener wrote:

> After weighing all possibilities, Army Group B decided upon an action without precedent in military history. Army Group will dissolve itself upon order by its command and in a disciplined manner. The date chosen was 17 April, at which time neither rations nor ammunition would be left …[109]

The date proved to be unrealistic, since on 14 and 15 April units of Army Group B, among them 15th Army, *Gruppe* Lüttwitz and some Divisions sent go-betweens to US Army units opposing them, and surrendered. Therefore Model switched the date from 17 April to 15 April. On that day he addressed his staff and other officers present. He said that he was no longer their commander and therefore he had no more right to issue any orders. He added that he felt his soldiers had the choice between three options. First, they could attempt to join a fighting unit outside the Ruhr Pocket. Second, they could join him and fight until the last bullet in some unit inside the *Kessel*. Third, "there was another way for all of you who have relatives nearby. I need not say more about this, you have undoubtedly understood what I intend to convey."[110]

General Wagener wrote further that surrender was unthinkable because the Geneva Convention would then no longer apply. This is not borne out by events. Even after Germany's unconditional surrender, the Geneva Convention continued to be in force and the military members of the Dönitz government continued to wear their uniforms with insignia and decorations. The Geneva Convention was no longer applied when German national sovereignty was formally abolished.[111]

---

108 *Windhund,* p.525.
109 Ibid, p.526.
110 Facsimile of the address in Model/Bradley, p.384 ff.
111 Wagener, p.561 ff.

8

War Crimes

"The problem does not consist in proving the self-evident, that Germans were not latent Nazis already in Tacitus' time, nor in attempting to show that a National-Socialist mentality existed with every German. One has rather to ask oneself, how one can bear to be confronted with a nation where the line separating criminals from ordinary people, guilty from innocent is so blurred, that in the coming Germany nobody will know if he meets a secret hero or a former mass murderer."

Hannah Arendt in a letter to her friend and mentor Karl Jaspers[1]

"Every officer and every soldier has to understand why the German command orders measures in the East which have no place in civilized countries".

Generalfeldmarschall Walter von Reichenau,1.11.1941[2]

S ebastian Haffner gives his personal definition of war crimes: "The understanding of the special aspect of Hitler's mass murders is blunted if they are classified as war crimes. Hitler's mass murders can only be understood if one is aware that they were not war crimes, but something 'entirely different'. The shooting of prisoners of war in the heat of combat, the executions of hostages in partisan warfare, the aerial bombing of civilian populations, the sinking of passenger vessels during the U-Boat war; those are all war crimes, certainly horrible, but better forgotten by both sides after the end of hostilities. Mass murder, planned extermination of entire population groups, killing of human beings like vermin, all these are things 'entirely different'."

In Haffner's eyes, 'things entirely different' are:
- the Shoah
- the Euthanasia Order
- the mass-murder of the Polish leadership and the Polish intelligentsia, with more than a million murdered
- the three million Russian prisoners of war who perished in camps run by the *Wehrmacht*[3]

Walter Model was involved in every war crime in the East. However, he was not a major perpetrator. He was not in the same league as Walter von Reichenau, Erich von Manstein, Hermann Hoth, Georg von Küchler, Hans von Salmuth, Max von Schenkendorff and Walter Braemer. He did no more, nor did he do less than the other *Wehrmacht* commanders in the East, who participated in all the crimes without taking major initiatives of their

---

1   L. Köhlert/H. Saner (Ed.) *Hannah Arendt-Karl Jaspers. Briefwechsel 1926-1969*, Munich 1985. p. 90 ff.
2   BA-MA, RH 26-100/23, Bl.6.
3   Haffner, p.181.

own. This is probably the reason why his name is only rarely mentioned in works dealing with German war crimes, especially the voluminous Shoah literature.

This chapter will cover in detail:

1. The Commissar Order
2. The *Gerichtsbarkeitserlass* (The *Barbarossa* order)
3. The Shoah
4. The fate of the Russian prisoners of war
5. The wilful famine enforced on the Russian population in occupied areas
6. The kidnapping of children fathered by German officers and soldiers with Russian women
7. The "scorched earth" policy carried out during the *Büffel* retreat at Rzhev
8. The shooting of American prisoners of war at Malmédy during the Ardennes offensive

Points 1 to 6 belong to "things entirely different". Points 7 and 8 are part of Haffner's "ordinary war crimes".

The two "criminal orders"

Historians use the term "criminal orders" in the East, with reference to the "Commissar Order" that demanded the execution of Red Army Commissars immediately upon capture, and without courts martial and the *Gerichtsbarkeitserlass*, also called the *Barbarossa* order, which gave the German military a free hand in committing atrocities against Russian civilians that would normally be punished by criminal law.

Rubicon in the East – Hitler's address to his senior commanders on 30 March 1941

On 30 March 1941, Hitler assembled a group of senior *Wehrmacht* officers in the *Reichskanzlei*. The group included the Generals who were foreseen to be the most senior commanders in the coming war with Russia. Hitler delivered a speech lasting two and a half hours. In it he outlined his directives for the conduct of the coming war. The *Barbarossa* plan of 18 December 1940 had already been communicated to the Generals. They therefore knew about the forthcoming war with Russia. In fact, by June and July 1940, Hitler had made no secret of his decision to attack Russia. We have already seen that a first operational plan had been prepared by General Erich Marcks already in July 1940.

The Generals were still "drunk with success" after their unexpectedly rapid and crushing victory over France. Their belief in Hitler's genius had strengthened, and the trauma of the First World War, which had affected a generation of German officers, was wiped out. There was no fear of a two-front major war – Hitler had emphasized in his speech that the situation in the West was not yet a serious threat. The German commanders were convinced that they would conduct a new *Blitzkrieg* that would end in victory, well before increased attention had to be given to other theatres. The strong anti-Bolshevik feelings of the German officer corps overrode policies of the past. Bismarck's favouring of cooperation with Russia had been erased from the German commanders' memories.

But Hitler's speech enlightened them as to the methods he was going to order in the East. After having listened to Hitler's address, none of the commanders who were present could ignore the fact that they would be issuing and obeying orders so terrifying that there was no precedent for them in any war of the past. Therefore the word "Rubicon" is a suitable for that fateful day. Claims by German Generals in their memoirs, that they were ignorant of the cruelties foreseen for the war in the East and that they opposed them when they occurred, can be dismissed. The appeals for murder, which a number of commanders issued in the weeks preceding the German attack, or during its first weeks, are a true reflection of their views. A few examples, taken at random, are given here.

Generaloberst Erich Hoepner, Commander of *Panzergruppe 4*, 2 May 1941:

> The war against Russia is the consequence of the fight that we are compelled to wage in order to preserve our existence. We have to guarantee the economic independence of Greater Germany, and all areas of Europe that have come under its domination. It is the old struggle of the Germans against the Slavs, the defence of European culture against the Muscovite-Asiatic flood, the throwing back of Jewish Bolshevism. This struggle must lead to the annihilation of today's Russia and requires methods of unprecedented brutality. Every military action has to be inspired by an iron will of a merciless destruction of the enemy. No mercy will be shown to the leaders of the Russian-Bolshevik system.[4]

On 6 July 1941, Hoepner issued an additional order, asking "for good and fair treatment of the loyal population". He added that "individual acts of sabotage should simply be charged to Communists and Jews."[5]

Generalfeldmarschall Walter von Reichenau, Commander of 6th Army, 10 August 1941,

> Executions of criminals, Bolsheviks and mostly Jewish elements, are carried out by units of the *SD* of the *Reichsführer SS* and chief of the German Police.[6]

General der Infanterie Karl von Roques, Military Commander, *Berück* of the rear area of Army Group South:

> If acts of sabotage occur, without the perpetrators having been discovered, search should not be made among Ukrainians, but confined to Russians and Jews. Any measures of reprisals are to be taken against them.[7]

General der Infanterie Carl-Heinrich von Stülpnagel, Commander of 17th Army, 30 July 1941:

> If an act of sabotage cannot be shown to have been committed by an Ukrainian, the village elders have to be ordered to name Jewish and Communist inhabitants instead. This will encourage the population to engage in denunciation … Many members of the Russian youth organisation, *Komsomol*, have remained behind. If urgency is required, they are easy to get hold of. In particular, Jewish members of the *Komsomol*

---

4   NOKW 2510.
5   Ibid.
6   H. Krausnick / H. Wilhelm, *Die Truppe des Weltanschauungskrieges. Die Einsatzgruppen der Sicherheitspolizei und des SD 1938-1942*, Stuttgart 1981, p.219 (henceforth Krausnick).
7   NOKW 2424.

have to be considered as standard bearers of sabotage, and as the leaders behind the formation of juvenile criminal bands.[8]

In a letter of 21 August 1941, to the department of propaganda at *OKW*, General von Stülpnagel had written:

Request to German propaganda: increased fight against Jewry. Total enlightenment about Jewry is a must."[9] Back in 1935, Stülpnagel had already written in a memorandum: "The 'snitching' attitude of the Commissars, who are mostly Jewish, reminds one of the worst years of the beginning of the Soviet system. Since Jews are averse to military duties, even in the Soviet Union, most Russian officers view them with distrust.[10]

General der Infanterie Hans von Salmuth, Commander of XXX Corps, 2 August 1941:

The fanatical will of the Communist party and the Jews to halt the progress of the German *Wehrmacht* must be broken at all costs. Special units are in charge.[11]

General der Panzertruppe Hans-Georg Reinhardt, Commander of XLI Corps, 6 May 1941:

It is the old struggle of the Germans against the Slavs, the struggle of European culture against the Muscovite-Asiatic flood, and the defence against Jewish Bolshevism.

Finally, an order by General Erich von Manstein, 12 June 1941:

This war demands acts, without mercy, against Soviet troublemakers, snipers, partisans and Jews.[12]

The extermination of the Jews was not mentioned in Hitler's speech. But the orders quoted above show that the Generals understood that it was part of Hitler's intention, and that they were happy to include it in their orders.

Several sources give different figures for the number of Generals who attended Hitler's address. Hürter's research arrives at the conclusion that it was around 100. The commanders in chief of the Army, von Brauchitsch, of the *Luftwaffe*, Göring, and of the *Kriegsmarine*, Raeder, accompanied by their chiefs of staff, Keitel, Jodl and additional officers of *OKW* were present. Others included the future high commanders in the East, the three *OB* of the Army Groups, *Feldmarschalls* von Bock, Ritter von Leeb, and von Rundstedt. Also present were the *OB* of the Armies,[13] *Generaloberst* von Küchler, *Generaloberst* Busch,

8   NOKW 1654 and 2716.
9   BA-MA, RW 4.
10   NOKW 2018.
11   BA-MA, RH 20-11/488.
12   NOKW 1691.
13   Among the Armies and *Panzergruppen* OB, Generals von Kleist and von Weichs were not present, since their time was taken up by the preparation of the imminent attack upon

Generalfeldmarschall von Kluge, *Generaloberst* Strauss, *Generalfeldmarschall* von Reichenau, General Carl-Heinrich von Stülpnagel, *Generaloberst* Ritter von Schobert, and the commanders of three of the four *Panzergruppen, Generaloberst* Hoepner, *Generaloberst* Guderian and *Generaloberst* Hoth.[14]

A summary of Hitler's speech was written down by several of the attending commanders. In most books, the shorthand notes of Halder are reproduced. Hürter shows that the notes made by Hoth are more to the point. Halder had obviously edited his notes to include them in his post-war memoirs, whereas Hoth's notes were not intended for publication and reflect Hitler's words as they were spoken at the time. Hoth's version is also more comprehensive. Both versions are included below, the stenographic style and the word for word translation are purposely maintained.

Halder's version with the italics as in the original:

11 am. Meeting with the *Führer*. 2½ hour address of the situation expected by 30 June. Mistake by England to waive possibility of peace. Describes war until now. Very critical of Italian performance and politics. Both advantageous to England.

England's hopes rest on USA and Russia. Russian transportation problems. We must clear up Russian situation. Only if we solve our problems on the ground, will we be able to find a solution to our problems on the seas and in the air. Aims in Russia: Destroy armed forces and shatter state. Russian *Panzer*. Respectable quality. Old models. In numbers Russia has the greatest amount of *Panzer* in the world. But only few of the large and heavy models.

Problems of the Russian space. Require concentration on decisive locations. *Luftwaffe* cannot control everything. Must concentrate on close cooperation with ground forces. The Russians will not be able to withstand the combined assault of *Panzer* and *Luftwaffe*.

No illusion about Allies. Finns will fight but too few and weakened. Nothing can be done with Romanians. May perhaps be used for holding lines along a wide river, and outside offensive locations. Antonescu has increased his armed forces instead of reducing and improving them. Fate of German units not to be allowed to depend on Romanians.

Pripet swamps. Defence, land-mines.

Russian retreat. Not probable because of the need for the Baltic Sea and Ukraine. If the Russians want to retreat, they have to do it early, otherwise they will not get away. After solution problem in the East, 50-60 Divisions of *Panzer* will be sufficient. Part of the ground forces will be discharged. Can be used in production for Navy and *Luftwaffe*. Part will be needed for other tasks, for instance Spain. *Colonial duties.*

War between two philosophies of life. Devastating judgment of Communism which is antisocial crime. Communism is an enormous danger for the future. We must retreat from traditional military comradeship. The Communist was never a comrade, and will never be a comrade. It is a war of extermination. Even if we do not understand this, we will still vanquish the enemy. But in thirty years from now

---

Yugoslavia and Greece. As *Oberquartiermeister* I, General Paulus should have been present, but on that day he was in Budapest.

14   Hürter, p.3 ff.

we will face the same Communist enemy again. We are not making war to preserve the life of the enemy.

War against Russia: Elimination of the Commissars and Communist intelligentsia. The new states to be created must be socialist states, without any 'intelligentsia' of their own. On no account can a new intelligentsia be permitted to develop. A primitive socialist intelligentsia is sufficient. War must be waged against the poison of subversion. This is no matter for courts martial. The commanders have to know their duties. They have to lead. Troops will defend themselves with the same means with which they are attacked. Commissars and GPU are criminals and will be treated as criminals.

Soldiers may not become detached from officers. Officers have to take their decisions in accordance with the feelings of their soldiers. Officers have to overcome any apprehension for themselves." Halder added his own note: 'War will be different from the war in the West. In the East, hardship looks mild when viewed against the future.

Note by Halder: Order by Commander in Chief of the Army[15]

Keeping his style to match the memoirs of German Generals, Halder declared after the war, that he wrote down his notes to show his disapproval. The truth is the opposite. Pursuant to Hitler's speech of 30 March 1941, Halder issued an order under his own signature, stipulating harsh measures against the civilian population in occupied Russian territory:

Any attempt of active or passive resistance by the civilian population has to be nipped in the bud with sharp measures. A self-assured and drastic attitude towards the hostile population is the best means for prevention. At an early stage, clear knowledge must be obtained as to whom the Army can rely on in occupied territories. Such parts of the Russian population, who are hostile to the Soviet state and system, must be made useful to German interests, if necessary by means of some material advantages and the granting of modest liberties.[16]

Hoth's version, starting from section 4:

4. Necessity of the attack against Russia.
   a. Moral justification. Stalin felt in autumn 1939 that Germany would bleed to death. If no victory, the Russian will be in Germany now. Their political agitation has not been stopped like ours. Espionage rings which serve Hitler or Stalin. History of German politics. Nerves.
   b. Criminal inclinations: Russia permanent home for antisocial elements.
   c. If England resists for 1-1½ years, American help will become effective. Then we will need *Luftwaffe,* AA equipment, navy, also battleships. Thus transfer of war production to air and sea. Only possible if Army reduced in size. 50 Divisions, strong *Panzer.* But first Russia has to be defeated. New A-A gun.

---

15 Halder personal diary, vol. II, p.336 ff.
16 OKH/GenStdH. Gen. Qu/Abt. *Kriegsverwaltung,* Nr. II/031 12/41, g Kdos. Chefs. 3 April 1941. BA-MA, RH 22/v.11.

    d.   Eliminate Russian-Asiatic danger for the future. Only thus Germany obtains freedom of action. Russian colossus weighs heavily.

    e.   Ideology. Fight against Bolshevism.

5.   Assessment Russia: Strong air force, strong *Panzer*. *Luftwaffe* cannot eliminate enemy air force. Losses in the West and space. Necessary concentration at few locations. Heavy Russian *Panzer* with long 7.5cm guns. Produced in Lithuania. Lethargic masses. Tough commanders. But leadership? Armament industry not particularly high standard. Examples."

6.   Aim of the attack: Destruction of the Russian state. Establish protectorates Lithuania, Belorussia, Ukraine. Socialist republics without intelligentsia. Keep on a low level. Take over or destroy Russian armament industry. Cut off from oil. Finns to Leningrad. Continue advance. Some plants important for Russian war effort such as optical plants. Maritime trade concentrated in Petersburg, therefore *Schwerpunkt* in this direction.

7.   Conduct of war against Russia: No pattern. Norway different from Poland. Justice is too humane. Always catches the same criminals. Keeps them alive instead of killing them. Crimes of the Russian Commissars. In every place where they appeared. Latvia, Galicia, Baltic states. Behaved like Asiatics. Deserve no indulgence. No courts martial, have to be shot immediately upon capture. Not to be shunted off to the rear.

8.   Illusions: Allies. Finns will fight courageously. But leadership and equipment? Nothing to be expected from Romania. Cowards, corrupt, spoiled. Always seek cover. Unreliable.

9.   Fight for our existence: Has to be fought once. Now we have a big advantage everywhere. Cannot be kept forever. *Führer* aware of his responsibilities. Cannot pass on this task to future generations. (1918: our children). Not wait like end 19th or beginning 20th century. Act by ourselves. Now, statesman and *Feldherr* matched in one person. Unprecedented march to victory. Difficult decision. Have wrestled long with myself. Situation not as difficult as Frederick the Great whose task was beyond solution. So much easier for us.[17]

After the war, Brauchitsch and Halder said that von Bock, von Rundstedt, Ritter von Leeb and some Army *OB* had come to them after Hitler left the room. They expressed their outrage and stated that this kind of war was intolerable. In his testimony at Nuremberg, Hoth contradicted them. He said that after Hitler left the room, everybody also left. There were no possibilities of talking with him, nor were there any conversations between the commanders.[18]

Information about the contents of Hitler's speech was conveyed to their Corps commanders by the Generals who were there. Hoth is known to have made his notes of Hitler's address available to his two Corps commanders, General Rudolf Schmidt and General Adolf Kuntzen.[19] *Generaloberst* von Küchler referred to the address at a meeting

---

17   Hürter p.7 ff.

18   Ibid, p.10.

19   BA-MA, RH 21-3/40.

with all his divisional commanders on 25 April 1941. He engaged in lengthy comments on Hitler's goals, which he described as

> establishing a German hegemony or domination over Europe, the conquest of an adequate *Lebensraum,* and the annihilation of an ideological arch-enemy. Only the Soviet Union remained an obstacle to Germany's domination of Europe and it was an Asiatic country, far removed from Germany and its ideology. The Soviet Union was a threatening cloud in the East which could break at any moment over the West. Therefore the present opportunity must be used to remove this danger for future generations, thanks to the strength of the *Wehrmacht.* It is not sufficient to push Russia into a geographical background. European Russia must be annihilated and Russia, as a state, has to disappear. We are faced with a *gewaltig* (gigantic) aim, and we have to accomplish gigantic tasks.[20]

Information was passed down to corps and divisional commanders. The orders of the day, issued by Generals who did not attend the meeting of 30 March 1941, are sufficient evidence of their knowledge of Hitler's address.

The Commissar Order

The IMT described the Commissar Order as "one of the most heinous, despicable orders ever issued by any Army."[21] The insistence is on the word "Army". Further, and even more atrocious orders had been issued by the Nazi regime such as the *Gerichtsbarkeitserlass,* and the Euthanasia Order of 1 September 1939, which was the forerunner of the Shoah. However, the drafting of the Commissar Order was prepared jointly by *OKW* and *OKH,* with the final version issued by *OKH.*

From 1917 Commissars could be found in all units of the Red Army, from Company upwards. At the lowest level, Company and Battalion, they were named *Politruks,* at higher levels *Zampolit*, and at more senior levels simply Commissars or War Commissars. Commissars were officers who had undergone special political training. They were given military commands according to their rank. In addition they had duties of political indoctrination and supervision. Their uniforms were ordinary officers' uniforms with collar patches of their rank[22] and special insignia on the sleeves identifying them as Commissars. At the very top, at Front and Theatre levels, Political Directorates were established. A Political Directorate was headed by a very senior political figure, among others Khrushchev, Zhdanov and Bulganin, who were given Generals' rank. The authorities of the Commissars were changed at regular intervals. On 9 October 1942, the institution of Commissars was abolished, only the Political Directorates were maintained.

The Commissar Order was given its final wording at *OKH* on 6 June 1941, and distributed in 340 copies to the commanders, down to division level:

---

20 BA-MA, RH 20-18/71.
21 IMT, Case 12 (OKW Trial), p.90.
22 Shoulder straps, similar to the shoulder straps of the Tsarist Army, were introduced after the battle of Stalingrad.

In the fight against Bolshevism, the enemy is not expected to act in accordance with maxims of humanity and international law. In particular, the Political Commissars, the mainstay of enemy resistance, can be expected to act in a hateful, cruel and inhumane manner against our prisoners of war.

Troops must remain aware:

1. In this struggle, forbearance and observation of international law towards these elements is out of place. They are a danger to our security and to the peaceful administration of conquered territory.

2. The Commissars are the creators of barbaric and Asiatic combat methods. They must be dispensed with immediately and with utmost severity. The troops must be given to understand that any mercy shown to Commissars endangers their own security, and the peaceful administration of conquered territory. Therefore, when captured during battle, or when resisting capture, Commissars must be executed immediately. Commissars are not recognised as soldiers. International law concerning prisoners of war is not applicable to them. They will be separated from other prisoners and liquidated."[23]

The remainder of the document contained detailed instructions of the procedures under which the order was to be executed. It required regular reports to *OKH* on the number of Commissars shot. Some Corps and Divisions sent daily reports, others lumped them together in communications at intervals of two weeks.

Purported objections by German Generals to the Commissar order on moral grounds have long been exposed as a myth. At Nuremberg, in his plea for *OKW* and the *Generalstab*, Dr Hans Laternser had stated, "When Hitler mentioned this plan, which had been prepared solely by him, in his address to the Generals in March 1941, he immediately encountered the strongest rejection from all commanders present. They had been raised in a spirit of humanity and soldierly ethos. All attempts of the Generals at *OKW* and *OKH* had failed to put a halt to formalising Hitler's views in a written order. When the Commissar Order was issued, the commanders of Army Groups and Armies either abstained from forwarding it to the units under their command, or they gave instructions to disobey it. They acted in full knowledge of their risk of being severely punished by their Supreme Commander for open disobedience of an order in wartime, An additional order by the Commander in Chief of the Army, Brauchitsch, to preserve discipline accomplished the desired effect. It gave the commanders at the front the tool they needed, to act according to their convictions. The military leadership thus knew that the Commissar Order was not complied with at Army Groups and Armies.[24]

The truth was the opposite. There never were "all efforts by *OKW* and *OKH*". Obviously, no commander could refuse to communicate the order to his subordinates. The "additional order" by Brauchitsch, 8 June 1941, stated that civilian Commissars, who are treated separately in the Commissar Order, who can be shown to have acted in a hostile manner against the *Wehrmacht,* or who can be suspected of having such intentions, have to be taken aside after capture, and shot in an inconspicuous (*unauffällig*) manner.[25] The

---

23 NOKW 1076.
24 Also quoted in Streit, p.45.
25 Nuremberg trial against the major Nazi criminals, vol.22, p.622.

reader will have to judge if "inconspicuous shooting" of civilian Commissars is a "softening" of an order mainly concerned with military political Commissars.

The most recent research, which is probably not yet exhaustive, shows that the Commissar Order was carried out in all Army Groups, Armies, Corps and at least 80% of all Divisions engaged in the East.[26] Since Commissars were reintroduced in the Red Army on 15 July 1941, during the first three weeks of the Russo-German War, there were no commissars at the outset of the campaign, yet daily reports from Wehrmacht units mentioned the execution of Commissars from the very first day of the war. Obviously, P.O.W. officers, who were shot at random after capture, were reported as executed Commissars. The total number of Commissars shot in accordance with the order has never been established. Many documents were removed in the later stages of the war. On being captured, many Commissars removed their insignia; often they were denounced by other prisoners. The reporting of executions started at the lowest level, by the soldier or, at best, the officer who did the shooting. Thereafter they were transmitted step by step upwards. Whatever protests were raised by German Generals were not based on moral grounds, but reflected the realization that the Commissar Order made the Commissars fight desperately, because they knew the fate that awaited them if captured.[27]

Statements made by Generals in their memoirs, that they had never received the order, have been exposed as lies. Guderian wrote that he had never seen the *Gerichtsbarkeitserlass* nor the Commissar Order. "Perhaps Army Group Centre had refrained from communicating them to my *Panzergruppe*".[28] An order from General Joachim Lemelsen, commander of XLVII *Panzer* Corps in Guderian's *Panzergruppe* 2, shows Guderian's statement to have been untruthful. General Lemelsen had protested, in general, against the shooting of prisoners of war, but added that "prisoners, who could be shown to have been Commissars, had to be immediately taken aside and shot, in each instance upon an order given by an officer to the firing squad."[29] The Ia of 17th *Panzer* Division in Lemelsen's Corps, confirmed that the Commissar Order had been transmitted to him through normal channels by direct instructions from Guderian.[30] Furthermore, Guderian reported directly to *OKH* that *Panzergruppe* 2 had taken only a few prisoners

---

26 F.Römer, *Der Kommissarnefehl. Wehrmacht und NS-Verbrechen an der Ostfront 1941/42*, Paderborn 2008. (henseforth Römer). Römer estimates that 10,000 Commissars were shot.

27 The only objections which contained a moral element came from Manstein who stated that the order was "not soldierly" (*unsoldatisch*) and from General Rudolf Schmidt, commander of XXXIX Corps in Busch's 16th Army. After stating the usual arguments about the negative effects of the Commissar order in its increasing Russian resistance, General Schmidt wrote that "the Russian people must be shown a future". (NOKW 2413) Yet both Manstein and Rudolf Schmidt had commissars shot. Manstein's sentence to 18 years included the execution of commissars at 11th Army. Streit shows that Schmidt's Corps had reported the execution of 20 commissars by 5 July and that additional figures were reported separately by Divisions of his Corps. (Streit, table of executed commissars, p.88 ff.).

28 Guderian, p.138.

29 C. Streit, *Keine Kameraden – Die Wehrmacht und die sowjetischen Kriegsgefangenen*, Stuttgart 1978, p.1978. Streit's main subject is the mistreatment of Russian prisoners of war, however part of his book contains detailed statistics about the execution of the Commissar order.

30 Minutes of the Nuremberg trial of major Nazi war criminals, vol. 53, p.156 ff.

of war during the first days of the campaign, but that by the beginning of August, 170 Commissars had been "shunted off" (*abgeschoben*).[31]

The statement that "the Commissar Order was not communicated to our units" can be found in a number of German post-war recollections.[32] That is easy to explain. When they received the Commissar Order, the Generals knew that it was contrary both to established rules of law, and to what remained of their honour as soldiers. In 1941, the Generals could not care less, because they had final victory in sight. After the war, they wanted to dissociate themselves from that order, as from other criminal orders of Hitler. The easiest way out was to claim that they had never received the Commissar Order. Since the reporting system under the order was deficient, and the exact number of Commissars executed in accordance with the Commissar Order could not be established, it was easy to say and to write: "Maybe other units executed the order, but I have never received it". At that time, detailed archive research was still in its infancy. The memoir-writing Generals were perceived by many as unblemished heroes who had become victims of "victors' justice."[33] Only *Generaloberst* Hermann Hoth admitted at his trial that he had received the order, that he was basically in agreement with it, and that he had communicated it to the units under his command.[34]

Model's 3rd *Panzer* Division was part of Guderian's *Panzergruppe* 2 and the Commissar Order was likewise carried out in his Division. On 28 July 1941, the Ic report of the Division read:

> 3rd *Panzer* Division, Lobkovich, 28, VII, p. 127.
>   Assembly point of prisoners of war at Karachev …
>   … The captured Commissar foreseen for execution is to be shot. The other Commissar, captured a few days before, is to remain a prisoner of war[35] …

---

31   BA-MA, RH 21-3/v. 423.
32   For instance, Reichhelm writes: "Some units have apparently received communication of the order. At 9th Army, this did not happen. General Weckmann, its chief of staff, prevented its distribution". (Reichhelm, Recollections, p.116). When I showed Reichhelm Streit's figures, which give details about commissars executed at 9th Army, (Streit, p.88 ff), he refused to believe what had been established in official documents. Already during the first weeks of the war, the representative of the German Ministry for Foreign Affairs with *AOK* 9 had stated in his report to Berlin: "Commissars are being thoroughly dealt with here. All political commissars are shot upon capture." (quoted by Hürter, p.397). The reports ends with a typical sentence: "In our sector, Russians wage war in an Asiatic manner."
33   Jodl was aware at an early stage that the Commissar Order was contrary to rules of civilized law. On one of the drafts submitted to him, he had pencilled a note: "Finally the paper has to be shown to the *Führer*. Since we can expect reprisals against captured airmen, we had better word the Commissar order as a reprisal of our own." (Streit, p.47).
34   Interrogation Hoth, IMT Case 12, 30 April 1948. Quoted by Hürter, p.395.
35   Commissars could be retained as prisoners of war for interrogation if they were believed to have useful information. After that they were generally handed to the SD which had them shot. Some commissars succeeded in surviving in prisoner of war camps.

Signed: von dem Knesebeck, Lieutenant[36]

By the end of 1941, the number of Russian prisoners of war decreased dramatically. Only a few more Commissars were captured. It had become apparent that the order had missed its original purpose. On 6 May 1942, Hitler decided to "suspend" the Order: "in order to strengthen the wish of the Russian soldier to surrender or to defect. For this purpose, an attempt should be made to show the Commissars that they can perhaps save their own lives."[37] The "suspension" remained in force until the end of the war.

The *Gerichtsbarkeitserlass (Barbarossa* Order)

The Order was issued on 13 May 1941, under Keitel's signature, and communicated to the troops in early June:

The prime objective of military justice is to maintain *Manneszucht*.[38] The wide extension of the operational territories in the East will dictate the form of the combats to come. The kind of enemy that will be encountered means that the military courts must shoulder with determination the tasks which they will be able to accomplish if they concentrate upon their traditional duties. This will be possible only if the troops ruthlessly protect themselves against any threat from the local civilian population. Therefore, the following rules will apply to the *Barbarossa* area which comprises the operational areas, the rear areas and the areas under political administration.

I: Treatment of criminal actions committed by enemy civilians:
1. Until further notice, criminal actions by enemy civilians no longer fall under the authority of courts martial and summary courts martial.
2. Enemy soldiers who have become detached from their units have to be shot without mercy, either in combat or in flight.
3. Any attempts of any kind by enemy civilians against the *Wehrmacht,* or units attached to it, have to be dealt with by the troops without delay, and by all means available, until complete annihilation.
4. If such measures have been neglected, or have not been instantly possible, suspicious elements have to be brought immediately before an officer, who will decide if they have to be shot.
5. If deceitful or malicious actions against the *Wehrmacht* take place in villages, and individual perpetrators cannot be immediately identified, collective reprisals will be conducted under the authority of officers with at least the rank of battalion commander.

---

36 BA-MA, RH 27 – 2/167. Further executions of Commissars by 3rd *Panzerdivision*, in Römer, p.640 ((BA-MA, RH 27-3/14,/16/29, 165, 166, 167, 170, 171,175,176,179/180,181/182,/226 /227/22)/230/231. BA-MA, MWg 2/533, 5354(Sr 394, RH 39/709(*Pz.Rgt.* 6), MSg 2/4651.
37 NOKW 1807.
38 The word *Manneszucht* refers to discipline by the troops, and is not used in the daily German language. It appears frequently in *Wehrmacht* documents. A literal translation is 'men's discipline'.

6.   It is forbidden to keep suspected perpetrators in temporary custody for the purpose of deferring them to military tribunals at a later date, when ordinary rules of military justice will again be applied.

7.   The Commanders in Chief of Army Groups, acting in cooperation with the relevant *Luftwaffe* and Navy commanders, are authorized to restore the authorities of military tribunals over enemy civilians, if they consider that the relevant areas are sufficiently pacified. For areas under political administration, this authority is restricted to the head of *OKW.*

II. Treatment of criminal actions, by officers and soldiers of the *Wehrmacht*, and of units associated with it, against enemy civilians:

1.   Actions against enemy civilians, by officers and soldiers of the *Wehrmacht,* and their aides, need not be prosecuted, even if they are crimes or other offences punishable by criminal law.

2.   Such deeds should be seen against the background of the military collapse of 1918. The suffering of the German people, and the internal struggle against National-Socialism, with its many victims, were decisively due to Bolshevik influence. No German is allowed to forget this.

3.   In each instance, the holder of judicial authority (*Gerichtsherr*) decides if a disciplinary measure is sufficient, or if legal action is required. Acts by officers and soldiers of the *Wehrmacht,* against enemy civilians, may only be deferred to courts martial, if this is required by maintaining *Manneszucht,* or by protection of the security of the troops. The latter is the case if the actions are viewed as serious crimes, having an unrestrained sexual background, if they result from a criminal disposition of the perpetrator, or if there are signs that the troops threaten to become dissolute. Legal action is likewise required if the acts under review result in damage to our troops, such as senseless destruction of their quarters, stocks and booty. Prosecution by courts martial requires a signed order by the *Gerichtsherr.*

4.   Testimonials by enemy civilians have to be examined with utmost care.

III. Responsibilities of commanders.
Commanders are personally responsible:

1.   That all officers subordinate to them are thoroughly acquainted with all the points under section I.

2.   That their legal advisers are made most thoroughly acquainted, in good time, of the contents of this order, and also of verbal explanations by the *OB,* of the political intentions of the leadership.

3.   That they are only allowed to confirm such sentences which are in conformity with the political intentions of the leadership.[39]

One is entitled to question which was more horrible, the order itself or the nonsensical attempt to justify it. In its criminality, the *Gerichtsbarkeitserlass* was worse than the Commissar Order. The Commissar Order was directed against one specific group, the

---

39   BA-MA, RW 22/155.

jurisdiction order against the whole Russian population. Every General and every officer, with even a minimum understanding of law, must have understood that the order was a break with every world-wide civilized principle of law . This was probably the reason that led Brauchitsch to issue an additional order on 24 May 1941:

> … All commanders have to keep in mind that individual acts of violence, committed by soldiers, cannot be permitted. They have to prevent any development of unruliness in their units. The individual soldier must never get the feeling that he can do what he likes in Russia. In every case he has to obey orders by his officers. I request that this be made totally clear, down to the smallest unit. Immediate steps by officers must strive to maintain *Manneszucht*, the foundation of our previous successes.[40]

In this additional order, Brauchitsch attempts to square the circle. Bringing the order and *Manneszucht* under a common denominator, would require the art of a magician. The Russian victims could not care less if they were killed by drunken hordes or by soldiers imbued with *Manneszucht*.

No further moral criticism was directed against the jurisdiction order, which was communicated in writing to every Division commander, with the Army Group and Army commanders adding sentences of their own, which thus increased the criminal character of the order.[41] In its lack of any protest, the *Wehrmacht* reached its lowest point. An almost incredible statement by Manstein at his trial must be mentioned. Manstein declared that the second part of the order was not illegal because the speed of the German advance did not permit the setting up of military tribunals in time. That requires no comment.

The compliance of Model's 3rd *Panzerdivision* with the *Erlass* is documented in the BA-MA archives.[42]

An address by General von Cochenhausen to his 134th Infantry Division is a typical example of the mentality of the German commanders in the East:

> Only brutal force makes an impression upon the enemy. Courts martial and summary courts martial are abolished. Whoever attempts resistance, even passive resistance, is to be summarily shot. Every officer can order an immediate execution of the death sentence. This is an order by the *Führer* which has to be communicated to every soldier." And then follows an almost unbelievable statement: "In the Germany of

---

40 OB.d.H./Gen.z.b.V./Gr.R.West. Nr. 80/41 g., Kdos.Chefs.) quoted in Hürter, p.250.

41 A typical example of reactions by *Wehrmacht* commanders can be found in a letter from von Bock to von Brauchitsch. *Feldmarschall* von Bock wrote that the order gave the German soldier the right to shoot any Russian whom he pretended or wanted to pretend to be an "irregular". The additional order by Brauchitsch was insufficient, because it was not sufficiently compatible with *Manneszucht*. When von Bock heard from Brauchitsch that *Manneszucht* was his main concern, he wrote in his diary: "Now I am satisfied". (In Poland, von Bock had ordered the burning down of villages). Hürter, p.251, Gerlach, p.1115 ff.

42 BA-MA, MSg 2/5354, p. 3 and BA-MA, RH 27-3/226. For details about compliance with the *Erlass,* article by F. Römer, ‚Im alten Deutschland wäre ein solcher Befehl nicht möglich gewesen. Rezeption, Adapation und Umsetzung des Kriegsgerichstbarkeisterlasses im Ostheer 1941/42', *Vierteljahrshefte für Zeitgeschichte*, vol. 1, January 2008, p. 53-99.

former times such an order would not have been possible, because nobody would have had the guts to issue it.[43]

Model's part in the Shoah

Anti-Semitism in the German Officer Corps

There is no reason to doubt that Model was an anti-Semite, as were practically all German officers. His anti-Semitism was an inheritance of the traditionally anti-Semitic Prussian Army. Although Jews theoretically enjoyed all political rights in Imperial Germany, certain self-styled elitist groups, such as the Army and the senior civil service, would not accept them in their ranks. Jews could not even become reserve officers. The rank of reserve officer was a status symbol in Imperial Germany. A well-known, apocryphal story tells of an old and famous professor to whom the Emperor had granted an audience, and to whom he promised the fulfilment of a request. The professor looked at the Emperor with his half-blind eyes, and asked with a trembling voice to be promoted to *Oberleutnant* in the reserve. Bismarck had once said that one becomes a man only with the appointment of Lieutenant. Carl Zuckmayer made use of Bismarck's dictum in his comedy *Der Hauptmann von Köpenick*. Adolf Wormser, the Jewish purveyor of military uniforms and their accessories to the Imperial court, tells an employee of the Köpenick administration, who comes to order a new uniform after having been promoted to Lieutenant in the Reserve: "I have always said that Darwinism begins with Corporal, but man only with Lieutenant." The historian Friedrich Meinecke had mocked the cult of the officer: "The active Lieutenant is God, the reserve Lieutenant is a demi-God".[44]

Among the Imperial German Armies, the Bavarian Army was more liberal. Jews could become officers of the reserve, in exceptional circumstances also active officers.

The anti-Semitism of the German Officer Corps, prior to the First World War, was not racist. If a Jew converted to Christianity the obstacles were removed. Neither was it vulgar in the style of Hitler's tirades.[45] At that time, it was a typical example of narrow Prussian provincialism. In no other major Western European countries, even in those with strong anti-Semitic tendencies, were there similar restrictions.[46] Neither in France, nor

---

43   BA-MA, RH 25-134/5. att.7.

44   V. Ullrich, *Die nervöse Grossmacht 1871-1918. Aufstieg und Untergang des deutschen Kaiserreichs*, Frankfurt 2004, p.400.

45   On 1 November 1925, in articles with the headline: "Hitler in Braunschweig" the *Braunschweiger Landeszeitung* wrote: …"Thereafter Hitler ranted against the Jews in his usual manner. Since everybody knows what the National-Socialists have against those German citizens, we can save paper and omit reporting what Hitler said." Quoted by Saul Friedländer in *Das Dritte Reich und die Juden. Die Jahre der Verfolgung 1933-1939*, Munich 2000, p.118. Hitler had an innate feeling to adapt his rhetoric to different audiences. In a speech on 28 February 1929 to the *Hamburger Nationalklub von 1919*, a nationalist-conservative body, he omitted to mention the Jews since the members present belonged to the high levels of society, including a number of high ranking officers in retirement. Ibid p.119. Hitler obviously understood that vulgarity was out of place in this auditorium.

46   Anti-Semitism was also prevalent in the US Army. In 1938, General George Van Horn Moseley, one of America's most decorated Generals and a former candidate for chief of staff, told a group of reserve officers that America should only accept Jewish refugees if they were first

in Austria, were Jews prevented from entering the military or the senior civil service. The French Armies of 1914-1918, and of 1939-1940 included Jewish Generals. The Austrian Army, before the *Anschluss,* numbered five Jewish Generals. The *Staatssekretär* (in Austria, the *Staatssekretär* was the deputy minister) of the Austrian Ministry of Defence was the Jewish Dr Julius Deutsch. The Jewish Dr Robert Hecht was one of the most influential officials in the Defence Ministry. The Polish Army had many Jewish reserve officers, also a few active officers. The Hungarian Army of the Austro-Hungarian Empire had a large number of Jewish officers. The Jewish *Generaloberst* Samuel Hazai, born Cohn, was Hungarian defence minister from 1910 to 1917. Between 1917 and 1918 he was commander in chief of the Replacement Army, (*Ersatzwesen*), the highest command in the Hungarian Army after the Chief of Staff.[47]

In 1916, anti-Semitism in the German Army reached its climax with the *Judenzählung.* It was a census of all Jews serving in the German armed forces, made under the pretext that there were complaints about many Jews being shirkers. The census showed that there was not only no substance in the premise of the *Judenzählung*, but that the percentage of Jewish soldiers in the front line combat exceeded the percentage of Jews in the German population. But no apology was forthcoming. The census cost Germany much of the sympathy which it had enjoyed among American Jews, who had previously been strongly opposed to the US entering the war on the side of the Entente.[48] The historian, Thomas Nipperdey, has written that while anti-Semitism in Imperial Germany at that time was less violent than in France, Russia and Austria, it has to be looked at, not only in the context of that period, but also in the later "sign of Auschwitz."[49]

After the First World War, the progressive radicalism of the political parties led to an increase in anti-Semitism. In the Weimar Republic, Jews reached increasingly high positions in all spheres of German politics, the economy, and all forms of cultural life. In turn, it led to an increase in German anti-Semitism, which was furthered by the increasing number of Eastern European Jews who established themselves in Germany. When Hitler took power in 1933, German anti-Semitism was already widespread.

---

sterilized, so that these "racial inferiors" would not procreate. While this caused an uproar, both General Marshall and General Eisenhower retained their admiration for Moseley as soldier and remained in close contact with him until his death in the 1950s. As late as the 1960s, Eisenhower wrote fondly of Moseley as a "patriotic American, unafraid to disagree with the consensus, whose outspoken reaction to public questions got him a bad press and created a distortion of what Moseley really represented." The four-star General Albert Wedemeyer, who had attended the German *Kriegsakademie* during the Nazi years as part of his staff training, was a staunchly pro-German racial anti-Semite. General George Patton stated in 1945 that "it was a mistake to believe that the displaced person is a human being, which he is not, and this applies particularly to the Jews, who are lower than animals." Quoted from an article by Joseph W. Bendersky, 'Racial sentinels: Biological Anti-Semitism in the US Army Office Corps 1890-1950. The Racial Mentality of an Anglo-Saxon Elite', in *Militärgeschichtliche Zeitschrift* 62 (2003) vol.2. pp.331-353.

47 E. Schmidl, *Jews in the Habsburg Armed Forces,* text in German and English, Eisenstadt 1989.

48 Details about the census in W. Angress, *Das deutsche Militär und die Juden im Ersten Weltkrieg in Militärgeschichtliche Mitteilungen 19* (1976) pp.77-146.

49 Quoted by S. Friedländer, *Das Dritte Reich und die Juden. Die Jahre der Verfolgung 1933-1939*, Munich 1998, p.95.

The attitude of German active officers towards Jews in general was one of indifference, coupled with a feeling of inborn superiority and disdain. Social contacts did not exist. The anti-Semitism of the officer corps paved the way for approval of the racial legislation of the Third Reich. Later, indifference led to participation in the "final solution". *Generaloberst* Gotthard Heinrici's wife was half Jewish. He refused to divorce her and had to request a *Deutschblütigkeits* certificate from Hitler for her and his son.[50] (Hitler decided personally, on a case by case basis, if a *Mischling* was to be considered to be of "pure German blood"). This did not keep *Generaloberst* Heinrici from inserting frequent vulgar anti-Semitic remarks into his voluminous correspondence with his wife during the war.[51] Strong anti-Semitic feelings can also be found among the officers who participated in the plot of 20 July. Generals Hoepner and von Stülpnagel have already been mentioned. *Generalmajor* Helmut Stieff, who was hanged after the failure of the plot, wrote to his wife on 21 November 1939 about the excesses in Poland: "I am ashamed of being a German". But then he added: "Łodz is a horrible city. Countless Jews have to wear a yellow band on their sleeves. At least half of the inhabitants of Łodz wear the yellow band. And how they look! Impossible to understand that such persons may exist."[52]

Feldmarschall Maximilian von Weichs, who had protested against the German brutalities in Poland, wrote after his visit to the Łodz ghetto: "Terrible run-down and dirty houses and shacks. Masses of the well-known types of "caftan Jews".[53] Von Weichs apparently ignored the fact that the dirty houses and shacks were located in an area of Łodz which had been assigned as a closed ghetto by the Germans. Before the war, few Jews inhabited that district, which was the most run-down part of the city. Since the whole Jewish population of Łodz was packed into the ghetto, "masses of the well-known caftan Jews" could not be seen elsewhere in the city. That this situation was created by the German occupiers seems to have been beyond the horizons of von Weichs' understanding.

In autumn 1939, General Theodor Groppe had heard that party officials in the Sarre area intended to organize a pogrom against the Jews who had remained there. He gave orders to his Division to protect the Jews and, if necessary, to shoot if the pogroms were to take place. But as a Captain in the 1920s, he had campaigned privately for the extreme right DNVP[54] and criticized the Catholic *Zentrum* party which had joined hands with the Social-Democrats and the "Jewish democrats".[55]

Einsatzgruppen

When the war against Russia began, four *Einsatzgruppen* were set up. *Einsatzgruppe* A was under Dr Walther Stahlecker. *Einsatzgruppe* B, which operated in the area of Army Group

50 B. Rigg, *Hitlers jüdische Soldaten*, Paderborn 2003, pp.204-245 ff.

51 J. Hürter, *Ein deutscher General an der Ostfront. Die Briefe und Tagebücher des Gotthard Heinrici 1941/42*, Erfurth 2001. Also J. Hürter: *Es herrschen Sitten und Gebräuche genau wie im 30-jährigen Krieg. Das erste Jahr des deutsch-sowjetischen Krieges in Dokumenten des Generals Gotthard Heinrici, Vierteljahrshefte für Zeitgeschichte 2000*, vol. 2, pp.329-403.

52 H. Mühleisen (ed.) *Helmuth Stieff Briefe*, Berlin 1991, p.108 ff.

53 M.von Weichs, 'Recollections' (unpublished), vol.3, BA-MA, N 19/7, Bl.18 ff. Quoted by Hürter, p.513.

54 At that time, the NSDAP was only in the process of formation.

55 J. Förster, ,Reichswehr und Antisemitismus', in J. Matthäus/K. Mallmann (ed.), *Deutsche Juden und Völkermord. Der Holocaust als Geschichte und Gegenwart*, Darmstadt 2006, p.22.

Centre, was commanded by the chief criminologist of the *Reich, Reichskriminaldirektor* Arthur Nebe. Nebe was already recognised as Germany's leading crime expert, before the Nazis took power.[56]*Einsatzgruppe* C was under Dr Otto Rasch, and *Einsatzgruppe* D was commanded by Otto Ohlendorf. *Einsatzgruppen* A, B and C consisted of approximately 1,000 men each. The smaller *Einsatzgruppe* D numbered 600.

Every *Einsatzgruppe* worked through sub-units, the *Sonderkommandos* (Sk) and the *Einsatzkommandos* (Ek). The Sk followed the front line troops closely. Originally, the Ek remained in the rear, but after an increasing number of Army commanders requested their presence, they were soon in the front line.

The duties of the *Einsatzgruppen*, and the general principles of their co-operation with the *Wehrmacht*, were first laid out in the "Wagner-Heydrich agreement". It was signed on 28 April 1941, between *Generalmajor* Eduard Wagner, Chief Quartermaster at *OKH*, and *SS Obergruppenführer* Reinhardt Heydrich, head of the *SD*.[57] General Wagner participated in the 20 July plot and committed suicide on 21 July 1944. Heydrich had been appointed *Reichsprotektor* of the Bohemia & Moravia Protectorate in 1942. He was killed that same year by Czech partisans in Prague. The agreement did not contain all the details concerning the tasks of the *Einsatzgruppen*. They can however be summed up as the organised killing of all communist functionaries, "Asiatic inferiors", Gypsies and Jews.

Co-operation between the *Wehrmacht* and the *Einsatzgruppen* was formalized in an *OKH* order, signed by Brauchitsch on 28 April 1941. Streit describes the separation between *Wehrmacht* and *Einsatzgruppe* as being a simple cliché.[58] *Einsatzgruppen* commandos were instructed to follow the troops at a short distance and to report to the commander of the rear area, the *Korück*. As the Sk came nearer the front line, reports were no longer sent as routine to the *Korücks*, but communicated directly to the Ic/AO of the front line units involved.

A representative of the security police and the *SD* was attached to the staff of every Army, to organise "centralised steering" of the activities of the *Einsatzgruppe* commandos. The representative was usually the chief of the *Einsatzgruppe* commandos attached to the Army. The commander of the *Einsatzgruppe* was its representative with the *Korück*. Duties of the representative were to bring the instructions of the SS main security office (*RSHA*) to the knowledge of the Army commander without delay, and to remain in close contact with the Army's Ic/AO. The Ic/AO was required to coordinate the activities of the *Einsatzgruppe* with his Army's military requirements.

---

56 Nebe was the first department head of the SD to volunteer for the command of an *Einsatzgruppe*. He also maintained some contact with the military and civilian resistance movements. Gersdorff mentions him repeatedly in laudatory words. He writes that "Tresckow knew that Nebe was a decided opponent of National-Socialism and a very decent man." (Gersdorff, p.85). On 15 August 1941, the "very decent man" directed personally an execution of Jews in Minsk which was attended by Himmler. During the five months of Nebe's command of *Einsatzgruppe* B, its Sk and Ek murdered 45,000 Jews, more than any of the other *Einsatzgruppen* during the same months. Leading members of the resistance such as von Tresckow, von Gersdorff, Georg von Boeselager were not only aware of what happened in the rear, they even added positive comments to the *Einsatzgruppen* reports. On 20 July 1944, Nebe disappeared. After some months he was discovered in the apartment of one of his many girlfriends and was hanged.

57 NOKW 2086.

58 Streit, p.51.

The first direct cooperation between *Wehrmacht* and *Einsatzgruppen* had thus been formalised. By February 1941, *Feldmarschall* von Brauchitsch had admonished the Generals who had opposed the excesses in Poland, to likewise understand Himmler's point of view.[59]

Only part of the murders were committed by the *Einsatzgruppen* alone. The first wave was more or less equally divided between the *Wehrmacht*, including the units of the "secret field police" (*Geheime Feldpolizei*), which were part of the *Abwehr*, and the *Einsatzgruppen* which advanced with the *Wehrmacht*. Christian Gerlach establishes that some 50% of the victims among civilians, both Jews and other nationalities, and prisoners of war in Belorussia, were murdered with active participation by the *Wehrmacht*.[60]

During the first weeks of the Russian campaign, Latvians and Lithuanians civilians organized massive pogroms. The *Wehrmacht* was witness but did not intervene. When informed about the massacres at Kaunas, Busch found nothing better to say: "Those are internal Lithuanian matters which do not concern us." From Busch such a statement could be expected, however the "conservative" *Feldmarschall* Ritter von Leeb said to his *Berück*, General Franz von Roques:

> We have no influence, we simply have to stay away. Roques told me that this is hardly the manner in which the Jewish problem can be solved. The best way would probably be the sterilization of all male Jews.[61]

In his recent work of 1,000 pages, the first complete and detailed book concerning the involvement of the ordinary police (*Ordnungspolizei*),[62] Wolfgang Curilla presents shocking statistics. They establish that more than 50% of the Jews in the occupied areas of the Soviet Union were killed with the active assistance of 21 police battalions, totalling 12,000 men, which accompanied *Wehrmacht* and the *Einsatzgruppen*.[63] In Belorussia, the police battalions participated in the murder of 300,000 Jews, corresponding to 57% of the total. In Eastern Galicia, the victims numbered 630,000 – 49% were killed by the police units. In the Ukraine 650,000 Jews were murdered, 300,000 with assistance from

---

59   Streit, p.51.

60   Gerlach, p.1151.

61   Hürter p. 540 ff., with quotation from Ritter von Leeb's diary.

62   Previous important works have dealt with individual police units. C. Browning, *Ganz normale Männer. Das Reserve Polizeibataillon 101 und die Endlösung in Polen*, Reinbeck 1993 (German edition), deals with Police Battalion 202. D. Goldhagen, *Hitler's Willing Executioners. Ordinary Germans and the Holocaust*, New York 1996, singles out some Police Battalions. C. Gerlach, *Kalkulierte Morde. Die deutsche Wirtschafts-und Vernichtungspolitik in Weissrussland 1941-1942*, Hamburg 1999, (henceforth Gerlach) concentrates mainly on Belorussia.

63   W. Curilla, *Die deutsche Ordnungspolizei und der Holocaust im Baltikum und in Weissrussland 1941-1944*, Paderborn 2006. (Henceforth Curilla). The three main branches of the German police were the 'Administration Police' (*Verwaltungspolizei*), the 'Criminal Police', (*Kriminalpolizei*), which included the *Gestapo* and the 'Ordinary Police' (*Ordnungspolizei*), which before the war had the daily duties of uniformed policemen worldwide, such as traffic control, maintaining public order, etc. The murders in the East were committed by battalions of the *Ordnungspolizei*, which had been set up at the beginning of the war. The chief of the German police was Himmler, the chief of the *Ordnungspolizei* was SS-*Oberstgruppenführer* Kurt Daluege. Daluege was hanged in Prague after the war.

police units. In the Russian republic, the police battalions acted on a more limited scale. There, the Jewish victims numbered 107,000, of whom 17,000, 16%, were killed by police battalions. Locally recruited Russian police, Ukrainian, Latvian and Lithuanian police units participated in the murders. The total number of Jewish victims in the Soviet Union is estimated at 2.1 million, with close to 1 million murdered by police battalions alone, or in participation with *Wehrmacht* and *Einsatzgruppen*.[64]

The murderous Reserve Police Battalion 101 has been the subject of two contradictory books, Christopher Browning: *Ordinary Men: Reserve Police Battalion 101 and the Final Solution in Poland*, New York 1992, henceforth Browning.) and Daniel Goldhagen: *Hitler's willing executioners. Ordinary Germans and the Holocaust*, New York 1996. Browning describes the policemen as men who really did not want to kill Jews but since the job had to be done, each man felt himself under pressure not to leave this unpleasant task to others. Goldhagen sees the murders as a direct result of an inborn German anti-Semitism, the like of which could not be found in other nations. Goldhagen's book led to the "Goldhagen debate" among historians both in Germany and in other countries. While Goldhagen's thesis is now rejected by most historians worldwide, the "Goldhagen debate" was an important element in searching for an answer to the question how men without a criminal background can be turned into ruthless murderers. [65]

Model's 3rd *Panzer* Division and *Einsatzgruppe* B

3rd *Panzer* Division had no active part in the first organized wave of killing Jews in the summer and autumn of 1941. However, that was not because of any opposition by Model to the actions of the *Einsatzgruppe* and other units that committed the murders. The Division was the spearhead of *Panzergruppe* 2. It had already left the cities by the time that Nebe's men, and the SS and police units arrived, and started committing their murders. During the swift advances of the first months of the Russo-German War, the participation of *Wehrmacht* front troop units was limited. Later, the front troops had their share of the murders.

Without doubt, officers and soldiers of Model's Division murdered Jews in their passage through the townships. That happened in every *Wehrmacht* unit. A number of *Wehrmacht* officers and soldiers had taken part in brutalities against Jews in German cities before the war. Later, they played their part in many murders in Poland. In the defenceless Russian Jews they saw new outlets for their inborn thuggish nature. All soldiers in the East had knowledge of the hate appeals launched by the Generals in the weeks preceding the invasion. They also knew that they would not be punished if they mistreated or even killed Jews during their passage through cities and villages. There are, however, no records of organized participation in the murders by 3rd *Panzer* Division. During the later killings things were different. Model's 9th Army had its share of the murders.

The lack of participation of 3rd *Panzer* Division, in the first wave, can be established by comparing the diaries of the Division and the reports by *Einsatzgruppe* B–EM, (*Ereignismeldungen* – reports of actions by the *Einsatzgruppe* and its Sk to *Panzergruppe* 2),

---

64 Complete statistical tables, in Curilla, pp.828-833.

65 The Reserve Police Battalion 101 consisted of 500 officers and men. By May 1943, this small unit had accounted for 83,000 Jewish victims. 38,000 Jews were shot, 45,000 were transported by the battalion to the extermination camps (Browning, p.189).

and TLB (*Tätigkeits und Lageberichte an das RSHA*), the regular reports of the *Einsatzgruppe* to the SS main office *(RSHA)*. The TLB were originally sent twice every month, thereafter on a monthly basis. Separate data of actions by the ordinary police units are taken from Curilla. Finally, some documents are kept at the post-war central office for research into war crimes at Ludwigsburg (ZStL).

Bobruisk

3rd *Panzer* Division was deployed around Bobruisk between 28 June and 1 July.

The first unit of Sk 7b, commanded by SS *Sturmbannführer* Rausch, appeared on 11 July.[66]

14 August: General Max von Schenkendorff ordered 225th Infantry Division to request the presence of the *SD*.[67]

September: 1st SS Cavalry Division shot 7,000 Jews near the airport.[68] A document in the TLB related to this action was signed by SS *Gruppenführer* Hermann Fegelein.

October: 380 Jews were murdered.[69]

The Police unit Waldenburg, (*Polizeikommando Waldenburg*), arrived in Bobruisk in November.[70]

December: 5,281 Jews were shot, and Bobruisk was declared "free of Jews".

Rogachev

3rd *Panzer* Division entered Rogachev on 7 July and remained in the area until 11 July.

Sk 7b was transferred from Mogilev to Rogachev during the last weeks of September. It was joined by the infamous Dirlewanger SS unit which was to take part in the massacres during the Warsaw uprising.[71]

The "police handling" of the Jewish population was completed in September.[72] (The *Einsatzgruppen* often used this and other euphemisms to avoid the word "killing")

Shlobin

3rd *Panzer* Division was in the Shlobin area on 9 July. During September, Jews were shot.[73] Total extermination took place on the same day as in Rogachev, and was reported in the same documents in the TLB. In the second half of September, exterminations were carried out simultaneously in some cities.

Mogilev

3rd *Panzer* Division was in the Mogilev area on 11 July. In August, "small scale" executions began with some 80 victims.[74] On 25 September, a ghetto was established.[75]

---

66 BstU 9, Vol. 31, p.3-17 and TLB 31, 23 July 1941.
67 BA-MA, RH 22/227.
68 ZstL II, 202 AR – Z 64/60 and BA-MA, RH 22-224.
69 TLB 6, 1-31 October 1941.
70 TLB 6, 1-31 October 1941.
71 TLB 90 and 133, 14 November 1941.
72 EM 90 and 133, 14 November 1941.
73 TLB 5, 15, 30 September 1941.
74 TLB 50, 67, 73, 12 August, 29 August and 4 September 1941.
75 Mogilev City Administration Order Number 51, 25 September 1941.

During the last ten days of October, Ek 8 headquarters was established within the city.[76] 836 mentally ill victims were reported as having been shot, but there was no indication of their religion. In reality, this was the first experiment with gas chambers.[77] In addition, 113 Jews were "liquidated" by other means.[78]

In October, 2,200 Jews were shot in the city and its surroundings.[79] On 19 October, 3,276 Jews were shot in the city.[80] In November, 13 Jews were shot.[81] An additional 153 were murdered in December.[82]

The Reserve Police Battalion 22 began its murders in November.[83]

Chausey

3rd *Panzer* Division was in Chausey on 16 and 17 July. In August, 31 Jews were shot[84] and in September an additional 20 were killed.[85] Total extermination of the Jewish population in Chausey and Mogilev took place on the same dates. It was reported in the same TLB without any mention of the numbers of victims.

Smolensk

3rd *Panzer* Division participated in the battle for Smolensk but did not enter the city. After the capture of Smolensk, the city became the headquarters of *Einsatzgruppe* B until the end of the year. Smolensk was not part of the former Jewish Pale settlement. Before the German invasion 12,000 Jews lived at Smolensk. When the Germans arrived most had fled. The Jews who had remained were first put into a ghetto and then shot.[86]

No police units participated in the killings.

Roslavl

3rd *Panzer* Division was at Roslavl on 1 August. Roslavl was the headquarters of SS *Standartenführer* Professor Six's "Advance Commando Moscow" unit which, according to documents in the TLB, took part in the shooting of 114 Jews.[87] Total elimination of the Jews in Roslavl occurred in November and December, after police units had joined the Advance Command Moscow. Documents in the TLB and other sources include this with other actions without listing the number killed.

---

76 TLB 90 and 133, 14 November 1941.

77 Krausnick/Wilhelm, p.544.

78 TLB 6, 1-31 October 1941.

79 TLB 133, 14 November 1941.

80 TLB 133, 14 November 1941

81 TLB 7, 1-30 November 1941.

82 TLB 8, 9, 1-31 December 1941.

83 Curilla, p.257.

84 TLB 3, 15-31 August 1941.

85 TLB 4, 1-15 September 1941.

86 Hilberg, p.309.

87 TLB 13 September 1941.

Starodub

3rd *Panzer* Division was in the Starodub area on 21 August. In the first half of October 272 Jews were shot there while building themselves a ghetto.[88] Total elimination of all Jews took place at the same time as the culmination of the Rogachev murders, and is reported in the same TLB.

Konotop

3rd *Panzer* Division captured Konotop on 11 September, moved on, and returned on 23 September after the closure of the Kiev *Kessel* The murder of the Jews at Konotop was carried out by the SS Cavalry Division during December, when 1,153 Jews were arrested and then shot.[89]

Kiev

3rd *Panzer* Division participated in the battle for Kiev but did not enter the city. The massacre at Babi Yar was carried out by *Einsatzgruppe* C assisted by troops of 6th Army.

Orel

3rd *Panzer* Division was in the Orel area on 30 September. No Jews had remained in the city. *Einsatzgruppe* B reported that "the mass flight of Jews continues. When the Sks entered Orel, Meden, and Maloyaroslavets, no Jews had remained."[90]

The cities that were captured by XXXI *Panzer* Corps, in the last weeks of the German advance toward Moscow, were recaptured by the Red Army in the counter-offensive. They were never entered by the *Einsatzgruppen.*

Smaller actions occurred in the cities mentioned herein, but they were not mentioned in the TLB or in other archive documents. The dates given for all the recorded actions show that Model and his Division were already far away when the killings began.

That Model was not involved in the mass murders of the *Einsatzgruppe B* was, basically, pure chance. How Model felt about the *Einsatzgruppen* is shown by a statement of *AOK* 9 on 20 May 1942, when Model was already *OB* of 9th Army: "Great value is attached to a smooth co-operation of all military departments with the *SD,* and to far reaching mutual assistance."[91] At that date, there were very few Jews left in the area of Army Group Centre. However, the *Einsatzgruppen* did not limit their murders to Jews. They killed many other innocent people, purported partisans, Communist functionaries, and others who were regarded as being hostile to the *Wehrmacht.*

How much did Model know?

The answer is simple. Model knew everything. So did all the German commanders in Russia and in others theatres of operations. Recent research has also shown that knowledge of the extermination camps was widespread, both in Germany and in the front areas.[92]

---

88 TLB 6, 1-15 October 1941.
89 BA-MA, O VI-3.
90 TLB 8, 1-31 December 1941.
91 BA-MA 20-9/276, quoted by Hürter p. 567.
92 Obviously the sudden disappearance of Jews wearing the yellow star was noticed in every city. Deportations from Germany were seldom individual, in most cases all the Jewish inhabitants of a city were assembled and deported within a few days. On 16 November 1941, Goebbels

After the war, *Feldmarschall* von Weichs admitted that he had heard rumours about the extermination camps in Poland, and had questioned Himmler about them. Himmler had replied: "Those are not rumours, they are the truth."[93] The conversations between the German Generals at the Trent Park POW camp, which were monitored by the British, show that all the Generals who had been in the East were fully aware of the mass murder of Jews. A number had witnessed shootings, others had taken an active part. General von Choltitz admitted that he had been one of the *Wehrmacht* commanders directing the mass murder of 15,000 Jews at the Crimean capital Simferopol. Many admitted that they had knowledge of the mass extermination camps. A recent video *Die Wehrmacht eine Bilanz,* largely based on the conversations between German POW officers at Trent Park, quotes a conversation between General Eberbach and his son, a junior naval officer. General Eberbach stated that the massacre of Jewish men may have been necessary, but that the indiscriminate killing of women and children was too much. His son disagreed and said that the children had to be murdered lest they became the avengers at a later date.

Furthermore, Model is known to have attended Himmler's speech at Posen, 26 January 1944, together with a sizeable group of *Wehrmacht* commanders.[94] Himmler never ranted like Hitler, he addressed his audience in a manner close to whining, and with self-pity about the "cruel tasks" he was given. Only Himmler's notes of that particular speech remain: "In the *Generalgouvernement,* greatest reassurance after solution of the Jewish question. Racial struggle. Total solution required. We cannot allow anyone to remain alive who will take vengeance on our children."[95]

The complete texts of similar addresses by Himmler, to the *Gauleiter* in Posen on 6 October 1943, and to several hundreds of *Wehrmacht* commanders in Sonthofen, on 24 May 1944, have been preserved. It is thus possible to reconstruct the text of Himmler's speech that Model attended. The relevant parts of the two addresses by Himmler are given as appendices. The real purpose of Himmler's addresses and their total candour was to turn his listeners into accomplices and to prevent them from pretending that they knew nothing.

Model likewise knew about the *Einsatzgruppen.* His *Panzer* Division did not participate in the first wave of murders, but his statement of 20 May 1942 shows that he was fully informed of their activities. We will see that as *OB* of 9th Army, he cooperated actively with the *Sk* 7a of *Einsatzgruppe* B.

Model had also seen the Reichenau order of the day of 10 October 1941, which was widely distributed over the whole Eastern Front. On 6 November 1941, *Generaloberst* Guderian had emphasised: "I fully endorse the Reichenau order. It is valid for the whole

wrote an article in the weekly *Das Reich*: 'Die Juden sind schuld' (The Jews are guilty). He recalled Hitler's speech of 30 January 1939 – "If Jewry will succed in unleashing another war, the result will be the annihilation of the Jewish race in Europe". The article continued: "We now witness the execution of this prophecy. Jewry is now suffering a fate which is cruel but deserved. It is being gradually destroyed." The article was printed in a special edition, distributed all over the country. (F. Bajohr, Dieter Pohl (ed.) *Massenmord und schlechtes Gewissen. Die deutsche Bevölkerung, die NS-Führung und der Holocaust* Frankfurt 2008 , p. 57.

93   Interrogation of Weichs by 7th US Army 30 May 1945, quoted by Hürter, p.599.

94   Goebbels diary, vol. 11/II, 26 January 1944.

95   B. Smith/A. Peterson (ed.) Heinrich Himmler. *Geheimreden 1933 bis 1945 und andere Ansprachen*, Berlin 1974, p.201. (Henceforth Himmler Geheimreden).

2nd *Panzer* Army."[96] *Generaloberst* Hoepner communicated the Reichenau order to the units of his 4th *Panzer* Army on 7 November 1941.[97] (Model's 3rd *Panzer* Division was initially one of the units of Guderian's *Panzergruppe* 2, later it was transferred to Hoepner's *Panzergruppe* 4). The Reichenau order and the Manstein order, its sequel, are given in the appendices to this chapter. Model obviously knew of the hate appeals launched by practically all high commanders at the onset of the war with Russia.

9th Army under Strauss had ruthlessly participated in the murder of Jews. Gottfried Münzer, a teacher who served in 9th Army, had witnessed a massacre of Jews at Vitebsk on 14 August 1941:

> Five SD men shot the Jews, one after another. The Jews who were shot fell into a ditch. The next group then had to stand in front of the ditch, and after being shot fell into the ditch over the corpses of the men already there. This massacre took place only three kilometres away from the headquarters of *Generaloberst* Strauss."

On 25 August 1941, 397 Jews were handed by the *Wehrmacht* to Sk 9 of *Einsatzgruppe* B, with the usual justification, "that they had acted against the *Wehrmacht*." Major Brotbrück, Adjutant of *Generaloberst* Strauss, had expressed the wish to assist at the execution. He went there, together with another officer. Apparently he liked what he saw, Nebe reported, on 28 August 1941: "The executions were carried out in the usual manner. Major Brotbrück said that he was impressed by the soldierly attitude of the men of the Sk and that he felt that the executions were undoubtedly conducted in a humane manner." Nebe's report was initialled by von Bock, General von Greiffenberg, Colonel von Tresckow, and Lieutenant Colonel von Gersdorff. [98]

On 22 September 1941, shortly before Model assumed command of 9th Army, *AOK* 9 issued the following order:

> Concerning Jews in occupied territories in the East.
>
> The following order has been issued by *OKW* on 12 September 1941:
>
> Some incidents make a reminder necessary of the *OKW* guidelines of 19 May 1941, concerning the behaviour of troops in the USSR.
>
> The fight against Bolshevism demands energetic and ruthless actions against the Jews, the main support of Bolshevism.
>
> Therefore any cooperation between the *Wehrmacht* and the Jewish population, whose attitude is of either open or hidden hostility to Germany, is not permitted.

---

96   BA-MA, RH 24-24/95, Bl.18.
97   BA-MA, RH 21-4/33.
98   BstU, ZUV 9, Bd.31. In August 1941 a massacre of up to 8,000 Jews took place at Borisov, where *Feldmarschall* von Bock had his headquarters. Apparently this was too much for von Bock, who requested "*Polizeigeneral* Nebel [sic]" to conduct his executions at some distance from his headquarters. (Diary von Bock, p.239.) Hürter describes von Bock's attitude – an attitude that was shared by many commanders: "Kill whom you want to kill, chose your methods and the place for your actions, but, please, don't do it in my immediate vicinity", Hürter, p.557. The massacre at Borisov was apparently a first eye-opener for von Tresckow and Gersdorff, both of whom had previously been very happy with their relations with Nebe and initialled the reports of *Einsatzgruppe* B, at times with positive comments.

This includes the utilization of individual Jews for assistance to the *Wehrmacht*. On no account are units of the *Wehrmacht* permitted to deliver certificates to Jews, mentioning that they performed tasks for the *Wehrmacht*.

Jews may only be employed in special columns under German supervision. This order has to be communicated to all units of the Army.

By order of *AOK* 9
signed: Weckmann, Chief of Staff of the Army."[99]

Rzhev – 9th Army's cooperation with *Sonderkommando* 7a of *Einsatzgruppe* B
Sk 7a was with 9th Army, from the beginning of the war in the East until November 1944.[100] It numbered around 100 men. Its first commander was Dr Walter Blume[101] who was replaced on 17 August 1941 by Dr Eugen Steimle.[102] Dr Steimle left *Einsatzgruppe* B on 10 December 1941. He was succeeded by SS *Hauptsturmführer* Kurt Matschke. On its way to Velish, where 9th Army had its headquarters, Sk 7a had conducted mass murders in Vilna, Minsk, Vileka, Vitebsk, Gorodov and Nevel. Thereafter it went to Velikiye Luki, and a small troop was sent to Toropec. It returned to Velish and in October it remained close to 9th Army in its advance to Moscow. It reported a number of *Judenaktionen* in its progress.[103] Cooperation with 9th Army was very close from the beginning. On 11 August 1941, *SS Obersturmführer* Foltis, a member of *Sk* 7a, complained to Army Group Centre that an officer of 9th Army had strongly criticized its actions at Velish. A Major von Klitzing had witnessed a mass execution of Jews by the *Sk* 7a. He had asked Foltis: "Do you wage war only against the Jews or also against the Russians?" Foltis replied: "Against both" and Klitzing told him: "Then see to it that you are at least well paid by whoever gives you such orders." 9th Army's Chief of Staff, Colonel Kurt Weckmann summoned Klitzing and gave him a dressing down. His report stated: "I have told Major von Klitzing in clear terms that his attitude was wholly out of order. The *Wehrmacht* knew that the elimination of Jews had been entrusted to special units by an order of the *Führer*. The *Wehrmacht* should be grateful to them and understand that they were saddled with a heavy task. Most of them would undoubtedly prefer to join the fight of the *Wehrmacht* against their common enemy. Major von Klitzing should be aware that the commander of the *Sk*, *Obersturmbannführer* Walter Blume, was a man beyond reproach [!] and that the trust which had been established between *AOK* 9 and the *Sk* could under no conditions be jeopardized. *Generaloberst* Strauss had been informed of the incident and had expressed his strong disapproval of Major von Klitzing's behaviour. Major von Klitzing received a

---

99   WF-03/17084, Bl.250. The order was distributed to units of 9th Army, down to division level.
100 After Arthur Nebe had left *Einsatzgruppe* B, it came under the command of SS-*Oberführer* Erich Naumann. Naumann was sentenced to death at the *Einsatzgruppen* trial (IMT Case 9) and hanged. Sk 7a was commanded in turn by Dr Walter Blume, Eugen Steimle, Albert Rapp, Helmut Looss from June 1943 until June 1944 and finally by Dr Gerhard Bast.
101 Dr Blume was sentenced to death at the IMT *Einsatzgruppen* trial (Case 9). His sentence was reduced to 25 years. He was released from jail after a few years and became a senior executive in an industrial company.
102 Dr Steimle was likewise sentenced to death. The sentence was reduced to 20 years.
103 EM 108, 123 124, 133: "…during the progress towards Moscow – 175 executions." Krausnick p.185.

severe official warning. Dr. Blume did not request further action after Colonel Weckmann assured him that *AOK* 9 would see to it that the mutual trust between it and the *Sk* would persist." At Army Group Centre, Colonel Weckmann's report was initialled by Tresckow and von Gersdorff. [104]

On 21 October, *Sk* 7a established its headquarters at Rzhev and reported that an order service and a Jewish council (*Judenrat*) had been set up.[105] Few Jews had remained at Rzhev. However, even the smallest numbers never prevented the *Einsatzgruppen* from searching for and murdering them. The city was outside the former Pale of Settlement, where Jews in Imperial Russia had to live, unless they had obtained a university degree or paid the taxes of a merchant of the first guild. But a number of Jews, who had fled eastwards when the *Einsatzgruppen* began their murders, had found temporary shelter in Rzhev. Between 1942 and February 1943, *Sk* 7a moved constantly with 9th Army's headquarters between Rzhev and Sychovka.

When Model became *OB* of 9th Army, *Sk* 7a was in Sychovka. The day Model assumed his command, *SK* 7 was under the command of *Obersturmbannführer* Dr Albert Rapp. Rapp had served in Department VI, the foreign countries section of the *RSHA*. In 1939, he was posted in Posen, as head of the local *SD*. He was also head of the department for the resettlement of Poles and Jews further east. In 1940 he became head of the "staff for the evacuation of Poles and Jews from the *Warthegau*", the Western provinces of Poland that had been incorporated into the *Reich*. They were responsible for the legal definition of Jews in those territories. In 1965, Albert Rapp was tried at Essen.[106]

At his trial, Albert Rapp stated:

> I was born in 1908, in Schornborn, Wurttemberg. After my *Abitur*, I studied law at Tübingen University, where I obtained my doctorate in 1936. I had joined the *NSDAP* in 1931. Between 1931 and 1937 I was in the *SA*, in 1937 I joined the *SS*. My last *SS* rank was *Standartenführer*. I was promoted to this rank in 1945. In 1936, I was taken into the *SD*.
>
> In February 1942, I became a member of *Einsatzgruppe* B and was named commander of *Sonderkommando* 7a. When I arrived at *Sk* 7a, I talked with the head of *Einsatzgruppe* B, SS *Oberführer* Erich Naumann. He was the first to tell me about the tasks of the *Einsatzgruppe*. The *Sk* was moving towards Sychovka, where

---

104 J. Hürter, *Militäropposition und Judenmord bei der Heeresgruppe Mitte im Sommer und Herbst 1941 Alte Erinnerungen und Dokumente*, p. 14.ff.

105 J. Hürter: *Militäropposition und Judenmord bei der Heeresgruppe Mitte im Sommer und Herbst 1941. Alte Erinnerungen und Dokumente*, 2009, pp.14-15. Gerlach lists the names of all officers involved in the 20 July plot who in one way or the other had taken an active part in the actions of the *Einsatzgruppen*, the secret field police units (*Geheime Feldpolizei*), which was under the authority of the *Abwehr* (*Wehrmacht* counter intelligenc), the police battalions and in other actions related to the Shoah: von Tresckow, von Gersdorff, Georg von Boeselager, General von Greiffenberg, chief of staff of v. Bock's Army Group Centre. Lieutenant Peter Yorck von Wartenburg, General Eduard Wagner, who committed suicide on 20 July, Lieutenant Fritz-Dietlof Graf von der Schulenburg.who was hanged after the collapse of the *Putsch*, General Georg Thomas, the *Wehrmacht* "economic strategist", who enforced the famine policy in the occupied areas of Russia. Gerlach, p.1104-1126.

106 After the war, Rapp had been in hiding under the name of Alfred Ruppert.

AOK Model [sic] arranged for our quarters. Upon arrival, I described my assignment to the Chief of Staff Krebs, and the Ic, whose name I cannot recall. [The Ic was Lieutenant-Colonel Georg Buntrock.] I saw it as my duty to move my *Sk* in the manner most suitable to the interests of 9th Army. My men were stationed with the various Corps of the Army, however they remained subordinate to me. It was agreed with *Generalfeldmarschall* [sic] Model, General Krebs and the Ic, that my *Sk* should work closely with the Ic of 9th Army's Corps staffs, and secure the area to the best of our abilities."

When questioned about the duties of the *Einsatzgruppen*, Albert Rapp stated that they basically consisted of the "liquidation" of Jews. "We called this *Sonderbehandlung*", (literally "special treatment". This was one of the many euphemisms used by the *Einsatzgruppen* for their murders.) "I don't remember if the people killed by us were Gypsies or Jews." When asked about the names of other members of the *Sk*, Rapp answered that he preferred not to reply to the question.[107]

On 29 March 1965, Rapp received a life sentence for having personally participated in ten actions of murder, totalling 1,180 victims.

In June 1943, Albert Rapp was succeeded by *Sturmbannführer* Helmut Looss. As a university student, Looss had been an active member of the National-Socialist students' association, (*Nationalsozialistischer Deutscher Studendentenbund*). After joining the party, he also entered the *SS*. He was taken into the *SD* and served first in department II, 113 *Politische Kirchen* (Political problems of the Churches) of the *RSHA*, headed by a former cleric Albert Hartl, who was also involved in the T-4 euthanasia program.[108] Looss was the head of an action by the *SD* against the diocese of Düsseldorf, within the framework of actions against a number of German dioceses.[109] In August 1942, Looss was appointed police attaché in Rome. In December 1942, he was transferred to the *SD* in Kiev.[110] From there he joined *Einsatzgruppe* B and became head of its *Sk* 7a.

---

107 *Zentrale Stelle der Landesjustizverwaltungen Ludwigsburg,* AR-Z 96/60, Band 6, Bl.1.403-1.499202.

108 The Catholic Church was viewed as a hostile element to the totalitarian state, because of its active part in state matters and in society. Unlike the Jews, the twenty million German Catholics could not be discriminated against as whole entity. The church policy of the party was directed against such activities within the church that were viewed as undesirable within the framework of National-Socialist ideology. Details about the church policy of the *RSHA* in W. Dierker, "'Niemals Jesuiten, niemals Sektierer". Die Religionspolitik des SD 1933-1941' in M. Wildt (Ed.), *Nachrichtendienst, politische Elite und Mordeinheit. Der Sicherheitsdienst des Reichsführers SS,* Hamburg 2003, pp.86-118.

109 Ibid. pp.108-110.

110 M. Wildt, *Generation des Unbedingten. Das Führungskorps des Reichssicherheitshauptamtes,* Hamburg 2003, p.405 (henceforth Wildt).

Looss was tried in 1960.[111] Lieutenant Colonel Herbert Lange, in 1943/44 Ic/AO of 9th Army, appeared as a witness.[112] Lange stated that he had taken up his post in October 1942. He described the various Ic departments in the units of 9th Army, adding that a "so-called" *Sonderkommando, Sk* 7a, was also stationed within its area. According to him, contacts between 9th Army and the *Sk* 7a were only loose, because the *Sk* 7a received its orders from Himmler, and reported to him. [In this spirit one could also say that every Regiment in the *Wehrmacht* received its orders from Hitler and reported directly to him. Between Himmler and a *Sonderkommando*, there were at least two layers of command, the *Einsatzgruppe*, which was subordinated to the *RSHA*, which in turn was subordinated to Himmler.]

I can't recall any reports from Rapp about his actions in combat against the partisans. It is however possible that such actions took place, since the *SD* often acted on its own initiative and responsibility, without referring to us.

Here Lange contradicts a later statement of his, in which he admits that he received the regular *Ereignismeldungen – EM*. Those reports were sent to the Ic/AO in every unit.

Question:

Has 9th Army requested participation by *Sk* 7a in an action against partisans?

Reply by Lieutenant Colonel Lange:

This question has to be put to Lieutenant Colonel Georg Buntrock, at that time Ic with 9th Army. Lieutenant Colonel Buntrock can also state if decorations were awarded by 9th Army to members of the *Sk* 7a. To the best of my recollections, *Sk* 7a received only food rations from 9th Army. 9th Army had no authority over *Sk* 7a. [This is also not true. The Wagner-Heydrich agreement required the Ic/AO to coordinate the activities of the *Einsatzgruppen*.]

Lange said further:

Both the commander of *Sk* 7a and other members paid regular calls on *AOK*. The visits were only for the sake of mutual information. On one such occasion, I got acquainted with *Obersturmbannführer* Rapp and with *Sturmbannführer* Looss. They paid regular calls upon the Ic and came to me on such occasions. We talked both about service matters and also personal questions in order to strengthen our

---

111 After the war, Looss had been in hiding under the name of August Freuwört. For ten years he was a teacher at a school at Bremen. When his identity was discovered. he was arrested and tried. Dr. Blume and Steimle, although immune from further prosecution after having already been prosecuted at the Allied *Eisatzgruppen* trial had to testify as witnesses after being threatened with coercive detention.

112 The questioning of Lange took place at a Munich hospital where Looss was undergoing treatment. The proceedings against Looss were halted because of the defendant's ill health. Loos died in 1988.

cooperation. I had knowledge of the actions of the *Sk* 7a, since its regular reports, *Ereignismeldungen* were addressed to me. But I have read them only superficially, to try to determine if they contained anything of interest for the *OB*. In such instances, I reported their content to the chief of staff, General Krebs, and to the *OB*, *Generaloberst* Model. A number of reports contained details about executions. I found them to be disgusting. I always had the impression that Model strongly disapproved of such acts of inhumanity.[113] None of the reports were kept, I always destroyed them after having read them. [The Ic/AO did not have authority to destroy documents addressed to the *AOK* or the Ic. The Ic, Buntrock, could destroy them, if he was ordered to do so by Model or by Krebs.][114]

Lange said that Rapp was always very polite and obliging.

I recall that Rapp's successor, Helmut Looss, once turned to me and said that *Reichsführer-SS* Heinrich Himmler had ordered him to have his troops in 9th Army's front line. I replied to Looss that according to orders by *OKH*, troops from the *Einsatzgruppen* have no business to be together with the front troops." [Himmler would have hardly bothered to involve himself in the positioning of an *Sk*. There was never any order from *OKH* with the content mentioned by Lange. Furthermore, a relatively low-ranking officer like Lange would hardly have waved aside a direct order from Himmler. He would have immediately run for cover. The Ic/AO was not an officer of the *Generalstab*. He had no direct access to the *OB*, all his communications were addressed to the Ic or the Army's Chief of Staff.]

Looss insisted, and requested a meeting with the Chief of Staff. He was then received by General Krebs, who told me that he had replied to Looss in the same manner as I had done. Looss had then requested a meeting with Model. Looss was received by Model on the evening of the same day. Model told him that he was bound by the *OKH* order. However, if Looss wanted to refer to his superiors, he authorized him to send a message to them by 9th Army's telex, or to phone them. Model insisted that an order by *OKH* could only be changed after consultation between *Reichsführer-SS* and either *OKW* or by *OKH*. My impression was that the Army had no interest in letting units of Sk 7a come into the front line.[115]

The only points worthwhile retaining from Lange's testimony is his admission that *AOK* 9 regularly received reports from *Sk* 7 and that its commanders met with Model and Krebs, who were both fully informed of the murders and gave assistance to the *Sk* 7a. The remainder is the bravado of an unimportant officer, who felt flattered at being heard as a witness for 9th Army, because his former commander and his former chief of staff were no longer alive.

---

113 If one disapproves of something, one obviously has knowledge of it.
114 This is perhaps the explanation why so few documents were preserved at 9th Army. The Ic/AO of Manstein's 11th Army, Major Ernst-Wolf Riesen, took great care to preserve every report. This has turned 11th Army's documents into a goldmine for historians.
115 *Zentrale Stelle der Landesjustizverwaltungen Ludwigsburg*, 202 AR-Z 96/60, Bd.2. Bl.202-242.

The total number of victims of *Sk* 7a, *Wehrmacht* and police battalions, up to 28 February 1942, was 29,953. During Model's time as *OB* 9th Army, they amounted to 24,928 Jews and "Gypsies".[116]

Again, the numbers are unimportant in the determination of the *Wehrmacht* commanders' responsibility. The relevant factor is that without the active participation of all the *Wehrmacht* commanders in the East, both at the front and in the rear, the murders in Russia could not have been carried out with such efficiency and on such a scale.

Extracts from the questioning of Fabian von Schlabrendorff by Robert Kempner, a senior member of the American prosecution team at Nuremberg, can be quoted:

Question: "How many members of the resistance, known by you, have signed such documents?" Kempner was referring to documents relative to the deportation of Jews.

Answer: "For instance, we had SS *Obergruppenführer* Nebe. He had to do with such things."

Question: "Don't you know, at least, that Nebe was involved in the mass slaughter of Jews in Russia?"

Answer: "On the contrary, I knew SS *Obergruppenführer* Nebe when he was head of *Einsatzgruppe* B in Russia. I have talked to him several times. I know that he had tried to do his best to prevent the murder of Jews and of Russians…"

Question: "Continue."

Answer: "…or, at least, reduce it to the strict minimum required…"

Question: "Continue."

Answer: "But he found himself in a terrible dilemma. Either he left his post and would be replaced by commanders who, instead of killing 10%, would kill 100%, or he could stay and reduce the number of victims to a minimum."

At that moment, Robert Kempner became exasperated and asked Schlabrendorff: "Mr. expert of the resistance movement, I put a final question to you. How many Jews may one kill, if the final aim is to get rid of Hitler? How many millions?"
  Schlabrendorff replied: "I would say, not a single one."
  Kempner simply said: "Thank you, no more questions."[117]

Kommandostab Reichsführer-SS (Command staff of the Reichsführer-SS) and *Waffen*-SS Cavalry Brigades

The authoritative work on the *Kommandostab* and the *Waffen-SS* units which operated in the rear areas of the Armies in the East is the recently published doctoral thesis by Martin

---

116 Table in Curilla, p.846 ff.
117 R. Kempner, *Ankläger einer Epoche. Lebenserinnerungen*, Berlin 1983. p.189.

Cüppers, *Wegbereiter der Shoah*.[118] To date, this is the only book that deals exclusively with this particular subject.

The *Waffen-SS* cavalry units rivalled the *Einsatzgruppen* in the murder of Jews in the East. However, they operated as separate units and were not subordinated to the *RSHA*. A directive issued by the *Kommandostab* in the late summer of 1941, stated: "The Jews are the best conveyors of information to the enemy. If any such suspicion arises, all the Jewish inhabitants of the relevant township have to be ruthlessly exterminated."[119] The directive was sent to the three brigades of the *Waffen-SS* that were stationed on the Eastern front. The *Waffen-SS* cavalry units had already taken part in the atrocities in Poland, but at that time they were under the same authorities as all other SS units.

The *Kommandostab* was set up on 7 April 1941, first under the name of *Einsatzstab Reichsführer-SS*. On 6 May 1941, the name was changed to *Kommandostab Reichsführer-SS*. The *Kommandostab* was under Himmler's direct authority. The chief of staff was *SS Brigadeführer*, later *Obergruppenführer*, Kurt Knoblauch. [120]

On 16 April 1941, Himmler and the General Quartermaster at *OKH*, *Generalmajor* Eduard Wagner, agreed upon the positioning of four "Higher Police and SS Commanders" (*Höhere SS und Polizeiführer, HSSPF*), in the areas foreseen for occupation. Not surprisingly, four of the most murderous high SS leaders were appointed to those functions, *Obergruppenführer* Erich von dem Bach-Zelewski, *Obergruppenführer* Friedrich Jeckeln, *Gruppenführer* Gerret Korsemann and *Obergruppenführer* Hans-Adolf Prützmann.[121] If the *Wehrmacht* was in need of assistance by the SS units, prior agreement of the *HSSPF* had to be obtained.

The first major action of the SS Brigades was the murder of 15,000 Jews who had found temporary refuge in the Pripet marshes. The *Wehrmacht* was held back by the difficulties of the terrain. The men of the SS Cavalry unit were likewise not successful. They called for the burning down of all villages in the area, and the driving of women and children into the marshes to have them drown. "SS men should be spared the burden of

---

118 M. Cüppers, *Wegbereiter der Shoah. Die Waffen-SS, der Kommandostab Reichsführer-SS und die Judenvernichtung 1939-1945*, Darmstadt 2005 (henceforth Cüppers).

119 Directives for the activities of the units subordinated to the *Kommandostab*, 17.9.1941, Cüppers, p.9.

120 Kurt Knoblauch was born in 1885. He became a *Fahnenjunker* (Officer Cadet) in 1905 after having passed his *Abitur*. During the First World War, he commanded at first a Company. In 1916 he became Battalion commander. He was highly decorated. He was taken into the *Reichswehr* and in 1933 was already a full Colonel. He left the *Reichswehr*, joined the *NSDAP* and entered the *SS*. He explained his decision by the lack of available Regiment commands. This sounds somewhat strange – to have became a full Colonel at the age of 48, before the rush of promotions after 1935, harboured the promise of a successful military career with a high General's rank at its termination. In 1949, the Munich court sentenced Knoblauch to two years.

121 Erich von dem Bach-Zelewski testified for the prosecution at Nuremberg. Many years later a German court sentenced him to life imprisonment for participation in the murder of communists in the 1930s. Friedrich Jeckeln was hanged by the Russians. Hans-Adolf Prützmann committed suicide in 1945. Gerret Korsemann was handed over to the Poles who sentenced him to 18 months. He returned to Germany and lived quietly until his death in 1968.

shooting them". But on 11 August 1941, SS *Sturmbannführer* Gustav Lombard reported that the order to have women and children drowned could not be carried out because the marches were not deep enough for the purpose.[122] Therefore Lombard's men had to revert to the "burdensome shooting."

Co-operation with 9th Army was close. On 28 June 1941, *Generaloberst* Strauss had his chief of staff, Colonel Kurt Weckmann, communicate his "heartfelt appreciation" to Knoblauch for his assistance.[123] At that date, the Brigade had not yet taken part in military actions, it had only engaged in the murder of Jews and other civilians. Commanded by Fegelein, it had participated in the murders in townships that had been passed previously by Model's 3rd *Panzer* Division. By December 1941, the official count of the *Kommandostab* victims had risen to at least 85,000. Cüppers feels that this figure is on the low side, because thousands of POW were taken to camps controlled by the Brigade, to die of hunger and exhaustion. A sufficient number of Jews had escaped during the first wave of the *Einsatzgruppe* B killings to warrant further search, followed by murder.[124]

In December 1941, 1st SS Cavalry Brigade was given its first combat duties in the area of 2nd Army, which was commanded by *Generaloberst* Rudolf Schmidt, in place of *Generaloberst* von Weichs who was on temporary sick leave. Its first action at Orel, ended in disaster, and its positions were overrun without much resistance. On 20 December 1941, a few days before Model became *OB* of 9th Army, the Brigade came under the command of 9th Army. It was taken by sledge to the areas around Rzhev. It took part in the battles of Rzhev. The presence of the SS Cavalry Brigade, which by then included the unit of the notorious criminal and rapist Dr Oskar Dirlewanger, gave 9th Army under Model the possibility to concentrate on the battles around Rzhev, while the Brigade committed mass murder in the rear. As Army *OB*, Model held territorial authority and was thus responsible for the well being of the civilian population in the area of his Army.

In the first half of 1942, the Brigades were increasingly subordinated to the *Wehrmacht* commanders. Their reports continued to be sent to Himmler, but the *Kommandostab* became increasingly passive. Between 35,000 and 45,000 German soldiers were killed in action by the partisans, who controlled increasingly large segments of occupied territories.[125]

Members of the *Kommandostab* who survived the war, and were not sentenced to death by Allied tribunals, had a relatively easy life after 1945. A total of 797 were taken prisoner of war, 40% by the US, 28.2% by the Soviet Union, 16.4% by Great Britain, 8.7% by France, 3.8% by Czechoslovakia, 1.5% by Poland and 0.3% by Canada. Only 1.4% were sentenced to more than ten years in prison. Jail sentences between six months and 10 years were meted out to around 30%.[126]

Many of the German trials of members of the SS Cavalry Brigades turned into the usual farce of such proceedings in the Federal Republic. Cüppers gives a number of examples.

---

122 J. Westemeier, Joachim Peiper. *Zwischen Totenkopf und Ritterkreuz. Lebensweg eines SS-Führers*, Bissendorf 2006, p.57.
123 Letter from OB 9th Army, 28 June 1941, BA-MA, RS 4/930. "Without the assistance from the SS, we would not have known what to do" – Cüppers, p.127.
124 Cüppers. p.237 ff.
125 Cüppers, p.244.
126 Tables in Cüppers, p.314 ff.

Hans-Walter Nenntwich was taken, with forged identity papers, into the foreign office, where he advanced to senior councillor (*Legationsrat*), under the name of Dr Sven Joachim Nansen. His real identity was discovered by the British. That did not prevent him from becoming director of a movie production company and later, owner of a sizeable motor construction plant. In 1963 he was indicted for participation in the murder of Jews in Russia, and sentenced to four years. Two days after the sentencing he managed to escape. He settled in Egypt, and wrote a number of letters to the court which had sentenced him, bragging of his ability to repeatedly fool the authorities.[127]

A certain Adolf K. (Cüppers does not give his name) told the court that he had acted in accordance with the Bible: "I am a deeply religious man and this has brought me into conflict with my superiors. But only this morning, I have read in the Bible that Moses likewise had men, women and children killed by the sword."[128]

Gustav Lombard, who had led the "cleansing" of the Pripet marches in summer 1941, during which 15,000 Jews were murdered, rose to SS *Brigadeführer* and Division commander. He was taken prisoner by the Russians and sentenced to 25 years for the rape and murder of a Russian girl, and the wanton shooting of purported partisans. He was set free in 1955, returned to Munich and was given a senior position in the Allianz insurance company. An investigation against him, for his part in the Pripet murders, was launched in 1962 by the Munich prosecution office. Lombard's defence was that the reports bearing his name had been forged by Fegelein. That defence was successful. Fegelein was a convenient scapegoat, since Hitler had had him shot in the Berlin Bunker, shortly before he himself had committed suicide. The charges against Lombard were dropped. On his 80th and his 90th birthdays his former comrades staged parties for him, and hailed him in speeches of congratulations. Lombard died in 1992, aged 97.[129]

---

127 Cüppers, p.319 ff.

128 Ibid. 329. Cüppers gives the minutes of a typical interrogation of a bank clerk, Ernst K. by the Bavarian police in 1969:

Question: Give us the details of your military career.

Answer: I don't remember them.

Question: What were your functions with the SS-Brigade?

Answer: I don't remember them.

Question: What were the names of your commanders?

Answer: I can't recall any.

Question: At what locations were you stationed in the USSR?

Answer: I can't remember.

Question: What do you know about the shooting of Jews?

Answer: I never heard of such things.

Question: Can you give us details about the activities of the Brigades?

Answer: After so many years, I can't remember any.

Question: We are now giving you the names of a number of cities and townships in Poland and in Russia.

Answer: I never heard those names before today. (p.319 ff.)

129 Article by Cüppers: 'Gustav Lombard – ein engagierter Judenmörder aus der Waffen-SS' in K. Mallmann/.Paul (ed.) *Karrieren der Gewalt. Nationalsozialistische Täterbiographien*, Darmstadt 2003, pp.145-155.

The career of the Austrian Friedrich Peter has amazing aspects. Peter was born in 1921. He had joined the *Hitlerjugend* (Hitler Youth), in 1939 and entered the SS in the same year. During the summer of 1941 he took part in murders by the SS cavalry units in Northern Ukraine. In 1942 he became an officer and entered the *Waffen SS* Division *Das Reich*. After the war he returned to Austria and became one of the founders of the right wing *FPÖ* party, later headed by Jörg Haider. In 1958, Peter became chairman of the *FPÖ*. The *FPÖ* supported the Socialist minority government of Bruno Kreisky, the first and only Jewish Chancellor in Austria's history. After Kreisky gained an overwhelming victory in the 1975 elections, he intended to offer Peter the position as Deputy Chancellor. Even for the Austrians, who had successfully spread the legend that Austria was Hitler's first victim, a government post for Peter proved too much to swallow. The "Nazi Hunter", Simon Wiesenthal, denounced Peter at a press conference. Peter withdrew his candidacy, after having engaged in lame attempts to defend his "reputation". "I knew nothing. I have only done my duty. The documents presented by the Russians are forgeries." In May 1983, his party made another attempt to bring him back into the limelight. It proposed him as candidate for Third Deputy Speaker of the Austrian parliament. In the meantime, new incriminating documents about Peter had come to light and he withdrew from active political life.[130] Wiesenthal's intervention led to a strong hostility against him by Kreisky.[131]

In Nuremberg, the *Waffen-SS* was judged to have been a criminal organisation but the cavalry units were overlooked and not included in the verdict. As a result, former members of the SS cavalry units were not subject to automatic indictment.

The tragic fate of the Russian prisoners of war

In his book *Keine Kameraden*, Christian Streit arrives at a total of 3 million Russian prisoners of war who perished in their camps. For years, German revisionist historians disputed Streit's figures, claiming that they were exaggerated. Alfred Streim wrote of 'at least' 2,530,000 victims.[132] Joachim Hoffmann, who saw the German attack on Russia as a preventive war, arrived at a figure of 2 million.[133] Whether 2 or 3 million Russian prisoners of war perished, as a result of ill-treatment in their camps, the guilt of the *Wehrmacht* remains the same. When Soviet intelligence became available, it showed that the data given by Streit were on the low side.

During the first four months of the Russo-German war, close to 4 million Russian soldiers were taken prisoner. A German argument, that such a number could not have

---

130 Cüppers, p.320 ff.
131 One can describe the Kreisky-Wiesenthal conflict as a typical post war Austrian comedy. A Jewish chancellor in one of the more anti-Semitic countries of Europe, who had been forced to flee Austria before the war and seek asylum in Sweden, engages in public attacks against another Austrian Jewish victim of National-Socialism, who spent the war years in Polish camps and who reveals the activities of a former SS officer during the Shoah. After the war, the Austrian Socialist party had constantly co-operated with former prominent Nazis. Its candidate for the position of the first commander in chief of the *Bundeswehr* was the former *Generaloberst* Lothar Rendulic, who had been cashiered from the Austrian Army in 1936 for illegal NS activities and who after the war had been sentenced to twenty years for war crimes.
132 A. Streim, *Sowjetische Gefangene in Hitlers Vernichtungskrieg, Berichte und Dokumente 1941-1945*. Heidelberg, 1982.
133 J. Hoffmann, *Stalins Vernichtungskrieg 1941-1945*, Munich 1995.

been foreseen, does not stand up. The Germans could fall back on their experience from previous campaigns. During the first three weeks of the battle for France, the Germans took more than 1.2 million prisoners of war.[134] The Germans expected a *Blitzkrieg* in Russia, with the usual *Kessel* formations of far larger size than the ones in the West in 1940 and it was obvious to them that enormous numbers of prisoners would be taken.

The documentary by Laurence Rees, *War of the Century*, shows horrifying pictures of gigantic deep ditches, with tens of thousands of Russian soldiers practically glued to each other, some of them naked. German soldiers are standing at the top of the ditch, mocking the prisoners or, from time to time, throwing them a piece of bread.

When the German offensive ran out of steam, the Germans suddenly discovered that the Russian prisoners were a potential work force. (Employment of prisoners in war production was contrary to the Geneva Convention, as was compulsory work of any kind for officers). But by the end of 1941, more than 2 million prisoners were dead from exhaustion, hunger and mistreatment.[135]

The top German commanders were at best indifferent. In August 1941, *Feldmarschall* von Bock made a lame protest against the brutality of the treatment of Russian prisoners. At the same time, he complained that their number could not have been foreseen, and that their transportation to the rear was difficult, due to the "special character of this war".[136]

The *OB* West, *Feldmarschall* von Rundstedt, recommended in October 1942 that Russian POWs should be sent to France to work. He praised the positive qualities of Russians, their hard work, modesty, simplicity. But he added: "If he does not knuckle under, just shoot him." (*Wenn er nicht pariert, kann er einfach erschossen werden*).[137]

On 13 November 1941, a meeting of the Army Group and Army chiefs of Staff at Orsa, was presided over by Halder and *Generalmajor* Eduard Wagner, quartermaster at *OKH*. Bock's chief of staff, *Generalmajor* Hans von Greiffenberg, brought up the question of the lack of sufficient food for Russian prisoners. It had brought prisoners to a state in which they could not be employed in production. Wagner instructed General von Greiffenberg: "Prisoners who are not yet engaged in production work have to starve to death in the camps."[138]

One typical example of the attitude of German commanders is shown by *Generaloberst* Adolf Strauss, at a time when Model's Corps was already part of his 9th Army. In November 1941, Strauss had requested more Russian prisoners be put into production work for the *Wehrmacht*. Strauss added: "The worn-down Russian soldiers who are close to starvation will consider themselves lucky if they were to receive two-thirds of the rations of German soldiers. Obviously the Asiatic sub-humans must stay in the camps."[139] Apparently some officers at *OKH* expressed the fear that the German soldier could be negatively influenced

134 *OKW* summary of operations in the West, 10 May to 4 June 1940, attached to the daily *Wehrmacht* communiqué of 4 June 1940.

135 According to the Geneva Convention, Russian prisoners of war would have been entitled to the same food rations as soldiers of the German *Ersatzheer*.

136 The protest by von Bock is not in the German archives. Its source is von Bock's diary, 22 August 1941. Hürter writes that the German commanders acted like swimmers who did not wish to get wet. Hürter, p.382.

137 NOKW 546.

138 Hürter, p.388.

139 BA-MA, RH 23/219, AOK 9, Ia Nr. 4346/41, 23.11.1941.

by close contact with the Russians. Strauss replied that the German soldier was well aware of his moral superiority. He further added that employment of the Russian prisoners would have positive effects for Germany after the war, since the Russians would have been taught discipline, and some elements of the German language.[140]

On 27 December 1941, one month before Model took over 9th Army, Strauss sent an order to the Army:

> I have been given to understand that many cases of frostbite could be avoided if the German soldiers were not careless and stubborn. Often, German soldiers, clad in their uniforms, guard prisoners who wear fur coats, fur hats and felt boots. Any consideration is out of place.[141]

In August 1943, 9th Army, at that date already under Model's command, handed over 72 prisoners of war to the *SD* units stationed in its prisoner of war camps.[142] Such handovers were common practice between 1941 and 1943. Army Group Centre delivered 10,000 prisoners of war, mainly Jewish officers and soldiers to units of *Einsatzgruppe* B in its POW camps. All were murdered.[143] Model must share the responsibility for the fate of the Russian prisoners of war, with all commanders in the East.

German famine policy in Russia

A deliberate famine policy was applied by the Germans in all parts of occupied Russia. On 2 May 1941, the Secretary of State of the nutrition ministry, *Reichsernährungsministerium*, Herbert Backe met with General Georg Thomas, head of the military economics and armaments department (*Wehrwirtschafts-und Rüstungsamt*) at *OKW*. It resulted in an agreement, on 23 May 1941, on a plan dividing the Soviet Union into two economic zones, the wealthy "black earth" regions and the "subsidy regions" (*Zuschussgebiete*). The latter were to be closed off from the "black earth" regions, the produce of which was primarily reserved for the *Wehrmacht* and the German homeland. The minutes of the meetings between Backe and Thomas contain the following points:

1. The war can only be continued if, during its third year, the *Wehrmacht* can totally live upon the food available in Russia.

---

140   Chapter by Jürgen Förster in *Der Angriff auf die Sowjetunion*, Stuttgart 1983, p.1059. Here again a strange statement by Reichhelm: "During the first weeks of the war, *Generaloberst* Strauss, OB of 9th Army visited together with me one of the numerous prisoner of war camps. Since the camps were close to the border, food was available in adequate quantity and prisoners were provided with tents and blankets. Apparently this changed for the worse later and I am sure that the German command has not taken appropriate measures for the well-being of the Russian prisoners." (Reichhelm, p.118.) The visit by Strauss and Reichhelm must have taken place on another planet.

141   BA-MA, RH 20-9/24. Order Strauss, AOK 9, 27.12.1941.

142   AOK 9, O.Qu./QU 2, BA-MA WF – 03/172277. Quoted by Gerlach, p.839.

143   Ibid. Another incredible statement by Manstein at his trial. The handing over of POWs to the SD was one of the points of Manstein's indictment. When questioned, Manstein said that he saw no difference here with his own handing over from POW status to the British Home Office.

2.   Millions of Russians will die of hunger if we take our needs out of the country.[144]

On 25 November 1941, Göring said to the Italian foreign minister, Count Galeazzo Ciano: "During this year, between 20 and 30 million people will die of hunger in Russia. Perhaps this has to be welcomed because some nations must be decimated."[145]

The *Wehrmacht* blockade of Leningrad resulted in one million civilian deaths, mostly as a result of the famine, more than twice the number of German victims of the aerial bombardments by the Allies.

The case of Kharkov, where the *Wehrmacht* for more than one year forbade all arrival of food supplies, is described in a number of books. Survivors appear in the documentary film by Laurence Rees, *War of the Century*. The famine policy was ruthlessly conducted by the *Wehrmacht* at all levels in the East. Even before 22 June 1941, the *Wehrmacht* commanders had abdicated their responsibilities to the *Wirtschaftsstab Ost* (Economic Staff East). The staff enforced its policy through its sub-units, the *Wirtschaftskommandos*. In their orders of the day, the German commanders made no effort to disguise their policy. Their approval was generally placed under a cloak of self-pity. The orders of the day, of Reichenau and Manstein, are examples in kind.[146] They are reproduced as appendices.

Walter Model had obviously taken no part in the decision-making of that policy. In 1941, he was one of several hundred Division commanders who were presented with a series of measures governing the German actions in the East. His responsibility is that he applied those measures, including the wilful famine, to the same extent as all the *Wehrmacht* commanders. In January 1943, an average of ten men, women and children died daily of hunger in Rzhev – the city had 40,000 inhabitants. [147]

"Children's' villages" – *Kinderdörfer*

German cruelty in the East extended to the treatment of children. In the Jewish ghettos, pregnant women were often executed upon discovery of their pregnancy. Gerlach quotes shocking examples where parents were shot and their children killed by blows to their skulls.[148] Children aged 10-14 years were forced to cut peat, with food rations which made their early death inevitable.

---

144 Gerlach, p.46. More details in Gerlach.p.1127 ff.

145 Ciano mentions this conversation in his diaries. (p.478.) Göring's statement was prompted by a conversation with Ciano about the famine in Greece, in which he advised Ciano not to take famine conditions there too seriously. (A detailed account of the famine policy is found in G. Aly/S. Heim, *Vordenker der Vernichtung. Auschwitz und die deutschen Pläne für eine neue europäische Ordnung*, Frankfurt 2004, pp.363-393)

146 His acknowledgment of his own part in the famine policy did not prevent Manstein from writing in *Verlorene Siege*: "The Army has done all that is possible to help the civilian population. The Chief *Quartiermeister* of 11th Army, Colonel Hauck and the excellent Army director (*Intendant*) Rabius have solved this problem in an exemplary manner, in spite of all the local difficulties." (p.247). Had Manstein known at that time that Hauck would testify against him in later years, calling his purported break-out order from Stalingrad a lie and admitting that 11th Army had put troops and equipment at the disposal of the *Einsatzgruppe* D in the Crimea, he would have worded this paragraph differently.

147 BA R-58/7/1146.

148 Gerlach, p.1075.

The stringent German racial laws did not prevent hundreds of thousands of Russian children from being fathered by German officers and soldiers. In a report to Hitler, of 8 September 1942, *Generaloberst* Rudolf Schmidt estimated the number of children born of German soldier parents at 1.5 million. As a result, a policy was introduced where such children, provided their "racial qualities" were irreproachable, were brought to Germany for adoption by "pure-blood" German families. At the same time, homeless children were looked upon as a danger which had to be concentrated in camps. Here the initiative was taken by Model's 9th Army, in close co-operation with the Sk 7a and Sk 7b of *Einsatzgruppe* B and the criminal police.[149] Such children were brought into provisional camps, (*Anhaltelager*). Some children were sent to Germany for forced labour, others were handed over to hospitals for medical experiments.[150]

Scorched Earth measures

During the *Büffel* retreat from Rzhev, Model employed ruthless scorched earth measures. The removal of tens of thousands of Russian civilians has already been mentioned. The historian Alexander Werth, who spent the war in the Soviet Union, reports the wilful destruction of 5,500 houses in Vyazma, 1,300 in Gzhatsk, 5,000 in Rzhev, and all the churches in Rzhev and the 137 villages in the area of Sychovka, where Model had his headquarters.[151]

Here we enter into the area of what Haffner calls 'ordinary' war crimes. In all major wars, centuries back, scorched earth measures were applied. Louis XIV burned down a large part of the infrastructure of the Palatinate. In his march through Georgia in the American Civil War, General Sherman ruthlessly destroyed towns and hamlets. During the first months of the Russo-German war, *Stavka* issued the following order, on 17 November 1941:

Order No. 0428: The *Stavka* of the Supreme Commander orders:

1. Every area where German troops are stationed has to be destroyed by fire up to 40-60 kilometres depth from the front line, and 20 to 30 kilometres on each side of the roads. Destruction has to be made by the air force, using rockets and artillery, by troops mounted on skis and partisan units who have to carry bottles containing incendiary material.
2. Every Regiment has to set up special commandos, consisting of 20 to 30 men, for the purpose of this destruction. Men who have performed outstandingly will be proposed for high decorations."[152]

When Model assumed command of Army Group Centre, the policy of *Tote Zonen* (dead zones) was already in practice. The idea of creating a "no-man's land" had first been applied on 5 September 1941, by Manstein's 11th Army in the Crimea.[153] In those "zones" all villages had to be evacuated and subsequently destroyed. If any Russian was spotted

---

149 Gerlach, p.1086 ff.

150 Ibid, p.1074 ff. Gerlach arrives at the conclusion that between 11,000 and 14,500 children were forcefully separated from their families (p.1090).

151 A. Werth, *Russia at War,* New York 1964, p.631.

152 Quoted by Volkogonov, p.617.

153 BA-MA, RH 20-11/341.

within such a zone, he was considered to be fair game and liable to be instantly shot by any German. A sizeable number of such orders had been issued by General Harpe, when he was commander of 9th Army.[154] Units of Caucasian and Cossack troops, which had been recruited by Colonel Claus von Stauffenberg and deployed around the "dead zones", were rabble. They terrorized the Belorussian villages, even those where the population had collaborated with the Germans. Rape by Caucasians was a daily occurrence.[155]

During the massive German retreat, in summer 1944, after the Russians had launched the *Bagration* offensive, many German troops began to run amok. Disorganized individual murders and destruction became a daily occurrence. Laurence Rees' documentary film *War of the Century* shows shocking pictures.

One German officer recalled burning whole villages. He described his actions with obvious satisfaction:

> We would pour gasoline upon the houses, surround them with straw, and set them on fire. Those who lived there were driven away and their cattle confiscated. I had no problems with the burning. The houses were primitive and not worth keeping. They were certainly not German, French, or British houses. They did not come up to our level of housing, but those people would somehow survive. If we took their cattle away, they could still find vegetables in the fields and in the woods. They would somehow survive bad weather conditions since they were very resourceful. Perhaps we committed a crime, but we were following our orders.

The producers of *War of the Century*, interviewed General Peter von der Groeben who was nearly 100 years old when the movie was produced. In 1944, he had been a Colonel and Ia of Model's Army Group Centre. He had some ties to the military resistance. General von der Groeben began by admitting that many "unpleasant things" had indeed occurred. When shown a report, bearing his initials, that mentioned the killing of 1,920 purported partisans with only some 30 rifles found after the action, he began to stammer. He said: "The troops were simply enraged, and I had so many urgent matters to attend to that I could not concern myself with adding up figures. After all, if the partisans had no arms at all, we would never have sent German soldiers against them."

A Belorussian peasant recalled that, when the Germans retreated through his village, he and other male inhabitants had been tied to each other, and forced to march in front of the Germans as human shields. He had been wounded and left for dead, but had survived to tell his story.

Christian Gerlach gave additional examples. Model certainly had heard of such happenings, since he was almost continuously with his troops in the front line. But he cannot be blamed for those excesses. The fact that as Army Group *OB* he had no territorial authority is irrelevant here. In the chaos of the battle, the Armies of Army Group Centre, and their Corps, had disintegrated. A number of high commanders had been killed in action, or had been taken prisoner. In many instances, Model exercised direct command of units down to Divisions that no longer had workable staffs. The concept of territorial authority, and its limits, had lost its meaning. When Model took over command of Army

---

154 Gerlach, p.1097.
155 For details, ibid, p.1100 ff.

Group Centre, chaos had already developed. More than twenty German Divisions had been torn to pieces. Under such conditions, discipline tends to become an empty word if it cannot be controlled by some kind of organized chain of command. But Model had inherited a situation where any chain of command no longer existed.

The massacre of American prisoners of war at Malmédy during the Ardennes offensive

On 17 December 1944, around 84 American officers and soldiers were shot after having surrendered.[156] The shooting took place under the order of a *Waffen SS* unit commanded by *SS Standartenführer* Joachim "Jochen" Peiper. That unit was part of Sepp Dietrich's 6th *Panzer* Army. The shooting caused an uproar in the US and Peiper was designated as "GI enemy Number 1".

All parties in the Second World War had engaged in the shooting of prisoners. When 45th US Division landed at Scoglitti in Sicily, a Captain and a Sergeant lined up and shot 79 German prisoners of war. Patton intended to pass the incident over in silence, however courts martial were ordered. Patton wrote to his wife: "Some 'fair-haired' boys are trying to say that I killed too many prisoners. Yet the same people cheer at the far greater killing of Japs. Well, the more I killed, the fewer men I lost."[157]

In the *Ruhrkessel*, 95th US infantry Division shot a number of German prisoners of war. One survivor recalled:

> Early morning 8 April 1945 we, 8 officers and soldiers of 116th *Panzer* Division, were captured. A few minutes later, 6 more prisoners were brought in. We had to face a wall. Suddenly some shots were fired from the surrounding houses. There was a short exchange of fire. When it was over, we were brought into a house. The bodies of American soldiers, who had been killed in action that day, were laid below the window of the room where we being held. We were ordered to walk past them. At 10.30 am, we were told that we, 14 officers and soldiers, would be shot around 6.30 pm. At 6 pm we were taken to the American command post. 11 of us were shot, 3 survived, among them myself, with several wounds.[158]

The wilful shooting at Malmédy did occur and Peiper was a Nazi of the worst kind. In his previous capacity as ADC to Himmler, he had participated in many crimes. He had accompanied Himmler on visits to concentration camps. He had toured the ghettos of Warsaw and Łodz. He had witnessed executions by the *Einsatzgruppen.* It is not established

---

156 The number is that determined by the official investigation conducted by the US Senate. 'Malmedy Massacre Investigation – Report of the Subcommittee of Committee on armed services – United States Senate – Eighty-first Congress, first session, pursuant to S. res. 42, Investigation of action of army with respect to trial of persons responsible for the massacre of American soldiers, battle of the Bulge, near Malmedy, Belgium, December 1944, 13 October 1949'. Overall, the investigation found evidence that members of *Kampfgruppe Peiper* had murered 362 US POWs during the Battle of the Bulge, and 111 civilians.

157 Bradley, General, p.220.

158 H. G. Guderian, the son of the *Generaloberst*: *Das letzte Kriegsjahr im Westen. Die Geschichte der 116. Panzer Division – Windhund Division,* Sankt Augustin 1994 (henceforth *Windhund*). The history of the US 95th Division does not mention the incident.

if he had personally taken part in the murders. However, in conversations with American observers during his trial, he expressed approval of their activities. The shooting at Malmédy was carried out by *Kampfgruppe Peiper*, which was part of 1st SS *Panzer* Division, named *Leibstandarte SS Adolf Hitler*. Peiper did not give the order for the shooting. He was not present when it occurred. The shooting was ordered by *Sturmbannführer* Werner Poetschke, who was killed in action shortly after.[159]

Peiper was a highly decorated officer. He had been awarded the swords to the oak leaves of his Knight's Cross. But the extent of his military capacity was the command of a Battalion. As a regimental commander he was a failure, he repeatedly lost control over his unit, which was simply butchered. That was particularly the case during the Ardennes offensive. Peiper surrounded himself with yes-men and discarded experienced commanders.[160] His *Kampfgruppe* was not an elite *Waffen-SS* unit, it was a mixture of SS, recently drafted *Hitlerjugend*, ethnic Germans from various countries in Eastern Europe, and units taken from penal battalions.[161]

The violent reaction in the US has to be seen against the background that the Allies were very severe about crimes committed against their own troops, which is logical. However, similar crimes committed, either by them against Germans, or by Germans against soldiers and civilians of other nations, were often viewed with a large amount of indifference.[162] SHAEF intelligence had been surprised by the German Ardennes offensive. That battle led to unusual nervousness in the American press reports and public opinion.

The Malmédy trial began on 16 May 1945, at a US military tribunal at Dachau. 71 officers and men from the *Waffen*-SS were on trial. Among them were three officers with General's rank, *Oberstgruppenführer* Sepp Dietrich, *Obergruppenführers* Hermann Priess,

---

159 A comprehensive biography about Peiper has been written by Jens Westemeier, *Joachim Peiper, (1915-1976) – Zwischen Totenkopf und Ritterkreuz. Lebensweg eines SS-Führers*, Bissendorf 2006. (Henceforth Westemeier). In 1996, Jens Westemeier had already published a book about Peiper, which was partially apologetic. In his later book, he distances himself entirely from his first work.

160 Westemeier, p.236 ff.

161 Ibid. p.188.

162 A typical example was Albert Kesselring's trial. The *Feldmarschall*'s defence team was aware of Allied practice and Kesselring had no qualms in admitting his ruthless *Bandenbefehle*, which were worded in the manner of the *Barbarossa* order in the East. The Italian *Resistenza* contained large numbers of units of the extreme left and in the Cold War climate Allied tribunals were often unconcerned with their fate. Kesselring likewise admitted his responsibility for the massacre in the *Fosse Ardeatine* in Rome, where 335 Italians were shot in reprisal for the killing of 33 German Military Police soldiers in Rome's *Via Rasella*. Kesselring's admission of his responsibility for the *Fosse Ardeatine* massacre provided him with an alibi in his denial of presence and knowledge of the execution of an American commando at La Spezia on the same day. General Anton Dostler had already been sentenced to death and shot for this event and Kesselring had reason to fear that he would share his fate. It was easier for him to assume the responsibility for *Fosse Ardeatine* which was a far more horrible massacre, but where the victims were Italians. For details, K.von Lingen, *Kesselrings letzte Schlacht. Kriegsverbrecherprozesse, Vergangenheitspolitik und Wiederbewaffnung: Der Fall Kesselring*, Paderborn 2004, and J. Staron, *Fosse Ardeatine und Marzabotto. Deutsche Kriegsverbrechen und Resistenza. Geschichte und nationale Mythenbildung*, Paderborn 2002.

Gruppenführer Fritz Krämer and, of course, Joachim Peiper. On 16 June 1946, all the defendants were found guilty. 46 were sentenced to death by hanging, 22 received life sentences, two were sentenced to 20 years, one to 15 years, and five to 10 years. None of the death sentences were carried out. The American defence lawyer, Colonel Willis Everett, laid bare many errors and neglects of judicial procedures in the trial. Undeniably, the prosecution had worked in an amateurish manner. Not surprisingly, Senator Joseph McCarthy persevered against the Jewish prosecuting attorney, William Perl. McCarthy accused the American tribunal of using Gestapo and NKVD methods. By 1951, all the death sentences had been commuted to life. By 22 December 1956, the day Peiper was released, all the defendants had been set free. After finding employment in Germany, Peiper spent the last years of his life in France. He died on 14 July 1976 when his house was set on fire. At first, there were rumours that he was murdered by Communist youths who had protested violently against his presence in France. However, the blaze turned out to have been an accident.

Through the intermediary of the Swiss legation in Berlin, the US government lodged a protest. They demanded a German investigation after the shooting. Army Group B and 6th *Panzer* Army were questioned. On 8 March 1945, the German Ministry for Foreign Affairs told the Swiss legation that there was no knowledge of any American prisoners having been shot.

Model obviously knew about the incident. Whether his knowledge was prior to the investigation, or a result of it, cannot be established. Regardless of that point, Model cannot be held responsible for what occurred at Malmédy. As Army Group Commander, he held no territorial authority, nor did he have territorial responsibility. The highest directly responsible person was Sepp Dietrich. But even Dietrich's part in the massacre remains an open question. At his trial, one of his officers testified that he had asked Dietrich what should be done with POWs. Dietrich replied: "You know what has to be done with prisoners". Dietrich did not deny his reply, but stressed that it was to mean that POWs had to be treated in accordance with international law.[163] Intended meanings can neither be proved nor disproved. Dietrich received a life sentence. He was set free in 1956. While he languished in jail, his wife left him and obtained permission to drop the name of Dietrich. Dietrich's freedom did not last long. In 1957 he was indicted by a German court for his part in the executions of the 30 June 1934. He was sentenced to 18 months, which he served in Landsberg prison. Dietrich died in 1966.

---

163 C. Clark, Joseph ''Sepp' Dietrich. Landsknecht im Dienst Hitlers', in R. Smelser/E. Syring (ed.) *Die SS. Elite unter dem Totenkopf. 30 Lebensläufe*, Paderborn 2000, p.128.

9

Orders of the Day

Orders of the day are a popular toy for Generals in all armies. They are seldom read by the troops. The main purpose of the Generals is to extol themselves in future history. In the *Wehrmacht*, the Generals wanted to make sure that their orders of the day were favourably viewed by Hitler.

Wehrmacht orders of the day were issued by all commanders of major units, on the eve of an attack on another country. If the new enemy was little known, like Russia, the orders of the day were read out and the troops absorbed the "education" that the Generals were providing. The way in which *Wehrmacht* officers and soldiers behaved in Russia, shows that the hate appeals issued by the Generals, at the outset of *Barbarossa*, were carefully read in all units of the *Ostheer*. The orders of the day from Generals von Reichenau, von Manstein and Hoth were likewise common knowledge. The three Generals made sure that they were communicated to every battalion of their units. The Reichenau order of the day was distributed all over the Eastern Front, with many commanders adding their own laudatory views.

If an order of the day by a General concerned a specific operation, its contents were repeated through the ranks, down to the Battalion commanders. Orders by Battalion commanders were carefully read by every soldier in their unit, since they concerned an action in which all the soldiers were going to take part. What the General had written was mostly disregarded.

Many orders of the day issued by Army and Army Group *OB* were written with the purpose of "motivating" the troops. Little if any attention was paid to them. Soldiers expected mail from home and were not interested in encouragement from their Generals. In exceptional circumstances, such as the Stalingrad *Kessel*, messages from above were read, since they might have harboured some sign of hope for relief. Under normal circumstances, the troops were sufficiently "motivated". They required no additional encouragement from lengthy and pathetic orders issued by their *OB* who was a remote figure. As the war progressed, their names were often not known to the rank and file, since commanders were replaced at ever-shorter intervals.[1] When "motivation" declined during the last months of the war, nothing that came out of the pen of a General could restore it.

"Motivation" orders issued by a *Wehrmacht* General would at times recall past history of the party. Written in National-Socialist style, they included standard phrases like "*Heil dem Führer*," or "Forward with the *Führer*," or "Forward to new battles to the glory of the

---

1   On 22 April 1944, Model, recently appointed *OB* of Army Group North Ukraine, issued a two page order of the day, honouring *Generaloberst* Hans Hube, who had died in an air crash the previous day. It is far from certain that many rank and file of Army Group North Ukraine were aware that Model was their new commander. Most soldiers who had never served under Hube ignored his name and could not care less about his fate. Facsimile of the Hube order in Model/Bradley, p.181 ff.

Führer". Similar orders of the day in the Red Army mentioned Stalin's name, and the battle cry of the Russian soldier: "For the homeland and for Stalin." A Japanese order always contained a message of devotion to the Emperor. In democratic states such as Britain or the USA, mentions of Winston Churchill or Franklin D. Roosevelt in military orders of the day were unthinkable. Had they occurred, the press would have had a field-day.

Model's orders of the day invariably contained a strong Nazi element. They provide an interesting picture of the changes which his personality gradually underwent during the war. His orders often included variations of a standard sentence: "No soldier in the world may be better than us." Some examples are given here.

The first order of the day to Army Group North on 1 February 1944:

During the coming battles I order that no soldier in the world may be better than us.[2]

On 31 July 1944, Model issued an order of the day to Army Group Centre, which ended with the words:

No soldier in the world may now be allowed to be better than the soldiers of our *Führer* Adolf Hitler. *Heil* to our beloved *Führer*.

However, this order contains an unpleasant element:

…In spite of the present superiority in numbers and equipment of the enemy, we will succeed in matching both by a total concentration of all our means. At home all the prerequisites will be taken care of by *Reichsführer-SS* Himmler and *Reichsminister* Dr. Goebbels …[3]

The references to Himmler and Goebbels certainly cause raised eyebrows. Granted, Himmler had succeeded *Generaloberst* Fromm as Commander of the *Ersatzheer*, and Goebbels had received responsibility for total mobilization after the fall of Stalingrad. But mentioning both Goebbels and Himmler in an order of the day indicates a continued strong proximity to the regime. Perhaps Model was under the influence of a meeting with Goebbels, in January 1944, which Goebbels recorded in his diary: "Model is aligned politically. He pleads for a ruthless war in the East. He understands the problems of Bolshevism, and he knows that we have to make short work of the Russians… Model makes an excellent impression."[4]

This order of the day had a very pessimistic undertone:

The enemy stands at the borders of East Prussia. He tries to penetrate our country. Our *Führer*, our German people, and our soldiers in the West and the South, expect you to bar his further advance … There is no way back … Have all our sacrifices been in vain? … Cowards are not allowed in our midst … There can be no doubt, a man who falters forfeits his life …

---

2   Facsimile in Model/Bradley, p.83.
3   Facsimile in Model/Bradley, p.237.
4   Goebbels diaries, part II, vol.11, p.176 – 26 January 1944. Quoted by Hürter p.601.

An order of the day of 9 November 1944, the anniversary of the Hitler *Putsch* on 9 November 1923, shows an attachment to the regime which comes close to hypertrophy:

In the middle of violent combats at the borders of the *Reich*, the Front and the whole country unite in remembrance of 9 November. The men who fell before the Munich *Feldherrnhalle* were a beacon of a small community of front line soldiers and young idealists. They were bound together by the barrages of the First World War which imbued them with National-Socialist ideas. Now they are the *credo* of all our people. The action of 9 November ignited the revolutionary spark in a period of weakness, error and blindness. The National-Socialist revolution succeeded because a growing community of idealists never lost faith, despite being surrounded by indifference and by hatred. We will likewise gain victory over the material superiority of the enemy, and his propaganda, if we fight with the same fanaticism, and belief in final victory... In this gigantic struggle, our beloved *Führer* is the source of our strength. Fate had chosen him to lead Germany out of distress to liberty. He created the miracle of German unity. And now, in spite of the fluctuations of the war, he will show us the path to victory... No soldier may be better than the soldiers of our *Führer* ... We will be victorious because we believe in Adolf Hitler and in the German *Reich*.[5]

Increasingly 'absurd' orders of the day

General August Winter wrote after the war that in summer 1943, Model's nerves had begun to show signs of exhaustion. General Winter felt that this had an adverse influence on the clarity of his leadership. This was not the case. In 1943 Model's military leadership was still unimpaired, it began to falter only during the last weeks of his life. But 20 July had made him increasingly close ranks with the regime. He had obviously become unable to cope with the gap between military reality and the hollow phrases of National-Socialist propaganda.

On 8 February 1944, Model issued an order of the day to Army Group North, worded in "*Lebensborn style*". The word *Lebensborn* cannot be translated into English. It was one of Himmler's bizarre creations calling for increased proliferation of the Aryan race. SS members of *Lebensborn* had to commit themselves to engender at least four children, either in marriage, or out of wedlock. *Lebensborn* had the responsibility for the upbringing of children in special *Lebensborn* homes. The first home had already been built in 1936. By 1944, 13 *Lebensborn* homes had been built, with 11,000 children as inmates.

Model's order of the day is reproduced in full:

Preservation of the German people's spirit. [Model used the word *Volkskraft*, an expression from Nazi jargon which literally means "popular strength" but does not have an exact corresponding term in other languages. The connotation is one of the mystical inner strength of the nation. Model used other Nazi jargon words in his order. For example, *Volkskörper*, which also cannot be translated. Yet another jargon expression was *Volkstod*.]

---

5   Facsimile in Model/Bradley, p.325.

The war waged against us, by enemies full of hatred, has gone on for four years. It has caused heavy losses of the best German blood. Further losses are caused by the criminal terror bombings of our cities, which show that the enemy is eager to destroy our people's core. If we suffer losses in our people's core, which cannot be remedied, we will lose the war even if we achieve military victory. Therefore, marriage and bearing children have become a matter of paramount importance. It is imperative that every commander concerns himself with this unconditionally, and in total solemnity. Every German man and woman must take care of the future of our people in the highest feeling of responsibility. Continued proliferation of our racial blood, and this has to be emphasized clearly, must be looked upon as a holy duty, which is not less important than courage in action. I request from every officer and soldier, who has not yet given thought to founding a family, to understand that he has to meet the danger of the gradual disappearance of the German people. It is 'unsoldierly' to delay this step until safer times. That can easily be too late. The soldier is expected to be bold when facing the enemy. He must be equally bold when deciding about the future of his personal life.

I order all commanders to give priority in instructing their officers accordingly, and to have this message conveyed to every unit, to the last man. In every instance, preference in leave must be given to soldiers who are family fathers or who intend to marry. Furthermore, I will see to it at the highest level that officers who have reached the age of 30 and are still unmarried, will be promoted more slowly than married ones, regardless if they are their equal in performance.[6]

Whatever prompted Model to issue this absurd order of the day remains a mystery. The private lives of his officers, who performed their duty, were none of his business. Perhaps Model recalled Himmler's directive for "procreation", of 28 October 1939. The complete text of that directive is given in Appendix VI. General Kinzel and his staff, who already had contempt for Model, must have been flabbergasted, and probably laughed. General Kinzel may well have said to his associates that Model's order of the day justified his statement that Model was completely insane. Incidentally, Model's two daughters never married.

On Christmas Eve 1944, Model sent an order of the day to Army Group B. It included the following absurd message:

Christmas is the greatest holiday of the German family. The candles of the Christmas tree reflect the profound ardour and the wonderful inner strength of our people. Christmas is the day of Peace on Earth. Our enemies do not want peace. They hate our German Christmas. Therefore, peace must be conquered with the sword... Now, during the Christmas days, we have to fight with unaltered courage and give Germany, and our *Führer* Adolf Hitler, the best Christmas gift, a German victory... A turn of events is within our reach. If Germany continues to fight, and to work with unbroken energy, the brightness of victory will be our reward. Then Christmas peace will descend upon Germany.[7]

---

6 Facsimile in Model/Bradley, p.103.
7 Facsimile in Model/Bradley, p.346.

A message to his troops on New Year's Day indulged in philosophy about "Belief" and "Faith." It began with the words: "To be a *Führer* means Faith." Then follows:

In difficult times of war, faith is the rousing and indispensable weapon of every soldier, every officer, and every General. At critical moments this truism is always forgotten. There is every reason to remember it.

1. A man who has no faith in himself and in his cause, who sees only difficulties, loses courage and finds no way to overcome the difficulties.
2. A man who loses faith becomes the play-thing of all adversities. He will remain the anvil and will never be the hammer.
3. Faith stems from the heart, not from reason. The heart and the spirit must inspire the will with fanaticism.
4. A man who does not believe in his cause is unable to convince and to rouse others.
5. Only a man convinced of the mission of his own people has the fervour, the strength, and the ardour to spur on others to the greatest performance, overcoming the unavoidable crises in every war.
6. A man who has no faith will transmit his despondency to others.
7. A man who loses faith loses himself and damages his cause.
8. War separates the true leaders from the fakes. Leaders without faith are a danger for the troops. They have to be stamped out ruthlessly.
9. A man who believes in his heart that difficulties must be overcome will be victorious. But if a man has doubts at the foot of the mountain, then he will not be able to climb it, and will falter even after the first hundred metres.
10. To be a leader implies faith.
11. Faith means: Never despair of our people's destiny, even if dark clouds cover the sky. If a man believes in the future of his people, he knows that the sun will dispel the clouds. We know that the sun will shine again over Germany. Our *Führer,* Adolf Hitler, is the symbol of this unshakable faith. We, the soldiers of greater Germany, will never permit anyone in the world to excel us in this belief.[8]

In fairness to Model, it must be mentioned that by 19 February 1942, *Generaloberst* Maximilian von Weichs, who belonged to the conservative Generals, had issued an order of the day in a similar spirit:

We had become used to forcing our initiative upon the enemy. We were spoiled by our previous victories. The initiative of the enemy has taken us completely by surprise. Parts of the officer corps have shown themselves not up to the strains of the crisis. Faint-heartedness, instances of disobedience and mistrust gained ground, and criticism did not even stop at the person of the *Führer*. Every officer has to be a model in his attitude towards the *Führer* and the state. The officer must be the guardian of morale and prohibit uncalled-for criticism and prophecy of doom. National-Socialism has taught us that faith must be added to the old soldierly virtues of fighting and obedience.[9]

---

8 Facsimile in Model/Bradley, p.363.
9 BA-MA, RH 20-296.

'Atrocious' orders of the day

On 12 March 1945, *Feldmarschall* Albert Kesselring was appointed *OB* West. Until then, he had commanded in the Mediterranean theatres. Rudolf von Gersdorff, who had risen to *Generalmajor* and was Chief of Staff of 7th Army, recalled his first meeting with Kesselring: "I had reported to Kesselring about the catastrophic situation of the Army. He interrupted me, and reminded me of his order to have every deserter hanged from the nearest tree. He had been driving around and not seen a single hanged man. Before he left, he admonished me to carry out his orders more faithfully."[10]

Kesselring issued orders of the day which can only be described as horrendous. They were written in first person singular and communicated to Model. Model could have been content in forwarding them to his subordinate commanders, but instead, he chose to append his own signature to Kesselring's and thus assumed responsibility for their content. The order of the day, 16 March 1945, is one such example.

> Order by Supreme Commander West:
> An important Rhine bridge has fallen into the hands of the enemy in spite of careful preparations for blowing it up. This was due to indecisive, irresponsible and cowardly behaviour of the officers responsible who had delayed the demolition, and abandoned the bridgehead.
>
> The five officers have been tried by summary court martial, and sentenced to death. One of them, a Captain, was tried *in absentia*. The sentences against four Majors and one Lieutenant have been carried out. The family of the Captain, who could not be found, has been arrested in accordance with *Sippenhaft*. [*Sippenhaft* means family accountability, and was introduced in 1944. It held the closest family members accountable for an officer who had been captured, if he was considered to have acted with cowardice.] This message must be communicated to all troops. He, who does not live in honour, dies in shame.
>
> I order again that every instance of failure be brought without delay before a summary court martial. I expect the courts to act without mercy."
> *OB* West, Kesselring, *Generalfeldmarschall*
> *OB* Army Group B, Model, *Generalfeldmarschall*" [11]

A further order of the day was issued by Model, on the same day, to the *General der Wehrmacht Ordnungstruppe*:[12]

> Who fears a death in honour, dies in shame. The summary courts martial, ordered by the *Führer*, has sentenced the commander of Remagen, Major Scheller, to death and

---

10 R. von Gersdorff, *Soldat im Untergang*, Darmstadt 1977, p.176 ff. (henceforth Gersdorff).

11 BA-MA, RH 19/IV, 226. The copy of the order with Model's signature added was first found in Eastern Germany. Ref: 167/90, Military Archives of the German Democratic Republic, WF – 03/5774, p.1104.

12 The *General der Ordnungstruppe* was in command of the various *Wehrmacht* bodies and other police units in charge of searching for deserters, arresting them and having them brought before summary courts martial. Every Army Group and every Army had a *General der Ordnungstruppe* attached to its staff.

loss of military honour, for disobedience in defending the bridgehead at Remagen and dereliction of duty in the field …

The remainder of the order is identical with the joint order by Kesselring and Model.[13] Model had already behaved dishonourably during the Remagen tragedy, and with these orders he added to his moral demise.

Model's last Order of the Day on 29 March 1945

This order of the day was the most senseless document Model issued during his entire military career. It was dated two days after elements of General Ridgway's American XVIII Airborne Corps had closed around Model's Army Group B, severing parts of it. They completely encircled the remainder, along with Model's headquarters, cutting off all retreat.

The full text of the 29 March order of the day are given below. It can be described as being simply insane. Americans would say, "The General has gone off his rocker".

From *OB* of Army Group B:
The enemy has crossed the Rhine on several wide fronts. In the East, the Bolsheviks have again made great progress.

The most difficult task now facing a commander is to convince his men of the prospects of continuing the war. The situation in the East, and in the South, and in the West, with its economic consequences, the absence of airpower, and the destiny of the homeland and the population, can give rise to doubt about the pursuit of the war.

More than ever, we have to dispute every inch of German soil. More than ever, everyone has to fight and sacrifice himself. More than ever, every commander has to raise his ability to convince his subordinates to reach the highest peak.

The physical well-being of the soldiers is still taken care of. But the degree to which their families are affected by the events, and the irregularity of mail from the front, requires a strong spiritual help from above. In particular, young officers who lack experience, have to be assisted with advice and support. Performance can only be expected from men who have been educated as uncompromising fighters for an idea.

The pressure of events shows that many segments of the German people, and also the soldiers, are still contaminated by the poison of Jewish and materialistic thought. This has led to failure on the part of soldiers in the East and in the West. It is now reflected in the attitude of part of the civilian population, who are more concerned with their property than the unconditional support of the fighting troops. Materialistic, petty-mindedness is not soldierly.

The example of the Generals of Army Group A, who have succeeded in breaking out with parts of their troops from some of the encirclement on the left bank of the Rhine river, shows what strength of will, without compromise and with uninhibited fighting power, can achieve. Such an attitude must be demanded from every officer, every non-com and every soldier.

The poet Walter Flex has written: 'To be a Lieutenant means to be a living example to his men. He has likewise to be an example in dying.'

---

13 BA-MA, RH 19/IV, 226.

Those words have to be the *credo* for every officer. They demand action and reject passive floating.

Too much is put into words, too little is left aside.

A dull issue and transmission of orders is worthless. Attention must be paid to the ways and means of enforcing them reasonably, immediately and without undue consideration. Officers have to be ready to sacrifice themselves, in their efforts to have orders reach the front line. An order which does not reach the man in the front line is worthless.

In critical times, immediate action, also without orders from above, is a self evident requirement. The energy of the German Army must be maintained at all costs. It must be promoted by every commander.

In previous times, wars were reserved for the military. They were fought and won by military means only.

This belongs to the past. During the French Revolution the fighting spirit of young, inexperienced soldiers, with inadequate arms, had the better of their enemies who were well-trained soldiers, but who lacked an ideal.

Unlimited passion, drastic hardship, total and fanatical belief in an idea, those are the prerequisites for victory today. Whoever has such qualities will be able to overcome material and personal inferiority.

Let us impart to our men the remaining assets of our war effort, the achievements of our submarines, the political dissent between our enemies, the dwindling of their resources and their growing lassitude. Let us fight like fanatical National-Socialists and educate our men in this spirit.

Wars are not won with a slide-rule or by a simple sense of duty. The will for victory and faith are essential. This is true for the simple soldier and for the highest commander. To be a *Führer* means to have faith. He who no longer believes in victory, can no longer fight with the required toughness and contempt for death. He is in the wrong place. He who does not have the unconditional will for victory is a weakling and a danger for the troops. All have to follow the spirit of Albrecht Dürer's painting, 'Knight, Death and the Devil'.

Let all abide by the words of Martin Luther. 'All annoyance stems from the Devil, courage and joy stem from God'.

Doubts have to remain silent. Duty, honour and faith have to guide every soldier.

One has to repeat time and again, that this war is waged to decide if Europe will be governed by the rules of Hitler, or of Stalin. America and Britain have considerable weight through their material resources, but spiritually they belong to the past, without future influence. This is shown by the Yalta conference. The only decision remains between Bolshevism, which wants to conquer the world, and National-Socialism, which wants to bring joy to the German people. In every conflict of ideas, the stronger will and unconditional faith have emerged victorious.

In our fight for the ideas of National-Socialism, against the void of materialistic Bolshevism, our victory is mathematically certain if our will and our faith can remain unshaken.

Every officer must be an example to his men, and must show relentless effort to persuade every soldier to fight on fanatically, and thus ensure final victory.

The victory of National-Socialism is not in doubt. The decision rests with us.

Model, *Generalfeldmarschall*.[14]

Professor Manfred Messerschmidt subjects this order of the day to scathing criticism. He wrote:

> In the last stage of the war, there was no limit to absurd appeals. The more absurd the appeals to fanaticism, the greater their chances of success. An example of this state of mind is shown by an order of the day of 29 March 1945, by the Commander in Chief of the troops already encircled in the *Ruhrkessel*, in which he tries to spur his soldiers to a final fanatical resistance … Model, who is looked upon as an 'unconditional believer' appears unhappy with the lack of uncompromising readiness to fight for an idea. By accusing segments of the German people and soldiers of being poisoned by Jewish and materialistic thought, this *Feldmarschall* endeavours to explain the catastrophe with the creation of a new stab in the back legend. He also has the nerve to require his soldiers to accept the residual nonsense of the National-Socialist catastrophe-psychology. 'In our fight for the ideas of National-Socialism, against the void of materialistic Bolshevism, our victory is mathematically certain if our will, and our faith, will remain unshaken'. Empty slogans, which every soldier can see through, but which a *Feldmarschall* has the nerve to present to his commanders in a situation where everything was falling apart. He said at the end of March 1945: 'The victory of National-Socialism is not in doubt. The decision rests with us!' *Feldmarschall* Model delivered the ideological funeral of the *Wehrmacht*. Reason had disappeared. Nonsensical philosophy had gripped military reason.[15]

The comments by Manfred Messerschmidt cannot be disputed. Perhaps there is too much pathos in his criticism of an order of the day to which certainly few, if any soldiers, paid attention. The order of the day was not printed, it was typed and mentions no distribution to units. Possibly no printing equipment was no longer available in the *Kessel*. At that time, the only thing most soldiers had in mind was to get out of the war unhurt. Model himself hardly believed what he wrote, since two weeks later he dissolved his Army Group. However, one can query why Professor Messerschmidt did not pour equal scorn on the infamous orders of the day from *Feldmarschall* von Reichenau on 6 October 1941 and from General von Manstein on 20 November 1941. Reichenau demanded from his troops "understanding for the harsh but deserved punishment of sub-human Jewry". General von Manstein of 20 November 1941, asked his soldiers to "understand the harsh punishment inflicted upon Jewry". While Model's order of the day was simply stupid, the orders by Reichenau and Manstein were direct appeals to murder. Yet Professor Messerschmidt writes that these commanders were still far away from perverted thinking. They looked upon their orders of the day as a psychological artefact to strengthen the morale and the combat readiness of their soldiers. He adds that the Generals did not even understand why Hitler found their orders of the day to be excellent.[16] Unfortunately the Generals,

---

14 Facsimile in Model/Bradley, p.378.
15 M. Messerschmidt, *Die Wehrmacht im NS-Staat, Zeit der Indoktrination*, Hamburg 1969, p.480.
16 Ibid, p.414 ff.

as well as the authors of the orders of the day, understood perfectly well. The Reichenau order of the day, which served as their model, was distributed by all the high commanders in the East, with added anti-Semitic slogans of their own.

Courts Martial

The criminal law system of the Third Reich was a disgrace. It had turned into an instrument of terror. Existing law codes had been maintained and most of their paragraphs were still valid. However, the addition of new laws and the increasing perversion of existing ones by many judges had turned the *Reich* into a constitutional vacuum. Principles which were part of the Roman legal system, and which had become the rule in every civilized country, had disappeared.[1] They included the non-retroactivity of law and penalty (*nullum crimen, nulla poena*) and the prohibiting of being tried more than once for the same offence (*ne bis in idem*). In 1933, Hans Frank was President of the Academy of German Law, and after 1939 he became the Governor of the Polish *Generalgouvernement*. Already in 1926, Hans Frank, at that time an attorney, had stated in a speech that the criterion of law is its benefit to the nation (*Recht ist was dem Volke nützt.*)

Apart from becoming increasingly cruel, many judges pronounced sentences according to *gesundes Volksempfinden* (healthy popular perception). This would permit the circumvention of any paragraph of the relevant codes. Since the Third *Reich*'s foundations were not State and Law, but *Volk* (people) and *Rasse* (race), everything that was judged contrary to healthy popular perception, could be physically eliminated. Few of the judges who had engaged in the perversion of the law were prosecuted in the Federal Republic. Those who were condemned were set free after a few years' imprisonment. Many continued to hold high legal office.

The Adenauer years were a refuge for former high-ranking Nazis in all spheres of public life. In 1959, the Socialist German students' league (*Sozialistischer Deutscher Studentenbund*) organized an exhibition in Karlsruhe. It listed 138 former high-ranking judges and prosecutors who had reached prestigious posts in the Federal Republic. The Chief Prosecutor of the Federal Republic, Max Güde, certified that the dates shown were correct. Fifteen had risen to chief prosecutors. Two had become Supreme Court justices. One was chief prosecutor at the Supreme Court (*Bundesgericht.*) Six former judges and prosecutors at the People's Court (*Volksgericht*) held high positions in the West German justice system.[2] In 1958, the creation of the Ludwigsburg central office for prosecution

---

1 The German Code of Civil Law (*Bürgerliches Gesetzbuch*) came into effect in 1900. Until that year, German civil law followed updated Roman law.

2 Details in J. Friedrich, *Die kalte Amnestie. NS-Täter in der Bundesrepublik*, Berlin 2007. (Henceforth Friedrich). Two examples, taken at random from Friedrich's book: In 1943, a court at Leslau, near the Polish border, had sentenced a Polish worker, Kasmierczak, to death. He helped smugglers and when he was caught, he was attacked by a police dog which he wounded with his knife. The court stated that hurting a dog was not in itself sufficient for a death sentence, but by stabbing the dog, the Pole had shown that he was predisposed to violence. Both the judge and the prosecutor of the court reached high positions in the Federal Republic. In another case, Frenchman Marius Carpentier, who had volunteered for work in Germany,

of crimes during the Nazi era led to some overdue redress. But a number of crimes came under the statute of limitations. Many culprits escaped justice on grounds of ill-health, real or purported.

During the war, around 1,000 military courts were set up. They consisted of one military justice official and two officers. Until the new military criminal law, *KstVO*, of 17 August 1938, the military justice system had three courts, courts martial, higher courts martial and finally the *Reichskriegsgericht, RKG*. The new law abolished the three-instance system and replaced it with a one-instance system. The presidents of a court martial (*Gerichtsherren*) had far-reaching powers.[3] They selected the assistant judges, gave instructions to the prosecutor and determined the date and place of each trial.[4] Their verdicts could not be increased, nor be reduced by higher courts that had only the right to confirm the sentences or to abrogate them.

In the *Wehrmacht*, Divisions and Armies had legal departments, with professional judges, and could act as courts martial. Most of the military judges had been lawyers, judges, prosecutors and attorneys before the war. Corps and Army Groups had no judicial authority and no legal departments. However, an Army Group *OB* had one or more legal advisers. An Army Group *OB* could not change a sentence rendered by an Army court martial. He could only object to it. A strong Army Group *OB* often prevailed against a verdict confirmed by a weaker Army commander. If the Army commander was a strong personality, he could disregard the Army *OB*'s objection. The Army Group *OB* had the right to request a court martial by the *Reichskriegsgericht, RKG*.

A typical example of the power of the *Gerichtsherr* in law perversion is the Navy military justice trial against Anton Mayer. Mayer was a first grade *Mischling* who had volunteered for service in the Navy in the hope of escaping racial persecution. When he volunteered, his racial background was not disclosed. When it was discovered, he deserted. On 17 January 1944, the Vienna naval court martial sentenced him to ten years' imprisonment. A naval legal expert, who was requested to review the sentence, found it too lenient and recommended its abrogation. The *Admiral*, who was *OB* of Naval Group West, and *Gerichtsherr*, took the advice of the expert and ordered a new trial. It sentenced Mayer to fifteen years. The judges of that court martial felt pity for Mayer and attempted to circumvent a directive of 27 April 1943 by the Supreme Commander Navy, *Grossadmiral*

---

had participated in the recoveries after a bombing raid in Berlin. On two subsequent days he had taken a belt, a pair of gloves, a tin of jam, and a domino from the rubble. The Berlin court sentenced him to death, because "he had shown such a degree of criminal disposition that he excluded himself from the community of decent men." Carpentier was 18 years old. After the war, the judge, who sentenced Carpentier to death, became a judge at the Berlin district court Schöneberg. (Ibid, p.381).

3   Hitler was the supreme *Gerichtsherr* of the *Wehrmacht*. On 26 April 1942, the *Reichstag* which he had summoned to a special session had formally stated that he could disregard existing laws. The background to this legislation was *Generaloberst* Hoepner's threat to sue for the respect of his accrued rights (*wohlerworbene Rechte*) after he had been cashiered. Apparently Hitler found it necessary to have such an unprecedented legislation passed with the blessing of the *Reichstag*, although the *Reichstag* had become a puppet assembly.

4   Detailed descriptions in M. Messerschmidt, *Militarismus, Vernichtungskrieg, Geschichtspolitik. Zur deutschen Militär-und Rechtsgeschichte*, Paderborn 2006, p.130-142 (henceforth Messerschmidt).

Karl Dönitz. Dönitz had ordered that no mercy could be shown to a deserter, unless he voluntarily rejoined his unit within a week. The court martial used the argument that the oath of a *Mischling* did not have the same value as an oath of an "Aryan" soldier. Dönitz then took personal charge of the case, abrogated the sentence and ordered a new court martial at the Berlin naval court. That court martial sentenced the soldier again to fifteen years. Dönitz abrogated the sentence once more and requested the head of the legal department at *OKM* to convince the court martial that it was not permissible to treat Mayer more leniently than an "Aryan" soldier. A fourth trial took place, and a death sentence was rendered on 20 July 1944. Mayer was executed on 20 August.[5]

According to §14 KStVO, a number of the offences came under the exclusive purview of the *RKG*:

- ordinary treason
- treason in times of war
- high treason
- crimes against the *Führer* and chancellor of the *Reich*
- crimes which fell under the law for the protection of the nation and the civilian population that were enacted by the President of the *Reich* in 1933 after the arson of the *Reichstag*[6]
- wilful damage to military equipment
- neglect to report criminal offences which were within the purview of the *Reichskriegsgericht*
- economic sabotage
- *Wehrkraftzersetzung* (causing damage to the *Wehrmacht*. The word is one of the many linguistic inventions of the Third *Reich*).

From September 1939, until October 1944, the *RKG* was presided over by *Admiral* Max Bastian, who had succeeded General Walter Heitz. When he took office, *Admiral* Bastian is supposed to have said: "Conscience may not be challenged. Better let one hundred guilty men go free, than to condemn one innocent."[7] One feels tempted to write an anthology of the high moral values expressed by *Wehrmacht* dignitaries and their application in reality. Up to February 1945, *RKG* had pronounced 1,189 death sentences. 1,049 sentences were carried out. Most were for *Wehrkraftzersetzung* which was given the largest possible sphere and covered any action that could be looked upon as causing harm to the *Wehrmacht*.[8] On 1 December 1939, the *RKG* Second Senate ruled that a man who did not intend *Wehrkraftzersetzung*, but was aware of its legal status, could likewise be

---

5   Messerschmidt.p.134 ff.
6   This law was retroactive. It made arson punishable with death by hanging and was passed on the day following the arson. Death by hanging did not exist at that time in Germany and the only man condemned in the *Reichstag* arson trial, Marinus van der Lubbe, was beheaded. However the law was invoked by the People's Court (*Volksgericht*) after 20 July 1944 in order to have the death penalties carried out by hanging.
7   M. Messerschmidt, 'Admiral Max Bastian', in G. Ueberschär (ed.) *Hitlers Militärische Elite. Vom Kriegsbeginn bis zum Weltkriegsende*, Darmstadt 1998, pp.1-11.
8   Clemenceau once said that it was sufficient to put "military" in front of any institution to deprive it of any sense. "Military justice has nothing to do with justice, just as military music is not music".

sentenced for it. This ruling meant the death sentence for people who had done nothing worse than make harmless political jokes. Up to 40,000 cases of *Wehrkraftzersetzung* had been handled by military courts. Among the victims of this law were the *Ernste Bibelforscher*, (Jehovah's Witnesses).[9] On 11 September 1939, Hitler had reached a decision, in principle, that Jehovah's Witnesses could not expect to be treated differently from others and be spared a death sentence. After a number of Jehovah's Witnesses had been sentenced to death during the first quarter of the war, the matter was again brought to Hitler's attention. Hitler decided that a death sentence for serious refusal to serve in the *Wehrmacht* could not be commuted. The motives of the refusal to perform armed service were not to be taken into account. Only if an accused declared himself ready to forswear his attitude, could clemency be granted.[10]

In 1941, an amendment to §5 *Kriegssonderstrafrechtsverordnung*, (*KSSVO*), special military penal regulations of 1.9.1938 stated that, "for a stubborn political offender like a *Bibelforscher*, the death sentence is usually mandatory, because his attitude has a propagandist effect". In other words, the degree of individual guilt was not a criterion. Only the interests of the national community (*Volksgemeinschaft*) were taken into account.

During the First World War, the Imperial German Army pronounced fewer death sentences than any Allied Army.

Crime	Total Number	Executed	Pardoned
Refusal of obedience in the front line	25	4	21
Desertion	27	10	17
Treason	49	18	31
Mutiny	9	2	7
Physical attack on a superior in the front line	8	3	5
Murder	32	11	21
Total	150	48	102

Thus 78.6% of death sentences rendered, and 77% of the sentences executed, concerned military offences.[11]

In the French Army 2,000 death sentences were rendered and 700 executed. The figures for executions after the mutinies of 1917 are not included, they remain secret. Corresponding figures for the British Army were 3,080 and 346. The Italian Army carried out 750 death sentences after judgments by regular courts (*da regolare sentenza*), and several

---

9   The Jehovah's Witnesses (*Bibelforscher*) was an association created by Charles Taze Russel in 1870 and led by Joseph Rutherford until 1942. Their *credo* was an imminent return of the Christ and a strict observance of all Christian legislation and rules. They were conscientious objectors, refused the oath of allegiance to Hitler and the *Deutsche Gruss (Heil Hitler)*. They were mercilessly pursued and in most instances sentenced to death. Civilian Jehovah's Witnesses were prosecuted under the law of insidiousness (*Heimtückegesetz*) and generally sent to concentration camps.

10   W. Messerschmidt, *Was damals Recht war…NS-Militär und Strafjustiz im Vernichtungskrieg*, Essen 1996, p.88.ff. (Henceforth Messerschmidt damals).

11   Table in van Creveld, p.134.

hundred executions after verdicts by summary courts martial. A large undetermined number of soldiers were shot by 'friendly fire' during mutinies or mass flights.

During World War II, the figures were reversed. In the *Wehrmacht*, a total of at least 17,055 death sentences were executed, of which 70% were for desertion and *Wehrkraftzersetzung*.[12] In *Mein Kampf*, Hitler had complained about the lack of severity of the German justice system during World War I. Apparently, the military judges of the Third *Reich* were haunted by the fear of being compared with their predecessors in World War I, and took the opposite path.

The death sentences rendered in the US Army, during World War II, totalled 443 of which 70 were carried out. Only one execution for desertion was carried out. 255 of the death sentences concerned criminal offences under common law.[13]

Wehrmacht death sentences for desertion were particularly cruel, since conscientious objections on religious grounds were equated with desertion and mercilessly punished.[14] Death sentences for desertion were carried out close to the date of Germany's unconditional surrender. Many soldiers deserted after the partial surrender to Montgomery on 5 May 1945. On 5 May 1945, *Generaladmiral* Walter Warzecha, head of the legal department in *OKM*, had a 19 year old soldier shot for desertion., although the *Führer* had "deserted his people" by committing suicide three days earlier.[15]

After Germany's unconditional surrender, death sentences continued to be carried out with the shameful consent of Allied occupation units. In one instance, a Canadian unit provided a German execution squad with rifles for execution of a death sentence one week after the unconditional surrender. Many soldiers who had been sentenced to

---

12 Ibid. p.135. Some historians arrive at even higher figures, Messerschmidt writes of an excess of 20,000 executions.

13 Ibid, p.134 ff.

14 One unique instance deserves to be mentioned. The town commander of Berlin, *Generalleutnant* Paul von Hase, was one of the most active members of the 20 July 1944 plot. He was sentenced to death at the first trial, 7-8 August 1944 and hanged on 8 August. As *Gerichtsherr* von Hase was particularly severe. On 24 April 1944 he sentenced a 34 year old Austrian soldier to death. During a talk with some university students, the soldier had said that there were organizations prepared to carry out a change of regime. One had to support the Communist Party. He was reported by one of the students. The court martial presided by General von Hase sentenced him to death on the grounds of his "considerable danger to public morale." On 23 June 1944, *Generaloberst* Fromm, *OB* of the *Ersatzheer*, confirmed the sentence. The mother of the soldier asked for a pardon through *Reichsleiter* Baldur von Schirach and said that she had already lost a son and foster son killed in action and another son was severely wounded. Baldur von Schirach asked if it was not possible to replace the death sentence by a prison term. General von Hase declined to reconsider and passed the matter on to General Fromm, with the mention that the request for pardon contained no new elements. General Fromm agreed on 16 July 1944, five days before 20 July. On the evening of 20 July, both Fromm and von Hase were arrested and Himmler replaced Fromm as commander of the *Ersatzheer*. Himmler acted differently from Fromm. He did not agree to a pardon, but he ordered that the death sentence not be carried out. The soldier was sent to a concentration camp. Messerschmidt, p.133 ff.

15 Messerschmidt damals, p.109.

prison were placed in penal battalions on their release. Their chance of survival in those units was practically nil.[16]

Wehrmacht courts during the war

During the war, the authority of the *Wehrmacht* justice system underwent a number of changes. In 1939, Hitler had objected to harsh verdicts, handed out by *Wehrmacht* courts against party members and the SS for atrocities against the civilian population in Poland. On 13 October 1939, separate new courts were created to try members of the SS, the *Waffen* SS, and the Police.

Summary courts martial were created on 1 November 1939. Under certain circumstances, a regimental commander, or a commander of lower rank, who had been given similar temporary authority, was permitted to preside as judge over the court martial. On 13 June 1940, the Commander in Chief of the Army, *Generaloberst* von Brauchitsch, issued a directive that summary courts martial could only be called under exceptional circumstances.

The *Gerichtsbarkeitserlass* of March 1941 transferred a number of offences which until then had been subject to the military penal code, to the authority of local troop commanders. A decree by Hitler of 21 June 1943 ordered the establishment of a special summary court martial for the *Wehrmacht*. This *Sonderstandgericht für die Wehrmacht* came within the framework of the *Reichskriegsgericht*. Final judicial authority was vested in Hitler himself.

Finally, in March of 1945, Himmler, in his capacity as Commander in Chief of the *Ersatzheer,* recommended the creation of *Fliegende Standgerichte* (flying summary courts martial). They were empowered to order the immediate execution of verdicts rendered by them. Hitler agreed. The military courts were retained but could not interfere with the verdict of a *Fliegende Standgericht*. Thus hundreds of officers and soldiers were executed during the last weeks of the war.

Wehrmacht military courts in 9th Army

The judicial system was the same in all *Wehrmacht* Armies.

In accordance with § 14 *KstVO,* courts martial at Divisions could not confirm death sentences, nor prison sentences of more than five years. Death sentences had to be confirmed by the Army Commander, who was likewise permitted to grant pardons.

Trials in which Model was involved

The trial of *General der Panzertruppe* Georg Stumme and *Generalleutnant* Hans von Boineburg-Lengsfeld

On 2 August 1942, the two Generals and a staff officer of General Stumme's Corps, were indicted for negligence in handling secret documents pertaining to the summer 1942 *Blau* offensive. The court martial was presided over by Göring. Model and *Generalleutnant* Wilhelm Ritter von Thoma acted as assessors. The three officers each received a short prison sentence, but were pardoned after one month's detention.

---

16 For details, N. Wachsmann, *Gefangen unter Hitler, Justizterror und Strafvollzug im NS-Staat,* Munich 2006.

As *OB* of 9th Army

Görlitz writes that Model never confirmed a death sentence.[17] As usual, Görlitz does not indicate specific sources. A majority of the legal files of 9th Army were lost during the war. However Görlitz's contention is unlikely. Model was *OB* of 9th Army during close to two years. Given the cruelty of the German military justice system and the number of death sentences carried out, it is hard to believe that Model acted differently from other Army *OB*.

As *OB* of Army Groups

Model was involved in three major trials that occurred at a time when he was *OB* of Army Groups. He held no judicial authority.

The trial of General von Choltitz

General von Choltitz recalled that he had met Model only once, on 17 August 1944, just after Model had relieved von Kluge. He had informed Model of the steps he had taken to send the demolition squads away without destroying the Seine bridges. Model had approved. Their conversation had been short. Model was very tired, after an exhausting journey of 36 hours from Rastenburg to Paris.[18]

Model cannot be blamed for his instructions to have General von Choltitz put on trial. The respectability of General von Choltitz's actions at Paris is beyond doubt. However, he had acted in contradiction to a formal order by Hitler. On 28 August 1944, Model informed *OKW* that he had requested the start of open court martial procedures against General von Choltitz:

> I have requested the President of the *Reichskriegsgerichthof* to initiate proceedings against General von Choltitz, and other officers under his command. General von Choltitz has not lived up to the expectations of a Commander of Paris. I am unable to judge if his failure is due to the stress of fighting, or to the weakening of his willpower, and of his capacity to reach decisions through the use of tranquilizers. This possibility cannot be excluded.[19]

Since General von Choltitz had already surrendered to the Allies, and become a prisoner of war, he was not in personal danger. However, his family was at great risk of *Sippenhaft*. Model was aware that von Choltitz's judgement was in no way impaired, since he had listened in on his last conversation with Speidel. But his statement, referring to a possible use of tranquilizers and that General von Choltitz was perhaps no longer master of his actions, can be viewed as an attempt to bend over backwards in order to spare the General's family the worst possible consequences.

In the end, this proved to have been unnecessary. General von Choltitz could have been tried *in absentia*, but this did not take place. Instead, the court focused on a technicality. The defendant was known to have signed his name "v. Choltitz" but, given

---

17 Görlitz, p. 180
18 Choltitz , p.238.
19 Facsimile in Model/Bradley, p.272.

the importance of the surrender document, he had signed it "von Choltitz."[20] The military court was convened at Torgau in March 1945. It immediately noticed the discrepancy in the signature and expressed doubts as to the authenticity of the surrender documents. Proceedings were postponed indefinitely.

The adventures of General von Schwerin and his trial

The many adventures of General Gerhard Graf von Schwerin are probably unique in the history of World War II. He emerged as one of the few German commanders endowed with genuine guts.

In 1939, before the outbreak of the war, Schwerin, at that time a Lieutenant Colonel and head of the department *Fremde Heere* (Foreign Armies), at the *Generalstab*, had paid a visit to Great Britain. He had warned his hosts that the British policy of appeasement to Hitler boded ill for the future of the world.[21] He had made the same comments to Sir Kenneth Strong, the British military attaché in Berlin. In 1945, Sir Kenneth Strong was G-2 at the Allied Expeditionary Force's European Theatre headquarters. Schwerin's talk with him before the war, and also his visit to Britain, stood him in good stead after the war.

Graf von Schwerin was nicknamed "Conte" and also "Monsieur Lévrier" (Schwerin's 116th *Panzer-Grenadier* Division bore the name *Windhund* – greyhound, or in French 'lévrier') He was an exceptionally brave officer, at the same time he was often prone to eccentric behaviour. During the battles in the area Nikopol-Krivoy Rog, he had been awarded the swords to the oak leaves of his Knight's Cross. Then criticism was levelled at the performance of his Division. He was relieved, together with his Ia, Major Heinz Günther Guderian, the son of *Generaloberst* Guderian.[22] Von Schwerin was furious and refused to accept the swords award to the Knight's Cross. He informed *Generalmajor* Viktor Linnarz, department head in the Army's personnel division accordingly and sent copies of his letter to *Generaloberst* Guderian and to General Heusinger. When General Schmundt told him that the criticism against his Division had been removed, he accepted the swords.

During the battles in Normandy, Schwerin had a violent quarrel with his Corps commander, *General der Panzertruppe* Hans von Funck. A misunderstanding had arisen about the date of an attack by 116th Division. General von Funck felt that Schwerin had 'cold feet'. On 7 August 1944, Funck insulted Schwerin over the phone: "*Graf* Schwerin, if 60th Regiment had any spark of honour left, this could not have happened. When will it finally attack? When can I expect that the Division will finally carry out orders by me?" Schwerin replied: "I will not stand for any insults to myself or to my Division."[23] General von Schwerin then left his command post for an advanced post, without disclosing its location.

Before Major Guderian could search for him, *Feldmarschall* von Kluge called and said that he had relieved Schwerin of his command. Schwerin was ordered to present himself to General Speidel at Kluge's headquarters at La Roche-Guyon. In a letter to the commanders in 116th Division, Schwerin wrote that General von Funck had repeatedly insulted the

---

20 Choltitz, p.272.
21 Meyer Heusinger, p.394.
22 Heinz Günther Guderian rose to Major General (two stars) in the *Bundeswehr*.
23 *Windhund*, p.62.

Division and that this had led to increasingly violent exchanges between General von Funck and himself. Schwerin added that he would state his case to *SS-Oberstgruppenführer* Paul Hausser, *OB* 7th Army.[24] On 17 August 1944, Kluge was relieved by Model.

Model reinstated Schwerin as commander of 116th Division, and put 21st *Panzer* Division and 22nd SS *Panzer* Division also under his command, now named *Gruppe* Schwerin. On 6 September, Colonel von Gersdorff, at that time Chief of Staff of 7th Army, wrote to Army Group B headquarters and requested that von Schwerin should be relieved. Conflicting reports had reached *AOK 7* as to the whereabouts of 116th Division. Given the chaotic situation in the West at that date, that was hardly surprising. Perhaps the following message, from General von Schwerin to the commanders in his Division, had reached *AOK 7*.

Graf von Schwerin had written:

> The retreat towards the German border was unavoidable. The soldiers want to go home. The German soldier is fed up with the war. He has no more hope, he wants to go home and that is it. The commander of 116th Division knows his men. He feels as do they, as do all the front commanders. But the high commanders think otherwise and are still clinging to illusions. The commander of 116th Division knows how his men are thinking. They would continue the hopeless fight on German soil. Only the front soldier can stop this madness. Commander of 116th Division will not disappoint his men. He will not continue to fight on German soil and open the homeland to destruction. He is firmly decided to act accordingly. But first he has to lead his Division back into Germany. He will not permit his Division to be destroyed by irresponsible orders from above.[25]

Schwerin led his Division back to Aachen. The town was of no operative significance, but it was the first sizeable German city to face capture. On 13 September 1944, Hitler issued an order: "If the enemy breaks through, every house is to be defended. No retreat is allowed."[26] The same day, General von Schwerin was appointed commander of the Aachen sector. The town commander, Colonel von Osterroth, was subordinated to him.

When the Allied forces reached the Aachen outskirts, panic broke out in the civilian population. On 10 September, three days before General von Schwerin arrived, Himmler had been in the city. He had addressed the inhabitants, assuring them that the enemy would never come close to Aachen and that no evacuation was contemplated.

On the night of 10 September, *OKW* instructed *Gauleiter* Josef Grohé to order the evacuation of the city. Grohé had issued an order which ended with the words: "Whoever disturbs evacuation measures, or refuses to let himself be evacuated, puts not only himself but also others into danger of death. He is a traitor and has to be dealt with accordingly." Evacuation was to be carried out by the *Kreisleiters*. But the next day, both they and the police officials were among the first to flee. Chaos erupted in the streets and at the railway station.

---

24 Ibid, p.565.
25 Ibid, p.135.
26 BA-MA, RH 24-81/101.

When General von Schwerin drove through the city on 12 and 13 September, he discovered that all officials had fled. He believed that the capture of the city was imminent. He wrote a letter, in English, to the American general who would attack the city and whose name he ignored: "To the Commanding Officer of the US Forces occupying the town of Aachen. I stopped the stupid evacuation of the civil population and ask you to give it relief. I am the last commanding officer here."[27] He dropped the letter into a mailbox. (The American general in command of the assault was Major General J. Lawton Collins). Schwerin had expected a capture of Aachen without resistance, but the Americans had halted their advance close to the city's outskirts.

On the afternoon of 13 September, the *Gauleiter* of the area were called to a meeting at 7th Army headquarters. Gersdorff informed General Krebs that a letter from General von Schwerin to an unnamed American general had apparently turned up at a post office. General Krebs informed General Westphal, Chief of Staff *OB* West, that he had ordered an official investigation. General von Schwerin was questioned that same evening by his Corps commander, *Generalleutnant* Friedrich Schack. He did not mention his letter.

On 14 September, the Americans succeeded in breaking through in the south of the city. Grohé went to General Schack and complained that the *Wehrmacht* was responsible for the chaos and that he would report this to Hitler. General Schack relieved General von Schwerin. On 15 September, a telex message from Himmler arrived at Army Group B: "Commander of 116th Division has apparently fled with his unit. Immediate report as to the whereabouts of General von Schwerin is ordered."

Himmler had been informed about General von Schwerin's letter by the deputy commander of the *Wehrkreis*, General Franz Mattenklott. In the meantime, General von Schwerin had tried to recover the letter. General Schack questioned him again. Once again, Schwerin did not mention his letter. After the meeting, General von Schwerin disappeared and could not be located. Before vanishing, he had written a personal letter to Himmler in which he rejected the charges by General Mattenklott. Himmler calmed down.

On the evening of 15 September, Model notified *OB* West that he had relieved Schwerin and had requested court martial procedures against him. In his message he strongly criticized the Party and Police authorities. He added that he had no doubt that Schwerin had always acted in accordance with his military duties, without sparing himself.[28]

During the next few days, General von Schwerin drove from one location to another. General Schack searched for him in vain. Reports that General von Schwerin could not be located continued to arrive at Army Group B headquarters. On 18 September, General von Schwerin informed General Schack that he would agree to meet with him, but only at his own divisional headquarters where he felt secure. By then Model had begun to lose patience. A telephone conversation between Krebs and von Gersdorff was recorded in the war diary of Army Group B of 18 September:

> *OB* Army Group insists that he will not agree to be confronted with further *harlequinades* and that this nonsense must be put to an end. General Schwerin must be placed in pre-trial detention, and after interrogation, brought to Supreme Command West headquarters. The interrogation must be conducted by *OB* 7th Army.

---

27 The original of the letter is in the Aachen city archives.
28 BA-MA, RH 19 IX/89.

Details must be agreed upon with the chief judge at *OB* West, thus preventing any differences with *Reichsführer* SS. *OB* Army Group describes the three day absence of Schwerin as a *Köpenickiade*.[29]

On 19 September, General von Schwerin was placed in pre-trial custody. The chief military judge at *OB* West, Henning von Beust, ordered his release. Model was furious and wanted a court martial. But General Brandenberger, who as *OB* 7th Army held judicial authority, stepped in and said "only over my dead body."[30] *Feldmarschall* von Rundstedt shared the opinion of his judge and Model was forced to back down.

The story had a curious conclusion. Hitler simply sent a warning to Schwerin and recalled his previous bravery. General von Schwerin wanted to be returned to the command of his previous Division. Model objected, because the events at Aachen had become widely known. General Schack was relieved and replaced by General Friedrich Köchling. Schwerin was promoted to General *der Panzertruppe* on 1 April 1945, and became commander of LXXVI *Panzer* Corps.

When discussions about the Federal German Republic's membership in NATO, and the creation of the *Bundeswehr* began in 1949, Sir Kenneth Strong remembered von Schwerin's visit to London in 1939. Strong talked to the governor of the British zone of occupation, General Sir Brian Robertson, who arranged for Schwerin to become Konrad Adenauer's first military adviser.[31] Not surprisingly, this resulted in intrigues by Generals Adolf Heusinger and Hans Speidel, who aspired to receive the top command positions in a new German Army and who looked at Schwerin as a possible rival.[32] A slander campaign against General von Schwerin was initiated and spread by them and their associates among former *Wehrmacht* Generals who held influence over the appointments to positions in the *Bundeswehr*. In September 1951, the duo Heusinger-Speidel succeeded in having Adenauer dismiss General von Schwerin, who was replaced by a civilian, Theodor Blank. General von Schwerin died in 1980.

---

29 Facsimile in Model/Bradley, p.304 *"Köpenickiade"* refers to an event which in 1906 made the headlines in Germany. Wilhelm Voigt, a cobbler, who had served a number of prison terms, donned the uniform of a Captain and succeeded in assembling a number of soldiers, whom he ordered to march to the town hall of the Berlin suburb of Köpenick. He arrested the mayor and made off with the money of the municipality. This episode showed the respect which uniform commanded in Imperial Germany. It conferred authority upon its bearer and commanded obedience by civilians. Model's link between the adventures of General von Schwerin and Wilhelm Voigt is, however, questionable.

30 Gersdorff, p.169.

31 Sir Bryan Robertson felt that it was necessary for the Federal Chancellor to have a military adviser, but he opposed "wild or irresponsible people like General von Manteuffel" or "sensible but indecisive men like *Generaloberst* Heinrich von Vietttinghoff". (Meyer, Heusinger, p.395).

32 Details about General von Schwerin's activities in Meyer, Heusinger, p.386-426. Georg Meyer's bias in favour of General Heusinger has to be taken into account. It led him to quote many disparaging remarks by Heusinger about former comrades, among them victims of 20 July such as General Stieff, who could not reply.

Vogelsang castle and the trial of General Straube

Vogelsang castle was one of the training schools for party officials. It was under the personal authority of Robert Ley. As head of the *Deutsche Arbeitsfront (DAF)*, the national trade union organization, Ley was one of the highest-ranking party leaders. The party schools were looked upon by Hitler as a symbol of prestige. On 7 February 1945, Lieutenant General George Patton's 3rd US Army had attacked in the southern Eifel region. Hitler had forbidden the surrender of any fortification of the West Wall, but the Americans had succeeded in breaching it in several places.

Model ordered the demolition of the Ruhr valley dams, and this led to an evacuation of the Dreiborn area, where Vogelsang was located. Ley felt that the *Wehrmacht* had not done enough to protect the castle and lodged an official complaint. The LXXXVI Corps Commander in charge of the area, General Erich Straube, one of his Division Commanders, and the commander of an artillery regiment, were all brought before a court martial. They were acquitted and the *OB* of 15th Army, General von Zangen, confirmed the verdict. The Vogelsang trial led to a strong personal hostility between Ley and Model, which Goebbels recorded in his diaries.[33]

Model disagreed. His relationship with von Zangen had always been strained. He requested a second court martial which again resulted in acquittal. Model remained unconvinced and questioned the accused personally. He then changed his mind and agreed with the court. Hitler demanded that the officers be brought to a special tribunal, but Model objected and prevailed.

Summary courts martial

On 15 March 1945, Model issued the following order: "Every soldier who is arrested away from his unit, on the roads, either alone or in groups, on first aid places without being wounded and who claims to have been dispersed and looking for his units, has to be brought before a summary court martial and shot."[34] On the same day, Kesselring had issued a similar order.

Already on 9 March 1945, Model had addressed the following order to his Army Group:

Soldiers of the Army Group! Fighters of the Rhine and the Eifel!
In this immense struggle for Germany and every German man and woman, the German soldier fulfils his heavy duty with courage and loyalty. Only a few betray their country in times of distress, by escaping from their duties. They move around behind the front lines and claim to have been dispersed.

The following orders have to be communicated to every soldier with the greatest possible urgency:

Fundamental order:

---

33 Entry of 15 March 1945: "Ley has a negative view of Model. His leadership has become nervous and erratic. The *Gauleiter* in the West have a low opinion of him." Ley was indicted at the trial of the major Nazi criminals. He committed suicide in his Nuremberg cell.

34 On 15.3.1945, Rundstedt has issued a similar order. M. Messerschmidt, *Stuttgart im Zweiten Weltkrieg*, Gerlingen 1989, p.482.

There will be no more dispersed soldiers, nor soldiers who have become separated from their unit. Whoever has lost touch with his unit, in combat, has to contact the nearest combat unit within 24 hours. Any troop in combat can be located through the noise. A soldier who does not act in this manner is an evil traitor of his people and will be treated like a criminal. Lame excuses such as: I have been dispersed and I am searching for my unit will no longer be accepted.

As a first step I order:

Until 16 March, every soldier who had been separated from his unit has to report without delay to the nearest unit in combat. The unit reached by him has to integrate him, without taking into account in which arm he had served previously. A return to his original unit is not urgent and will be subject to separate rules. Model, *Generalfeldmarschall*."[35]

By that time, summary courts martial had become a daily occurrence in all *Wehrmacht* units. In all German cities, roads and in the countryside, which were not yet occupied by the Russians and the Western Allies, soldiers and civilians were hanging from trees and lamp-posts, marked: "I am a traitor" and "I have made a deal with the Bolsheviks", all an increasingly common sight. During the first week of April 1945, one month before Germany's unconditional surrender, *Grossadmiral* Karl Dönitz saw it fit to issue the following order: "Our duty as soldiers which we are sworn to, makes us stand as a rock of resistance, bold, tough and faithful. A soldier who does not act so is lower than a miserable cur. (*Hundsfott*). He has to be hanged with a poster around his neck: 'Here hangs a traitor who in his cowardice has caused the death of German women and children whom it was his soldierly duty to protect.'"[36] Given the increasing chaos in the last weeks of the war, the exact number of victims of summary courts martial will never be established.

---

35 Facsimile in Model/Bradley, p.368.
36 quoted by J. Zimmermann, *Pflicht zum Untergang. Die deutsche Kriegführung im Westen des Reiches 1944/45*, Paderborn 2009.

Photographs

Generalfeldmarschall Walter Model, a photograph taken during the
early stages of the Campaign in Russia (Biblio Verlag)

Model in discussion with Hitler Youth, October 1944. (Bundesarchiv 183-J28036)

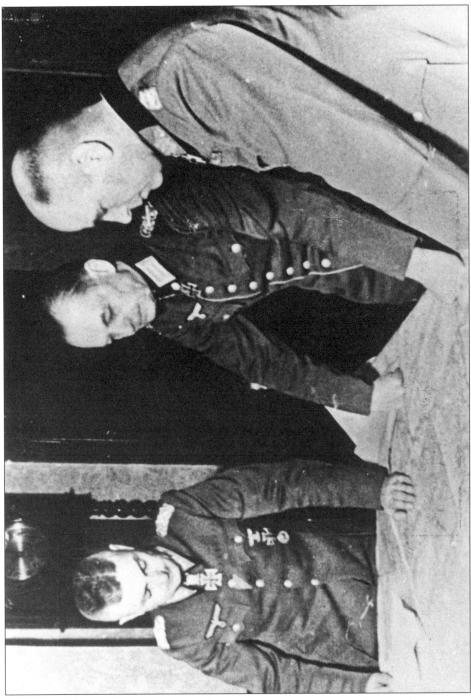

Model discussing preparations for the forthcoming Ardennes offensive with
Generalfeldmarschall Gerd von Rundstedt (centre) and *General der Infanterie* Hans Krebs
(right), Bad Tönisstein, Villa Brandenburg, November 1944 (Bundesarchiv 146-1978-024-31)

Generalfeldmarschall Fedor von Bock (Bundesarchiv 146-1977-120-11)

Generalfeldmarschall Wilhelm Keitel (Biblio Verlag)

Generalfeldmarschall Günther von Kluge (Bundesarchiv 146-1995-002-09A)

Generalfeldmarschall Georg von Küchler (Bundesarchiv 183-R63872)

Generalfeldmarschall Erich von Manstein (Private collection)

SS Oberstgruppenführer Sepp Dietrich (Bundesarchiv 183-J27366)

Generaloberst Ludwig Beck (Private collection)

Generaloberst Johannes Friessner (Bundesarchiv 146-1984-018-27A)

Generaloberst Heinz Guderian (Biblio Verlag)

Generaloberst Franz Halder (Biblio Verlag)

Generaloberst Josef Harpe (Bundesarchiv 146-1981-104-30)

Generaloberst Alfred Jodl (Private collection)

Generaloberst Georg Lindemann (Bundesarchiv 183-L08017)

General der Infanterie Dietrich von Choltitz (Bundesarchiv 183-E1210-0201-018)

General der Infanterie Gustav-Adolf von Zangen in conversation with *Reichsminister* Prof. Albert Speer, Autumn 1944. (Bundesarchiv 183-H28061)

General der Panzertruppe Hasso von Manteuffel (Bundesarchiv 146-1976-143-21)

Appendix I

Goebbels' speech of 19 April 1945

At a moment of the war when the enemy, perhaps for the last time, has loosed all his hate and means of destruction against us from East, West, South-East and South, I appear once more before the German people. I have done this every year since 1933. Now on the eve of 20 April, I will speak again about the *Führer*.

I can only repeat that the present time, with all its sadness and weight of hurt, has found its only worthy representative in the *Führer*. If Germany is still alive, and if Europe and the entire civilized West have not yet been absorbed by the maelstrom of the dark abyss, we have only him to thank. He will remain the Man of the Century.

But if it is manly and German for the *Führer* of a great and brave nation to face this challenge alone, trusting in his own strength and the help of the Almighty, to continue fighting, refusing to surrender to the powerful enemy, then it behoves the German people to follow the example of such a *Führer*. Unconditionally, without any restrictions, rejecting any feeling of weakness or inconsistency, we must continue to believe in the bright star above us. Even if covered by dark clouds, we shall not be cowardly, but will replace the white flag of surrender with the flag of the swastika. We thank the Almighty that he has made us the gift of a real *Führer* in such terrible times.

The war is nearing its end. The madness of our enemies has already passed its zenith. The heads of the enemy conspiracy have already been shattered by fate. It was the same fate that preserved the *Führer* on 20 July 1944. Surrounded by rubble, dead and wounded, he remained upright and unhurt, and able to complete his mission. He has to do this with pain, and increased challenges, but this had been dictated by providence. The German people have borne him, elevated him on their shield, and elected him as their *Führer* in free elections. The German people know his achievements in peace time, and are now determined to follow him to the victorious end of the war which was forced upon us.

Who else but the *Führer* can show us the way out of the world crisis? His work is the work of order. All that his enemies are able to oppose him with is a diabolic mixture of anarchy, and destruction of countries and their peoples. Above all, if the world still lives today, not only we but others have to thank the *Führer*. They may revile him, cover him with dirt and express their base hatred of him, but they will change their minds, and bitterly regret their present views. The *Führer* is the core of resistance against the destruction of the world. He is Germany's bravest heart and he represents our people's ardent will. I allow myself a judgment which has to be proclaimed loudly today: If the nation still breathes, if a possibility of victory remains, if there is a way out of the danger, we have to thank him for it.

We look up to him in hope and in unshakeable faith. We stand behind him, soldiers and civilians, men, women and children, inspired by faith and the will to fight, and determined to do our utmost in preserving life and honour.

We stand by him as he has stood by us in Germanic loyalty. We remain true to our oath. We need not tell him that, because he knows this himself. *Führer*, order us and we will follow you. We feel him within ourselves and around us. May the Almighty give him strength, keep him in good health, and protect him from danger. We will take care of the rest.

Germany remains the nation of faith. Germany will celebrate the greatest triumph even when in danger. History will never relate that a *Führer* abandoned his people, or that the people abandoned their *Führer*. And this is victory. If on this day, in good times, we have turned to the *Führer*, now, in the hour of suffering and danger to all of us, we have a more urgent appeal to him: He has to remain what he is for us, and what he always was for us: Our Hitler![1]

---

1   Taken from J. Thorwald, *Das Ende an der Elbe*, Stuttgart 1953, p. 73 ff.

Appendix II

Extracts from Himmler's address to the *Gauleiters,* Posen, 6 October 1943

I may now come to a matter, in this private auditorium, that you consider has become the most difficult problem to face in our lifetime, the Jewish question. You consider it obvious, and a matter of joy, that no more Jews are to be found in your towns. Every German, apart from individual exceptions, is well aware that we would not have survived the bombing of our cities, nor partisan warfare, and that we may face even harder challenges in the coming years, had we remained with these pestilential bacteria in the body of our nation. The sentence 'all Jews must be physically annihilated' is easy to say. For those who have to carry it out, it is the hardest imaginable duty. Look, of course it is Jews, it is evident that it is only Jews. But think how many, even party members, have made the well-known request to me and to others. They wrote, 'of course all Jews are swine, but Mr X is a decent Jew who should not be harmed.' I dare say that if I sum up all such requests, there must have been more decent Jews in Germany than the total number of Jews in our country. I mention this because I am sure that you at home certainly know respectable National-Socialists, all of whom know one decent Jew.

I will ask you to only listen to what I have to say now, and to talk to no one about it. We had to ask ourselves what to do with women and children. I decided in favour of a clear solution. I did not find it possible to kill the men, or to have them killed, and then to let the children and grandchildren become the avengers. I had to face the difficult decision to have this whole people disappear from the earth. For the organization that had to carry out this order, it was the most difficult assignment ever. I can affirm that this has been carried out by men and women who have suffered no damage to their soul. There was such a danger. The path between becoming cruel and heartless, losing respect for all human life, or becoming soft and suffering a nervous collapse, is as narrow as the passage between Scylla and Charybdis. To have walked past 100 or 1,000 or more, executed corpses, and to have remained decent[1], is an immortal page of glory in our history which will never be told.

We have turned over all the property we have confiscated from the Jews to the state treasury, and it is of astronomical size. I have always had one principle: If we want to win the war, we have a duty to our people, and to our race, and of course to our *Führer,* who finally, after 2,000 years, has been given to us. We must act with consequence and show no meanness. But we have not the right to take one penny from the confiscated Jewish property. I have established the rule that SS men who take as little as one mark,

---

1 Himmler had the habit of using the word *anständig* (decent) in almost any address, regardless of the subject.

are subject to the death penalty. Only this week, let me say it in total frankness, I have confirmed a dozen of such death sentences. [This statement was a brazen lie. All the executioners, the men of the *Einsatzgruppen*, the policemen and the *Wehrmacht* officers and men rivalled each other in plundering the corpses of their victims.] One has to be without pity, else the solution to the problem will not be complete. I had to tell you this without inhibition. In the countries occupied by us, the Jewish question will be entirely solved by the end of this year. Perhaps some isolated Jews will remain in hiding. Then we will tackle the problem of Jews who have married Christians, and the fate of the half-Jews, in a reasonable and logical manner.

You can believe me that I had to overcome serious problems with many economic bodies. I had to clean up a number of ghettos. In Warsaw we have had four weeks of street-fighting in the ghetto. Four weeks! We have taken out some 700 bunkers. This ghetto produced fur coats, clothes and other wear. Had we tried to destroy the ghetto earlier, we would have heard: 'Stop! You are hurting war economies, you are hurting armament production'. Of course, this was not said by Speer. Those were alleged war production plants which Speer, together with me, will clear out during the coming weeks and months. We will do this without sentimentality, just as we abstain from sentimentality in all matters which have to be completed unflinchingly for Germany.

This is what I had to say about the Jewish question. You are now informed and you will keep it to yourselves. Later we can decide if we should inform the German people of the details. I feel that, since we have assumed the responsibility, not only for the idea but also for the action, it might be better to take those secrets to our graves.[2]

---

2 *Geheimreden*, pp. 169-171.

Appendix III

Extracts from Himmler's address to high ranking *Wehrmacht* commanders, Sonthofen, 5 May 1944

Another vital question for the security of the *Reich,* and for all of Europe, was the Jewish problem. We have solved it by giving the necessary orders, and in full understanding of its implications, in a manner without any compromise. (Applause from the audience). I believe you know that I am not a bloodthirsty man and that I have no personal pleasure or enjoyment in the actions which I am compelled to undertake. But also I have sufficiently strong nerves, and an overriding sense of duty, to accomplish what I decide to do without compromise. With regard to the Jewish women and children, I could not justify letting the children live, to later become the avengers against our fathers and our grandchildren. I would consider this to be cowardly. Therefore I solved the problem without compromise. At this moment we are sending 100,000 Hungarian Jews into concentration camps. Another 100,000 will follow. They will be engaged in the construction of underground industrial plants which will never be seen by the German people. But I have a firm belief. I would take a dim view of the Eastern Front in the *Generalgouvernement*, if we had not solved the Jewish question there, if the ghetto in Lublin still existed, and if we had not destroyed the gigantic Warsaw ghetto, with its 500,000 inmates, last year. That took five weeks of street fighting. We had to use *Panzer* and other heavy arms to clear 700 bunkers ... [1]

---

1   *Geheimreden*, p. 203.

Appendix IV

Reichenau's order of the day of 10 October 1941

Subject: Behaviour of the troops in the East

There is insufficient clarity about the behaviour required of troops toward the Bolshevik system. The main purpose of the war against the Jewish-Bolshevik system is the annihilation of all its means of power, and the extermination of Asiatic influence on European culture.

This confronts the troops with duties which go beyond one-sided traditional soldierly norms. The soldier in the East is not only a fighter, in accordance with the art of war, he is likewise the bearer of a relentless popular ideology. He is the avenger of all the bestialities committed against the German people, and the nations related to her by common blood.

Therefore the soldier has to have full understanding of the necessity of the just punishment inflicted upon sub-human Jewry. It is likewise necessary to put down any attempts of uprising in the rear that are usually instigated by Jews.

The battle against the enemy, behind the front, is not taken seriously enough. Malicious and cruel partisans, and degenerate women, are still treated as prisoners of war. Snipers in civilian clothes or wearing parts of uniforms, and tramps, are treated like decent soldiers and sent to prisoner of war camps. Russian officers who have been captured, tell with a sneer of contempt, that Soviet agents are roaming peacefully in the streets of captured cities and are often fed by German field kitchens. Such an attitude by the troops is simply thoughtless. Time has now come for their superiors to awake them to the requirements of the present struggle.

Giving food at field kitchens to the civilian population, and to prisoners of war who are not performing work for the *Wehrmacht*, is just as much misunderstood humanity, as the giving away of cigarettes and bread. The soldier is not allowed to give away to the enemy what the homeland lacks under great privations, or what has been carried to the front with the greatest difficulty. This prohibition also extends to goods captured from the enemy. They are a necessary part of our catering.

During their retreat the Soviets have set many buildings ablaze. Troops must only be interested in extinguishing the fires if the buildings can be preserved as their quarters. In all other eventualities, the destruction of symbols of the former Bolshevik system, even buildings, is part of the framework of the war of destruction. Historic or artistic considerations cannot be given credence in the East. Commanders will issue the necessary orders for preserving raw material resources, and production entities that are necessary to our war effort.

Disarmament of the population in the rear of the fighting troops has total precedence, given the difficult transportation conditions to the front. Whenever possible, captured arms and equipment have to be carefully preserved and put under guard. If circumstances do not permit this, all captured arms and equipment have to be immediately destroyed. If armed partisans are discovered in the rear, draconian measures must be implemented.

Such measures must also extend to local male civilians, who may possibly avoid the fighting, or avoid taking up arms, or attempt to stay away from areas of fighting. The indifference, shown by many who pretend to be hostile to Bolshevism, has to give way to a clear decision to actively participate in the fight against it. If this does not happen, no one has the right to complain, if he is considered to be an adherent to the Soviet system, and treated as such. Fear of German measures must be stronger than apprehension of the loose remainder of Red Army units.

While remaining remote from future political considerations, the soldiers have to comply with two overriding duties.

Total destruction of Bolshevik heresy, the Soviet State and its Army.

Merciless annihilation of alien maliciousness and cruelty, thus preserving the security and life of the German *Wehrmacht* in Russia.

Only in this manner will we be true to our historic mission to liberate the German people, for all time to come, from the Asiatic-Jewish peril.

The commander in chief

Signed: von Reichenau, *Generalfeldmarschall.*[1]

[On 28 October 1941, *OKH* communicated the Reichenau order to the three Army Group Commanders in the East with an accompanying letter:

By order of the Commander in chief of the Army, an order of the day by the commander of 6th Army on the conduct of the troops in the East is attached, which the *Führer* considers to be excellent. The Commanders are requested to issue orders of a similar content, if this has not already been done. Signed: Wagner, by order. *Feldmarschall* von Rundstedt, commander of Army Group South, wrote to three of his Army commanders, von Manstein (11th Army), Hoth (17th Army), von Kleist (1st *Panzer* Army), and his *Korück*, that he was in full agreement with Reichenau's order of the day. He asked them to consider issuing similar orders, provided they had not already done so under their own initiative, after adapting them to local considerations.]

---

1 NOKW, D-411.

Appendix V

Manstein's order of the day of 20 November 1941

Since 22 June, the German people are engaged in a life and death struggle against the Bolshevik system. This war is not conducted in traditional manner, solely against the Russian Army, and it does not follow European rules of war. Fighting continues behind the front. Partisans and snipers in civilian clothes attack individual soldiers. Small units attempt to destroy our supply with mines and other infernal tools. Bolsheviks, who have remained behind, continue to impose terror and disquiet upon a population liberated from Bolshevism, and thus attempt sabotage of the political and economic pacification of the country. Industrial plants and harvests are destroyed, and the urban population is exposed to famine.

Jewry is the centre, between the enemy in the rear, and the remaining units of the Red Army which are still capable of fighting. More than anywhere else in Europe, it holds all keys of political leadership and administration, trade and handcraft, and it is the cell of all disturbance and potential uprisings.

The Jewish-Bolshevik system has to be exterminated for all times. It must never again be permitted to penetrate our European *Lebensraum*.

The German soldier has not the sole duty to destroy the military means of this system. He is also the standard bearer of a popular idea, and an avenger of the cruelty against himself and the whole German people.

Combat in the rear is not paid sufficient attention. The soldier has to participate actively in disarming the population, in controlling it, and in arresting all deserters and civilians. He has to see to the removal of all Bolshevik symbols. Every incident of sabotage has to be punished immediately and with the most radical means. Every event has to be reported without delay.

The food situation in Germany makes it necessary for the troops to live with what is available in occupied areas, and to see that a maximum quantity of available foodstuff is sent to the homeland. In enemy cities, much of the population will have to remain hungry. Humanitarian sympathy, arising from a lack of understanding, cannot be permitted to divert food from the homeland by distributing it to the civilian population, and to prisoners of war, unless they work for the *Wehrmacht*.

The soldier has to show understanding for the harsh punishment meted out to Jewry, the spiritual flag bearer of Bolshevik terror. This punishment is necessary, to nip in the bud all attempts of uprising that are mostly inspired by Jews. Commanders of all ranks have to keep their soldiers constantly aware of the spirit of the present struggle. Carelessness must not be permitted to aid the Bolshevik struggle in the rear of the front line.

Ukrainians who are not Bolsheviks, also Russians and Tartars must be expected to accept the new order. The indifference of many purported anti-Bolshevik elements has to be replaced by an unequivocal readiness to work actively with us, in the struggle against Bolshevism. If this is not done voluntarily, it has to be enforced by us.

A voluntary participation in the reconstruction of the country by the population is an absolute prerequisite for attaining our desired political and economic objectives. It makes it incumbent upon us to show justice to such parts of the population that have been fighting heroically against Bolshevism over many years.

Our domination of this country makes it incumbent upon us to show performance and hardness towards ourselves, and to refrain from consideration of individuals. The behaviour of our soldiers is under constant observation. It has to render enemy propaganda invalid and prevent any such attempts. If a soldier takes the last cow, the last chicken, the last breeding sow, the last seeds from the farmer, the economy cannot be revitalised.

Immediate result of our measures is not a cornerstone of our success. Future and lasting effects have to be taken into account.

Religious customs, especially those of the Moslem Tartars, have to be respected.

Future measures of the administration have to be assisted by explanations via propaganda, to the population. There must be encouragement of local initiatives, such as premiums, increasing participation in the fight against partisans, and the development of a local police force.

Our aim requires:

Active co-operation by the soldier against the enemy in the rear. Every vehicle has to be provided with sufficient arms. Attitude towards the population must be contained, restraint has to be shown toward prisoners of war and women, waste of foodstuff must be prohibited.

No arbitrariness and selfishness, no unruliness and lack of discipline, and no violation of soldierly honour will be tolerated.

To be distributed down to Battalion level.

Signed: The commander in chief
v. Manstein" [1]

---

1 BA-MA, RH 20-11/519.

Appendix VI

Himmler's directive for procreation – 28 October 1939

Reichsführer SS und Chef der deutschen Polizei im Reichsministerium des Inneren

SS–Order for the SS and the Police

Every war is a blood-letting of the best blood. Many victories of arms meant likewise a devastating defeat of the people's vitality and its blood. The unfortunate death of the best men, regrettable as it is, does not represent the worst consequence. Much worse, is the absence of children who, during the war, have not been fathered by the living.

The perennial wisdom, that only a man who has children may die with a peaceful mind, has to be the gospel for the SS during this war. A man dies with a peaceful mind if he knows that his *Sippe* (family), with all that was desired and achieved by his ancestors and by himself, will find a continuation in his children. The greatest gift, for the widow of a fallen soldier, is the child of the man whom she has loved. But beyond the conventions of civil law and traditions, which may perhaps be necessary in other circumstances, it will be a high duty, of German women and girls of good race, to bear children out of wedlock. This is not a sign of youthful abandon, but of a profound and ethical desire to be the mother of children, of soldiers going into battle. Only fate can decide if they will return or if they will die for Germany.

Men and women, who remain home by order, have likewise the sacred duty to become parents of children.

We must never forget that the victory of the sword, and the bloodshed by our soldiers, would be meaningless if it were not followed by the victory of the child, and the settlement of new areas.

During the First World War, many soldiers decided not to father children, out of a feeling of responsibility towards their wives, who would have to bear a heavy burden if he failed to return. Men of the SS, you need not have such concerns.

1. The care of all children of good blood, born in marriage or out of wedlock, will be taken care of by special delegates of mine who will become their tutors. We will stand by their mothers, and will take care of their moral and material needs, until they come of age, thus preventing any plight for the mother and the widow.
2. The SS will take care of all mothers and children born during the war, either in marriage or out of wedlock, if they are in plight or in distress. If the fathers return after the war, the SS will generously satisfy their founded requests for economic assistance.

Men of the SS, and mothers of the children hoped for by Germany! Give evidence that your faith in the *Führer,* and your devotion to the eternal life of our people, and our blood, will show you equally brave in fighting and dying for Germany, and in transmitting new life for Germany.

Reichsführer SS, Heinrich Himmler.[1]

[This directive led to a protest by General Theodor Groppe, who stated to the troops of his Division, that this message was removing Germany from civilized nations.[2] The importance which Himmler attached to his directive is shown by his repeated mentioning of the 'Groppe incident' in his address to the *Gauleiter,* and other party functionaries, on 29 February 1940: "…Some of you *Gauleiter* in the West know the incident with *Generalleutnant* Groppe, who criticized my directive in a course for non-commissioned officers of his Division. He said that I had soiled the honour of the family… I am used to much, but this was beyond boundaries … I have immediately complained to *Generaloberst* von Brauchitsch…*Generalleutnant* Groppe has been relieved of his command. This measure has hopefully caused any uneasiness to disappear …"[3]]

1   H-A Jacobsen: 1939-1945. *Der Zweite Weltkrieg in Chronik und Dokumente*n, Darmstadt 1951, p. 409 ff.

2   K.-J. Müller: *Das Heer und Hitler. Armee und nationalsozialistisches Regime 1933-1940,* Stuttgart 1969, pp. 459-462.

3   *Geheimreden,* p.122 ff.

Abbreviations

Many abbreviations refer to documents in the footnotes. They are basically of interest only to readers who know German and who are consulting archive documents. A number of abbreviations are likewise in the text of the book. The German meaning will be given, followed by a translation into English.

AA	Auswärtiges Amt	Ministry for Foreign Affairs
Abs.	Absatz	Paragraph
Abt.	Abteilung	Department
Abw.	Abwehr	Counter intelligence
A.K.	Armeekorps	Corps
Anl.	Anlage	Attachment
Anm.	Anmerkung	Comment
AOK	Armeeoberkommando	Command of Army and Army Group
Az.	Aktenzeichen	File
BA-MA	Bundesarchiv-Militärarchiv	Freiburg Military Archives
Bd., Bde	Band, Bände	Volume, volumes
Bl.	Blatt	Page
BstU	Unterlagen Staatsicherheit DDR	Records state security GDR
Chefs.	Chefsache	Document for/by commander
Div.	Division	Division
Dok.	Dokument	Document
Dulag	Durchgangslager	POW transit camp
Ebd.	Ebenda	Ibid
Ek	Einsatzkommando	Subunit Einsatzgruppe
EK	Eisernes Kreuz	Iron Cross
EM	Ereignismeldung	Report by Einsatzgruppe
g.	geheim	secret
geh.	geheim	secret
Gen. Kdo	Generalkommando	Corps command
geh. Kdos.	geheime Kommandosache	secret order document
Gen. Qu.	Generalquartiermeister	Quartermaster General
Gen. Stab	Generalstab	German General Staff
Gen.St.d.H.	Generalstab des Heeres	General Staff Ground Forces
Gestapo	Geheime Staatspolizei	Secret State Police
GFP	Geheime Feldpolizei	Secret Field Police
gez.	gezeichnet	signed
Gr.	Gruppe	Group
Hg.	Herausgeber	Editor
HSSPF	Höherer SS und Polizeiführer	Higher Police and SS commanders

Ifz	Institut für Zeitgeschichte, München	Institute for Contemporary History, Munich
i.G.	im Generalstab	Member of the General Staff
IMT	Internationaler Militärgerichtshof	International Military Tribunal
i.V.	in Vertretung	by order
Kdo.	Kommando	commando
Kdr.	Kommandeur	commander
Kdt.	Kommandant	commandant
K.G.	Kommandierender General	Corps commander
Kgf.	Kriegsgefangene	prisoners of war
KTB	Kriegstagebuch	War diary
KZ	Konzentrationslager	Concentration camp
MG	Maschinengewehr	machine gun
NKVD	Narodny Kommissariat vnutrennych diel	USSR Interior Ministry [secret police]
Nr.	Nummer	Number
NS	Nationalsozialism	National-Socialism
NSDAP	Nationalsozialistische deutsche Arbeiterpartei	National-Socialist German Worker's Party
OB	Oberbefehlshaber	Commander Army and Army Group
OB.d.H.	Oberbefehlshaber Heeres	Commander in Chief Army
Offz.	Offizier	Officer
OKH	Oberkommando des Heeres	Supreme command Army
OKL	Oberkommando der Luftwaffe	Supreme Command Air Force
OKM	Oberkommando der Marine	Supreme Command Navy
OKW	Oberkommando der Wehrmacht	Supreme Command Wehrmacht
Op.Abt.	Operationsabteilung	Operational department
O.Qu.	Oberquartiermeister	Chief Quartermaster
Prop.	Propaganda	propaganda
Pz.AOK	Panzerarmeeoberkommando	Command Panzer Army
Pz.Div.	Panzerdivision	Panzer Division
Qu.	Quartiermeister	Quartermaster
Rgt.	Regiment	Regiment
RSHA	Reichsicherheitshauptamt	SS main security department
S.	Seite	Page
SA	Sturmabteilung	Storm troopers
SD	Sicherheitsdienst	SS Security Service
Sk	Sonderkommando	Subunit of Einsatzgruppe
SS	Schutzstaffel	SS
SU	Sowjetunion	Soviet Union
t.to.	Tonne	ton
UdSSR	Union der Sozialistischen Sowjetrepubliken	Union of Soviet Socialist Republics
vgl.	vergleiche	compare
VO	Verbindungsoffizier	liaison officer

WFSt.	Wehrmachtführungsstab	Staff OKW
Wi	Wirtschaft	economy
z.b.V.	zur besonderen Verfügung	for special disposition
zgl.	zugleich	simultaneously
zit.	zitiert	quoted
z.Zt.	zur Zeit	at this time

Bibliography

Absolon, R. (ed.): *Das Wehrmachtstrafrecht im Zweiten Weltkrieg, Sammlung der grundlegenden Gesetze, Verordnungen und Erlasse*, Kornelimünster 1958.

Absolon, R.: *Wehrgesetz und Wehrdienst, Das Personalwesen in der Wehrmacht*, Boppard 1960.

Alexander, M.: *The Republic in Danger. General Maurice Gamelin and the politics of French defence 1933-1940*, London 1992.

Aly, G., Heim, S.: *Vordenker der Vernichtung. Auschwitz und die deutschen Pläne für eine neue europäische Ordnung*, Frankfurt 2004.

Aly, G.: *Macht, Geist, Wahn. Kontinuitäten deutschen Denkens*, Frankfurt 2005.

Aly, G.: *Rasse und Klasse. Nachforschungen zum deutschen Wesen*, Frankfurt 2003.

Aly, G.: *"Endlösung" Völkerverschiebung und der Mord an den europäischen Juden,* Frankfurt 2005.

Aly, G.: *Hitlers Volksstaat. Raub, Rassenkrieg und nationaler Sozialismus*, Frankfurt 2005.

Aly, G . (ed.): *Volkes Stimme. Skepsis und Führervertrauen im Nationalsozialismus*, Frankfurt 2006.

Alberti, M.: *Die Verfolgung und Vernichtung der Juden im Reichsgau Wartheland 1939-1945*, Wiesbaden 2006.

Angress, W.: 'Das deutsche Militär und die Juden im Ersten Weltkrieg' in *Militärgeschichtliche Mitteilungen* 19 (1976) pp.71-84.

Angrick, A., Klein, P.: *Die Endlösung in Riga. Ausbeutung und Vernichtung 1941-1944*, Darmstadt 2006.

Angrick, A. : *Besatzungspolitik und Massenmord. Die Einsatzgruppe D in der südlichen Sowjetunion 1941-1943*, Hamburg 2003.

Arad, J. (ed) *The pictorial history of the Holocaust*, Jerusalem 1990.

Archiv Peter (ed.): *Spiegelbild einer Verschwörung. Die Kaltenbrunner-Berichte an Bormann und Hitler über das Attentat vom 20. Juli 1944. Geheime Dokumente aus dem ehemaligen Reichssicherheitshauptamt*, Stuttgart 1961.

Arnold, K.: *Die Wehrmacht und die Besatzungspolitik in den besetzten Gebieten der Sowjetunion. Kriegführung und Radikalisierung im "Unternehmen Barbaraossa"*, Berlin 2005.

Arntz, H. Dieter: *Kriegsende 1944/45 — zwischen Ardennen und Rhein*, Euskirch 1984.

Aron, R.: *Histoire de la Libération de la France*, Paris 1959.

Asprey, R.: *The German High Command at War — Hindenburg and Ludendorff and the First World War*, London 1993.

Bagramyan, I.: *So schritten wir zum Sieg*, Berlin 1984.

Bajohr, F., Pohl, D.: *Massenmord und schlechtes Gewissen. Die deutsche Bevölkerung, die NS-Führung und der Holocaust*, Frankfurt 2008.

Balck, H., General der Panzertruppe: *Ordnung im Chaos, Erinnerungen 1893-1948*, Osnabrück 1981.

Barnett, C.: *Hitler's Generals*, New York 1989.

Bartov, O.: *Hitlers Wehrmacht. Soldaten, Fanatismus und die Brutalisierung des Krieges*, Reinbek 2003.

Beck, B.: *Wehrmacht und sexuelle Gewalt. Sexualverbrechen vor deutschen Militärgerichten 1939-1945*, Paderborn 2004

Beck, L.: *Studien,* Stuttgart 1955.

Beevor.A., Vinogradova L.: *A writer at war. Vasily Grossman with the Red Army 1941-1945*, London 2006

Benz, B., Graml, H. (eds.): *Biographisches Lexikon zur Weimarer Republik*, Munich 1988.

Benz, W.: *Paul Carell. Ribbentrops Pressechef Paul Karl Schmidt vor und nach 1945*, Berlin 2005.

Besymenski, L.: *Sonderakte Barbarossa*, Reibeck 1973.

v. Below, Nicolaus: *Als Hitlers Adjutant 1937-1945*, Mainz 1980.

Bialer, S.: *Stalin and his Generals, Soviet Military Command, Memoirs of World War II*, London 1984.

Birn, R.: *Die Höheren SS-und Polizeiführer. Himmlers Vertreter im Reich und in den besetzten Gebieten*, Düsseldorf 1986.

Birn, R.: *Die Sicherheitspolizei in Estland 1941-1944. Eine Studie zur Kollaboration im Osten*, Paderborn 2006.

Böddeker, G.: *Der Untergang des Dritten Reiches*, Berlin 1985.

Böhler, J. (ed): *Grösste Härte. Verbrechen der Wehrmacht in Polen September-Oktober 1939*, Warsaw 2006.

Böhler, J.: *Auftakt zum Vernichtungskrieg. Die Wehrmacht in Polen 1939*, Frankfurt 2006.

Bonacker. M.: *Goebbels' Mann beim Radio. Der NS –Propagandist Hans Fritzsche (1900-1953)*, Munich 2007.

Bradley, F., Petersen A. (eds.): *Heinrich Himmler. Geheimreden 1933 bis 1945 und andere Ansprachen*, Frankfurt 1972.

Bradley, O.: *A General's Life*, New York 1983.

Bradley, O.: *A Soldier's Story*, New York 1951.

Breloer, H.: *Speer und Er. Hitlers Architekt und Rüstungsminister*, Berlin 2005

Brett-Smith, R.: *Hitler's Generals*, London 1976.

Brochhagen, U.: *Nach Nürnberg. Vergangenheitsbewältigung und Westintegration in der Ära Adenauer*, Hamburg 1994.

Broszat, M.: 'Soziale Motivation und Führer — Bindung des Nationalsozialismus' in: *Vierteljahrshefte für Zeitgeschichte* 18, 1972.

Broucek, P.: *Ein General im Zwielicht. Die Erinnerungen Edmund Glaises von Horstenau*, Vienna 1988, 3 Bände.

Browning, C.: *Die Entfesselung der "Endlösung". Nationalsozialistische Judenpolitik 1939-1943*, Munich 2003.

Browning, C.: *Ordinary Men: Reserve Police Battalion 101 and the Final Solution in Poland*, New York 1992

Brüne, L., Weiler J.: *Remagen im März 1945— Eine Dokumentation zur Schlussphase des 2. Weltkrieges*, Friedens-Museum "Brücke von Remagen e.V." 1994.

Bryant, A.: *The Turn of the Tide*, London 1957.

Bryant, A.: *Triumph in the West*, London 1959.

v. d. Bussche, A.: *Eid und Schuld*, Göttingen 1947.

Carell, P.: *Unternehmen Barbarossa*, Frankfurt 1966.

Carell, P.: *Verbrannte Erde*, Frankfurt 1972.

v. Choltitz, D.: *Soldat unter Soldaten*, Zürich 1951.

v. Cochenhausen, F.: *25 Lebensbilder von Feldherrn aller Zeiten*, Berlin 1930.

Cole, H.: *The United States Army in World War II, The Ardennes: Battle of the Bulge*, Washington 1965.

Conquest, R.: *The Great Terror — A Reassessment*, New York 1990.

Cooper, M.: *The German Army 1933-1945, Its political and military failure*, London 1978.

van Creveld, M.: 'Die deutsche Wehrmacht: eine militärische Beurteilung' in: Müller, R., Volkmann, H. (eds.): *Die Wehrmacht: Mythos und Realität im Auftrag des Militärgeschichtlichen Forschungsamts*, Oldenburg 1999.

van Creveld, M.: *Kampfkraft. Militärische Organisation und Leistung der deutschen und amerikanischen Armee 1939-1945*. Graz 2005.

van Creveld, M.: *The changing face of war. Lessons of combat from the Marne to Iraq*, New York 2006.

Cüppers, M.: *Wegbereiter der Shoah. Die Waffen-SS, der Kommandostab Reichsführer-SS und die Judenvernichtung 1939-1945*, Darmstadt 2005.

Curilla, W.: *Die deutsche Ordnungspolizei und der Holocaust im Baltikum und in Weissrussland 1941-1944*, Paderborn 2006.

Dahlmann, D., Hilbrenner, A. (eds.): *Zwischen großen Erwartungen und bösem Erwachen, Juden, Politik und Antisemitismus in Ost-und Südosteuropa 1918-1945*, Paderborn 2007.

Davidson, E.: *The Trial of the Germans. An Account of the Twenty-Two Defendants before the International Military Tribunal at Nuremberg*, New York 1966.

Dawidowicz, L.: *Der Krieg gegen die Juden 1933-1945*, Munich 1979.

Dirks, C: *"Die Verbrechen der anderen". Auschwitz und der Auschwitz-Prozess der DDR. Das Verfahren gegen den KZ-Arzt Dr. Horst Fischer*, Paderborn 2006.

Dönitz, K.: *Zehn Jahre und zwanzig Tage*, Frankfurt 1962.

Domarus, M.: *Hitlers Reden und Proklamationen 1932-1945*, Munich 1963, 4 Bände.

Dziennik Hansa Franka, Warsaw 1957.

Eberle, H., Uhl, M. (eds.): *Das Buch Hitler. Geheimdossier des NKWD für Josef W. Stalin zusammengestellt aufgrund der Verhörsprotokolle des persönlichen Adjutanten Hitlers, Otto Günscheund des Kammerdieners Heinz Linge, Moskau 1948/49*, Bergisch Gladbach 2005

Ehlert, H., Lang A., Wegner B.: *Manfred Messerschmidt. Militarismus, Vernichtungskrieg, Geschichtspolitik. Zur deutschen Militär und Rechtsgeschichte*, Paderborn 2006.

Encyclopaedia Judaica, Jerusalem 1973.

Encyclopedia of the Holocaust, Jerusalem 2000.

Enzensberger, H.M.: *Hammerstein oder der Eigensinn. Eine deutsche Geschichte*, Frankfurt 2008

Eisenhower, D.: *Crusade in Europe*, New York 1948.

Erickson, J.: *The Road to Berlin*, London 1983.

Erickson, J.: *The Road to Stalingrad*, London 1973.

Erfurth, W.: *Die Geschichte des deutschen Generalstabes 1918-1945*, Göttingen 1957.

d'Este, C.: *Decision in Normandy. The Unwritten Story of Montgomery and the Allied Campaign*, London 1983.

v. Faber du Faur, M.: *Macht und Ohnmacht — Erinnerungen eines alten Offiziers*, Stuttgart 1955.

Fall 7 IMT— Das Urteil im Geiselmordprozess, Berlin East 1963.

Fall 9 IMT – Das Urteil im Einsatzgruppenprozess, Berlin East, 1963.

Fall 12 IMT- Das Urteil im OKW Prozess. Berlin East 1965.

Faschismus-Getto-Massenmord. Dokumentation über Ausrottung und Widerstand der Juden in Polen während des zweiten Weltkrieges, Berlin East 1961.

Fest, J.: *Das Gesicht des Dritten Reichs — Profile einer totalitären Herrschaft*, Munich 1963.

Fest, J.: *Staatsstreich — der lange Weg zum 20. Juli*, Berlin 1994.

Fest, J.: *Ich nicht. Erinnerungen an eine Kindheit und Jugend*, Hamburg 2006.

Förster J.: *Die Sicherung des Lebensraumes in Das deutsche Reich und der Zweite Weltkrieg*, vol.4, Stuttgart 1983.

Förster, J.: *Die Wehrmacht im NS-Staat. Eine strukturgeschichtliche Analyse*, Munich 2007.

Förster, W.: *Ein General kämpft gegen den Krieg — Aus nachgelassenen Papieren des Generalstabschef Ludwig Beck*, Munich 1949.

Förster, W.: *Generaloberst Ludwig Beck — Sein Kampf gegen den Krieg*, Munich 1952.

Foertsch, H.: *Schuld und Verhängnis, Die Fritsch-Krise im Frühjahr 1938 als Wendepunkt in der Geschichte der nationalsozialistischen Zeit*, Stuttgart 1951.

Frey, N.: *Vergangenheitspolitik. Die Anfänge der Bundesrepublik und die NS-Vergangenheit*, Munich 2003.

Friedländer, S: *Das Dritte Reich und die Juden. Die Jahre der Verfolgung 1933-1939*, Munich 2000.

Friedländer, S.: *Die Jahre der Vernichtung. Das Dritte Reich und die Juden 1939-1945*, Munich 2006.

Friedrich, J: *Freispruch für die Nazi-Justiz. Die Urteile gegen NS-Richter seit 1948. Eine Dokumentation*, Hamburg 1983.

Friedrich, J.: *Das Gesetz des Krieges*, Munich 1997.

Friedrich, J.: *Die kalte Amnestie. NS-Täter in der Bundesrepublik*, Berlin 2007.

Friessner, J.: *Verratene Schlachten*, Hamburg 1956.

Frieser, K.: *Blitzkriegs-Legende. Der Westfeldzug 1940*, Munich 1996.

Frieser, K.: 'Schlagen aus der Nachhand – Schlagen aus der Vorhand. Die Schlachten von Charkow und Kursk' in: Förster, W. (ed.), *Gezeitenwechsel im Zweiten Weltkrieg? Die Schlachten von Charkow und Kursk in operativer Anlage, Verlauf und politischer Bedeutung*, Hamburg 1996.

Frieser, K.: *Krieg hinter Stacheldraht. Die deutschen Kriegsgefangenen in der Sowjetunion und das Nationalkomitee Freies Deutschland*, Mainz 1971.

Fröhlich, S.: *General Wlassow, Russen und Deutsche zwischen Hitler und Stalin*, Cologne 1987.

Gerber, K.(ed): *Generalfeldmarschall Fedor von Bock. Zwischen Pflicht und Verweigerung. Das Kriegstagebuch*, Munich 1993

Gerlach, C.: *Kalkulierte Morde — Die deutsche Wirtschafts- und Vernichtungspolitik in Weissrussland 1941 — 1944*, Hamburg 1999.

Gerlach, C.: *Krieg, Ernährung, Völkermord. Forschungen zur deutschen Vernichtungspolitik im Zweiten Weltkrieg*, Hamburg 1998.

Gerlach, C., Aly, G.: *Das letzte Kapitel. Der Mord an den ungarischen Juden*, Stuttgart 2002.

v. Gersdorff, R. Frhr.: *Soldat im Untergang*, Berlin 1977.

Gilbert, M.: *Endlösung — Ein Atlas*, Reinbeck 1982.

Gilbert, M.: *The Holocaust, The Jewish Tragedy*, London 1986.

Giordano, R.: *Die zweite Schuld oder von der Last Deutscher zu sein*, Cologne 2000.

Giordano, R.: *Die Traditionslüge. Vom Kriegerkult in der Bundeswehr*, Cologne 2000.

Giziowski, R.: *The Enigma of General Blaskowitz*, London 1997.

Goebbels, J.: *Tagebücher aus den Jahren 1942-1943*, Zürich 1948.

Goebbels, J.: *Tagebücher 1945*, Hamburg 1977.

Görlitz, W.: *Der deutsche Generalstab*, Frankfurt 1959.

Görlitz, W. (ed.): *Generalfeldmarschall Keitel, Verbrecher oder Offizier?*, Göttingen 1961.

Görlitz, W.: *Model — der Feldmarschall und sein Endkampf an der Ruhr*, Berlin 1992.

Goldhagen, D.: *Hitler's Willing Executioners. Ordinary Germans and the Holocaust*, New York 1996.

Gorbatov, A.: *Years off my Life — The Memoirs of a General of the Soviet Army*, London 1964.

Greiner H.: *Die oberste Wehrmachtführung 1939-43*, Wiesbaden 1952.

Grigorenko, P.: *Erinnerungen*, Munich 1981.

Guderian, H. : *Erinnerungen eines Soldaten*, Wels 1951.

Guderian H. G. (son of Generaloberst Guderian): *Das letzte Kriegsjahr im Westen, Die Geschichte der 116. Panzer-Division — Windhunddivision*, Freiburg 1994.

Gumbel, E.: *Verschwörer, Zur Geschichte und Soziologie der deutschen nationalistischen Geheimbünde 1918-1924*, Heidelberg 1979.

Gyseke, G: *Der Fall Priebke. Richtigstellung und Dokumentation*, Berg 1997.

Hachmeister, L.: *Der Gegnerforscher — die Karriere des SS-Führers Franz Alfred Six*, Munich 1998.

Haffner, S.: *Anmerkungen zu Hitler*, Berlin 2001.

Halder, F.: *Hitler als Feldherr*, Munich 1949.

Halder, F.: *Kriegstagebuch 1939-1942*, Stuttgart 1962.

Hamann, B.: *Hitlers Wien, Lehrjahre eines Diktators*, Munich 1998.

v. Hammerstein, K. Frhr.: *Spähtrupp*, Stuttgart 1963.

Hartmann, C.: *Halder als Generalstabschef Hitlers, 1938-1942*, Paderborn 1951.

Hartmann, C., Hürter, J., Jureit U.: *Verbrechen der Wehrmacht. Bilanz einer Debatte*, Munich 2005.

Hartmann, C., Hürter, J., Lieb, P., Pohl, D. (eds.): *Der deutsche Krieg im Osten 1941-1944. Facetten einer Grenzüberschreitung*, Munich 2009

Harvey A., Uhle-Wettler F.: *Kreta und Arnhem. Die grössten Luftlandeoperationen des Zweiten Weltkrieges*, Graz 2004.

Hamerow T.: *Die Attentäter, der 20. Juli — von der Kollaboration zum Widerstand*, Munich 1999.

Heer, H., Naumann, K. (eds.): *Vernichtungskrieg, Verbrechen der Wehrmacht 1941-1944*, Sammelband, Hamburg 1995.

Heer, H.: *Hitler war's. Die Befreiung der Deutschen von ihrer Vergangenheit*, Berlin 2005.

Heiber, H. (ed.): *Hitlers Lagebesprechungen — Die Protokollfragmente seiner militärischen Konferenzen 1942-1945*, Munich 1963.

Heidkämper, O.: *Witebsk*, Heidelberg 1954.

v. Herwarth, H.: *Zwischen Hitler und Stalin, Erlebte Zeitgeschichte 1931-1945*, Frankfurt 1982.

Herbert, U. (ed.) *Nationalsozialistische Vernichtungspolitik 1939-1945. Neue Forschungen und Kontroversen*, Frankfurt 2001.

Heuer, G.: *Die deutschen Generalfeldmarschälle und Grossadmirale*, Baden 1979.

Heusinger, A.: *Befehl im Widerstreit — Schicksalsstunden der deutschen Armee 1923-1945*, Stuttgart 1952.

Heydecker, J., Leeb, J.: *Der Nürnberger Prozess — Bilanz der tausend Jahre*, Cologne 1979.

Hilberg, R.: *Die Vernichtung der europäischen Juden*, Frankfurt 1990, 3 Bände.

Hilberg, R.: *The Destruction of the European Jews*, Frankfurt 1984.

Hilberg, R.: *Täter, Opfer, Zuschauer, Die Vernichtung der Juden*, Frankfurt 1992.

Hilberg, R.: *Die Quellen des Holocaust. Entschlüsseln und interpretieren*, Frankfurt 2002.

Hillgruber, A.: 'Die ideologisch-dogmatische Grundlage der nationalsozialistischen Politik der Ausrottung der Juden in den besetzten Gebieten der Sowjetunion und ihre Durchführung 1941-1944' in: *German Studies Review*, Vol.1. 1. II, Nr. 3, October 1979.

Himmler, K.: *Die Brüder Himmler. Eine deutsche Familiengeschichte*. Frankfurt 2007.

Hirschfeld, G., T. Jersak (eds.): *Karrieren im National-Sozialismus. Funktionseliten zwischen Mitwirkung und Distanz*, Frankfurt 2004.

Hitzfeld, O: *Ein Infanterist in zwei Weltkriegen, Erinnerungen 1898-1980*, Osnabrück 1983.

Huger, G., Meyer, A.: *The Incompatible Allies — A memoir history of German-Soviet relations*, New York 1953.

Hinze, R.: *Der Zusammenbruch der Heeresgruppe Mitte im Osten 1944*, Stuttgart 1980.

Hitler, A.: *Mein Kampf*.

Höhne, H.: *Der Orden unter dem Totenkopf— die Geschichte der SS*, Munich 1978.

Hoffmann, P.: *Claus Schenck, Graf v.Stauffenberg und seine Brüder*, Stuttgart 1992.

Hoffmann, P.: *Claus Schenk Graf von Stauffenberg. Eine Biographie*, Munich 2008

Hoffmann, P.: *Widerstand, Staatsstreich, Attentat, Der Kampf der Opposition gegen Hitler*, Munich 1979.

Horn, A.: *To lose a battle. France 1940*, Boston 1969.

Hossbach, F.: *Zwischen Wehrmacht und Hitler — 1934-1938*, Göttingen 1965.

Hubatsch, W.: *Hitlers Weisungen für die Kriegsführung 1939-1945*, Frankfurt 1962.

Huber, E.: *Heer und Staat in der deutschen Geschichte*, Hamburg 1938.

Huber, E.: *Verfassungrecht des Grossdeutschen Reiches*, Hamburg 1939.

Hürter, J.: *Hitlers Heerführer. Die deutschen Oberbefehlshaber im Krieg gegen die Sowjetunion 1941/42*, Munich 2006.

Hürter, J.: *Ein deutscher General an der Ostfront. Die Briefe und Tagebücher des Gotthard Heinrici*, Erfurt 2001.

Hürter, J.: *Wilhelm Groener. Reichswehrminister am Ende der Weimarer Republik 1928-1932*, Munich 1993.

Hürter, J.: 'Nachrichten aus dem Zweiten Krimkrieg (1941/42) Werner von Hentig als Vertreter des Auswärtigen Amtes bei der 11. Armee', in: *Internationale Beziehungen im 19. und 20. Jahrhundert, Festschrift für Winfried Baumgart zum 65. Geburtstag*, Paderborn 2003.

International Military and Defense Encyclopedia, Vol.5, Washington 1991.

Istoria Velikoi Otetschestvennoj Voiny Sovietskojo Sojuza — 1941-1945 (IVOVS), Moscow, 1963, 6 volumes.

Jacobsen, H.-A.: *Der Zweite Weltkrieg in Chronik und Dokumenten*, Darmstadt 1961.

Jacobsen, H.-A., Rohwer, L. (eds.).: *Entscheidungsschlachten des zweiten Weltkrieges*, Frankfurt 1960.

Janssen K., Tobias F.: *Der Sturz der Generäle-Hitler und die Blomberg-Fritsch Krise 1938*, Munich 1994.

Jodl, L.: *Jenseits des Endes — Leben und Sterben des Generalobersten Jodl*, Munich 1976.

John, O.: *Falsch und zu spät — der 20 Juli 1944*, Munich 1984.

Jünger, E.: Strahlungen. D*as zweite Pariser Tagebuch. Kirchhorster Blätter. Die Hütte im Weinberg*, Munich 1995.

Kaiser, W. (ed): *Täter im Vernichtungskrieg. Der Überfall auf die Sowjetunion und der Völkermord an den Juden*, Berlin 2002.

Keilig, W.: *Die Generäle des Heeres*, Friedberg 1983.

Keilig, W.: *Rangliste des deutschen Heeres 1944/45*, Friedberg (undated).

Kersten, F.: *The Kersten Memoirs —Totenkopf und Treue*, London 1956.

Kershaw, I: *Hitlers Macht. Das Profil der NS-Herrschaft*, Munich 2000.

Kershaw, I.: *Hitler 1889-1936*, Stuttgart 1998.

Kershaw, I.: *Hitler 1936-1945*, Stuttgart 1998.

Kesselring, A.: *Soldat bis zum letzten Tag*, Bonn 1953.

Klee, E.: *Das Personenlexikon zum Dritten Reich. Wer war was vor und nach 1945*, Frankfurt 2003.

Klein, P. (ed.): *Die Einsatzgruppen in der besetzten Sowjetunion 1941, Die Tätigkeits – und Lageberichte des Chefs der Sicherheitspolizei und des SD*, Berlin 1997.

Kleist, P.: *Zwischen Stalin und Hitler*, Bonn 1950.

Klink, E.: *Das Gesetz des Handelns — Die Operation Zitadelle 1943*, Stuttgart 1966.

Koehler, L., Saner, H. (eds.): *Hannah Arendt-Karl Jaspers. Briefwechsel 1926-1959*, Munich 1985.

Kogon, E.: *Der SS- Staat*, Frankfurt 1946.

Kondratew, O.: *Die Schlacht von Rshew – Ein halbes Jahrhundert Schweigen*, Munich 2000.

Konev, I.: *Das Jahr 1945*, Berlin 1969.

Kosthorst, E.: *Die Geburt der Tragödie aus dem Geist des Gehorsams — Deutschlands Generäle und Hitler*, Bonn 1998.

v. Kotze, H. (ed.): *Heeresadjutant bei Hitler 1938-1943, Aufzeichnungen des Major Engel*, Stuttgart 1974.

v. Krannhals, H: *Der Warschauer Aufstand 1944*, Frankfurt 1962.

Kratkaja Istoria Velikoi Otetschesvennoj Vojny Sovietskogo Soyusa, Moskau 1964.

Krausnick, H., Wilhelm, H.: *Die Truppe des Weltanschauungskrieges — Die Einsatzgruppen der Sicherheitspolizei und des SD 1938-1941*, Stuttgart 1981.

Kroener, B.: *"Der starke Mann im Heimatskriegsgebiet", Generaloberst Friedrich Fromm. Eine Biographie*, Paderborn 2005.

Khrushchev Remembers, Toronto 1970.

Krushchev Remembers, The Last Testament, London 1974.

Kunz, A.: *Wehrmacht und Niederlage. Die bewaffnete Macht in der Endphase der nationalsozialistischen Herrschaft 1944 bis 1945*, Munich 2007.

Lapp, P.: *General bei Hitler und Ulbricht. Vinzenz Müller – eine deutsche Karriere*, Berlin 2003.

Laternser, H.: *Verteidigung deutscher Soldaten*, Bonn 1956.

Leide, H.: *NS-Verbrechen und Staatssicherheitsdienst. Die geheime Vergangenheit der DDR*, Göttingen 2006.

Leppa, K.: *Generalfeldmarschall Walter Model, von Genthin bis vor Moskaus Tore*, Nuremberg 1962.

Leverkühn, P.: *Verteidigung Mansteins*, Hamburg 1950.

Liddell Hart, B.: *The Other Side of the Hill*, London 1978.

Liddell Hart, B. (ed.): *The Rommel Papers*, New York 1953.

Liddell Hart, B. (ed.): *The Soviet Army*, London 1956.

v. Lingen, K.: *Kesselrings letzte Schlacht. Kriegsverbrecherprozesse, Vergangenheitspolitik und Wiederbewaffnung. Der Fall Kesselring*, Paderborn 2004.

Littell, J.: *The Kindly Ones*, London 2009.

Löw, A.: *Juden im Getto Litzmannstadt. Lebensbdingungen, Selbstwahrnehmung, Verhalten*, Göttingen 2006.

Löw, A., Robusch K., Walter, S. (eds.): *Deutsche – Juden – Polen. Geschichte einer wechselvollen Bezeihung im 20. Jahrhundert*, Frankfurt 2004.

Longerich, P.: *"Davon haben wir nichts gewusst". Die Deutschen und die Judenverfolgung 1933-1945*, Munich 2006.

Longerich P.: *Heinrich Himmler. Biographie*, Munich 2008.

Ludewig, J.: 'Stationen eines Soldatenschicksals: Generalfeldmarschall Walter Model' in: *Military History Notebook* 4, 4th quarter 1991, 1st Year, Bonn, 1999.

Ludewig, J.: 'Walter Model – Hitlers bester Feldmarschall?' in: Smelser, R., Syring, E. (eds.): *Die Militärelite des Dritten Reiches, 27 biographische Skizzen*, Berlin 1955.

Mac Donald, C., *The United States Army in World War II, The European Theatre of Operations, The Siegfried Line Campaign*, Washington 1963.

McKee, A.: *The Race for the Rhine Bridges, 1940, 1944-45*, London 1971.

de Maizière, U.: *In der Pflicht — Lebensbericht eines deutschen Soldaten im 20. Jahrhundert*, Hamburg 1989.

Malaparte, C.: *Kaputt*, Frankfurt 2007.

Malinowski, S.: *Vom König zum Führer. Sozialer Niedergang und politische Radikalisierung im deutschen Adel zwischen Kaiserreich und NS- Staat*, Berlin 2003.

Mallmann, K., Angrick, A. (eds.): *Die Gestapo nach 1945, Karrieren, Konflikte, Konstruktionen*, Darmstadt 2009.

Mallmann, K., Cüppers, M.: *Halbmond unter dem Hakenkreuz. Das Dritte Reich, die Araber und Palästina*, Darmstadt 2006.

Mallmann, K., Riess V., Pyta, W. (eds.): *Deutscher Osten 1939-1945. Der Weltanschauungskrieg in Photos und Texten*, Darmstadt 2003.

Mallmann, K., Paul, G. (eds.): *Karrieren der Gewalt. Nationalsozialistische Täterbiographien*, Darmstadt 2005.

Mallmann, K, Musial B.(eds.): *Genesis des Genozids. Polen 1939-1941*, Darmstadt 2004

Mallmann, K., Böhler, J., Matthäus, J. (eds.): *Einsatzgruppen in Polen. Darstellung und Dokumentation*, Darmstadt 2008

Manig, B.: *Die Politik der Ehre. Die Rehabilitierung der Berufssoldaten in der früheren Bundesrepublik*, Göttingen 2004.

Mann, G.: *Erinnerungen und Gedanken – Eine Jugend in Deutschland*, Frankfurt 1968.

v. Manstein, E.: *Aus einem Soldatenleben*, Bonn 1958.

v. Manstein, E.: *Verlorene Siege*, Bonn 1955.

v. Manstein, R., Fuchs, T.: *Soldat im 20. Jahrhundert*, Munich 1981.

Macksey, K.: *Guderian — Panzer General*, London 1975.

Martin, B., Lewandowska, S. (eds.): *Der Warschauer Aufstand 1944*, Warsaw 1999.

Masson, P.: *Die deutsche Armee — Geschichte der Wehrmacht 1935-1945*, Munich 1967.

Matthäus, J., Kwiet, K., Förster, J., Breitmann, R.: *Ausbildungsziel Judenmord. "Weltanschauliche Erziehung" von SS, Polizei und Waffen-SS im Rahmen der "Endlösung"*, Frankfurt 2003.

Matthäus, J., Mallmann, K. (eds.): *Deutsche Juden und Völkermord. Der Holocaust als Geschichte und Gegenwart*, Darmstadt 2006.

Maunz, T.: *Geltung und Neubildung modernen Kriegsvölkerrechts*, Freiburg i.Br. 1939.

Megargee, G.: *Hitler und die Generäle. Das Ringen um die Führung der Wehrmacht 1933-1945*, Paderborn 2006.

v. Mellenthin, F.: *German Generals of World War II as I saw them*, Oklahoma 1977

v. Mellenthin, F.: *Panzerschlachten*, Neckargründ 1963.

Merridale, C.: *Iwans Krieger. Die Rote Armee 1939-1945*. Berlin 2006.

Messerschmidt, M.: 'Die Wehrmacht in der Endphase, Realität und Perzeption' in: *Stuttgart im Zweiten Weltkrieg*, Gerlingen 1989.

Messerschmidt, M.: *Die Wehrmacht im NS Staat*, Hamburg 1989.

Messerschmidt, M.: *Was damals Recht war, NS-Militär – und Strafjustiz im Vernichtungskrieg*, Essen 1996.

Messerschmidt, M., Wüllner, F.: *Die Wehrmachtjustiz im Dienste des Nationalsozialismus, Zerstörung einer Legende*, Baden-Baden 1987.

Meyer, G.: 'General Heusinger und die Anfänge der Generalstabs- und Admiralstabs ausbildung in der Bundeswehr' in: *Clausewitz Studien*, Jahresband 1997, Munich 1998.

Meyer, G.: *Generalfeldmarschall Wilhelm Ritter v. Leeb, Tagebuchaufzeichnungen und Lagebeurteilungen aus zwei Weltkriegen*, Stuttgart 1976.

Meyer, G.: *Adolf Heusinger, Dienst eines deutschen Soldaten 1915 bis 1964*, Hamburg 2001.

Michalka, W. (ed.): *Der Zweite Weltkrieg, Analysen, Grundzüge, Forschungsbilanz*, Munich 1989.

Merezkow, K.: *Serving the People*, Moskau 1971.

Militärgeschichtliches Forschungsamt (Eds.) *Anfänge westdeutscher Sicherheitspolitik 1945-1956, Band 1: Von der Kapitulation bis zum Pleven-Plan*. Munich 1982.

Model, H.: *Der deutsche Generalstabsoffizier, seine Auswahl und Ausbildung in Reichswehr, Wehrmacht und Bundeswehr*, Frankfurt a. M., 1968.

Model, H.: 'Der Führer dem Generalfeldmarschall Model – Geschichte eines Marschallstabes' in: *Decorations and Militaria Journal*, Notebook 14, September 1976.

Montgomery, Sir B.: *The Memoirs of Field Marshal Montgomery*, New York 1958.

Moorehead, A.: *Montgomery, A Biography*, New York 1964.

Morozow, M.: *Die Falken des Kreml — die sowjetische Militärmacht von 1917 his heute*, Munich 1982.

Müller, K.-J: *Das Heer und Hitler –Armee und nationalsozialistisches Regime 1933-1940*, Stuttgart 1969.

Müller, K.-J. .: *Generaloberst Ludwig Beck, Studien und Dokumente zur politisch-militärischen Vorstellungswelt des Generalstabschef des deutschen Heeres 1933-1938*, Boppard am Rhein, 1980.

Müller, K.-J.: *Generaloberst Ludwig Beck. Eine Biographie*, Paderborn 2008

Müller R., Volkmann H. (eds.): *Die Wehrmacht — Mythos und Realität*, Oldenburg 1999.

Münzel, M.: *Die jüdischen Mitglieder der deutschen Wirtschaftselite 1927-1955. Verdrängung-Emigration-Rückkehr*, Paderborn 2004.

Naumann, K.: *Generäle in der Demokratie. Generationsgeschichtliche Studien zur Bundeswehrelite*, Hamburg 2007.

Nazi Conspiracy and Aggression, U.S. Government Printing Office, Washington 1948.

Nehring, W.: *Die Geschichte der deutschen Panzerwaffe 1916-1945*, Berlin 1969.

Neitzel, S.: *Abgehört. Deutsche Generäle in britischer Kriegsgefangenschaft*, Berlin 2006.

Nekrich, A., Grigorenko, P.: *Genickschuss — Die Rote Armee am 22.6.1941*, Frankfurt 1969.

Nekrich, A., Heller, M.: *Die Geschichte der Sowjetunion 1940-1980*, Königstein 1982.

Newton, S.: *Hitler's Commander. Field Marshal Walther Model – Hitler's favorite General*, Cambridge (USA) 2005.

Niepold, G.: *Mittlere Ostfront Juni '44, Darstellung, Beurteilung, Lehren*, Bonn 1985.

Niepold, G.: *Panzer-Operationen, 'Doppelkopf und Cäsar,' Kurland — Sommer '44*, Bonn 1985.

Oldenburg, M.: *Ideologie und militärisches Kalkül. Die Besatzungspolitik der Wehrmacht in der Sowjetunion 1942*, Cologne 2004.

Paul, G. (ed.): *Die Täter der Shoah. Fanatische Nationalsozialisten oder ganz normale Deutsche?*, Göttingen 2003.

Paul, G., Mallmann K.: *Die Gestapo im Zweiten Weltkrieg. Heimatfront und besetztes Europa*, Darmstadt 2000.

Pehle, W. (ed.): *Das Judenpogrom 1938. Von der "Reichskristallnacht" zum Völkermord*, Frankfurt 1999.

Philippi, A., Heim, F.: *Der Feldzug gegen Sowjetrussland 1941-1945, Ein operativer Überblick*, Stuttgart 1993.

Picker, H. (ed.): *Hitler's Table Talks 1941-1944*, London 1953.

Pöppel, W.-K., Prinz v. Preussen, KH., v. Hase, K.-G., (eds.): *Die Soldaten der Wehrmacht*, Munich 1998.

Pohl, D.: *Verfolgung und Massenmord in der NS-Zeit 1933-1945*, Darmstadt 2003.

Primor, A.: …*"Mit Ausnahme Deutschlands". Als Botschafter Israels in Bonn*, Berlin 1999.

Pogue, F.: *United States Army in World War II, The European Theater of Operations, The Supreme Command*, Washington 1954.

Pohl, D.: *Verfolgung und Massenmord in der NS-Zeit 1933-1945*, Darmstadt 2003.

Poliakow, L., Weil, J.: *Das dritte Reich und seine Diener*, Berlin 1956.

Pufelska, A.: *Die "Judäo-Kommune", ein Feindbild in Polen. Das polnische Selbstverständnis im Schatten des Antisemitismus 1939-1948*, Paderborn 2007.

Pyta, W.: *Hindenburg. Herrschaftzwischen Hohenzollern und Hitler*, Munich 2007.

Raeder, E.: *Mein Leben*, Tübingen 1965.

Rees, L.: *Hitlers Krieg im Osten*, Munich 1999.

Reichhelm, G.: *Verantwortung und Gewissensnot*, Würzburg, 2002.

Reitlinger, G.: *The Final Solution, The Attempt to Exterminate the Jews of Europe 1933-1945*, London 1953.

Reitlinger, G.: *The House built on Sand*, London 1960.

Reitlinger, G.: *The SS—Alibi of a Nation*, London 1956.

Rendulic, L.: *Gekämpft, Gesiegt, Geschlagen*, Heidelberg 1952.

Richardson, W., Freidin, S.: *The Fatal Decisions*, London 1956.

Rigg, B.: *Hitlers jüdische Soldaten*, Paderborn 2003.

Rohland, W.: *Bewegte Zeiten, Erinnerungen eines Eisenhüttenmannes*, Stuttgart 1978.

Röhricht, E.: *Pflicht und Gewissen, Erinnerungen eines deutschen Generals 1932 bis 1944*, Stuttgart 1965.

Rokossovsky, K.: *Soldatski Dolg*, Moskau, 1970.

Römer, F.: *Der Kommissarbefehl. Wehrmacht und NS-Verbrechen an der Ostfront 1941/42*, Paderborn 2008

Ruge, F.: *Rommel und die Invasion, Erinnerungen*, Stuttgart 1959.

Ryan, C.: *A Bridge Too Far*, London 1974.

Ryan, C.: *The Last Battle*, London 1966.

Ryan, C.: *The Longest Day*, London 1960.

Rybakow, A.: *Prach i Pepel*, Moskau 1996.

Schäfer, K.: *Werner von Blomberg – Hitlers erster Feldmarschall. Eine Biographie*, Paderborn, 2006.

Schellenberg, W.: *The Schellenberg Memoirs*, London 1956.

v. Schlabrendorff, F.: *Offiziere gegen Hitler*, Zürich 1959.

Schmelser, R., Syring, E., (eds.): *Die Militärelite des Dritten Reiches —27 biographische Studien*, Berlin 1995.

Schmiedecke, J., Steinbach, P. (eds.).: *Der Widerstand gegen den Nationalsozialismus — Die deutsche Gesellschaft und der Widerstand gegen Hitler*, Munich 1985.

Schmidl, E.: *Jews in the Habsburg Armed Forces*, Eisenstadt 1989.

Schmidl, E.: *Der "Anschluss" Östereichs. Der deutsche Einmarsch im März 1938*, Bonn 1994.

Schmidt, M.: *Albert Speer. Das Ende eines Mythos*, Berlin 2005.

Schmitt, C.: 'Totaler Feind, totaler Krieg, totaler Sieg', in: *Völkerbund und Völkerrecht*, 4. Jahrgang, 1937/38.

v. Schramm, W.: *Verrat im Zweiten Weltkrieg— Vom Kampf der Geheimdienste in Europa, Berichte und Dokumentation*, Düsseldorf 1967.

Shtemenko, S.: *The Soviet General Staff at War*, Moskau 1970.

Seaton, A.: *The German Army 1933-1945*, New York 1982.

Seaton, A.: *The Russo-German War 1941-1945*, London 1971.

Seaton, A.: *Stalin as Warlord*, London 1976.

Seidel, R.: *Deutsche Besatzungspolitik in Polen. Der Distrikt Radom 1939-1945*, Paderborn 2006.

Seidler, F: *Die Militärgerichtsbarkeit der deutschen Wehrmacht 1939-1945. Rechtsprechung und Strafvollzug*, Munich 1991.

Seidler F.: *Die Kollaboration 1939-1945. Zeitgeschichtliche Dokumentation in Biographien*, Munich 1995.

Sereny, G.: *Albert Speer, Das Ringen mit der Wahrheit und das deutsche Trauma*, Munich 1995.

v. Senger und Etterlin, F.: *Krieg in Europa*, Frankfurt 1960.

v. Siegler, F. Frhr. (zusammengestellt und erläutert): *Die höheren Dienststellen der Wehrmacht 1933-1945, im Auftrage des Instituts für Zeit- geschichte Munich*, Stuttgart 1953.

Smith, B., Peterson, A. (eds.): *Heinrich Himmler, Geheimreden 1933 bis 1945 und andere Ansprachen*, Frankfurt 1974.

Sokolovsky, V.: *Military Strategy — Soviet Doctrine and Concepts*, New York 1963

Speer, A.: *Erinnerungen*, Berlin 1976.

Speidel, H.: *Invasion 1944 – Ein Beitrag zu Rommels und des Reiches Schicksal*, Tübingen, 1949.

Sprenger, M.: *Landsknechte auf dem Weg ins Dritte Reich. Zur Genese und Wandel des Freikorpsmythos*, Paderborn 2008.

Springer, H.: *Stationen eines Lebens in Krieg und Frieden — Zeitgeschichtliches Zeugnis des SS-Sturmbannführers und Ritterkreuzträgers der Leibstandarte-SS 'Adolf Hitler'*, Berlin 1996.

Stahlberg, A.: *Die verdammte Pflicht. Erinnerungen 1942-1945*, Berlin 1994.

Staron, J.: *Fosse Ardeatine und Marzabotto. Deutsche Kriegsverbrechen und Resistenza, 1944-1999*, Paderborn 2002.

Stein, M.: *Generalfeldmarschall Erich von Manstein, Kritische Betrachtung des Soldaten und Menschen*, Mainz 2000.

Stein, M.: *Generalfeldmarschall Walter Model – Legende und Wirklichkeit*, Bissendorf, 2001.

Stein, M.: *Österreichs Generäle im Deutschen Heer 1938-1945, Schwarz/Gelb-Rot/Weiss/ Rot-Hakenkreuz*, Bissendorf 2002.

Stein, M.: *Die 11. Armee und die "Endlösung" 1941/42. Eine Dokumentensamlung mit Kommentaren*, Bissendorf 2006.

Stein, M.: *Field Marshal von Manstein – The Janus Head. A Portrait*, Solihull 2007.

Stieff, H. (Mühlheisen, H. – ed.): *Briefe*, , Berlin 1991.

Steinberg, J.: *Deutsche, Italiener und Juden — Der italienische Widerstand gegen den Holocaust*, Göttingen 1992.

Streit, C.: *Keine Kameraden — Die Wehrmacht und die sowjetischen Kriegsgefangenen*, Stuttgart 1978.

Taylor, T.: *The Breaking Wave, The German Defeat in the Summer of 1940*, London 1967.

Taylor, T.: *Die Nürnberger Prozesse — Kriegsverbrechen und Völkerrecht*, Zürich 1951.

Taylor, T.: *The March of Conquest — The German Victory in the West 1940*, London 1959.

Taylor, T.: *Munich — The Price of Peace*, New York 1980.

Taylor, T.: *Sword and Swastika*, New York 1952.

Teske, H.: *Die silbernen Spiegel, Generalstabsdienst unter der Lupe*, Heidelberg 1952.

Thorwald, J.: *Das Ende an der Elbe*, Stuttgart 1950.

v. Tippelskirch, K.: *Geschichte des zweiten Weltkrieges*, Bonn 1959.

Tschuikow, W.: *Garde auf dem Weg nach Berlin*, Berlin 1976.

Ueberschär, G.,Vogel W.: *Dienen und Verdienen, Hitlers Geschenke an seine Eliten*, Frankfurt, 1999.

Ueberschär G. (ed.): *Hitlers militärische Elite— Vom Kriegsbeginn bis zum Weltkriegs ende*, Darmstadt 1998.

Ueberschär G. (ed.): *Hitlers militärische Elite — von den Anfängen des Regimes his Kriegsbeginn*, Darmstadt 1996.

Ueberschär, G. (ed.): *NS-Verbrechen und der militärische Widerstand gegen Hitler*, Darmstadt 2000.

Uhle-Wettler, F.: *Erich Ludendorff in seiner Zeit. Soldat, Stratege, Revolutionär. Eine Neubewertung*, Berg 1995.

Ulrich, V.: *Die nervöse Grossmacht 1871-1918. Aufstieg und Untergang des deutschen Kaiserreichs*, Frankfurt 1999.

Urban, T.: *Polen*, Munich 2009

U.S. Army Archives

The Ardennes: The Battle of the Bulge, Washington, 1965.

The European Theatre of Operations, United States Army in World War II, Washington, n.d.

Siegfried Line Campaign, Washington, n.d.

The Supreme Command, Washington 1956.

Vasilevsky, A.: *Delo Vsei Zhisni*, Moskau 1974.

Venohr, W.: *Stauffenberg — Symbol der deutschen Einheit — eine politische Biographie*, Berlin 1986.

Volkogonow, D.: *Stalin, Triumph and Tragedy*, London 1991.

Volkogonow, D.: *Trotzki*, Düsseldorf 1992.

Wachsmann, N: *Gefangen unter Hitler. Justizterror und Strafvollzug im NS-Staat*, Munich 2004.

Walde, K.: *Guderian*, Berlin 1976.

Wagener, K.: 'Kampf und Ende der Heeresgruppe B im Ruhrkessel', in: *Wehrwissenschaftliche Rundschau* 1975, Heft 10, Berlin 1975.

Warlimont, W.: *Im Hauptquartier der deutschen Wehrmacht 1939 bis 1945*, Bonn 1962.

Weber, M.: *Wirtschaft und Gesellschaft*, Tübingen 1972, 5. revidierte Auflage.

Weinberg, G. (ed.): *Hitlers zweites Buch*, Stuttgart 1962.

Weinberg, G.: 'Zur Dotation Hitlers an Generalfeldmarschall Ritter von Leeb' in: *Militärgeschichtliche Mitteilungen* Nr.2/1979, pp. 97-99.

Wegner, B.: *Hitlers politische Soldaten: Die Waffen-SS 1933-1945*, Paderborn 1997

Wehrmachtberichte 1939-1945, München, 1985, 3 Bände.

Weinke, A.: *Die Verfolgung von NS Tätern im geteilten Deutschland. Vergangenheitsbewältigungen 1949-1969 oder eine deutsch-deutsche Beziehungsgeschichte im kalten Krieg*, Paderborn 2002.

Weiss, H. (ed.).: *Biographisches Lexikon zum Dritten Reich*, Frankfurt 1998.

Werth, A.: *Russia At War 1941-1945*, New York 1964.

Werth, G.: *Verdun, die Schlacht und der Mythos*, Bergisch Gladbach 1979.

Westemeier, J.: *Joachim Peiper. Zwischen Totenkopf und Ritterkreuz. Lebensweg eines SS-Führers*, Bissendorf 2006.

Westphal, S.: *Erinnerungen*, Mainz 1975.

Westphal, S.: *The German Army in the West*, London 1952.

Wette, W. (ed.): *Zivilcourage. Empörte, Helfer und Retter aus Wehrmacht, Polizei und SS*, Frankfurt 2004.

Wette, W.: *Die Wehrmacht. Feindbilder, Vernichtungskrieg, Legenden*, Frankfurt 2002.

Wette, W. (ed.): *Handlungsspielräume im Vernichtungskrieg der Wehrmacht*, Frankfurt 2003.

Wette, W. (ed.): *Stille Helden. Judenretter im Dreiländereck während des Zweiten Weltkrieges*, Freiburg 2005.

Wheeler Bennett, J.: *The Nemesis of Power — The German Army in Politics 1918-1945*, London 1956.

Wildt, M.: *Generation des Unbedingten. Das Führungskorps des Reichssicherheitshauptamtes*, Hamburg 2003.

Wildt, M. (ed.): *Nachrichtendienst, politische Elite und Mordeinheit. Der Sicherheitsdienst des Reichsführers SS*, Hamburg 2003.

Wildt, M.: *Volksgemeinschaft als Selbstermächtigung. Gewalt gegen Juden in der deutschen Provinz 1919 bis 1939*, Hamburg 2007.

Wistrich, R.: *Wer war wer im Dritten Reich*, Munich 1983.

v. Wrochem, O.; *Erich von Manstein. Vernichtungskrieg und Geschichtspolitik*, Paderborn 2006.

Yahil, L.: *Überlebenskampf und Vernichtung der europäischen Juden*, Neuwied 1998.

Zabecki, D. (ed.): *World War II in Europe, An Encyclopedia*, New York 1999.

Zehnpfennig, B.: *Hitlers Mein Kampf – Eine Interpretation*, Munich 2000.

Zeidler, M.: *Reichswehr und Rote Armee 1920-1933. Wege einer ungewöhnlichen Zusammenarbeit*, Beiträge zur Militärgeschichte in Militärgeschichtliches Forschungsamt Band 36, Munich, 1993.

Zentner, C., Bedürftig, F., *Das grosse Lexikon des Dritten Reiches*, Munich 1985.

Zhukov, G.: *Vospominiania i Rasmishlenia*, Moskau 1965.

Zimmermann, J.: *Pflicht zum Untergang. Die deutsche Kriegführung im Westen des Reiches 1944/45*, Paderborn 2009.

Related titles published by Helion & Company

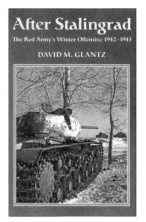

Under Himmler's Command. The Personal Recollections of Oberst Hans-Georg Eismann, Operations Officer, Army Group Vistula, Eastern Front 1945
Helion WWII German Military Studies
Volume 2
Hans-Georg Eismann
144pp, photos, maps   Hardback
ISBN 978-1-874622-43-7

After Stalingrad. The Red Army's Winter Offensive 1942-1943
David M. Glantz
536pp, photos, maps
Hardback
ISBN 978-1-906033-26-2

Forthcoming titles

Barbarossa Derailed. The Battles for Smolensk 10 July-10 September 1941 Volume 1: The German Advance, The Encirclement Battle, and the First and Second Soviet Counteroffensives, 10 July-24 August 1941
David M. Glantz   ISBN 978-1-906033-72-9

Entrapment. Soviet Operations to Capture Budapest, December 1944
Kamen Nevenkin   ISBN 978-1-906033-73-6

HELION & COMPANY

26 Willow Road, Solihull, West Midlands B91 1UE, England
Telephone 0121 705 3393   Fax 0121 711 4075
Website: http://www.helion.co.uk